Developing Ports as Business Ecosystems

Developing Ports as Business Ecosystems provides professionals in freight transport and maritime logistics, and specifically the ports industry, with a better conceptual understanding of the ports industry. It includes key insights and best practices for port management and development and an overview of new trends and developments relevant to developing winning strategies.

This second edition explains how a rapidly changing energy landscape and the advancing transition toward sustainability have deeply impacted port development in recent years. It provides an even more coherent, comprehensive contribution to port management, development and policies. The book uniquely features in-depth explanations of the port as an ecosystem, port governance and port policy choices, including public financing of ports. The new edition presents further developed analysis on the changing port landscape and the opportunities for business development in ports.

This book will broaden professionals' conceptual understanding of the ports industry and provide insights into the latest developments in this area. For students, this book provides an industry-focused and non-technical "essential reading" for gaining a deep understanding of the ports industry.

Peter W. de Langen is the owner and principal consultant of Ports & Logistics Advisory, based in Malaga, Spain. He is also a professor (part-time) at Copenhagen Business School, where he develops cutting-edge research in ports and logistics, and is co-director of the knowledge dissemination platform www.porteconomics.eu. Peter is included in the Stanford list of 2% best scholars in the field of logistics and transportation, a regular provider of executive education and speaker at industry conferences.

"A modern and well-rounded book on the port industry. Peter de Langen brings a fresh look into traditional topics, such as port governance, and gives an insight into current technologies which are reshaping the role of ports and the industry."

Duna Uribe, *Executive Commercial Director,*
Pecém Industrial Port Complex, Brazil

"In this book Peter de Langen explores the complexities of ports as business ecosystems and offers an in-depth view on how ports contribute to the increase of trade by providing added-value services to make consumers and producers better off."

Santiago Garcia-Mila, *Subdirector General,*
Estrategia I Comercial, Port de Barcelona, Spain

"Peter de Langen's book provides an impressive round-up of the key challenges seaports are facing today, from vertical and horizontal concentration to societal demands on the sustainability of port operation, and how the port industry should respond."

Jan Hoffman, *World bank, Global Lead,*
Maritime Transport and Ports

Developing Ports as Business Ecosystems

Port Development, Management and Policy for a Better Ports Industry

Second Edition

Peter W. de Langen

Routledge
Taylor & Francis Group
LONDON AND NEW YORK

Designed cover image: Peter W. de Langen

Second edition published 2026
by Routledge
4 Park Square, Milton Park, Abingdon, Oxon, OX14 4RN

and by Routledge
605 Third Avenue, New York, NY 10158

Routledge is an imprint of the Taylor & Francis Group, an informa business

First edition published as *Towards a Better Port Industry* by Routledge 2020

British Library Cataloguing-in-Publication Data
A catalogue record for this book is available from the British Library

ISBN: 978-1-041-04972-2 (hbk)
ISBN: 978-1-041-04969-2 (pbk)
ISBN: 978-1-003-63078-4 (ebk)

DOI: 10.4324/9781003630784

Typeset in Times New Roman
by codeMantra

Contents

Figures

Tables

About the author

Dr Peter de Langen has over 25 years' experience in the ports industry. Peter is the owner and principal consultant of Ports & Logistics Advisory (Malaga, Spain) and professor (part-time) at Copenhagen Business School (CBS). Previously, Peter was a professor of cargo transport and logistics at Eindhoven University of Technology (2009 to 2016), corporate strategist at the Port of Rotterdam Authority (2007–2013) and researcher and team leader at Erasmus University Rotterdam (1997–2007), where he obtained his PhD in 2004.

Peter is co-director of the knowledge dissemination platform www.porteconomics.eu and a regular speaker at industry conferences on ports. Peter provides (executive) education on ports in various programs, including the Maritime Economics and Logistics MEL) program at Erasmus University Rotterdam, and the shipping bachelor's program at CBS. In addition, he has developed and provided tailor-made executive education programs in Brazil, South Africa, Korea, Portugal, the Netherlands, Ghana, Ivory Coast, Gabon, Sudan and Saudi Arabia.

At the Port of Rotterdam, Peter was involved in and led various strategic renewal projects, such as the development of a Corporate Strategy and the Port Vision 2030. He also contributed to various international projects at the Port of Rotterdam, including Brazil, Romania, Oman and Indonesia.

Throughout his career as a consultant, corporate strategist and researcher, Peter de Langen has shared knowledge through (academic) publications, both peer-reviewed journal articles and books, book chapters, discussion papers and contributions to industry magazines. Peter de Langen contributes regularly to *Port Strategy* (under the tag *The analyst*). His work is widely read and cited, and Peter is included in Stanford's list of the World's Top 2% Scientists in their fields – even though he only a small part of his professional career has been dedicated to research.

With Ports & Logistics Advisory, Peter aims to provide high-impact contributions to projects and organizations and is active in boardroom advisory, research and executive education in ports and logistics worldwide. Peter has worked for leading companies and governments in the ports industry, among others the Port of Rotterdam, the Port of Barcelona, the European Seaports Organization, the World Bank, the Asian Development Bank, the United Nations and the Panama Canal Authority, and has experience with ports in more than 55 countries.

Preface

This book is the result of a lifelong interest in ports, which was undoubtedly nurtured by my grandfather, who lived in Rotterdam – at the time the largest port of the world – and had a vivid interest in ports and shipping, and my father, who also was drawn to "ports and transportation". Therefore, studying Economics at Erasmus University Rotterdam, specializing in Urban, Port and Transport Economics, starting my career at Erasmus as a researcher and consultant in the field of ports, and joining the Corporate Strategy team at the Port of Rotterdam were all natural choices. More than 25 years later, the "fire is still burning".

This book presents what I have learned in the past 25+ years working in the ports industry. It combines insights developed through academic work and insights from first-hand involvement in developing ports, port policies and port strategies and port reform processes. These experiences and insights have led to a coherent approach to ports as business ecosystems, which is presented in this book. It is therefore also a personal book, in the sense that it presents insights I have developed in my career and that I think are worth sharing. I hope the insights presented in this book contribute to better ports that create value for users and society at large.

Even though I am now based in Malaga, Spain, and have worked in over 55 countries, my perspective on ports is deeply influenced by my experiences in Rotterdam. Nevertheless, this book could not have been written without international experiences, many of which I developed through working with international organizations like the World Bank, United Nations, ESPO and various ports around the world. I am deeply grateful for these opportunities and deeply enjoyed working in these international environments.

This book contains material and insights from joint work with a variety of co-authors, work that has been published in academic journals. I have learned a lot from working together and have developed friendships in the process. As the list of scholars I worked with is too large to include in full: I am thankful to all of you for working together and trust you all recognize how this book builds on joint previous work, while at the same time it presents my distinct approach to ports.

Finally, many thanks to my family, Maria, Niels, Álvaro and Adrián. At times, it is a balancing act to combine international work with family life. I am very thankful for your support.

Preface

Structure of the book

Developing Ports as Business Ecosystems provides professionals in freight transport and maritime logistics, and specifically the ports industry, as well as students in these fields, with a better conceptual understanding of the ports industry. It includes key insights and best practices for port management, development, and policymaking and an overview of new trends and developments relevant for developing winning strategies.

After an introduction, Chapter 2 provides the most relevant insights for understanding the traditional view of ports as transport nodes, and Chapter 3 develops a new and additional perspective: the ports as a business ecosystem. Chapter 4 explains how new trends and developments affect port development and argues that assuming "business as usual" often leads to major port development mistakes. These introductory chapters provide the basis for Chapter 5, which offers a new perspective on port governance, in which public interests, corporatization, state-ownership and shareholder policies take a central role, and the model of an independent, state-owned *port development company* is presented. Chapter 6 describes the main challenges of developing port policies and discusses the required economic regulation of ports. Chapter 7 deals specifically with the important issue of cooperative initiatives in port business ecosystems.

Chapter 8 deals with port development and discusses major port development challenges, including granting concessions, developing a port vision, crafting stakeholder support, choosing port performance indicators and creating a port innovation system. The final chapter deals with port development strategies and includes themes such as the business model of the port managing body, portfolio analysis, pricing principles, the importance of "synergy services" in port business ecosystems and business development.

This book will broaden professionals' conceptual understanding of the ports industry and provide insights into the latest developments in this area. For students, this book provides an industry-focused and non-technical "essential reading" for gaining a deep understanding of the ports industry.

1 Introduction

1.1 Ports: often overlooked but critical nodes in global value chains

Seaports are indispensable nodes in the global trade system. There are more than 7500 ports worldwide that together accommodate the vast majority of world trade volumes. Cargo handling operations form the core of ports, but most seaports have evolved into logistics and industrial clusters, often with a huge impact on society, for instance, through their contribution to the overall economy, their role in attracting foreign direct investment (FDI), and their role as a hub in changing energy systems.

Ports thus play an important role in efficient, reliable, safe and sustainable global value chains. Yet, various obstacles and problems often hamper port development. This can deeply hurt countries, especially developing countries.

How ports have shaped cities

It is nowadays hard to imagine that the major world cities today have emerged largely because of port activities. London was the world's largest port in the 19th century, to be overtaken by New York, while currently Shanghai is the largest port in the world. All these – and many other historical world cities such as Venice, Hong Kong, Singapore, Tokyo, Buenos Aires and Barcelona – flourished in their early age as ports. The arrival, storage and trade of goods in these port-cities led to an agglomeration effect that re-enforced itself: ports attracted other economic activities, which led to population growth, which led to more economic activities and so on. In the words of Fujita, Krugman and Venables – leading scholars in economic geography, Krugman winning a Nobel Prize in Economics in 2009 for his work (2001, p. 236):

> Nearly all great cities are major ports (or were at one time), but many have long since ceased to be mainly port cities … There is nothing paradoxical in the fact that the Erie Canal made New York – and is now no more than a tourist attraction.

DOI: 10.4324/9781003630784-1

Most people only notice ports when they do *not* work. Consumers take efficient intercontinental transport of the products they purchase for granted. Likewise, many multi-nationals heavily rely on efficient intercontinental transport, but hardly pay attention unless a disruption threatens their supply chains.

But when a disruption occurs, ports turn out to be critical. For instance, in 2002, the US president, George W. Bush, intervened in a labor dispute on the US West Coast, where labor unions blocked port operations for ten days. He argued that the national interest was at stake. Indeed, large manufacturers, including companies such as Boeing (with a main plant located near Seattle), had warned they had to halt production because of the strikes. A calculation of the impact of the strike suggested an economic damage of US$2 billion per day.[1] When port operations on the West Coast started up again, over 200 ships were lined up outside ports waiting to unload and pick up containers and recovery of all delays took six to seven weeks. The significance of a disruption of port operations is easily understood, given the dependence of the US, like most other developed economies, on trade. For instance, about 90% of apparel bought by US consumers is imported by sea; the same applies to roughly 80% of all footwear and about 60% of all computers. As soon as the supply is disrupted because ports no longer operate, consumption is affected, with severe adverse economic effects.

In a similar case, the French government intervened in a labor union lockout of the French port of Marseille. In this case, the effect of a disruption in ports was also immediate: in France, the gasoline and diesel supply to cars and trucks depends on crude oil imports to refineries. The refineries have some stock, but heavily depend on port infrastructure for smooth operations. Thus, after some days the strike in the port provoked fuel shortages in the country. An additional example of the impact of disruptions in ports is the COVID-19-induced shipping capacity shortage in 2020. This disruption also shows the critical nature of ports and maritime logistics. Recent studies suggest that the number of disruptions has increased in recent years (UNCTAD, 2025a).

Disruptions with lasting effects: The case of Kobe

The Japanese port of Kobe was struck by an earthquake in 1995. It took several months to restore normal port operations, but Kobe never recovered the central position in the Japanese – and northeast Asian – port system it occupied before the crisis. A part of the cargo that was *transhipped* in Kobe (i.e., transferred from one ship to another ship) was lost, mostly to ports outside Japan, such as Busan in South Korea. A part of the cargo that was transported from Kobe to the Japanese "*hinterland*" shifted to other Japanese ports. The disruption of the port thus had lasting adverse effects for the regional economy.

Such disruptions clearly show the importance of a well-functioning port. Apart from disruptions, *malfunctioning ports can structurally constrain trade.* In Australia, queues of ships waiting for loading bulk cargoes, mainly coal, were the rule rather than the exception from 2006 to 2010. These queues are costly from a supply chain perspective (average waiting times of over 30 days were reported, and queues of over 70 ships) and constrain Australia's coal export at large. Similarly, port capacity and service quality issues constrain Brazil's exports of agricultural goods. In Guatemala, serious shortcomings in the ports on the east coast constrain exports of agricultural goods, such as bananas and citrus, especially to Europe (a non-traditional market for agricultural produce exporters). In South Africa, the underperformance of ports and rail freight constrains the export of mining products, with a direct negative impact on employment levels in the mining industry. The high logistics costs also seriously threaten the competitiveness of export-oriented industries such as car manufacturing.

Finally, the non-performance of ports is often *invisible*. Ports only thrive if they attract investments from private sector firms such as terminal operators and logistics service providers. The most important challenge is not exploitation, but rather the *development* of the port. Thus, the core risk is a lack of development, as indicated by lagging or absent investments, for instance, due to a lack of space or attractive investment conditions. Not attracting such investments may have serious consequences for the regional and national economy, as large development opportunities may remain untapped. For instance, the port of Lome (Togo, West Africa) is a relatively well-performing container hub but has no space to accommodate investments in logistics and processing industries. Thus, while the demand is there, these opportunities remain untapped, with serious detrimental effects on Togo's economy.

This book is focused on port development

In this book, the focus is on port development, i.e., all the activities to secure the port complex continues to create value, both for users and society. These activities range from investments in port expansion to making land-use decisions and securing stakeholder support for port activities. Port development is about developing the port business ecosystem.

Port development differs radically from terminal management. The management of terminals (including issues such as IT systems, equipment, operations management, and safety and security) requires strong capabilities in operations. It is widely accepted that the management of terminals is best done by the private sector. In the past decades port reform has made the "landlord model" in which terminals are operated by private companies the reference model.

Currently, the main challenges in the ports industry are related to port development. For instance, there is considerable debate about the best governance model for port development and the best port policy framework. This book provides a better understanding regarding port development, port management and port policies.

The above examples show that ports are a crucial enabler of international trade and important elements in global value chains. Disruptions, in which ports come to an abrupt standstill, receive widespread attention, make the seaport a temporary "boardroom issue" and lead to attention of politicians and policymakers. However, less visible structural *inefficiencies* in port operations and *untapped development opportunities* often are even more important impediments to economic development and international trade. Ports deeply affect the economic prosperity of countries and regions, in positive and negative ways. Efficient ports promote trade while inefficient ones provide barriers to trade. Well-developed ports attract large volumes of (foreign direct) investments, while neglected ports constrain investments. In many international supply chains, port costs are important components of overall transport costs.

While ocean transport is generally an open market where technological advances and increasing volumes have significantly reduced rates, ineffective port operations still abound. As one example, a World Bank study from 2004 shows that when a country manages to improve port efficiency, so that it moves from being among the 25% most inefficient countries to being among the best 25% of countries, overall transport costs reduce by more than 12%. Such an improvement subsequently leads to a boost in trade. The study shows that if a country like Peru or Turkey increased its seaports' efficiency to a level similar to Australia's, it would be able to increase its trade by approximately 25% (Clark et al., 2004). A recent World Bank report on port performance in the container segment shows that waiting times in many ports are high and add costs to international supply chains (World Bank, 2025b).

The precise effect of ports on trade and supply chain efficiency differs per port and changes over time, but the overall conclusion is clear: improving ports leads to reduced transport costs, more investments and increasing trade flows. All of this makes consumers and producers better off.

On top of their impact on economies and trade flows, understanding ports is relevant for a second reason: port development often is relevant from a *geopolitical perspective*. Various countries, including China, the US, India, Singapore and the European Union, actively aim to establish influence over the development of ports in emerging economies and use this influence to help achieve geopolitical goals. These countries often compete with each other in developing partnerships for port development.

Finally, the ongoing transition toward zero carbon of energy systems and global value chains, coupled with the potential growth of maritime trade, creates a need for investments in ports, as well as an opportunity for ports to attract large-scale investments, for instance, is clean energy production.

Based on estimates of the investment needs of European ports (see ESPO, 2024) as well as estimates of the investment needs of around €46 trillion investments to decarbonize in line with the 1.5C pathway, I estimate that *total private and public investments in ports may be expected to be around €2 trillion over the next ten years*, to a large extent driven by evolving trade flows and decarbonization. Accommodating such investment flows is a major challenge, both in developing economies, where port governance often is a major hurdle and access to finance a huge problem, and in ports in developed countries, where societal support for port development is often limited and environmental concerns and planning processes hamper adaptive port development.

1.2 A port as a transport node and as a business ecosystem

In this book, a seaport is broadly defined as "the set of economic activities related to handling ships – cargo and passenger – as well as all additional activities in global value chains that have located in the port area, including logistics, manufacturing, leisure and trade activities".

In port studies, the perspective that regards ports as "transport nodes" is well established. Key concepts and insights from this perspective are discussed in Chapter 2 of this book. But the main contribution of this book lies in the detailed discussion of insights from an additional perspective in which the port is treated as a *business ecosystem*. This perspective complements the "transport node perspective" and provides a richer basis for the understanding of the challenges related to port governance, port development, and strategies of port development companies. Central in the business ecosystem perspective is the recognition that interdependent firms cluster together in port regions, with various forms of coordination and resource sharing as a consequence. The transport node perspective is more narrowly focused (see Table 1.1).

I argue that the "business ecosystem" perspective is increasingly relevant for port development. This is partially because the direct local economic impact of the terminal activities is decreasing. While in earlier days, these activities generated a lot of direct and indirect employment, that is no longer the case. In Rotterdam, for example, employment in terminal activities has declined from around 25,000 jobs in the 1960s to less than 6000 in 2024, while in this period the volume of goods handled in Rotterdam more than doubled. This is due to mechanization and automatization. Both have had a positive impact on port users and work conditions in ports. However, the declining direct impact of terminal activities has also forced

Table 1.1 The transport node and business ecosystem perspective on a port

	Port as a transport node	*Port as a business ecosystem*
Performance indicator	Throughput volume	Investments and value added in the PBE
Frequently mentioned determinants of competitiveness	Maritime accessibility Geographic location Hinterland connections	Competitive energy prices Availability of land A qualified labor pool A good port innovation system
Research issues	The position of ports in liner shipping networks Hinterland accessibility Initiatives in ports for sustainable shipping	Synergies in the PBE Ports, special zones and FDI The governance of the PBE

policymakers and port developers to find ways to create a larger economic impact. The approach generally has been to develop the port from a transport node to a larger business ecosystem of industrial, logistics and leisure activities.

In addition, the energy and raw materials transition, critical for achieving a sustainable economy, creates a huge demand for new private investments in activities like production, assembly, storage and maintenance of offshore windmills, hydrogen plants to convert sustainable energy into hydrogen and ammonia, plants for biofuels and circular recycling and production activities. Such investments often cannot be located anywhere, but only in *logistics-industrial "islands"* (islands in a metaphorical sense, though in some cases true industrial islands are under development). Port business ecosystems often are prime examples of such logistics-industrial islands in an otherwise increasingly nuisance-free service economy. For instance, even though Maasvlakte II in Rotterdam is not a true "island", it is still developed as a special logistics-industrial island, with a specific regulatory, planning and policy approach. The same is the case for ports such as Raahe (Finland), Huelva (Spain) and Duqm (Oman). The business ecosystem perspective is also relevant to understand the various "freeport" initiatives, which also aim to expand and diversify port business ecosystems.

Ports as "islands" in an increasingly nuisance-free service economy.

Beyond being nodes in transport networks, ports have – often over centuries – evolved as diverse ecosystems that have attracted investments in activities such as manufacturing, logistics and leisure. As diverse industrial-logistics ecosystems, ports increasingly become metaphorical "islands" in an economy that is increasingly dominated by services, but where they serve society with valuable access for their material needs in the form of energy, consumer goods and raw materials and intermediate goods as inputs for the local, national and international industries. As such they contribute to the competitive position of nations.

The metaphorical "port industrial islands" sometimes may take the shape of real islands, where offshore wind is converted to hydrogen and ammonia and used in downstream production activities. Such an island is being built in Belgium – with financial support from the EU. In other cases, such as the Maasvlakte in Rotterdam, ports may not literally be "islands" but resemble them. More importantly, large scale port-industrial ports often are/would like to be considered "islands" in terms of planning and regulation. Freeport regulation is an example of regulation specifically designed for port industrial "islands", i.e., demarcated areas with a special tax and labor regimes. In my view, all non-landlocked countries benefit from developing a special regime that enables the flexible development of one or a few large-scale port-industrial islands.

1.2.1 Scale economies in port development

The previously mentioned estimate of around 7500 ports worldwide sounds a lot. However, in most countries the number of cargo handling ports is limited and only a relatively small number of those account for the vast majority of volumes. The *geographical concentration* of port activities in a few large-scale ports has increased over time. For instance, the Netherlands had well over 40 ports in the 16th century; at the time, all cities were port cities. Vessels were much smaller and could sail up the rivers, enabling all ports to trade internationally. Currently, the Dutch government has identified only five ports of national interest, and Rotterdam alone accounts for well over 75% of all volume handled in the Netherlands. This increasing geographical concentration has taken place everywhere, because of the increasing ship size and the associated increases in the size and draft of port facilities has allowed *scale economies*. These scale economies are relevant for shipping, but also for ports. For instance, investments in breakwaters and maritime access are very costly and "indivisible". Ports therefore have a large minimum efficient scale. The synergies between terminal infrastructure and adjacent logistics and industrial land further promote concentration of port activities. Given the scale of ships, only a few ports develop the international connections that attract industrial and manufacturing activities to ports. Finally, the increasing use of intermodal hinterland connections further increases the minimum scale of ports and thus their geographical concentration. Because of these economies, countries do not have a scattered distribution of terminals along the coastline, but a few large-scale ports.

1.3 The port managing body

In most ports around the world, one organization, often termed the port authority or port company, plays a central role in port development. In this book I use the term "port managing body" (PMB) as the generic term for all organizations tasked with port development. PMBs can be distinguished based on their governance model and classified into three types:[2]

1. A private port development company (PO-PDC).
2. A corporatized state-owned port development company (SO-PDC).
3. A public sector embedded port authority (PA).

The private port development company model (PO-PDC) has emerged in a relatively limited number of countries following reform. For instance, the UK and Greece have private port development companies, while in other countries (such as Brazil and India) some PDCs are private, while others are state-owned. For state-owned entities, two types are distinguished: the SO-PDC and the PA.

The core difference between the SO-PDC and the PA is that the PA is embedded in the public sector (which is the case in countries such as the US and Spain), while the SO-PDC is a *corporate entity* with real autonomy and consequently no (or very limited) involvement of civil servants and/or politicians in decision-making. The SO-PDC model is used in the majority of ports worldwide. Countries with this model include Canada, the Netherlands, Belgium, the UAE and Chile. In this book (Chapter 6), I argue that the corporatized state-owned port development company (SO-PDC) is generally a more appropriate port model than the public sector embedded port authority (PA). However, there are many hurdles to effective corporatization and various cases of ineffective corporatized PDCs. These cases and further reform steps are also discussed in Chapter 5.

Terminology

In this book, I will often use the abbreviation *PBE* for the *port business ecosystem*, i.e., the total of all interrelated economic activities in cargo handling, transport, warehousing, processing and maritime leisure that are co-located in and around the port area. I use *PMB* as the generic term for all *port managing bodies* whether publicly or privately owned and regardless of their business model. Chapter 9, on strategies of port managing bodies is relevant for the three types of PMBs distinguished above, i.e., the PA, the SO-PMB and the PO-PMB. I pay specific attention to the *state-owned port development company* (SO-PDC), as this is, as I argue later in this book, in my view the appropriate governance model for the vast majority of ports.

1.4 Outline of this book

The key insights regarding the role of the port as a transport node are discussed first (Chapter 2), followed by a detailed treatment of the port business ecosystem in Chapter 3. Next, the drivers of change in the ports industry are discussed, as a deep understanding of these is needed for effective policies and strategies. Based on insights from these three chapters, Chapter 5 discusses considerations for getting port governance right. Chapter 6 discusses the port policies that are needed to make sure that ports create value for society. Next, I discuss how cooperative initiatives between government, the PMB and third parties active in the PMB can create value for all parties involved. Chapter 8 provides concepts and insights for port development. The concluding chapter deals with strategies of PMBs. In each of the last five chapters, a short concluding paragraph provides a summary of the *good practices* that have been described in this chapter. All of these good practices together provide a short practical summary aimed to help the reader to contribute to a better ports industry.

Notes

1 This estimate was later criticized as too high, but still, the economic impact was clearly significant.
2 The vast majority of ports around the world can be classified in these three categories, even though there are some "grey areas". On top of this distinction, some PMBs are active nationally (i.e., a centralized model, such as in Kenya, South Africa and Sri Lanka), while in other countries various PMBs are active and compete with each other. This is for instance the case the Netherlands, the US, Brazil and India. Finally, PMBs are embedded in political systems in place in the country in which they operate, which can range from autocratic to democratic. These national political systems also deeply influence policy frameworks for ports investments.

2 The port as transport node

In this chapter, first, I discuss the main commodities handled in ports, second, I discuss the rankings of ports, the third paragraph discusses the position of ports in maritime networks, while the fourth provides key insights with regard to the hinterland of ports. The final section reviews available performance metrics and statistics regarding ports.

2.1 Commodities and global trade

In the last few decades, trade flows have grown rapidly due to a reduction of trade barriers, reduced costs of international transport, and increased globalization of production networks. World trade is measured in value. But for freight transport and ports, what matters more is the volume of transported goods: one shipping container carries over US$1 million worth of iPads, while US$1 million of iron ore translates in 6000–7000 tons, the equivalent of several fully loaded barges or trains.

Trade growth in *value* has been much faster than the increase in throughput *volumes*. This is mainly because the growth of trade was especially strong for *intermediates and finished goods*, and less for raw materials. These latter still account for the largest flows in terms of volumes. Table 2.1 shows the composition of worldwide shipping volumes.

Table 2.1 The composition of worldwide shipping volumes

Cargo type	*Global volume (*million tons)*
Dry bulk	5400
Oil	3000
Containers	1800
General cargo (incl RoRo)	1000
Other liquid bulk (including chemicals and LNG)	1000
Total	12,200

Source: Based on UNCTAD (2025a).

DOI: 10.4324/9781003630784-2

Liquid bulk volumes have grown moderately in the past decades, the main dry bulk commodities and other dry bulk cargoes (including roll-on–roll-off (RoRo)) somewhat faster, and containers most rapidly. An estimate of global volumes handled in ports based on extrapolating available data from Europe suggests that the global port throughput is around 31 billion tons per year. This is in line with the total shipping volumes from Table 2.1, because cargo is loaded and unloaded, and some cargo is handled *four* times, as it is transferred from one ship to another ship in an intermediate port. In addition to transporting around 1.8 billion tons of goods in containers, around 150 million TEU of empty containers are handled. The weight of these empty moves (around 150 million tons) is also included in the port statistics.

2.2 Port rankings

Based on data from the UN LO/CODE system and Marine Traffic,[1] there are about 14,000 commercial (i.e., cargo handling) ports worldwide, whose growing volumes give rise to substantial needs for additional investments. The global port volume estimates and number of ports suggest an estimated average port volume of around 2 million tons. This is substantial and has increased over time; due to scale economies, both regarding port infrastructure and regarding ships, the concentration of port volumes in a relatively limited number of ports has increased over time.

The distribution of the 31 billion tons over the total number of ports is very uneven. Table 2.2 shows the 25 largest ports worldwide in total cargo throughput in 2023. Ningbo-Zhoushan was the first port to handle more than 1 billion tons of cargo and currently handles about 4% of the total global port volumes. The top 25 combined handle about one-third of total global port volumes.

Table 2.2 The 25 largest ports worldwide in total cargo throughput in 2023

Port	*Country*	*Volume 2023**
Ningbo-Zhoushan	China	1300
Tangshan	China	806
Shanghai	China	700
Qingdao	China	600
Singapore	Singapore	592
Port Hedland	Australia	574
Suzhou	China	566
Rizhao	China	522
Guangzhou	China	500
Tianjin	China	500
Yantai	China	485
Busan	South Korea	440
Rotterdam	The Netherlands	439
Qinhuangdao	China	392
Huanghua	China	330
Dalian	China	316
Shenzhen	China	310
Antwerp	Belgium	271

(*Continued*)

Table 2.2 (Continued)

Port	*Country*	*Volume 2023**
Houston	United states	267
South Louisiana	United states	225
Yingkou	China	220
Los Angeles & Long Beach	United states	195
Nagoya	Japan	190
Hongkong	China	175
Chiba	Japan	156

Source: Author, based on data reported on port websites and national statistical agencies; in some cases, estimates from news items were used.

The rise of Chinese ports: Ningbo-Zhoushan and Shanghai

Due to Shanghai's location at the mouth of the Yangtze River, an enormous natural hinterland, the port was already important in the 16th century. In the 1930s it was an important trade centre in Asia. However, partly due to the closed Chinese economy at the time, Shanghai's rise to its current status as largest container port in the world started slowly. The first standard container service started in 1978, more than ten years after the first container services between Europe and the United States. In the 1980s, the first-generation container terminals were built. The facilities were small; in 1992 Shanghai handled less than 750,000 TEU, compared to more than 6 million in Singapore and Hong Kong.

In the early 1990s, the national government of China made the decision to develop Shanghai into an international container port. This decision was followed up with the development of a new set of terminals in the Pudong area, enabling a steep increase in throughput to more than 10 million TEU in 2004. Further expansion took place in the Yangshan deepwater port area, about 30 kilometres off the coast of Shanghai. The first facility opened in 2009. In 2011 Shanghai handled more than 31 million TEU, of which more than 12 million tons in Yangshan. Fast port development accommodated China's double-digit growth.

Around 2012, Ningbo-Zhoushan took over Shanghai's position as largest port worldwide. Ningbo-Zhousan is also located close to the Yangtze River, around 100 km. south of Shanghai. The five largest ports worldwide in volume terms are in China. They rose to these positions due to China's rapid manufacturing-led economic development.

2.2.1 The largest container ports worldwide

Next to the total freight volume, rankings of container ports receive widespread attention. Table 2.3 shows the 20 largest container ports worldwide. Different accounting methods are used, but the data do provide a reliable, broad picture.

Table 2.3 The 20 largest container ports worldwide

Rank	*Port*	*Country*	*Location*	*Volume 2013 (Million TEU)*	*Volume 2024 (Million TEU)*
1	Shanghai	China	Yangtze Delta	33.6	51.5
2	Singapore	Singapore	Malacca Strait	32.2	41.1
3	Ningbo-Zhoushan	China	Yangtze Delta	17.4	39.3
4	Shenzhen	China	Pearl River Delta	23.3	33.4
5	Qingdao	China	Yellow Sea	15.5	30.9
6	Guangzhou	China	Pearl River Delta	15.3	26.1
7	Busan	South Korea	Korean Strait	17.7	24.4
8	Tianjin	China	Yellow Sea	13.0	23.3
9	Dubai	UAE	Arab Peninsula	13.6	15.5
10	Port Klang	Malaysia	Malacca Strait	10.4	14.6
11	Rotterdam	Netherlands	North Sea	11.6	13.8
12	Hong Kong	Hong Kong	Pearl River Delta	22.4	13.7
13	Antwerp	Belgium	North Sea	8.6	13.5
14	Xiamen	China	Taiwan Strait	8.0	12.3
15	Tanjung Pelepas	Malaysia	Malacca Strait	7.6	12.3
16	Los Angeles	USA	West Coast	7.9	10.3
17	Tanger-Med	Morocco	Strait of Gibraltar	1.8	10.2
18	Suzhou	China	Yangtze Delta	5.9	9.7
19	Long Beach	USA	US West Coast	6	9.7
20	Laem Chabang	Thailand	Gulf of Thailand	5.7	9.6

Source: World Shipping Council (2025).

2.2.2 *The fastest-growing ports*

As another relevant ranking, Table 2.5 shows the fastest-growing large ports in the period 1992–2023 (31 years). The ports are ranked by annual growth rate. As may have been expected, Chinese ports have grown much faster than the ports in advanced economies.

Particularly, Chinese seaports have recorded elevated growth rates in the past 30 years. The large growth differences between ports located in the same region are worth noting. For instance, while Hong Kong's growth stalled, Shenzhen continued to grow throughout the whole period.

2.3 The roles of ports in maritime networks

The competitiveness of ports as transport nodes depends critically on their position in *maritime networks*. In bulk shipping, ships generally follow the cargo and shipping lines do not offer specific routes. This shipping segment is commonly termed "tramp shipping". In contrast, for container flows, as well as for ferry traffic and car carriers, shipping lines offer specific service networks (liner shipping). In most

It's all about containers

The annual ranking of largest container ports in the world receives widespread attention. Media often fail to mention that the container market is only a fraction of all cargo handled in ports. For example, 23% of all cargo handled in European ports was containerized in 2023 (see Table 2.4).

Table 2.4 Distribution of cargo volumes in the EU port system

Cargo type	*Volume 2023*	*Share*
Liquid bulk goods	1,263,904	38%
Containers	757,449	23%
Dry bulk goods	719,658	22%
Ro-Ro	424,580	13%
Other	173,002	5%
Total	3,338,593	

Source: Own calculation based on data from Eurostat (2025a).

It is easy to understand why so many people equate containers with ports and forget about the rest. After all, the container industry was the fastest growing market for ports in the past few decades and is expected to continue to grow substantially. Most investments in new port infrastructure are focused on the container market. Furthermore, container transport is the backbone of global trade. In *value terms*, the container market handles over 90% of all seaborne trade and is used for a huge variety of commodities, ranging from scrap and paper pulp to electronics and food. Over the last decade, various commodities have become increasingly containerized. Examples include fruit, cars and non-ferro metals.

Table 2.5 Average annual growth of the largest ports worldwide 1992–2023

Port	*Country*	*Average annual growth 1992–2023*
Rizhao	China	21%
Ningbo-Zhoushan	China	17%
Qingdao	China	15%
Tianjin	China	14%
Busan	South Korea	14%
Port Hedland	Australia	12%
Guangzhou	China	11%
Qinhuangdao	China	9%
Kandla Deendayal	India	9%
Dalian	China	8%
Shanghai	China	7%
Houston	United States	7%
Shenzhen	China	7%

(*Continued*)

Table 2.5 (Continued)

Port	*Country*	*Average annual growth 1992–2023*
Los Angeles and Long Beach	United States	6%
Antwerp	Belgium	5%
Singapore	Singapore	4%
South Louisiana	United states	4%
Hongkong	China	4%
Rotterdam	The Netherlands	2%
Nagoya	Japan	2%
Chiba	Japan	–0.5%

Source: Based on data from websites of port authorities and national statistical agencies.

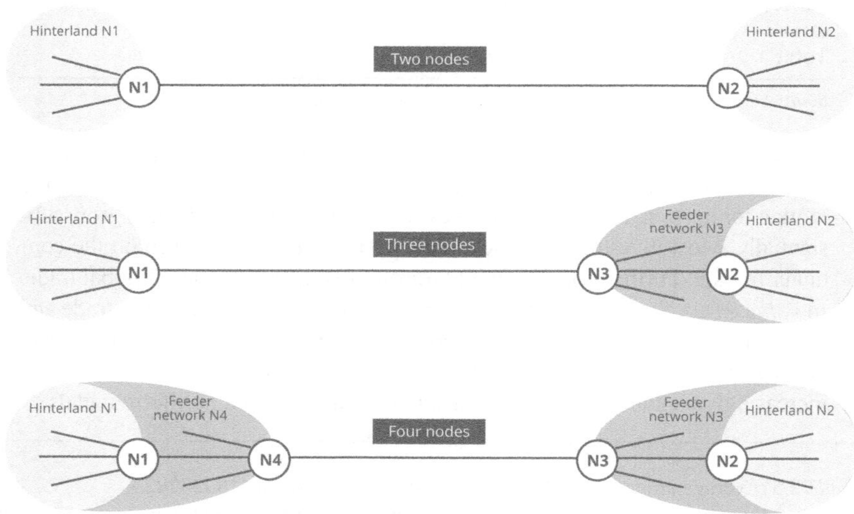

Figure 2.1 Nodes and their links

of these service networks, more than two ports (this is the minimum – one port for loading and one for unloading) are used. In such a network, cargo is shipped from a small port to a large *hub* port to be combined with other cargo. This network structure is efficient because of the scale economies in shipping. As a result, a *hub and spoke* system arises, in which smaller volumes are transported in relatively small vessels and over relatively small distances to hub ports, where they are combined so that large ships can be deployed between hubs. Figure 2.1 illustrates the use of intermediate nodes in scheduled shipping services.

Nodes N3 and N4 are hubs. These are the central ports from where smaller ports (N2 and N1) are served.[2] Achieving a "hub status" is attractive because it leads to substantial volumes. A hub status is also attractive for the economy at large, as hub ports have better maritime connectivity, and this connectivity reduces trade costs and thus increases volumes of trade.

Hub and spoke networks – mainly but not exclusively used for scheduled services

Even though the hub and spoke network is most advanced in container shipping, other commodities are also shipped through intermediate hubs. For instance, car carriers (which transport new cars, as opposed to ferries, which transport cars and passengers) often use hub ports as well, from which cars are transported to final import ports. As an example, Toyota uses a terminal in Malmö as such a hub, for cars destined for one of the Baltic countries.

Likewise, a small number of ports also serve as hubs in the global oil trade. Rotterdam is an example, as it is used as a hub for oil products from Russian refineries that are sent to Asia. In a similar fashion, some ports are hubs for LNG, from which "small scale" LNG is shipped to smaller destination ports, for instance to supply LNG to ships. As with containers, for all commodities where such a hub pattern has emerged, the hub function tends to lead to additional investments in storage and processing.

2.3.1 Four port types in container shipping

The complexity of the liner shipping network is increasing, because the number of container ports is rising, transport volumes are increasing substantially, ship sizes have increased and may further increase, and liner shipping companies are increasingly investing in terminal facilities.

There is a huge literature on liner shipping networks and port typologies (starting from Taaffe et al., 1963). The following main stylized roles of ports in maritime networks can be distinguished: hub port, gateway port, regional port and minor port (see Table 2.6).

Hub ports are generally located near the main routes of the global maritime networks. The main function of these ports is a transhipment function: generally, more than 60% of the cargo handled is sea–sea transhipment, but this percentage may be above 90, as is the case in Algeciras, Tanger-Med, Port Said and Singapore. The hinterland is mostly relatively close to the port, with road being the dominant hinterland mode. Hub ports are located at maritime routes because at such locations, the "deviation distance" is the smallest: shipping lines hardly have to make a detour to call these ports. For instance, Port Said is next to the Suez Canal, so all ships between Asia and Europe pass by the terminal.

Load centers are ports that serve a large hinterland of over 300 km from the port, generally including one or more metropolitan areas. Transhipment is (much) less important than hinterland transport. Load centers generally have relatively good intermodal hinterland connections. Examples include Rotterdam, Barcelona, New York/New Jersey, Buenos Aires and Melbourne.

Table 2.6 Container port types and their characteristics

Aspect	*Characteristic*	*Hub port*	*Load center*	*Regional port*	*Minor port*
Logic of location	Maritime network	Located strategically near (the intersection of) major shipping routes	Peripheral in the maritime network	Unimportant position in the maritime network	Unimportant position in the maritime network
	Hinterland network	Limited natural hinterland	An extensive and voluminous hinterland	A substantial industrial/ metropolitan hinterland	Local traffic base
Hinterland and transhipment role	Transhipment	>60% (sea/sea) transhipment	<40% sea/sea transhipment	Minimal sea/sea transhipment	No transhipment
	Hinterland modes	Limited local hinterland	>60% direct to hinterland substantial share (at least 10%) of origins/ destinations >300 km	At least 90% of the volumes with origin/ destination <500 km	Direct local hinterland, at least 90% of the volumes with origin/ destination <100 km
	Intermodal connections	Intermodal connections of limited importance	Intermodal connections are important in the modal split	A limited number of intermodal services	Hardly any intermodal facilities
Service characteristics	Vessel size	The largest vessels are at least 12,000 TEU	The largest vessels are at least 12,000 TEU	The largest vessels are up to 8000 TEU	Largest vessels up to 1000 TEU
	Service calls	Frequent calls of major services, in some cases dominance of one shipping line	Frequent calls of the major services of a number of shipping lines	Calls of secondary services (shortsea, feeder and secondary intercontinental services)	Feeder and shortsea services
	Indicative minimal annual volume	>1 million TEU cargo	>2 million TEU cargo	>150,000 TEU	<200,000 TEU

Note that some ports function both as a hub *and* as a gateway port. Examples include Shanghai (which is the gateway both to the metropolitan area of Shanghai and to the Yangtse River, as well as a hub for cargo to/from regional ports in Japan, China and Korea) and Rotterdam (which serves a large European hinterland and is a hub port, where containers are transhipped to smaller ports in the UK, Ireland and the Baltic).

Regional ports are ports mainly serving manufacturing or population regions of a moderate size. They are well located to serve their region, but do not attract transhipment, nor do they serve vast hinterlands. Regional ports are regularly served by medium-sized vessels and handle above 150,000 TEU annually. Regional ports can develop into load centers, mainly through the growth of the import export volumes.

Minor ports are located near small manufacturing or population centers. They arise when volumes are sufficient to make the presence of a small container facility economically viable[3]. Such a facility is, in general, served only by small vessels.

This port typology can be used for analyzing *network dynamics* in liner shipping. Maritime networks change constantly, driven by increasing ship sizes, mergers and alliances (the current industry structure with a limited number of competing alliances, each with a global service network, leads to more concentration of transhipment flows in a limited number of hub ports[4]), and investments in port infrastructure.

Given the effect of better maritime connectivity on trade, countries often consider ports as strategic infrastructure and thus invest in port infrastructure aimed at improving the position of ports in maritime networks. Examples of countries that have developed explicit policies to improve maritime connectivity through investments in ports include Morocco (Tangier-Med and, in a later phase, Nador-West), the Ivory Coast (Abidjan), Sri Lanka (Colombo) and Egypt (Port Said). New investments in port and terminal infrastructure can lead to adaptations of maritime network structures. In the case of West Africa, for instance, the region starts to attract direct deep-sea calls of large ships, whereas it used to be a region served by feeder ships. The changes in liner shipping networks will present opportunities for some ports and threats for others.

Evolving maritime networks: Gemini's Asia–Europe services

The joint network offered by Maersk and Hapag Lloyd in their alliance (called Gemini) is one recent example of a newly developed maritime network. This network is innovative in the use of transhipment to serve large "gateway ports" that traditionally have attracted "direct calls" on the mainline services. As an example, the Gemini network from Asia to Europe will not include a direct call in a port in Japan (which will be serviced through Shanghai), and Europe's second largest port, Antwerp, will also not be called directly, but instead be serviced through Tanger/Rotterdam. Apart from the large ports included in Figure 2.2, well over 100 feeder ports in Europe are connected to the services network.

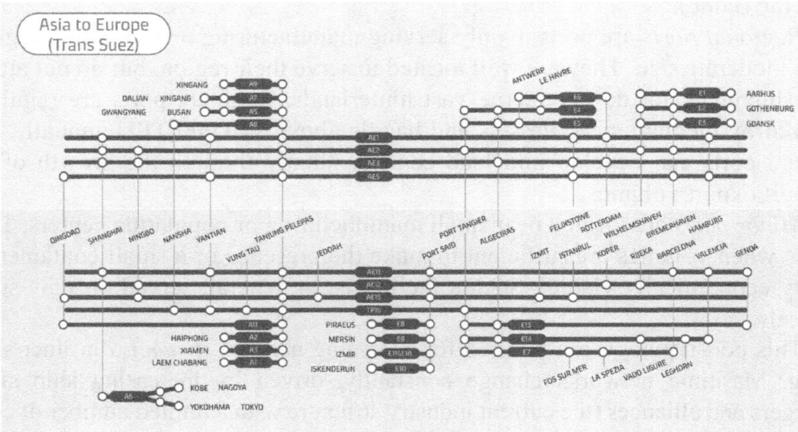

Figure 2.2 Gemini's announced Asia–Europe network, June 2024

Source: Maersk (2025).

2.4 The roles of ports in hinterland networks

Apart from the maritime network, the hinterland network of a port determines its ability to capture transport flows. The port connects port users, both consumers and producers, in the *hinterland* of a port with overseas markets. The "hinterland" can be loosely defined as the area inland from the port to which cargoes from overseas are distributed and from which cargoes with destinations overseas are shipped. Figure 2.3 shows a stylized port hinterland network.

Figure 2.3 shows a stylized port network, with five components:[5]

1) Inland terminals: These are the intermodal terminals that serve regional markets. Generally, important users are located in the direct vicinity of these inland terminals.
2) Inland hubs: These are intermodal terminals that function as hubs, and from where cargoes continue their intermodal journey to inland terminals. Generally, such hubs are located at intersections of hinterland corridors.
3) Satellite terminals: These are inland terminals located outside the (congested) port area, which serve as an alternative to the deep-sea port for trucks. Thus, trucks drop off and collect containers at the satellite terminal instead of at the deep-sea terminal.
4) Connections: These are connections between the port and the above-mentioned inland terminals, hubs and satellite terminals.
5) Logistics zones: These are zones in the hinterland that often have developed areas adjacent to intermodal terminals.

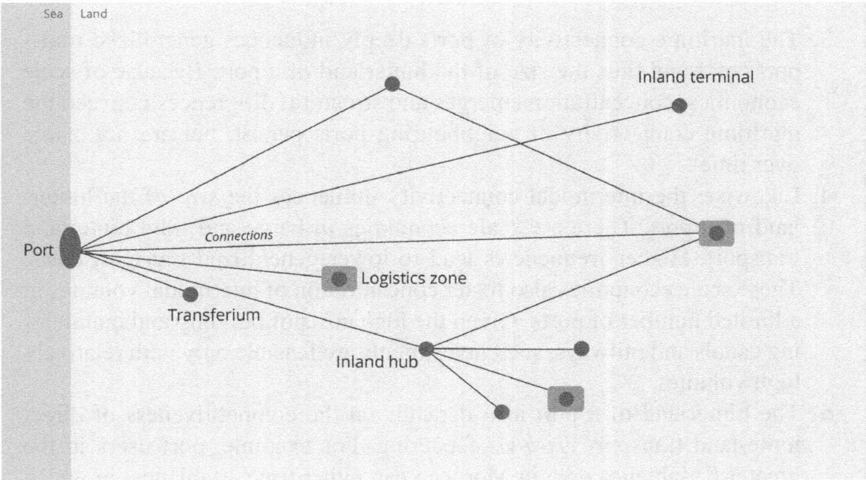

Figure 2.3 A stylized port hinterland network

The distinction between inland terminals, inland hubs and satellites is in practice blurred. Some inland nodes may have characteristics of two of these types.

The size of the hinterland of a port

The size of the hinterland of a port is elementary for understanding the business the port may attract. However, it is also complex to analyze port hinterlands. The hinterland of Port A would consist of all areas where this port has similar or lower generalized costs than competing ports. A method to analyze whether or not a port has a generalized cost advantage is complex for a number of reasons:

1. The hinterland of a port is "relational" in the sense that it depends on the overseas origin/destination of the cargo. For instance, the hinterland of the port complex of LA & LB covers, say, as much as 60% of the whole US territory for goods to/from north-east Asia, while it may be as limited as 15% of the US territory for goods to/from Europe.
2. The hinterland of a port also depends on the characteristics of the cargo, mainly its "value of time". For instance, Swiss may be a hinterland of ports in the south of Europe (e.g., Genoa, Venice) except for cargoes with a low value of time, for which Swiss may be Rotterdam's hinterland, due to the availability of low-cost but time-consuming barge services.

3. The maritime connectivity of ports deeply influences generalized transport costs and thus the size of the hinterland of a port. Because of scale economies, concentration emerges and structural differences between the maritime connectivity of neighbouring ports persist, but are not stable over time.
4. Likewise, the intermodal connectivity influences the size of the hinterland of a port. There are scale economies in barge and train hinterland transport. Higher frequencies lead to lower generalized transport costs. These scale economies also foster concentration of intermodal volumes in a limited number of ports. Given the high costs of building and maintaining canals and railways, such investments are feasible only with relatively high volumes.
5. The hinterland of a port also depends on the competitiveness of direct hinterland transport *vis-à-vis* feedering. For example, port users in the greater Casablanca area in Morocco can either use Casablanca, in which case most containers will be transhipped (in either Tangier-Med or another transhipment hub), or truck their cargo directly to the port Tangier-Med, which has many *direct calls* to destinations in Asia, Europe and elsewehere.
6. Institutional aspects, such as tax regimes and border crossing procedures, also influence the size of port hinterlands, generally favouring "domestic ports" over the use of foreign ports.

Given the characteristics of hinterland discussed above, port hinterlands are 'path dependent', in the sense that past developments in ports affect the future development path of these ports.

Past developments, such as investments in infrastructure, affect the further development of ports and hinterlands through *first-mover advantages*. These explain why ports that have developed certain hinterlands often continue to serve regions with lower generalized transport costs, even though from a purely geographic point of view, other ports may be better positioned. For instance, Hamburg has a huge market share in Bavaria due to its first-mover advantage, even though from a geographic perspective, other ports like Rotterdam, Koper or Trieste are better positioned to serve that hinterland. Hamburg has a large market share and, as a result, a very good intermodal connectivity in Bavaria, with more than 70 weekly trains to various destinations in Bavaria. Other ports face an uphill battle in increasing their market shares, and may also need investments in infrastructure whose business case (and "value case"[6]) is problematic given the fact that they duplicate existing infrastructural connections to Bavaria.

A simple model of a port's hinterland

A simple model of a port's hinterland can provide a first rough indication of the hinterland of a port. The method is based on three variables:

1. Road distance to the region relative to the distance from other ports.
2. Maritime distance relative to the maritime distance from other ports.
3. Maritime connectivity of the port (function of ship calls and call size), compared to the maritime connectivity of other ports.

For a specific hinterland region, based on data on each of these three variables, the most optimal port for a certain overseas destination region can be assessed. The calculation can be treated as a calculation to assess the utility o. ctain port for cargo between a certain hinterland region and a certain overseas region:

$$U_{p,h,wr} = \alpha_0^{p,h} + \alpha_1 RD_{p,h} + \alpha_2 MD_{p,wr} + \alpha_3 MC_p$$

$U_{p,h,wr}$ is the utility of a certain port p for cargo between a certain hinterland region *h* and a certain overseas region *wr*; $RD_{p,h}$ is the road distance between port p and hinterland region *h*; $MD_{p,wr}$. is the maritime distance between port p and a certain world region. MC_p is the maritime connectivity of port *p*. The alphas α_1 to α_3 represent the weight of the variables; α_0 can be regarded as an error term. These coefficients can be based either on estimates in other countries or on empirical analysis for the country to which the model is applied.

The weights of the variables can be based on empirical analysis. The most basic model would include these three variables; more variables can be added to this function based on specific considerations. Examples may include border crossings or the presence of locks. There is a substantial literature on hinterland networks (see Caballé Valls et al., 2020; Talley & Ng, 2022).

2.4.1 *Captive and contestable hinterlands*

A distinction can be made between captive and contestable hinterlands. This distinction is similar to the distinction made by Morgan (1951) between primary hinterlands, the area where the port is well established, and secondary hinterlands, with rivalry among ports. All regions where one port has a substantial competitive advantage because of lower generalized transport costs belong to the captive hinterland of this port. Consequently, this port handles the vast majority of all cargoes to/from these regions. Contestable hinterlands consist of all those regions without a single port with a clear cost advantage over competing ports. As a consequence, various ports will have a share of the market.

It is often argued that captive hinterlands have declined. This can, for instance, be due to increasing intermodal options to reach hinterlands (see, for instance, Cuadrado et al., 2004). However, many ports, especially in emerging economies, still have substantial captive hinterlands. As illustrations: Container cargo to/from Catalonia is rather captive for the port of Barcelona, the greater New York area is captive for the port of New York and New Jersey, and the whole of the Ivory Coast is captive for Abidjan. This may give rise to dominant market positions of terminal operators in the port or the port development company. This issue is addressed in more detail in Chapter 4 on port policies.

Austria as a case of a contestable hinterland

Austria is a case of a contestable hinterland.[7] Figure 2.4 shows the main seaports serving Austria.

The ports serving Austria can be grouped together into the "North ports" (Hamburg & Bremen), the West ports (Antwerp and Rotterdam) and the South ports (Trieste, Koper and Rijeka). Figures 2.5 and 2.6 show the evolution of market shares of the North, West and South ports from 1989 to 2019 for imports and for exports; more recent statistics are not available. Statistics for specific commodities are also not available; imports are mainly bulk products, and exports are mainly containers.

These data allow four important conclusions. First, new large-scale infrastructure can lead to substantial shifts between ports. The rising market share of Rotterdam and Antwerp (for imports from under 20% to over 50% for various years) can be attributed to the opening of the Rhine-Main Donau Canal. This has led to a

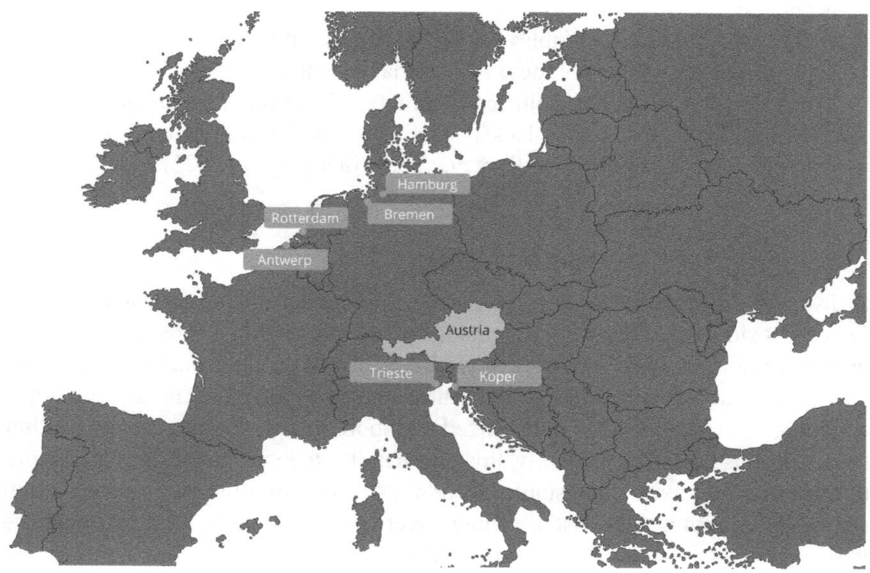

Figure 2.4 The main ports serving Austria

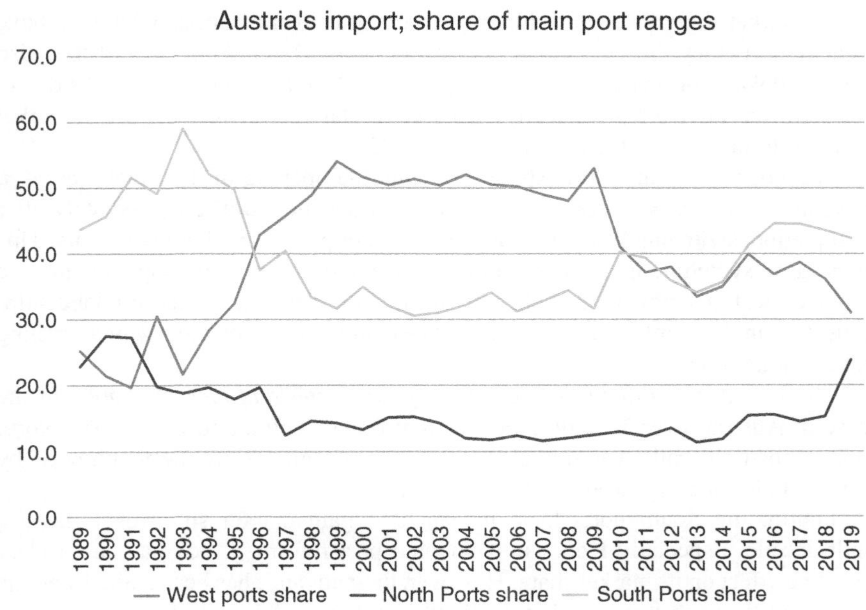

Figure 2.5 Austrian market shares of North, West and South ports; imports 1989–2019

Source: Verkehr (2020).

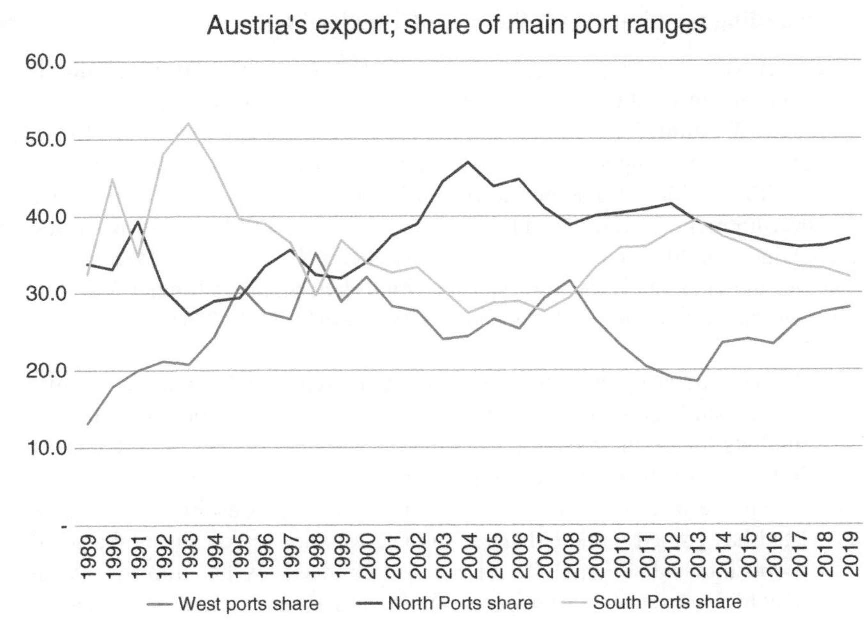

Figure 2.6 Austrian market shares of North, West and South ports; exports 1989–2019

Source: Verkehr (2020).

larger market share for inland shipping, from which Rotterdam and Antwerp have benefited, as they are well connected to the Rhine River. Another port that also benefited was Constanza (Romania), a port that played no role in the 1980s due to the Iron Curtain, but has gradually increased its share of the market, with a market share of around 7% of the total volume in 2023.

Second, the rise in market share following the opening of the canal *has taken roughly a decade*. Whereas a new highway attracts new traffic immediately after completion, switching from one transport mode or port to another takes years. This is because switching incurs costs. For instance, the structure of supply chains and storage locations may need to change, or firms may need to invest in inland shipping terminals or inland barges. These "switching costs" explain why switching takes a long time.

Third, *hinterland distance does not explain hinterland market shares*. In the case of Austria, over 35% of export freight flows continue to flow to the North ports, mostly by rail, even though Austria is also connected to the South ports by rail, and distances are around 500 km longer.

Fourth, the South ports have managed to gain market share over the last half-decade. Especially Koper implemented port reform, which has had a clear positive effect on its market share. However, their advance has been stalled, and the most significant shift was within the South ports, from Trieste to Koper.

Expanding the hinterland: the case of Tangier-Med

Tangier-Med is a major port development located on the Strait of Gibraltar and at the northern edge of Morocco. Tangier-Med attracted transhipment traffic immediately after opening (96% of its almost 3 million TEU in 2016 were transhipped) and is increasing hinterland traffic step by step. In 2024, Tanger-Med surpassed the 10 million TEU mark, of which still >90% is transhipment. Tangier-Med handled less than 11% of Morocco's domestic containers in 2017, compared with Casablanca's 74%. Tangier-Med mainly serves the Tangier–Tétouan region. The hinterland share of Tangier-Med has grown due to two different mechanisms (see World Bank, 2018):

1. A manufacturing growth effect. Tangier-Med's hinterland has grown faster than Morocco as a whole due to the presence of the port. The immediate hinterland region has a thriving auto components and assembly industry, as well as textile, clothing and light manufacturing industries.
2. A "shift effect" of cargo that was routed through Casablanca. Tangier-Med has gained market share in the Fès-Meknès region (in total around 4.4 million inhabitants). Tangier's road connectivity has improved with new highway stretches between Tangier and Meknès and Fès, further investments are under way.

2.4.2 Intermodal transport and the role of inland terminals

Driven partly by a policy focus on sustainable mobility, partly by the policy aim to promote international trade and export competitiveness, many countries aim to increase the share of rail and barge (where inland waterways are available) transport in the "modal split", i.e., the distribution of freight flows over different transport modes. This has given rise to increased attention to intermodal transport.[8]

Intermodality, co-modality, synchromodality and dry ports

Various relatively new terms have been developed to clarify how hinterland transport is organized. Intermodality refers to seamless transport in which various modes are used, "comodality" broadly means the combined use of the various modes of transport as complementary options. "Synchromodality" is the flexible allocation of cargo to different modes and routes in a network based on real-time information on delivery requirements (i.e., if stock levels are high, the cheapest and slowest mode would be used, but if there is a need for fast delivery, the truck is used; see Van Riessen et al. (2015), for an overview of research issues on synchromodality). Finally, "dry port" is a bit of an ambiguous term; it is most widely taken to be an inland terminal with as distinctive feature the ability of to perform customs clearance in the dry port instead of in the seaport. This can be an important benefit for port users, as it may enable them to postpone customs clearance (which may have benefits in terms of postponing payments) and it may lead to lower transaction costs if customs processes in the dry port are more efficient.

Policymakers in various countries aim to increase the share of intermodal transport because of its lower environmental impact and the positive effect of shifting cargo to intermodal transport on road congestion. For instance, in Europe the policy aim is to shift 30% of EU road freight over 300 km to rail and waterborne transport by 2030 and achieve a shift of 50% by 2050.

Intermodal connectivity in Europe – some empirical findings

Intermodal connectivity is relevant for port users in the same way that maritime connectivity is relevant. However, the body of knowledge on intermodal connectivity is still limited. The following findings from an analysis of intermodal connections in Europe are relevant:

First, rail and barge are complementary, in the sense that the number of overlapping OD pairs is limited and that barge is strong in relatively short distance transport, while rail generally is used for longer transport distances.

Second, the lowest transport distances are much lower than often assumed. Services over short distances are feasible, especially between ports and for mountain crossings. Nevertheless, even for more "regular" port to hinterland services, various cases of services at a distance below 100 km exist.

Third, service frequencies are on average very substantial (at least three times a week). These frequencies diminish with distance. This may be related to the efficient deployment of equipment, which may require higher frequencies on shorter trajectories.

Fourth, barge transport is barely used for inland-to-inland services; for rail, port hinterland connections are also much more common than services between two inland locations.

2.5 Metrics for the performance of ports as transport nodes

Various indicators have been developed to evaluate the performance of the port as a transport node. Some of these are discussed in more detail in Chapter 9 on goals and performance indicators for PMBs. Below, the following indicators are discussed:

- Liner Shipping Connectivity.
- Modal split.
- Container terminal productivity.
- Time spent in ports.

2.5.1 The Liner Shipping Connectivity Index

The Liner Shipping Connectivity Index is the most popular indicator of maritime networks. Published annually by the United Nations Conference on Trade and Development (UNCTAD) since 2004, it is a national (not port-level) index, focusing on container shipping market integration of national economies in global container shipping networks. The Liner Shipping Connectivity Index is constructed from globally available information on shipping routes and shipping activity.

The index consists of normalized averages of indicators of the number of ships calling in a country, average and maximum size of ships calling in the country, container throughput, number of services, and number of shipping companies linking to other countries. In 2014 the UNCTAD launched the Liner Shipping Bilateral Connectivity Index, a second indicator measuring how well a pair of countries is connected.

2.5.2 Modal split

The modal split of a port refers to the split of the hinterland volumes over different transport modes: road, rail, inland waterways and pipeline transport. Modal split data are mostly used for container transport. Mainly because of its location at the mouth of the river Rhine, Rotterdam is a port with a relatively low share of road transport (55%) and high shares of barge (35%) and rail (10%). An example of a port with a very unusual high share of rail transport is the port of Prince Rupert (located in Canada, about 750 km north of Vancouver), where more than 95% of all volumes are transported to the hinterland by rail.

2.5.3 Container terminal productivity

The World Bank and S&P Global Market Intelligence jointly publish an annual report on container Port performance. The study develops a container port productivity index, based on the total time a container ship spends in a port, in relation to the ship size and *call size* (the number of containers handled). The aim is "like-for-like" comparisons between ports, between ships with a certain size and call size (for instance, a capacity between 5000 and 8000 TEU and a call size of 1501–2000 containers). The required data for this analysis is provided by the shipping lines (in 2023, almost 200,000 port calls, 250 million container moves at 876 container terminals in 508 ports) and supplemented with vessel movement data from AIS.

The complexity of benchmarking terminal performance

The have been various initiatives to benchmark terminal performance, but developing like-for-like comparisons is complicated. The World Bank port performance indicator is the most advanced effort for such a benchmark, but also needs to be understood keeping in mind its weaknesses:

- The indicator is partial and developed from the perspective of the shipping line. This obviously is an important customer of the port and highly relevant, but no attention is given to items such as landside performance (how reliable, efficient and competitively priced is the landside operation, for instance the pick-up of the container by a truck) and berth/equipment utilization levels. Underutilized ports are likely to score better on the CPPI than higher utilized ones.
- The indicator includes ship waiting time even though that is not necessarily the result of poor port performance. The waiting time is a significant part of total port time and may be caused by factors such as out-of-window arrivals and tidal windows.
- The complexity of handling operations is not the same across ports. The clearest difference is between transhipment (T/S) and gateway operations. T/S operations are generally less complex, and thus ports with large T/S volumes would be expected to have shorter port stays (all else equal).

As a result of the above, especially ports with low utilization and high T/S volumes do well in the ranking.

2.5.4 Time spent in the port

UNCTAD has developed an indicator on the time ships have spent in a port, based on AIS data. The median time in port (in days) is used to ignore statistical outliers, i.e., ships that spend weeks or months in a port, for example, for repairs. The data do not allow a "like-for-like" comparison, since there are no data on ship size and volumes (un)loaded. Table 2.7 shows findings for a selection of countries (more and more recent data is available at https://unctadstat.unctad.org/datacentre/dataviewer/US.PortCalls).

Containerships in general are handled faster than liquid and dry bulk ships, partly because they are smaller, partly because the value of both the cargoes and the ship is higher. Japan and Singapore stand out with low port times, while the US is above the global average for all three commodity types.

Table 2.7 Average port stay in days of three ship types 2023

Country	*Liquid bulk*	*Dry bulk*	*Container*
World	0.99	2.13	0.71
Australia	1.3	1.67	1.44
Canada	1.07	0.36	1.46
China	1.11	2.01	0.6
Germany	0.44	2.52	1.02
Indonesia	1.32	2.69	0.97
Japan	0.32	0.9	0.35
South Korea	0.74	2.71	0.65
Netherlands	0.54	1.07	0.8
Norway	0.66	0.86	0.3
Singapore	0.64	0.76	0.85
US	1.71	2.25	1.08

Source: UNCTAD (2025a).

Dwell time as performance indicator?

The World Bank's Logistics Performance Index uses various data sources, the 2023 version included Tradelens (a blockchain initiative from Maersk and IBM, that was terminated end of 2023) data on the door-to-door transport time of maritime container shipments. The major "source" of the variation of total door-to-door transport time is related to the time containers spend in ports and dry ports. Especially in the "import port" dwell times (i.e., the time the container spends at the terminal before onward transport to the final destination) differ substantially between countries, and not always as would intuitively be expected: the average import dwell time is much higher in advanced economies (8.3 days in Belgium, 7.6 in Germany, 7.2 in The

Netherlands and the US) than in emerging economies such as China (5.5) India (2.6) and Cambodja (2.1). The lowest import dwell time is found in Japan: 1.0 days.

While I agree in principle with the World Bank that lower dwell times are part of a better logistics performance, in some cases, containers remain at the import port to optimize the logistics chain. The most important issue for shippers is a) the ability to freely decide when to pick up their goods/ containers and b) fast truck turnaround times at the terminal. When shippers can freely decide when and how to pick up their containers, they may opt to leave containers at the terminal until the goods are needed.

Another caveat to keep in mind is that modern large (semi-)automated are designed for an average dwell time of around 5–7 days, while container operations at older terminals with a limited yard space may have to adjust their pricing policies to secure low dwell times and reach an acceptable terminal efficiency. In short, a deep understanding of drivers of high dwell times is needed to make sense of the data.

Notes

1 See www.marinetraffic.com
2 Serving smaller ports from a hub port over sea is called "feedering". Smaller ports are therefore referred to as "feeder ports" in maritime networks.
3 Since investing in such a facility becomes more viable when other port facilities are further away, many minor ports are located in peripheral locations.
4 A relevant example is Piraeus, where following the Cosco concession for the terminal, the services from the Ocean Alliance (which includes Cosco China Shipping) have increased, with a surge in container volumes as a result.
5 Note that this figure regards infrastructure as a given.
6 The term "value case" is used for the policy perspective, i.e., the value case includes not only the direct revenues from the investments but also the external and indirect effects. The value case can be calculated with the use of a "cost–benefit analysis" (CBA).
7 Austria is a relatively small, open and prosperous landlocked economy in Europe. Both imports and exports are more than 35% of the country's GDP.
8 Defined by the OECD as "Movement of goods (in one and the same loading unit or a vehicle) by successive modes of transport without handling of the goods themselves when changing modes". See https://stats.oecd.org/glossary/detail.asp?ID=4303

3 The port as a business ecosystem

Anyone who drives around in a seaport, takes a boat tour in a port or flies over a port will note that ports are complexes consisting of many different activities, such as terminals, warehouses, chemical plants, tank storage companies, container depots, rail terminals and food processing plants. Some of these activities are closely interrelated (like an oil terminal and a chemical plant), while others are more "loosely coupled" to each other. All these companies together form a *port business ecosystem* (PBE). Huge synergies arise from the co-location of such interrelated companies in ports. Many of these benefits arise "spontaneously". For instance, the Siemens plant for offshore wind blades in the port of Hull will use port facilities for receiving parts and transporting the blades to the offshore wind locations. Siemens in Hull will also use energy from nearby power plants and use transport operators located in the port area. These transactions among companies in the PBE make Siemens and the other companies more productive.

The business ecosystem concept in management

In strategic management, the concept of *business ecosystems* has become increasingly popular. Rothschild (1990) and Moore (1993) were early scholars using the term "ecosystem" for an economic community of interdependent firms. Business ecosystems are argued to emerge when synergies are strong enough for coordination in an ecosystem to arise, but not strong enough to lead to one integrated corporate hierarchy. Some authors, such as Jacobides et al. (2019), have developed a precise definition of a business ecosystem, allowing a distinction between business ecosystems and related concepts such as networks or alliances.

The key insight is that large companies do not compete "in isolation", but instead develop and shape business ecosystems that compete with other business ecosystems. For instance, the Windows ecosystem, developed by Microsoft but composed of thousands of additional companies, compete with the Mac OS/iOS business ecosystem. Likewise, the North American and European business ecosystems for design and production of aircraft, shaped by Boeing and Airbus, respectively, compete with each other.

DOI: 10.4324/9781003630784-3

In addition to the synergies that arise "spontaneously" due to the market transactions of the involved companies, other co-location benefits can be created through a well-functioning *port business ecosystem developer*, in cooperation with firms in the PBE. The PMB in many ports increasingly acts as such a PBE developer. This issue is further detailed below and in Chapter 9, which deals specifically with strategies of the PMB.

Business ecosystem vs cluster

The cluster concept, popular in regional studies and with regional policy-makers, has increasingly been applied to the port industry. The port of Valencia has embraced the port cluster concept and positions itself as a leader in *port cluster governance*; Korea aims to further develop its ports as logistics clusters; and UNCTAD and World Bank publications advise for the development of port and logistics clusters. Sheffi, a widely cited scholar from MIT, has written a book on logistics clusters (Sheffi, 2012), most of which are centered around port activities. I have applied the cluster perspective to ports (De Langen, 2004). A key novelty of the business ecosystem concept is the attention for business models and strategies of business ecosystem developers. To align with that literature and because I draw on insights from that literature, I use the term *port business ecosystem*. A port cluster can be considered to be a special case of a localized business ecosystem. While the PBE consists of geographically co-located companies, other business ecosystems (as the Windows ecosystem) consist of companies that are not co-located yet do form part of one business ecosystem.

The business ecosystems perspective adds to the understanding of ports in four important ways.

First, the business ecosystem perspective yields relevant insights for *port governance*. The business ecosystem perspective regards a port and industrial zone as one PBE. Following this logic, the optimal governance model for the development of this PBE is an integrated model in which the PMB is also responsible for the development of the industrial and logistics zones in the port area. The second important governance implication is that the development of a PBE is a deeply commercial activity, so the appropriate governance model for the developer of this ecosystem is a *corporatized* model – not a public administration model.

Second, the business ecosystem perspective provides insights regarding the *strategy* and *business model* of the PMB. For instance, the perspective leads to a better understanding of why and how the PMB can create value for firms in the business ecosystem through providing ecosystem services such as a digital port community platform, open access pipelines and innovation services. In addition, the business ecosystem perspective helps to understand the choice of the PMB between in-house service provision and attracting a third party to develop activities in the port business ecosystem.

Third, the business ecosystem perspective informs the *policy approach to port development*. More specifically, port policies benefit from a deep understanding of the *value creation* that results from the development of a PBE, both economic value creation and societal value creation. The limitations regarding capturing the economic and societal value that port development creates often make port development commercially unfeasible. For this reason, designing effective mechanisms for public funding of the development of the PBE has a central place in port policies, just as planning policies are needed to enable the development of a world-class PBE.

Finally, the business ecosystem perspective also provides a new perspective on indicators of port performance. More specifically, from the business ecosystem perspective, *investment levels* of third parties in the ecosystem are critical for its long-term competitiveness.

Due to various trends and developments, the port business ecosystem perspective is *increasingly* relevant. First, due to ongoing productivity gains and automation, the direct economic impact of the terminal activities is declining. In addition, the spatial requirements for new terminal activities are also limited, especially in advanced economies, where the expected growth of transport volumes is moderate. Thus, policymakers and PMBs aim to develop the port from a transport node to a larger business ecosystem of industrial, logistics and leisure activities, to create a larger economic impact as well as a more competitive port.

Second, ports as logistics-industrial "islands" are critical for accommodating new investments driven by the energy and (raw) materials transition. Such investments in the production, assembly, storage and maintenance of offshore windmills, in hydrogen plants to convert sustainable energy into hydrogen and ammonia, in plants for biofuels and circular recycling and production activities, are often best located in PBEs.

Third, a thriving PBE can play a critical role in the policy ambitions of many countries to advance their strategic autonomy, through increased energy independence and better access to critical raw materials.

Fourth, many PBEs face a huge *transition challenge*, as industries often located in the port area, such as oil refineries, steel plants, coal-fired power plants and chemical plants, need to transition or run the risk of becoming *stranded assets*. Generally, achieving such a transition requires a PBE perspective. For instance, transitioning a steel plant (as is relevant in the PBEs in Amsterdam, North Sea Port and Taranto, to name a few) requires availability of gas and hydrogen, which in turn requires initiatives and investments of the PBE. In cases where some activities close down, the PBE perspective is also relevant for the redevelopment of these areas. For instance, in the port of Newcastle (Australia), initiatives are taken to re-develop the site of a former steel plant to attract circular and clean energy activities, as these may complement and diversify Newcastle's PBE (see Schulz et al., 2025).

Port business ecosystems and freezones

Port business ecosystems may also function as freezones. There are more than 5000 freezones worldwide, many of them in ports or in the direct vicinity of ports. Many governments have used freezone policies to spur the industrial development of port business ecosystems. This approach has already been in place for centuries; the port city of Hamburg is a good example of an early "freeport", though currently that status is no longer very relevant.

Freezones can be defined as geographic areas where goods may be imported, stored, handled, manufactured or reconfigured and re-exported under specific customs regulation – generally with lower/no customs duties. The integrated development of port infrastructure and a freezone regime can be a powerful method for economic development, especially in areas with a large land availability. Many ports have benefitted substantially from a freeport status. Examples include Jebel Ali and Shenzhen. The most critical factor in explaining the rapid growth of the Chinese ports in the period 1980–2010 is China's policy to develop freezones in China's coastal areas. Recent large-scale port and freezone developments include Misurata Free Zone (Libya), Khalifa Port Free Trade Zone (UAE) and the Coega Special Economic Zone (South Africa). As discussed in more detail later, there often is a separation between "port development" and "freezone development" entities, even though this goes against the concept of an integrated PBE developer, focused on attracting terminals as well as manufacturing and logistics activities.

3.1 The co-location of companies in ports

Marshall one of the most important 19th-century economists, observed that related activities tend to co-locate together geographically. He developed the term *external economies*, "economies arising from an increase in the scale of production, dependent on the general development of the industry" (Marshall, 1890, p. 266). Three external economies drive co-location: a shared labor market, the presence of customers and suppliers and knowledge spill overs.[1] These mechanisms promoting co-location are also relevant for the co-location of activities in a PBE.

First, the presence of suppliers and customers is an advantage since "trade costs" (which include transport costs) for transactions between firms in the same PBE are lower than for transactions when one partner is located outside the PBE. The petrochemical business ecosystem in Houston and the automotive ecosystem ("Toyota village") are archetypal examples of business ecosystems that have emerged due to this external economy.

Second, the presence of a variety of firms with a similar labor demand promotes the development of skilled labor. Because of the "constant market for skill", it is attractive for workers to invest in specific training and education, and specialized training and education centers emerge. Availability of specialized labor is part of the reason why energy companies, chemical companies and logistics companies locate in PBEs.

Third, co-location in a PBE can improve access to specific knowledge and information. This is related to the fact that most knowledge is tacit, rather than formalized, and thus flows most efficiently through (unplanned) face-to-face meetings. This mechanism is also visible in ports, which aim and often succeed in attracting start-ups in maritime logistics to strengthen the PBE. This topic is further discussed in Chapter 8.

The two main constraints on the development of PBEs are land scarcity and congestion. Since space is limited, land becomes scarce and expensive. These high land prices reflect the strength of the PBE, but induce some firms to locate outside the PBE. For instance, while a food processing firm may ideally prefer a location in a port business ecosystem, this either may not be feasible (insufficient available land), or the land lease costs may be too high. Various PBE developers take initiatives to invest in "satellite locations" that they consider extensions of their PBEs. Congestion is a second constraint on the number of activities that can be co-located in a PBE. This explains the initiatives of the PMB as well as other stakeholders to improve the efficiency of transport to and from and within the PBE.

3.2 Four components of a port business ecosystem

Four components of a PBE can be distinguished[2] (see Figure 3.1).

The function of the port as a transport node is at the center of the PBE: cargo handling at terminals is the *raison d'être* of the port infrastructure. Since the port is an element of a transport chain from origin to destination, transport companies, as well as related specialized activities, such as storage, ship repair and ship

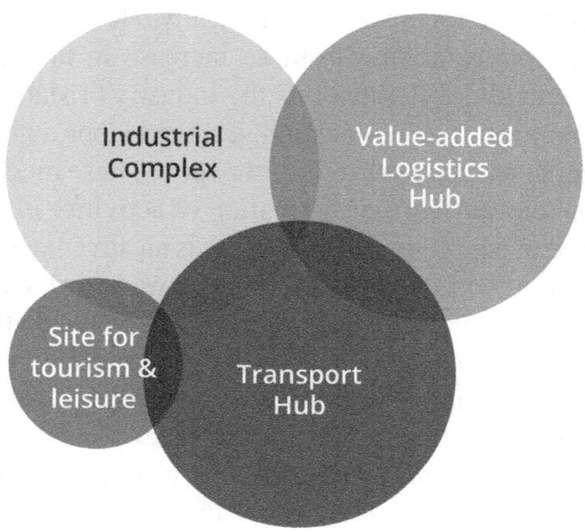

Figure 3.1 Four components of a port business ecosystem

management, are located in ports. All these activities can be regarded as elements of the function of the port as a transport hub.

Logistics activities, such as storage, re-packing and assembling, are frequently located in seaports. Logistics activities include all activities that add value to the goods, without involving a major transformation – in that case, these activities would be manufacturing activities.

Two reasons explain the presence of logistics activities in seaports. First, cargo is almost always temporarily *stored*, because of the scale differences between ships and inland modes (indicatively), transferring goods from a ship with a capacity of say 300,000 tons to trains (with an indicative capacity of say 3000 tons) barges (way a capacity of say 5000 tons) or trucks (with a capacity of about 25 tons) requires temporary storage of goods, in sheds, silos, stockpiles or container yards. This necessity of storage provides a rationale for locating logistics activities (such as blending and re-packing) in seaports: ports are natural (de)consolidation points.

Second, the availability of a large number of (intermodal) transport services makes a port an attractive location for logistics activities. Goods are delivered to end markets, both by land and by sea. This makes location in a port business ecosystem attractive, as the intermodal, shortsea and deep-sea connectivity of ports is very high. Thus, logistics zones in ports are often used not only to serve immediate regional markets, but also more distant markets. Perhaps the best example of this role is Jebel Ali (UAE), from which many other Gulf countries are served.

In addition, because ports have often gone hand in hand with urban agglomeration, many ports are located in metropolitan areas and thus well located for distribution facilities to these metropolitan regions. Included under the logistics category are also *trade activities*. Traditionally, trading and storage (in a port) are closely linked. All major port cities developed as commercial hubs. Although the strength of links between storage and trade has diminished, for some commodities (for instance, fruit, crude oil and grain), trading and related service activities are still related to storage and cargo handling and trading companies are located in the port. The links between ports and trade also explain why many of the free trade zones are located in direct proximity to ports. Some of the most successful free trade zones (FTZs), such as the Colon FTZ and the Jebel Ali FTZ, are located in the port area and form a part of the port business ecosystem.

Examples of *manufacturing activities* frequently strongly linked to ports are energy production, steel production, shipbuilding and repair, oil refining, chemical production and food production. Manufacturing activities in seaports are directly related to commodities handled in the port. Figure 3.2 shows the presence of manufacturing sectors in European ports, based on data from the European Seaports Organisation (ESPO, 2016).[3]

Manufacturing activities include large-scale plants that serve international markets. In addition, ports may also be attractive locations for small-scale manufacturing, as well as combinations between manufacturing and service activities. The rationale for locating manufacturing activities in ports generally stems from *supply chain efficiency* or *manufacturing synergies* due to a location in a port. With regard to supply chain efficiencies, the example of offshore wind components is

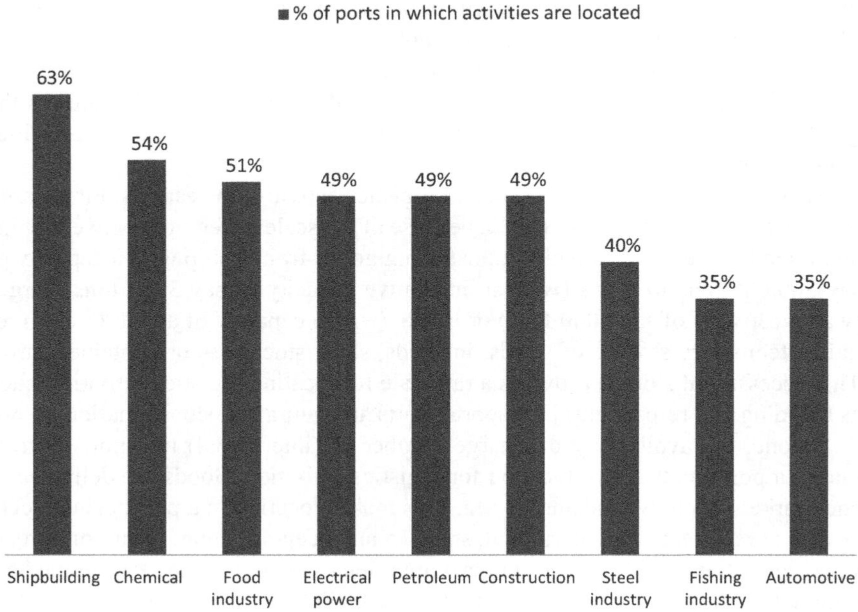

Figure 3.2 The presence of manufacturing sectors in European ports

Source: Based on data from ESPO (2016).

illustrative: such components are very large and heavy. Thus, producing such components in inland locations leads to high supply chain costs, as these components need to be transported to a port for installation offshore. Locating the manufacturing or assembly of these components in the port generates huge supply chain cost reductions. This explains why component manufacturers often locate in ports, such as Rotterdam, Bilbao and Hull. Ports often enable manufacturing synergies as utilities and sustainable energy are available and reliable, and companies can re-use heat and benefit from infrastructure to capture carbon.

Finally, ports increasingly also function as *leisure sites*. Ports accommodate cruises and (mega)yachts and may host tourism and leisure facilities such as hotels, restaurants, shops and museums. In addition, parts of the port-city areas no longer useful for terminal activities may be converted into public space. Because of the attractiveness of waterfronts, many ports have grasped the potential for leisure-related developments and have developed as sites for tourism and leisure. While such developments may be somewhat isolated from the freight-oriented activities in ports, there are synergies with other activities in the PBE. For instance, Roll-on Roll-off (RoRo) vessels carry passengers, part of them tourists, as well as freight. And cruise companies may take bunkering facilities into account when selecting ports of call. Table 3.1 shows activities often included in each of the four components of a PBE.

Table 3.1 Activities often included in each of the four components of a PBE

Transport hub	*Logistics value-added hub*	*Manufacturing cluster*	*Tourism and leisure*
Terminals (e.g., for containers, oil and oil products, chemical products, LNG, agribulks, biofuels, cars, iron ore, coal, construction materials), pilotage, towage, rail and inland waterways transport and trucking.	Warehousing and storage of consumer goods; heavy/special equipment storage and stockholding; storage of strategic commodities (oil, critical materials); fuel blending; refrigerated warehousing; Container freight stations.	Food processing; energy production; chemicals; steel and metal industries; offshore wind manufacturing; shipbuilding and ship repair/maintenance; circular economy materials processing.	Cruise activities; marinas (including for mega-yachts); congress, hotel and leisure facilities.

3.2.1 The importance of trading and other services in the port business ecosystem

In the four components of PBEs, trading and other services (finance, insurance) are not explicitly distinguished as a specific component of the PBE. In my view, these activities are best included as related to one of the four components discussed above. Especially trading activities can have important positive effects on the attractiveness of the PBE, especially when a PBE becomes a *pricing center* for commodities. Pricing centers can be regarded as physical places where both demand and supply of commodities are high and where reference prices are set. These prices are often also used in contracts. Pricing centers attract trade volumes. Examples of pricing centers for bunkering fuel include Rotterdam, Houston, Singapore and Fujairah. For these PBEs, expanding their role as pricing centers to new commodities such as ammonia is an important challenge, as it would strengthen their ecosystems (see Van Son et al., 2023).

3.3 Ports as locations of world-scale processing and manufacturing activities

Ports are especially attractive for *world-scale* facilities. Such facilities use feedstocks, such as iron ore, coal, oil, chemical products, grains, other ores, lithium and scrap and waste material from global markets and on top of that produce products, like steel, diesel, gasoline, ammonia, offshore wind components and batteries, solar panels and cars, that are also sold in global markets. World-scale facilities thus use the port both for imports and for exports. For these reasons, a location in a port business ecosystem is the “first best” location. Even a location at a short distance from the port may not be as attractive as a location directly in the port, due to additional transport and logistics costs.

An example of a world scale facility: the Shell refinery in Rotterdam

Most value chains are international and rely on ports. The Shell refinery in Rotterdam is one of the largest refineries in the world. Roughly 20 million ton of crude oil is refined to products such as petrol, gasoil and intermediate chemical products. Roughly 75% of the output consists of transport fuels, the remaining part are inputs for chemical processes. The crude oil arrives by ship, from various destinations, including the Middle East, Russia, Venezuela and the North Sea basin. The crude oil is partly sourced through long term contracts with oil producing companies and partly bought on the "spot market".

Crude oil comes in different varieties (e.g., with varying percentages of hydrogen or sulphur). The Shell refinery can handle different oils, including oil with high sulphur percentage and switches frequently between oil types, based on the price difference between them.

Traditionally, the refinery output was destined to Northwest Europe. Pipelines connect Rotterdam to this area (e.g., a Kerosine pipeline to Schiphol airport). As there is overcapacity in Europe, European refineries increasingly compete in the *Atlantic basin* (Europe, the east coast of the Americas and Africa's west coast). Thus, the Shell refinery traditionally served a local market, but increasingly competes on world scale. Significant volumes of refinery products are exported overseas.

Given the overcapacity, profit margins are very low, and tight cost control is required. The relatively high labour costs and tight regulations are important competitive disadvantages of refineries in the Netherlands. Low supply chain costs have to make up for that. These costs are relatively low because of scale economies of the refinery, the presence of chemical plants and the location of the refinery in an important seaport. Compared to refineries in inland locations, the Shell refinery has cheap access to a broad range of crude oil types, while overseas markets can be served relatively cheaply. Initiatives to further lower supply chain costs are required for sustained competitiveness in this industry.

This example shows a supply chain that has become increasingly global. This has an impact on ports, which need to continue to create value to ensure they remain a vital component of such a global supply chain.

3.4 Ports as locations of energy production

In line with the above logic, ports often are also important hubs for energy production, storage and distribution. Many energy commodities are globally traded (for instance, diesel, gas, ammonia and kerosene) and need storage and distribution facilities in ports. In addition, given the position of ports at the interface of land and sea, ports often are landing points for electricity generated offshore. Finally, the large energy demand often also makes ports logical nodes in energy networks. For all of these reasons, ports have attracted large investments in generation, storage and distribution of energy, and can be expected to attract a large share of investments in sustainable energy production. Energy companies have already invested in facilities such as electrolyzers and biobased fuel production in ports. For instance, seven out of the 12 large (>100 MW) hydrogen plants currently under construction or planned in Europe are in ports. This shows the relevance of ports for the energy transition, as well as the opportunities for ports to attract green energy production.

Ports as locations for energy production

Ports are attractive locations for power plants because of:

1. Low transport costs for energy sources (such as coal, biomass and so on).
2. Substantial local demand for energy, for instance by port related chemical plants and terminals. The new generation of automated container terminals are also heavy energy users.
3. The opportunities for re-using heat and steam brought about by the clustering of economic activities in ports.

For instance, about 40% of coal powered energy plants in the UK were located in a port. Coal-fired plants inland were closed first, while those on the coast have survived, and some new plants were built in the 1990s. In Belgium, most energy plants that use biomass are located in ports. New investments in energy plants rely predominantly on imported energy sources. Thus, it comes as no surprise that most of the newly proposed power plants are located on the shore, in port areas. For instance, three of the five proposed LNG power plants in the UK are on the coast.

Ports often aim to attract power plants, as they can strengthen the port complex, and secure long lasting and stable commodity flows. A number of ports actively seek to position themselves as biomass and sustainable energy complexes. For instance, two biomass energy plants in Port Talbots, UK (the latest opening in 2019) use the port for biomass imports. However, while initially the aim was to use imported wood pellets (more than a million ton per year), wood waste from municipalities across the UK is now used, thereby reducing the need for imports.

Ports are often also attractive locations for wind energy. The large-scale infrastructure in ports (together with the windy location on the shoreline) may be well suited for wind farms. For instance, the ports of Bristol, Cleveland, New York, Zeebrugge and Rotterdam have placed windmills in the port area. In New York, the wind energy is used to supply the terminal activities, thus making the port operations more sustainable.

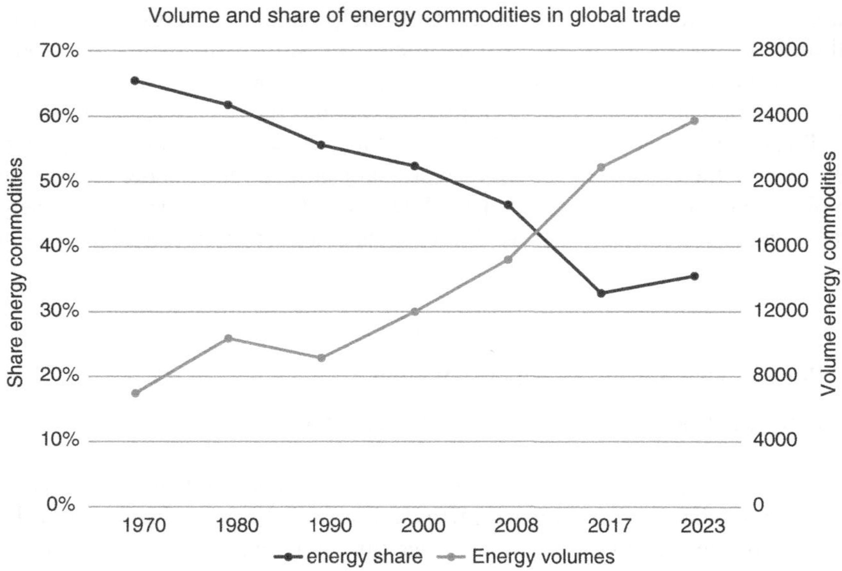

Figure 3.3 The share of energy commodities in global shipping

Source: Based on data from UNCTAD's Review of Maritime Transport (2019).

3.4.1 The importance of energy commodities

Energy commodities were by far the most important maritime trade commodities in 1970, with a combined share of over 65% of all freight flows in ton-km. This share has been declining due to the rapid rise of trade in intermediates and finished products. In 2000, this figure was still more than 50% (see Figure 3.3), in 2017 less than 30%. Nevertheless, in absolute volumes, shipping volumes of energy products have grown substantially, and energy commodities remain the cornerstone of many ports.

Commodity chain activities in a PBE

When analyzing activities in a specific PBE, analyzing *commodity chains* is a good starting point. Table 3.2 shows examples of activities frequently located in a seaport. There are clear advantages of co-locating different activities in one single commodity chain in a seaport.

Table 3.2 PBE activities in different commodity chains

Commodity	*Cargo handling and transport*	*Logistics*	*Industrial complex*
Dry bulk	Dry bulk terminal	Storage and blending bulk commodities	Steel production
Liquid bulk	Tank terminal, pipeline operations	Blending and tank storage	Oil refining, chemical production
Fruit	Container terminal, in some cases specific fruit terminals	Sorting and re-packing	Production of fruit juices
Containers	Container terminal, barge rail and road transport	Warehousing	Assembly lines, e.g., for cars

3.5 The critical role of the developer of the port business ecosystem

One key insight from strategic management scholars is that some companies actively develop a business ecosystem. Such companies need a specific set of capabilities and have a specific business model. Port managing bodies develop a business ecosystem. This issue is addressed in more detail in the chapter on business development in ports.

Even though most port business ecosystems are developed by state-owned entities, private companies also develop port-industrial ecosystems. Examples include:

- DP World develops a London gateway, where it will operate a terminal, but also develop a huge logistics park, where the aim is to attract investments from other firms that strengthen the business ecosystem. DP World develops a network of logistics and free trade parks in port areas. Their portfolio includes Jebel Ali (JAFZA, the home base), Chennai Logistics park (300 hectares), Djibouti Free Zone, and Orangeburg Logistics park (1300 acres).
- Port of Açu is the largest private industrial port complex in Latin America, located in the North of Rio de Janeiro State. It has been in operation since 2014, with investments from 22 companies and 11 private terminals. Contrary to virtually all Brazilian ports, Açu is an integrated port-industrial complex with over 4000 hectares of land for development. This combination has attracted substantial FDI flows, with further investments to be expected.
- Shell (for instance, on the site in Rotterdam) and BASF (for instance, on the site in Antwerp) manage a site that hosts >20 different companies. Both aim to attract companies to strengthen this complex.

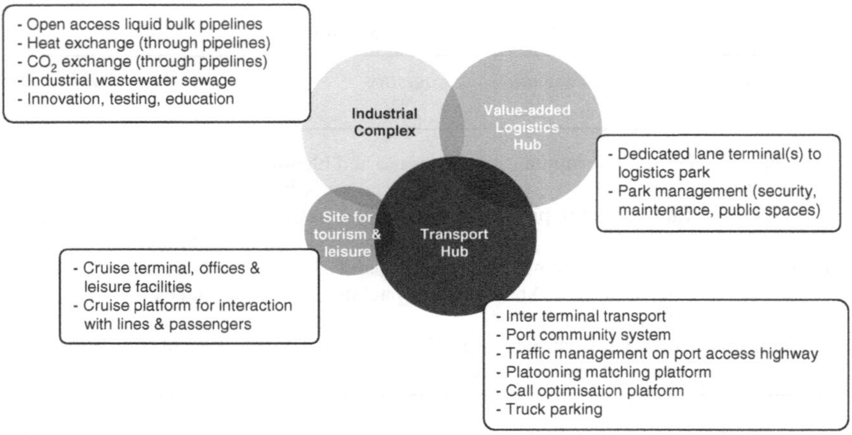

Figure 3.4 Synergy services for each of the components of the port business ecosystem

- Katoen Natie develops Loghidden City, a high-tech logistics complex covering some 260 hectares in the port of Antwerp. They aim to attract investments from other firms (e.g., in warehousing).

The considerations for the choice between state-owned or private port ecosystem developers are further discussed in Chapter 5.

3.6 Synergy services in port business ecosystems

One of the core challenges in developing the port business ecosystem is creating synergies. While these emerge to some extent spontaneously, initiatives focused on creating more synergies can create value for firms in the PBE. Figure 3.4 shows examples of frequently relevant synergy services for each of the components of the PBE.

The core challenge of developing synergy services is creating value for users and, perhaps more complicated, capturing the value that is created through charges. This issue is further explored in Chapter 5.

Notes

1 A distinction is made between "urbanisation economies", with forces towards the concentration of economic activities in cities (e.g., the presence of all kinds of business services), and "localisation economies", for specific industries. For port clusters, the localization economies are relevant.

2 Furthermore, services specific to the above-mentioned activities, such as ICT ship finance or truck maintenance, are part of the PBE.

3 In most of Europe's ports (69%), the manufacturing companies active in the port operate based on long-term lease contracts, not on private land.

4 The changing landscape of the ports industry

4.1 Introduction

This chapter discusses the most relevant trends that affect the ports industry. Trend analysis is extremely relevant for port development. Port development initiatives are too often based on "business as usual". *Disruptions* to business as usual deeply affect port development.

Illustrations of the risk of assuming business as usual

Various examples show how organizations tend to ignore signals that disruptions may impact the industry. This also applies to the ports industry. For instance, various studies in the late 1960s dismissed the value of containers in maritime transport. Likewise, various fruit terminal operators stuck to classical reefer port facilities even though containerization increased rapidly in this segment. Energy companies invested in LNG facilities in the US, even though shale gas later destroyed the value of such facilities.

Examples of port development impacted by disruptions include, Rotterdam's Maasvlakte I, which was constructed in the 1970s for the steel industry, but only used in the 1990s and for a different segment: containers. Some decades later. Maasvlakte II was constructed for containers, logistics and chemicals. By the time construction was finished (2015) it was clear that land uptake for chemicals was unlikely, as were the logistics activities initially foreseen. For containers, the spatial productivity was much higher than estimated, leading to large deviations compared with the initially estimated land uptake. Unforeseen activities did find a place at Maasvlakte II, mostly related to offshore wind. In Antwerp actual developments also differed radically from those planned: the "Left Bank" was developed for manufacturing but is used for containers and distribution.

Business as usual is often assumed in forecasts of traffic volumes in ports. The Port of Rotterdam (PoR) made projections shortly before the oil crisis in 1973. The projections foresaw a crude oil throughput of more than 200 million tons in 1980 and more than 300 million tons in 1990. The realized throughput of crude oil peaked in 1976, with almost 150 million tons, and declined to slightly less than 100 million tons in 1990.

DOI: 10.4324/9781003630784-4

On the other hand, when PoR made forecasts after the 1979 oil crisis (and after a period of economic stagnation), the overall forecasted volume for 2010 was between 270 and 330 million ton, a huge underestimation compared to a realized throughput of over 420 million tons.

In 2004, conventional breakbulk volumes in Antwerp were around 20 million tons. The forecasts at that time for 2015 were roughly between 17 million (low growth scenario) and 22 million (high growth scenario). However, partly due to rapid containerization of flows, breakbulk throughput declined to less than 15 million tons in 2015.

These cases demonstrate that "business as usual" is often assumed while in practice, business is generally not "as usual". Even though "perfect foresight" is impossible, a deep understanding of trends and developments that affect the industry is indispensable for port development.

4.1.1 Mental maps

Both individuals and organizations have mental maps. Such mental maps can be loosely defined as pre-fixed schemes that help in making sense of data/information. As a simple example, we use mental maps to assess whether or not we can cross the road with cars at a certain distance.

Mental maps are useful, but at the same time lead us (both at the individual and organizational level) to ignore data that do not fit in our mental maps. And this is where the risks come in: mental maps hamper the identification of disruptive new developments as well as the understanding of the impact of such developments.

On mental maps

Various studies suggest the relevance of mental maps. For instance, homogeneous teams are associated with lower performance of new ventures than diverse teams (Ensley & Hmieleski, 2005), a difference that may be explained by the lack of one shared narrow vision in diverse teams. Likewise, outside supervisory board members improve innovation performance of a firm if they come from another industry with a high innovation dynamic (Balsmeier et al., 2014). This suggests that experience from other industries leads to a more open view on the impact of change, resulting in a better innovation performance. Long tenures of the same CEO are associated with a lower innovation performance (Jia, 2017). The argument that mental maps may prevent fast adaptation to new dynamics is also convincingly presented in Levitt (2008).

Scholars have also argued that the strong embeddedness of firms (in a network, business ecosystem or region) may also lead to a shared mental map and consequently a reduced openness for disruptive developments.

Fixed mental maps threaten the performance of all organizations; they are even more relevant in organizations with a hierarchical culture. In such organizations, dominant views at the top remain often unchallenged, resulting in high risks of outdated strategies and operations. State controlled organizations often are hierarchical. This is relevant for the ports industry, where in many countries SO-PDCs have a central role.

For organizations that need to make investment decisions with a long-term perspective, like port development companies, terminal operators and shipping lines, it is imperative to acknowledge the risk of assuming "business as usual" and to develop a *process* to make assumptions about the future explicit and challenge them. This is the main reason for the success of *scenario analysis*, first developed at Shell and later applied more widely. A systematic analysis of drivers of change is an important part of a process to challenge assumptions regarding future developments.

This chapter provides a framework for analyzing drivers of change that affect port development. In addition, important developments are discussed. However, this chapter is not a comprehensive overview of all potential disruptive changes that affect port development.[1]

4.2 A framework to identify drivers of change

The framework from Figure 4.1 is helpful for analyzing trends and developments that impact port development. It is all-encompassing and thus leads to a structured

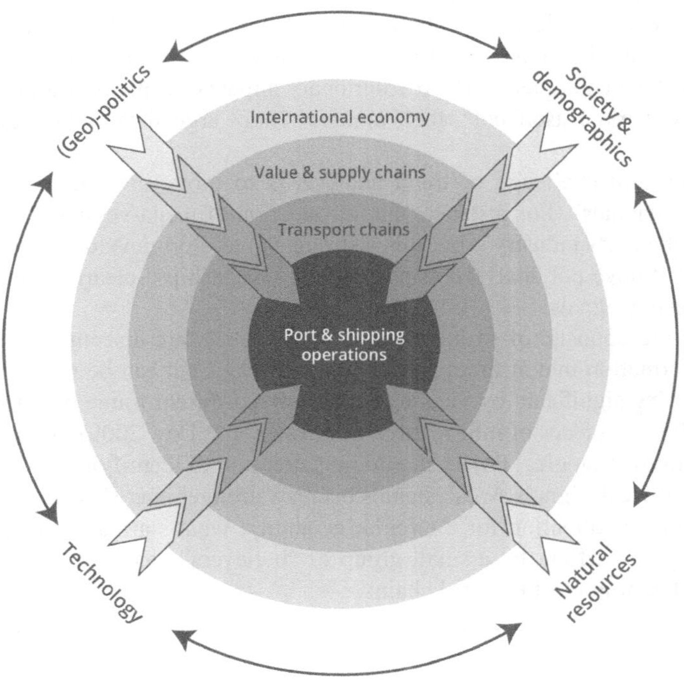

Figure 4.1 Drivers of change in the ports industry

overview of changes in various different fields – all of which can deeply impact port development.

Figure 4.1 makes a distinction between four layers of activity. While developments in all layers affect the other layers, the dominant mode of influence runs from the outside inwards.

The layer "international economy" encompasses the global economic production and trade system and includes international trade relations as well as overall macro-economic trends. The layer "value and supply chains" consists of the international value chains and networks that have emerged and lead to the provision of goods and services to companies and consumers. The third layer consists of transport chains, with a focus on freight transport chains, that are put in place to enable efficient operations in supply chains. The final layer "port operations" consists of all operations in a port and includes terminal, logistics and manufacturing operations in the port. These four layers are interrelated: while global trade patterns evolve and affect supply chains, freight transport and port operations, the opposite is also true: the containerization, for instance, has led to a boost in international trade (Hummels, 2007).

These four layers all deal with the spatial and organizational structure of the production of goods and services (i.e., economic activity).

Identifying trends beyond the "strong signals"

Various widely known cases show the risk of missing signals that in hindsight seem very clear. That applies for instance to the 2008 credit crisis, the value of mobile phones (that many companies missed) and the advantages of maritime containers. "The revolutionary impact of containerisation … has largely worked itself out", the *Financial Times* argued in 1976 (Levinson, 2016).

The core challenge of trend analysis is to move beyond the obvious "strong signals". For instance, the introduction of mega-vessels deeply impacts the ports industry – but it is a strong signal. Port development companies that have not analysed trends beyond "megaships" clearly run the risk of missing signals.

As the opposite of strong signals, *weak signals* are disconnected pieces of information that at first appear to be irrelevant but can be recognized as something significant by viewing it through a different frame or connecting it with other pieces of information (Schoemaker & Day, 2009). In the development of strategies, PMBs should pay attention to identifying and making sense of weak signals. Weak signals become stronger over time. An example includes the attention for a circular economy: what started out as a small activity carried out by a small group of "believers" has gradually become mainstream in most material chains.

4.2.1 Four drivers shape economic activities across all four layers

Figure 4.1 includes four categories of factors that influence economic activities across all four layers: technology, (geo)politics, societal and demographic developments, as well as developments of natural resources and ecosystems.

These "non-economic" factors deeply influence ports. As an example, geopolitical and policy issues gave rise to the US regulation that prevents the use of foreign ships for domestic services (the "Jones Act"). This leads to high maritime shipping transport costs and consequently more use of land-based transport modes, with a direct effect on the volume handled in ports.[2]

The benefit of using this broad framework is that it leads to a broad perspective on relevant trends and developments. I use this framework to discuss key trends and developments, relevant to port development, strategies of firms in the ports industry, growth prospects of ports and policies to improve port competitiveness.[3] Inevitably, this discussion is all-encompassing; references to publications focused on specific trends are provided in the references.

After discussing relevant trends for the ports industry, I identify ten *opportunity spaces* for port development[4] that emerge because of the changing landscape in which ports operate.

4.3 New technologies

Technological developments deeply affect all four layers of economic activities (terminal operations, freight transport chains, value chains and the overall global economic development). The impact of new technologies is so diverse (ranging from technologies for solar panels on ship hatches to technologies for extracting CO_2 and H_2 from seawater) that a complete overview of technological developments is impossible. Six important technological trends for ports are briefly described below.

4.3.1 Digitalization

Digitalization is converting information into a digital format, exchanging the resulting data and processing this data with the use of advanced and often automated data processing methods. Digitalization includes well-known technology catchwords, such as "big data", "internet of things", artificial intelligence and "blockchain".

Digitalization enables digital supply chains in which data, for instance, supply and demand data, becomes available for all supply chain partners. The resulting visibility allows all players, including customers, to plan ahead (in different scenarios). The digital supply chain thus can increase in terms of both *resilience* (the ability to adapt to changing circumstances) and *responsiveness* (the speed of responding to customer demand). The digital supply chain covers elements such as production, procurement, warehousing and logistics, and spare parts management. The digitalization of supply chains is discussed in more detail in the section on trends in supply chains.

Digitalization as enabler of precision agriculture

One of the perhaps less-known areas where digitalization is making a major impact is agriculture. Digitalization enables "precision agriculture". In this approach variability in crop development between specific areas is measured and translated into specific interventions to improve output of lesser performing parts of large agricultural plots. This optimizes returns on inputs and enhances output.

Precision agriculture has been enabled by precise geo-spatial data about crop yield, terrain features, organic matter content, and nitrogen levels, derived from sensors, drone images and satellites. Precision agriculture can substantially raise land productivity, which is badly needed given the growing global population. It may also give rise to growth of maritime transport of agri-commodities.

4.3.2 Autonomous transport

Technological advances toward autonomous transport are relevant for shipping (maritime and inland) and road and rail transport. Most attention, as well as investments, in R&D have gone into road transport. Various players aim to launch driverless cars in the late 2020s, based on advances in operating connected vehicles as well as capabilities for automated lane keeping, parking, acceleration and braking. A growing list of nations, including the US, Germany, Japan, China, France, Australia, Canada, Singapore, South Korea, the Netherlands, Sweden, the UK and Spain, have driverless vehicle legislation in place. Multiple companies are actively competing for leadership in this new "opportunity space". Autonomous vehicles are poised to transform industries like agriculture, mining, retail and passenger transport, while also having a huge impact on urban development, for instance, because driverless vehicles do not require nearly as much parking space as the current vehicle fleet.

For freight transport, the trend toward driverless trucks is also underway. The immediate step is truck *platooning*, which is piloted among others in Singapore and the Netherlands. Platooning has significant energy savings in the first stage, and in later stages will also reduce labor costs, either because truck drivers can rest or because trucks drive without a driver. Fully autonomous trucks are currently operating in the mining industry (over 2000 autonomous trucks in total). Their introduction on roads is also widely expected, in part because of large driver shortages in markets like the US and Europe. Most likely, autonomous trucks will for a substantial period operate with "constrained autonomy", only on specific freight routes, based on "geofenced" areas where autonomous trucks are permitted to travel (subject to weather and visibility conditions). The most likely corridors where autonomous trucking is permitted are corridors from seaports to inland logistics parks, directly adjacent to highways. In the US, an alliance of Aurora, Continental and NVIDIA plans to start producing driverless trucks at scale in 2027. In China, technology company Pony.ai has tested unmanned truck platoons for containers on a corridor between Beijing and the port of Tianjin. In Europe, advances are also being made, for instance by Scania, Volvo and Daimler, but regulatory steps are required to enable large-scale driverless trucking operations.

The development of autonomous *shipping* is also well underway, with leading companies such as Rolls-Royce, Maersk and Daewoo investing heavily in the technology. The approach is not generally aimed at replacing human actions but combining autonomous operations and human interventions, such that humans can take over control of ships, for instance, in busy areas or adverse weather conditions. Autonomous vessels will still require crews as well as human support from land. Consequently, connectivity with the ship is crucial. The benefits are substantial, most importantly cost savings (an estimate by Rolls-Royce suggests about 20%, mainly through fuel savings, crew savings and optimized vessel designs) and a reduction of accidents. Autonomous ships are expected to contribute to more safety, reduced costs and less pollution. This can lead to significant cost savings for shipping companies and a lower environmental impact. In March 2023, Kongsberg's Yara Birkeland, one of the world's first fully autonomous electric container ships, completed its maiden voyage in Norwegian waters, entirely self-guided. More investments in autonomous ships are on the horizon.

4.3.3 Cost reductions of sustainable energy technologies

There is a global transition away from energy production based on fossil fuels and toward sustainable energy sources. This transition is driven partly by active government policies (e.g., the UK decision to phase out coal) and partly by reduced costs of sustainable energy production and storage due to technological advances. These electricity prices are competitive with fossil-generated electricity (see Figure 4.2).

Offshore wind parks in Europe can now be developed without large subsidies. Worldwide, prices of sustainable energy production continue to decline. For instance, the Saudi Power Procurement Co. (SPPC) procured electricity from solar plants for around $0.013/kWh. The expectation is a further decline in sustainable energy prices.

There is a variety of sustainable energy technologies, including future nuclear technologies, which all play a part in the supply of energy. However, solar technologies are regarded as the highest potential technology. There are substantial differences per region in terms of the costs of solar electricity production. Figure 4.3 shows the solar power potential in different regions.

Figure 4.3 clearly shows the advantages of countries such as Australia, Saudi Arabia, Oman, Angola and Chile for the production of electricity from solar panels. This provides these countries with a strong export potential for hydrogen, hydrogen-based fuels generated from electricity. Furthermore, these countries – especially if they develop strong port business ecosystems – become very attractive locations for energy-intensive industries, such as the production of metals, fertilizers, chemicals, plastics and cement.[5]

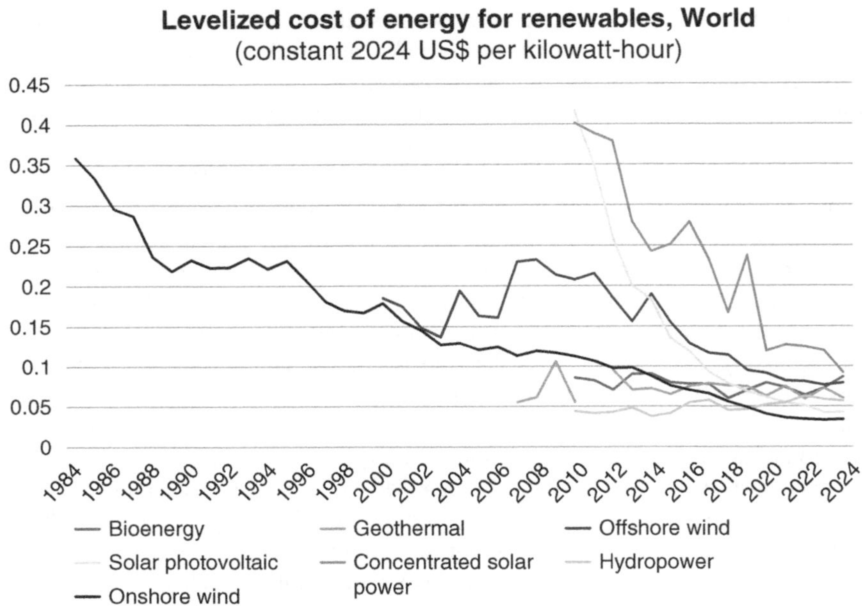

Figure 4.2 The evolution of electricity generation costs of sustainable technologies

Source: IRENA (2025) with major processing by Our World in Data.

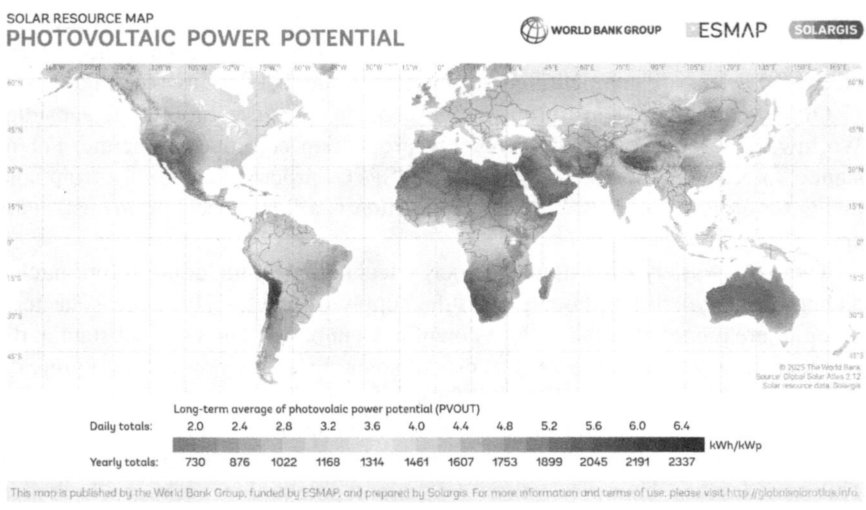

Figure 4.3 The solar power potential in different regions

Source: Global Solar Atlas 2.0 (2025).

Energy trends and geopolitics

A focus on energy security pushes countries to use the resources available domestically. Oil rich countries (the US, Saudi Arabia and Russia) aim to preserve their earnings through a policy focused on continued use of fossils. Europe, China and other resource-poor countries focus on clean energy, including substantial investments in small modular nuclear reactors.

China has developed a competitive advantage in clean energy, with leadership in solar, batteries, and electric vehicles (supported by secured access to critical minerals). China's aims to accelerate exports of low cost cleantech to emerging markets. This leads to trade tensions, especially with the US. Energy also plays a role in the race for dominance in artificial intelligence (AI). The increasing energy needs for datacenters and AI motivates tech firms to develop clean energy technologies that deliver reliable emissions free power, including small modular reactors, nuclear fusion and hydrogen. All large countries support such initiatives in view of their impact on the "AI race".

The evolving battery markets

A specific segment of the energy market with rapid technological advances is the battery market. The battery market is rapidly growing: investments in batteries in 2023 were >$30 billion, which is higher than investments in wind and solar combined. The innovation intensity is very high, and as a result battery technology is evolving in three different directions: first, the *costs* of energy storage are falling. Second, innovations increase the *energy density* of batteries and third, the *capacity/size* of batteries increases. For large batteries, 20/40-foot shipping containers have become standard sizes, both for mobile and "stationary" applications. This is because of the ease of transport of such a large battery container. Given the standardization of large batteries in containers, battery containers are likely to be used in barge and shortsea shipping, as container batteries can be "swapped" so that empty containers are replaced by full battery containers. Similar swapping models are also being developed for electric trucks.

Battery price levels are expressed in US$ per kWh. In the automotive industry, which is most advanced in the use of batteries, battery prices have declined rapidly to levels of around US$125– US$150 per kWh. A further decrease is widely foreseen; Goldman Sachs assumes a price level of around $70 per kWh in 2030. Prices for a large stationary battery container (which is used to balance the grid) are substantially higher (about US$180– US$200 per kWh by the end of 2023); this price difference is likely to become smaller or disappear as demand for larger batteries grows. Currently, price levels of battery containers for shortsea or barge applications are substantially higher (>US$350 per kWh) than those for "stationary" battery containers.

With regard to energy density, the current storage capacity of 20-foot energy containers used in maritime transport is about 3 MWh. However, new containers with higher storage capacities (6 to 10 MWh) have been announced. Battery containers with other materials may further increase storage capacity. The rapid decline of battery costs may have huge implications for inland waterways, shortsea and even deep-sea shipping, as electrification may become a feasible zero-emission option.

4.3.4 The spread of additive manufacturing (3D printing)

3D printing (additive manufacturing) builds objects in layers. 3D printing has the potential to allow the local, on-demand production of final products or parts thereof. It is possible to 3D print metals, ceramics, plastic objects and various forms of food. 3D printers use various resources in liquid form, such as polycarbonate (PC), nylon, bioplastic and metal (nano)particles. The 3D printing industry serves distinct market segments, from healthcare (where 3D printing is well established), to aerospace (SpaceX uses 3D printed components), to food and consumer goods.

The market for personal 3D printers is also growing as publicly available 3D product designs can be easily uploaded and 3D printed. 3D printing technologies are also well-suited to improve the circularity of value chains; end-of-life material can be converted relatively easily into source material for 3D printed products.

One example of a 3D printing application: meat

Current meat production is unsustainable, from an animal welfare perspective, and also from an environmental perspective (a large share of CO_2 emissions are associated with meat production, and potential energy sources are used as animal feed). In addition, there are health issues associated with the mega-farm meat production model. An emerging alternative is 3D printed meat grown from beef stem cells. Stem cells extracted from cow muscle tissue are cultured with nutrients to grow rapidly. These are mixed with fat and coloured using 3D printing technology. The resulting pink substance, whether in its raw or cooked form, looks, feels and tastes like "traditional meat", but is based on vegetable ingredients. The technology is more expensive, but this is offset by the huge reduction of resources needed. While this process is in its infancy, experiences from other industries suggest that once introduced with sufficient mass, costs will decline and such printed synthetic meat will become an alternative.

4.3.5 Robotization in manufacturing

Industrial robots have been around for a couple of decades and continue to become smarter, faster and cheaper, with increasing capabilities for sensing and learning, often based on artificial intelligence. As a result, more activities can be outsourced to robots, such as picking and packaging, testing products, or assembling minute electronics. In general, robots do not replace human workers, but instead lead to higher productivity of humans.

Robotics systems capable of "machine learning" enable the transfer of knowledge to other similar plants elsewhere in the world without investments in talent, training, set-up time and related costs.

Various companies offer "robotics as a service", enabling manufacturers to reduce costs. The "robot density" in manufacturing industries is somewhat below 200 robots per 10,000 workers across all industries. This density is higher in specific countries and industries. For instance, in the automotive industry in South Korea, one robot is deployed per fewer than four workers). Annually, more than half a million new robots were installed in 2023, more than 50% of these in China. A further increase is expected (around 4% per year, according to the International Federation of Robotics).[6] Higher levels of robot density imply higher productivity levels in manufacturing and a decline in the importance of wage level differences in location decisions.

4.3.6 *Technologies to advance the circularity of value chains*

A final important technological development is the introduction of new technologies to re-use end-of-lifecycle (EOL) products. Due to technological progress, an increasing number of value chains become "circular", in the sense that EOL products are re-used or recycled. Table 4.1 shows some technologies that enable increasing recycling rates.

Table 4.1 Technological advances enabling circularity for selected products

Commodity/ product	*Technology enabling circularity*
E-waste	Automated artificial intelligence-powered sorting systems with sensors, electrostatic separation, automated shredding and the use of high temperatures to extract valuable metals from e-waste. Specifically for batteries, lithium-ion battery recycling recovers lithium, cobalt and nickel.
Bio-waste	Advances in biological treatment methods and fermentation to recycle or upcycle bio-waste.
Construction and demolition waste (CDW)	Technologies to crush end-of-lifecycle concrete, allowing re-use of sand, gravel and cement. Such technologies can close the cement loop and make it 100% carbon-neutral.
Wastewater	Technologies to extract phosphate from wastewater (secondary phosphate). Traditionally, phosphate is mined and mainly used as fertilizer. Phosphate is often not recovered from water/sewage and ends up at the bottom of the ocean.
Car tires	New technologies to recover valuable high-quality "carbon black" that typically accounts for 20–25% of the total mass of car tires, a high-volume commodity for which recycling rates are typically low (<40%).

Source: Adapted and updated from de Langen and Sornn-Friese (2019)

4.4 Politics and geopolitics

Political and geopolitical developments deeply affect international trade. Geopolitics can both enable trade (new free trade agreements) and constrain it (bans or barriers on imports and exports). In the current geopolitical climate, all major countries (like the US, China, India and Brazil) or economic blocks (like the EU) have moved away from globalization and increasingly strive for *strategic autonomy*. Furthermore, the introduction of trade barriers as an instrument in geopolitical conflict has become more normalized and is widely used by the US. Countries continue to be open for international trade but no longer hesitate to take measures if trade negatively impacts their strategic autonomy. Furthermore, countries that are partners in geopolitical conflicts increasingly reflect that in favorable trade agreements, leading to "*friendshoring*", i.e., investing in partner countries, as that reduces risks of disruptions in global supply chains. These geopolitical events have implications for trade, especially for specific commodities:

- Energy commodities; all major countries aim for energy independence. This also includes initiatives, such as the EUs initiative to set up corridors and partnerships for the supply of energy from countries like Chile and Angola, which are considered friends in the geopolitical arena.
- Technologically advanced products such as (the latest generation of) semi-conductors.
- Medical supplies and medicine.
- Products of global industries that are considered strategic, such as steel, metals, chemicals and cars.

For a large number of countries, especially from the "Global South", the quest for strategic autonomy is well aligned with policies to be open for beneficial trade deals with OECD countries, on the one hand, and China, on the other hand. These two geopolitical blocks are vying for domination, but most developing countries aim for strong ties with both as this best serves their interests. This approach leads to careful maneuvering to prevent "choosing sides". This is directly relevant for port development, as governments consider ports as important assets in geopolitical competition.

4.4.1 Competition for leverage through control over freight corridors and ports

The most relevant global geopolitical initiative in the area of freight transport is the Chinese Belt and Road Initiative (BRI). BRI aims to strengthen connections and trade between the highly developed East Asia and Western Europe and the less developed countries in between, for instance, in Central and South Asia (Kazakhstan, India, Pakistan), East Africa (Kenya) and the Middle East (Oman). BRI is a core element of the Chinese foreign policy. BRI is purposefully developed as a rather loose concept, of which all countries can all form part.

Some countries of the European Union (EU), and the G20 have cooperative agreements with China under the umbrella of the BRI. However the EU regards the BRI as a geopolitical initiative of a geopolitical adversary (China) that increases China's global influence. As a result of pressure from the EU, the US, Italy (December 2023) and Panama (February 2025), respectively, have exited the BRI.

Important port development projects associated with BRI include Piraeus (Greece, the Mediterranean hub of COSCO, China's state-owned container shipping company), Hambantota (Sri Lanka, a widely criticized port development project) and Chancay (a newly developed mega port in Peru).[7]

China positions BRI as an open and inclusive development, aimed at creating mutual gains between all countries involved. The advantages for China include the impact of BRI on the Western part of China, as well as increasing export opportunities for Chinese companies that face a mature market domestically, such as construction and steel. China invests considerably in BRI and has developed instruments such as the Silk Road Fund and the Asia Infrastructure Investment Bank (AIIB). In addition, leading Chinese as well as foreign companies play a role in the BRI initiative.

In addition to serving Chinese economic interests, BRI is widely regarded as an instrument to increase the Chinese influence in Central and South Asia, as well as European and West African countries. The NATO countries, as well as India, have voiced concern about what they view as the interrelations between BRI and China's military capabilities.

Ports as strategic assets – geopolitics of port financing

Port infrastructure financing by national and international development banks has a clear geopolitical dimension. Given the significance of ports for society, many governments around the world consider ports as strategic assets for their economy and their international presence. Even though most governments retain some form of control over port assets, some of them rely on third parties, such as the World Bank, other multinational financial institutions or foreign governments, for support in financing port investments. The latter, usually in the form of bilateral loans and even grants, give the lending country leverage on international trade flows and thus political influence. This explains why providing financing for port development has a geopolitical dimension.

For instance, the European Union regards ports as strategic assets that have been designated as "critical infrastructure" (European Commission, 2006). Given the emergence of China's Belt and Road Initiative (BRI), a platform with mechanisms to provide financial support for port development, and certain Russian investments (for instance, in pipelines), Europe is reconsidering offering instruments for port financing for current and prospective trade partners, especially in North Africa, as a mechanism to secure the geopolitical interests of the EU.

The Partnership for Global Infrastructure and Investment (PGII) can be regarded as the response from the US and EU to China's BRI initiative. An India–Middle East–Europe economic corridor was announced at the G20 in 2023. This corridor initiative foresees a rail connection between Saudi Arabia, the UAE, Jordan and Israel. This agreement followed an improvement of relations between the involved countries – and especially Israel and Saudi Arabia. Such a rail connection – and the trade facilitation initiatives/hydrogen pipeline, as also announced in the agreement, could benefit supply chains within the Middle East and promote economic integration in the region. But progress since 2023 has been limited. Other PGII projects include the Lobito Corridor in Angola, the Trans-Caspian Transport Corridor (TCTC) and the Luzon Corridor (Philippines). PGII is also active in port projects through "Just Energy Transition Partnerships", for instance, in Senegal and Indonesia.

The EU has further developed its international activities in ports, under the umbrella of its "Global Gateway" initiative, a new European strategy to "boost smart, clean and secure links in digital, energy and transport sectors". One of the focus areas is Africa, and the countries around the Mediterranean. In this respect, the EU aims to integrate the African and European multimodal transport networks.

4.4.2 The role of SOEs in geopolitics

One of the core differences between BRI and the PGII is the key role of Chinese State-Owned Enterprises (SOEs) in the form of shipping companies, port companies, construction companies and logistics companies in the BRI. These SOEs are very effective instruments in investing in ports abroad in a commercially oriented manner. However, ultimately, the SOEs may be expected to put the country above profit – unlike the privately owned enterprises headquartered in OECD economies. This calls for regulatory scrutiny of overseas SOE activity. This issue is further addressed in Chapter 6 on port policies.

4.4.3 Geopolitical competition for control over rare earth metals

Rare earth metals (REMs) are critical components of various advanced products. REMs are critical in the shift toward sustainable energy. Solar plants, wind farms,

SOEs in ports and shipping

There traditionally is a significant state ownership of shipping companies, terminal operators and PDCs. Table 4.2 lists the main state-owned shipping companies and terminal operators. Not included is the PMB, which is owned by the state, either as a SO-PDC or as a PA, in the vast majority of countries. In China, most of the port companies are owned by the provincial government.

Table 4.2 The main state-owned shipping companies and terminal operators

SOE	*Country*	*Extent of state ownership*	*Description owner*
COSCO Shipping	China (PRC)	Majority state-owned	Owned by the Chinese state
Hapag Lloyd	Germany	Minority state owned	~25% owned by Saudi Arabia and Qatar ~14% owned by the city-state Hamburg.
Yang Ming	Taiwan	Minority state-owned	Minority ownership by the Taiwanese state
COSCO Ports	China (PRC)	Majority government owned	Owned by the Chinese state
PSA International	Singapore	Fully government owned	Fully owned by Temasek Holdings, the national wealth fund of Singapore.
DP World	UAE	Majority government owned	Owned by Dubai World Corp, the national wealth fund.
Shanghai International Port Group	China (PRC)	State-owned	Owned by the city government of Shanghai.
HHLA	Germany	Majority state-owned	Majority owned by the city government of Hamburg.

Source: own analysis, based on company websites

The implications for ports of decoupling between trade blocs

The policy logic and consequences of *decoupling* the Chinese and US economies is increasingly discussed. Some decoupling of both economies can already be observed, as both countries seem to be keen to reduce their interdependencies. This has led to "friendshoring": several studies have found that intra-bloc trade has been growing faster than inter-bloc trade. Further decoupling between China and the US may be expected.

However, the picture in Europe is less clear. Contrary to the US, no decoupling has taken place, at least if measured by the importance of China as a trade partner of the EU. Such decoupling may, however, be on the horizon, partly because of trade conflicts especially regarding electric cars, and partly because of the gradual recognition in Europe of the need for increased strategic autonomy. This emerging picture has led to a lower share of intermediates in global trade, as commodity chains become less trade intensive. Contrary to services trade, goods trade growth has been lagging GDP growth since the economic and financial crisis in 2008/2009.

All of this suggests maritime freight volumes growth will be very moderate, if there is growth at all. Furthermore, trade growth can be expected to vary between partner countries, with most of the growth arising with partners in the same "block", for Europe probably most importantly Turkey and Morocco. Trade prospects with the US are more uncertain, giving the potential for conflict on a variety of topics, from regulation of tech companies, to climate policies and relations with China.

In this changing landscape, it may be worthwhile for ports to perform a kind of "stress test" somewhat similar to the stress test of banks: "in the most adverse environment we can imagine, with a breakdown of global trade, do our investments still create sufficient value for users and society"? A positive answer is reason for comfort, a negative answer may lead to a re-think in terms of options to reduce risks, for instance through more phased approaches.

electric vehicles and batteries need REMs. The same applies to electronics and semi-conductors. Demand for REMs is expected to increase rapidly. China is the dominant supplier of REMs to the global market, accounting for around 85–95% of the total supply since the late 1990s. Japan, the US, the Netherlands, South Korea, and Italy source REMs from China.

In 2010, amidst the ongoing territorial disputes between China and Japan over the sovereignty of the Senkaku/Diaoyu Islands, China issued a warning regarding the potential withholding of REM exports to Japan. Likewise, in the 2025 trade conflict with the US, China announced a REM export ban. Given the increasing strategic relevance of REMs, countries have sought control over REMs produced in other countries. This control may be exerted through mining concessions, but also through control of REM export chains, including ports.

Most REMs are not available in pure form, but are refined from lightly processed mining outputs called concentrates. Refining is expensive and has adverse environmental effects. China dominates both mining and refining of REMs: China controls 87% of global rare earths refining capacity, according to the International Energy Agency. Western initiatives aim to develop processing technologies that are faster, cleaner and cheaper. For instance, the Port of Argentia, a heavy industrial seaport located in Newfoundland, Canada, explicitly aims to attract REM processing.

The metal with the greatest public attention is lithium. Australia is the world's leading supplier of lithium, but its production process is carbon-intensive. Lithium can be sourced in a more sustainable way in the so-called "lithium triangle" – a high-altitude area covering Chile, Argentina and Bolivia, which holds 56% of the world's lithium reserves. Chile has developed a National Lithium Strategy to secure sufficient state control over mining and exports. The Chilean ports are best positioned for exports from the lithium triangle. In this context, Chile aims to develop the small port of Arica into a large port industrial complex, and is actively seeking international investors, including from China, as China is an important export destination for lithium.

4.5 Societal and demographic developments

Demographic developments, for which long-term forecasts are made by the United Nations,[8] deeply impact economic growth, as well as trade growth. In terms of demographics, many developed countries are faced with the prospect of population decline, a major disruption from the population growth prevalent in the previous centuries. This is caused by falling birth rates and an aging population. Birth rates are very low in most developed economies (including China and Europe). Furthermore, population growth in countries like India and Bangladesh is no longer due to high fertility rates (in both countries, the average fertility rate is around 2), but due to a changing "age pyramid", as the average age is increasing. This implies the population will stall and start to decline in these countries, too.

As a consequence of declining birth rates, the number of children in the world has stopped growing. This moment in time was given the term "*peak child*". The data and projections suggest the number of under-5s peaked in 2017, the number of people under 15 peaked in 2021, and the number of under-25s most likely peaked in 2024. This implies the total global population will peak in a couple of decades.

Many advanced economies have fertility rates well below 2.1 children per woman, the rate that would lead to stationary population levels. Various developed countries are well below that rate, including the US (around 1.6), China (around 1.2) and Korea (around 0.8). The same applies to most European countries. Europe's population is set to decline, and without migration – which is a politically sensitive topic, with increasing numbers of votes for anti-migration parties – Europe may have a population in 2100 that is around 30% lower than currently. The long-term impact of declining populations on economic growth, trade volumes and activity in ports is substantial.

South Korea: the country facing the most dramatic population decline

South Korea is the country with currently the lowest fertility rate. Its population could plummet to just 15% of its current level by 2125 if the nation's ongoing demographic decline continues unabated, according to a long-term forecast from the Korean Peninsula Population Institute.

Under the institute's worst-case scenario, South Korea's population could drop to 7.5 million by 2125 – a sharp fall from the current 51.7 million. This would be even less than the current population of the city of Seoul alone, which is over 9.3 million. Even under the most optimistic assumptions of life expectancy, the population would shrink to 15.7 million, or less than one-third of its current size. This decline has a compounding effect: With fewer people in each successive generation, the pool of potential parents shrinks, further accelerating the decrease. The population decline also tips the balance between the retired and active: in 75 years, for every 100 people of working age (15 to 64) there will be up to 140 seniors aged 65 or older, compared to a current ratio of 100 to around 30 seniors. The report also suggests policy measures to increase fertility rates and also argues in favour of immigration. Thus, the bleakest forecasts are unlikely to materialize. Nevertheless, thinking through the effects of these scenarios on industrial production, consumption and global supply chains will lead to a different perspective on port development: it suggests the focus needs to be on managing transition and decline, not expansion.

Besides demographic developments, the most important societal trend is urbanization. The movement of people toward cities has accelerated in the past 40 years, particularly in the less-developed regions, and the share of the global population living in urban areas has increased.[9]

Africa remains the least urbanized region, though the population share living in urban areas has increased rapidly. Urbanization is projected to continue in the coming decades. According to the United Nations, around 67% of the world's population will live in cities by 2050. The majority of future urban population growth will take place in small- to medium-sized urban areas in developing countries.

Urbanization thus drives the growth of cities. Cities occupy less than 5% of the world's landmass, but they account for around 70% of the population, global energy consumption and greenhouse gas emissions. The urban areas expand rapidly: expansion of urban areas is on average twice as fast as urban population, as population densities decline.

The urbanization has important consequences for ports and shipping. More flows (of freight and passengers) will be transported between urban areas. In addition, in those urban areas, the pressure on land use will increase as the urban regions grow. This puts pressure on the land use of port activities. In addition, urbanization increases the need for efficient urban distribution systems; this presents an opportunity for ports. Finally, urban areas generate huge amounts of waste, which can increasingly be re-used and recycled. All in all, this suggests it may be sensible to plan for a large "port industrial complex" in close proximity to large metropolitan areas.

Urbanization and mobility

The urbanization, coupled with technological advances, in fuel and automated driving, will result in a decline in the demand for cars. Car ownership in urban areas is relatively low compared to rural areas. Car ownership in cities is also declining due to increasing mobility options, thanks to technologies for car-sharing and automated cars. Urban mobility is also frontrunner in the transition to electric cars, partly because policy initiatives in urban areas to reduce car emissions.

The third important societal trend is the increasing relevance of the voice of nearby residents in port development projects. These residents are mainly concerned about the local negative effects of port activities, through pollution, noise and road congestion. Because of the increasing relevance of these stakeholders, port development projects are increasingly *contested projects*. This calls for an inclusive approach to port development.

Contested port expansion, the case of Doel, Antwerp

Antwerp's plan to construct a major new tidal dock called "Saeftinghedok", which took shape in the late 1990s, has been fiercely opposed for years by Doel 2020, a group of residents of the small village of Doel (and their supporters). This village, according to the port development plans, had to be destroyed to make way for the new basin. The group Doel 2020 successfully contested government decisions by bringing the case to national and European courts, where the decision to dismantle the village was revoked. For years, the dispute was a David vs Goliath-like encounter, where Doel 2020 earned sympathy (see, for instance, a *New York Times* article on Doel in 2016, www.nytimes.com/2016/04/28/world/europe/belgium-east-flanders-doel.html) but was widely expected to ultimately lose the fight to preserve the village. However, a major breakthrough came with an agreement in 2018 between the Flemish Government, Doel 2020 and other stakeholders including Antwerp's port authority. This development plan enables port development while preserving the village of Doel. A final decision on the project has not been taken, and criticism of cost estimates (which may be around 5 billion Euro, higher than the previously communicated figure of 3.5 billion) has re-opened the debate on the logic of the investment. However, the original plans to destroy Doel will not be revived. Thus, whatever the final outcome, this case one of the most telling examples of the impact of local residents on port development initiatives.

4.6 Natural resources and ecosystems

Roughly 40%[10] of all worldwide maritime flows consist of energy sources (coal, crude oil, mineral oil products, LNG, and, in much smaller volumes, ethanol, biofuels and biomass). Changes in the mix of energy sources are a very relevant *driver of change* in the ports industry. The sources of energy worldwide are still dominated by fossil fuels. Oil, coal and gas together account for about 80% of all energy sources (source: International Energy Agency, 2024). This number has been slowly declining; in 1980, the share of these three fossil fuels was more than 90%. Scenarios on the future energy mix show the share of renewables will rise rapidly – but how much depends on policy initiatives. More data is provided in Chapter 7.

Three major energy users can be identified: industry, households and transport. These three together account for over 90% of all energy used (other activities include, for instance, agriculture).

Industry, mainly the steel industry, still heavily relies on coal, electricity and gas. A transition to sustainable industrial activity is underway, but advances slowly. Generally, initiatives to electrolyze industries and use hydrogen play a central role in reducing emissions in industries. However, after initial visions of widespread use of hydrogen, areas where it is expected to be deployed have been narrowed down. Furthermore, given the high price of "green hydrogen", most initiatives focus on "blue hydrogen", produced from natural gas.

With regard to transport, oil products (gasoline, diesel, kerosene) are still dominant, but a transition toward cleaner fuels is underway, driven by government policies. For passenger cars, the use of batteries and sustainable electricity is the dominant transition; for trucks, inland shipping and coastal shipping, various alternatives are actively being introduced, but the transition to a post-fossil era is a major challenge. Households worldwide use combustibles (mainly wood), electricity and gas. Reducing emissions can be achieved most easily through electrification, for instance, of cooking and heating.

4.6.1 Future energy demand and supply

How will the demand and supply of energy evolve over time? On the demand side, there is widespread agreement: energy demand will grow considerably, mainly in emerging economies. The largest oil company in the world, Exxon, annually publishes an energy outlook and projects a global increase of energy demand of more than 15% in 2050 compared to 2023, driven by a growing population and rising prosperity in developing nations. While energy demand in the developed OECD countries is expected to stabilize, a huge growth is expected in developing countries, especially in the Asia Pacific, but also in Latin America and Africa. The growth in energy demand for transport is especially large in developing economies, mainly because of increasing car ownership. In developed economies, a growing energy use in transport is also expected, mainly due to the expected continued freight transport growth.

The substantial growth in demand, combined with the scarcity[11] of fossil energy sources and increasing awareness of the need to reduce CO_2 emissions, poses a huge challenge. Some analysts argue that in the coming decades, *all* energy sources, including fossil ones, are needed to meet future energy demand; others argue for a faster transition toward sustainability to keep CO_2 emissions within targets set in the Paris agreement. WWF has developed a path toward sustainable energy provision (i.e., without the use of fossil fuels) by 2050. Others, including Exxon and the International Energy Agency (IEA), argue that fossil fuels will probably be used beyond 2050. Energy scenarios and specifically scenarios for shipping fuels are discussed in more detail in Chapter 7.

The Bloomberg New Energy Finance (BNEF) Outlook 2024

Bloomberg notes that capital investment in clean energy technologies has surged to record levels, yet emissions remain stubbornly high. BNEF expects radical cost reductions of solar and offshore wind, making costs of sustainable electricity lower than fossil. However, BNEF argues there are no fully decarbonized production routes for industry and hard to abate transport sectors that are cheaper than unabated production. That makes either subsidies, or some form of carbon pricing, crucial to emissions reductions. With regard to shipping, BNEF argues that "We believe a multi-fuel future is less likely to play out than one with a single clean marine fuel" – even though it is hard to specify which fuel will ultimately win out. The adoption of all net-zero marine fuels on offer today is currently miniscule, meaning there is a high degree of uncertainty over the sector's future direction and fuel of choice.

4.7 The international economy and international trade flows

4.7.1 Economic growth forecasts

Accurately forecasting economic growth is impossible, given the inherent uncertainty and the potential disruptive influence of events such as wars, pandemics and natural disasters. However, the economic growth potential depends on four structural factors.

First, demographic factors (as discussed previously in this chapter play a key role and will negatively impact the growth of countries with declining workforce populations, including Europe, China and Japan). Other labor market considerations also impact economic growth, most importantly, female participation, which is still low in developing economies and likely to increase. In addition, average working hours impact economic growth; most analysts expect a further decline in working hours in advanced economies.

Second, productivity is a key driver of economic growth. The AI revolution may be expected to have a positive impact on productivity growth. However, this impact is not the same in all economies. It may be expected that the US, which is leading in AI technologies and has virtually no legal hurdles to the development of AI, will benefit more than Europe.

Third, global openness to trade has a substantial impact. Some "strategic decoupling" (in sectors like batteries, biotech, medicine, data and chip-making) is widely expected. But more radical decoupling (for instance, driven by import tariffs) is also a plausible scenario. Decoupling negatively impacts economic growth, with a larger negative effect for China than for the US and Europe.

Fourth, military conflicts and political instability deeply affect economic growth. A large number of "low-income countries" (as defined by the World Bank) were very unstable in the past decades and often engaged in military conflict. Many of these countries have stagnated: on average, their inflation-adjusted GDP per capita has grown by less than 0.1% annually over the past 15 years – i.e., virtually no growth at all. Based on these considerations, *forecasts of global long-term GDP growth generally assume a gradual decline in GDP growth rates.*

4.7.2 Understanding trade growth

When trade flows change, so does freight transport and consequently, so do throughput volumes of ports. In general, if the economy grows, trade flows grow as well. In the period 1986–2016, world trade grew faster structurally than world GDP. However, this trend, at least for trade in goods expressed in volume terms, has been reversed (see Figure 4.4).

Historically, the growth of trade is closely related to trade policies. In periods where governments introduced barriers to trade, trade declined. In the period 1880–1914, with free trade policies, trade flows worldwide grew rapidly. The period 1914–1945, on the other hand, shows how trade flows fall due to the introduction of trade barriers.

Free Trade Agreements are one of the main sources of trade growth in the past decades. Research based on past trade agreements shows that a Free Trade Agreement between two countries will on average increase the trade between these

Figure 4.4 The evolution of trade as a share of GDP – the US, China and Europe.

Source: Based on World Bank (2025c) World Development Indicators.

countries by about 86% after 15 years (Baier & Bergstrand, 2007). For example, trade growth between Mexico and the US grew more than 140% in the first seven years after the NAFTA agreement in 1994, compared to only 40% growth of US trade overall.

Even though trade tariffs are now substantially lower than two decades ago, for specific commodities (cars, agricultural products) and specific countries (the US, Brazil, India and South Africa) tariff and non-tariff trade barriers[12] are still substantial. In addition, in 2025, we witnessed a reversal of the long-term trend toward reduced trade barriers. New trade barriers were initiated by the US and will have a lasting effect on global trade.

Imports vs local production

A substantial part of past trade growth was due to the substitution of local production by imports. For most commodities, the share of EU imports has increased, so that commodities such as toys, carpets and ores are almost fully imported. The same applies to large batteries, solar panels and medical equipment.

Declining generalized transport costs as driver of trade growth

Next to GDP growth and trade policies, the level of transport costs also influences trade growth. The larger the distance between countries, the lower trade flows between them, as a larger distance translates into higher transport costs.[13]

Generalized transport costs have fallen strongly in the last three decades. These generalized transport costs include the "out-of-pocket" expenditure for transport, as well as inventory costs for cargo during transportation, insurance costs for transport and costs associated with the stock levels held to cope with the uncertainty of international transport. It is important to look beyond just the out-of-pocket transport costs: a large part of the cost reductions has materialized in *faster transport*. While out-of-pocket costs have remained stable, the transit times have decreased, resulting in lower generalized transport costs. Increased reliability and security of freight transport has also lowered generalized transport costs. The same applies to the transaction costs; while previously, lots of time was dedicated to searching transport service providers, negotiating, and tracking shipments, all of this can now be done in a digital and automated way.

There is a substantial potential for additional reductions in transport costs, which will drive the growth in trade volumes. The potential for trade growth through reduced transport costs is substantial in countries with inefficient ports and inland logistics.

GDP growth, trade barriers and transport costs drive the development of trade volumes. These drivers suggest future growth of trade volumes may be expected: GDP will continue to grow, and transport costs will continue to fall,[14] due to increasing productivity in shipping, terminals and hinterland transport. However, the future of trade barriers is uncertain, especially as the US has normalized the use of tariffs.

Transport costs and tariff duties

In the 1950s, transport expenditures were *half* as much as tariff duties for US imports. In the 1960s tariff duties were reduced, and transport expenditure was roughly equal to tariff duties. By 2004, aggregate expenditure on shipping was *three times higher* than aggregate tariff duties paid for imports. In this situation, reduced generalized transport costs (due to increased services, more productive ports and so on) will increase trade. However, the rise of trade barriers negatively influences trade, as is clear from the declining exports from China to the US following the introduction of tariffs.

4.7.3 A changing direction of trade

Changing trade patterns can substantially impact the fortunes of ports. Changes in the direction of trade are mainly driven by macro-economic developments. On a global level, two major changes can be observed. First, more than 40% of the goods exported by developing economies go to other developing economies, double the share in 2000. This changing orientation is reflected in maritime flows, with strong growth of "South–South" flows.

Second, intra-Asia trade is becoming more important. Intra-Asia trade accounts for over 13% of total worldwide trade, much more than the Asia–North America (6%) or Asia–Europe (5%) trade. This intra-Asia trade is expected to gain further importance in the coming decades, given the growth prospects of Asian economies. In the container segment, intra-Asia trade accounts for 40% of global container trade.

The impact of a change in the direction of trade – the case of Liverpool

The best case to illustrate the relevance of the direction of trade is Liverpool. Liverpool once was the UK's largest seaport but declined in importance after UK trade shifted from the US to Asia. Liverpool and Manchester (also a port on the west coast, so well located for trade with North America) had a combined share of 15% of total UK port throughput in 1965, compared to no more than 7.6% in 2010. This has close to nothing to do with the performance of both ports and is simply due to shifting geographies of trade. A similar story applies to the US Atlantic coast ports that accounted for over 44% of total US TEU traffic in 1996, compared to less than 40% 15 years later. The third illustration of changing directions of trade is Poland. In 1985 (in the communist era), Polish exports to Germany accounted for only 8% of total Polish exports, compared to almost 28% in 2023.

4.7.4 The future of trade and freight flows

The overview of the drivers of trade (GDP, liberalization and transport costs) suggests that trade volumes may be expected to continue to grow, albeit with a slower pace than in the previous decades. How much depends on many contingencies and cannot be accurately forecasted.

Trade patterns that do not seem to make sense

Trade flows arise spontaneously, as a result of decisions of individual companies. For individual companies, trading makes sense, but some of these trade flows do not seem to make sense when looking at the bigger picture. For instance, who would think that Saudi Arabia actually imports sand? However, it does import high-quality sand for the glass industry.

A widespread strange trade pattern concerns intra-product trade: many countries import goods that they also export. This is widespread, for such products as cars (for instance, Germany exports substantial amounts of cars to France and at the same time imports substantial amounts of cars from France) as well as for commodities such as crude oil and steel. Furthermore, the case of Italian ham producers that import raw meat (say from Germany) process it into ham and then export it back to the origin country are well known. Such trade flows seem irrational and are not incorporated in classical trade models. Often, trade emerges due to regulation, imperfect information and networks and capabilities of traders. Overall, the combination of strongly reduced generalized transport costs with the increasing use of digital platforms to purchase goods leads to a world in which purchasing goods from third countries often goes unnoticed. For instance, around 1 billion small packages were imported into the US in 2022, through e-commerce platforms, up from 400 million in 2018. Similar volumes arrive to the EU. However, both in the US and the EU, policy initiatives to secure more control over imported goods introduce new trade barriers and may also lead to higher costs for such flows.

4.8 International supply chains

The decisions about the "high-level" organization of supply chains can be termed *supply chain design.* Relevant choices include:

- The choice between activities organized in-house and the outsourcing of logistics activities.
- The choice between producing on demand or on stock.
- Choices regarding the international footprint of supply chains.
- The use of warehousing facilities and transport modes.

Supply chain design is generally done mainly by large multi-national companies that produce and sell goods, large retailers or large trading companies. Examples of product brand companies include Anheuser-Busch InBev (beer), Volkswagen (cars), Inditex (fashion), DSM (chemical materials), and ASML (high-value machinery for printing microchips). Examples of *retailers* include IKEA and Walmart. *Trading companies* that design supply chains include Cargill and Capespan.

All these companies have a strong position in the overall value chain /value network.[15] Because of this position, they (have to) increasingly focus on the efficiency, agility and sustainability of the overall chain/network, from raw material to end-product. These companies make strategic decisions to meet challenges in their industries, which can radically change the design of their supply chain structures. Below, the most important trends in supply chains are discussed.

4.8.1 Digitalization of supply chains and transport operations

The continuous improvement of technologies for information exchange and automated decision-making based on information availability is a key trend in supply chains. The technologies are very briefly discussed below.

Relevant technologies for supply chains and transport operations

The following technologies are especially relevant for supply chains and transport operations:

- Technologies and standards for automatic internet-based data exchange.
- Technologies that enable transmission of data to/from vehicles.
- Technologies that provide accurate position and speed information of vehicles, container or other cargoes (e.g., based on GPS or RFID).
- Sensors that can track variables such as temperature and corrosion. RFID is a major new technology in this field.
- Agent technology, with autonomous software agents that communicate with others (users, software agents) and automatically respond to changes in the environment.
- Open ICT platforms where third parties can provide services.
- Automatic detection and identification technologies, for instance of trucks and passenger vehicles.
- AI technologies that vastly improve the accuracy of predictions of items such as sales and resulting stock levels.
- Blockchain technology, which creates a decentralized, immutable record of transactions and operations. This facilitates real-time tracking of goods, reduces fraud, and streamlines data exchange. This enhances transparency, traceability, security, and efficiency.

The availability of digital technologies drives changes in supply chains; six important changes are discussed below.

New ICT-based business models

One "radical" effect of advances in ICT is that they create opportunities to develop *new business models* in supply chains and transport operations. New ICT-based ventures create value by lowering transaction costs and enhancing the efficiency of operations.

As an example, new digital intermediaries offer online freight booking platforms. These business models challenge the traditional role of forwarding companies. As a second example, digital entrants provide brokerage services to exchange cargo between different transport operators. Different firms submit their transport routes, and the service provider identifies win-win cargo exchanges between transport operators, based on advanced planning and routing optimization. If the transport firms decide to exchange cargo (e.g., a container), the intermediary receives a fee.

Cheaper and more reliable data exchange in supply and freight transport chains.

Even without the introduction of new business models, digitalization helps to substantially reduce *transaction costs* in supply chains. For example, whereas traditionally firms provide information to customs on paper, advanced digital systems automatically feed data to customs, thus reducing transaction costs. Or similarly, automatically generated information on the status of shipments leads to automatic invoicing and payment for freight transport.

ICT also improves information exchange in intermodal freight transport. Huge amounts of data exchange are required along freight transport chains. As an example, to enable efficient moves of containers from a ship to a train, the exchange of data such as the estimated and actual arrival time of a ship, the stowage plan, the inland destination of containers, the customs status of containers, the loading list for a train, the estimated and actual time of arrival of a train at the rail terminal, the departure schedule and the loading and unloading list for the inland terminal, is essential. All this data exchange is costly if data needs to be manually processed, partly because of inevitable mistakes in manual work. Thus, automated data exchange allows substantial cost savings. For ports, *port community systems* can be beneficial. This explains why these PCS systems have emerged, for instance, in Singapore, Rotterdam, and Valencia. A more detailed overview of PCS systems and other trade facilitation platforms is provided in a World Bank publication (see Ollivier et al., 2024).

Dynamic planning of vehicles and freight flows across different firms

Third, better information availability and processing capabilities allow for better planning across different firms along a supply chain. Data availability along the supply chain enables *decentralized* intelligent planning systems, with autonomous decision-making of individual units based on the access of these units to relevant

A port community system

Most freight transport companies have company-specific (global) systems and standards for planning and data exchange. These systems are internal, and generally not well integrated with information systems of other firms in the transport chain, or different public authorities to which data have to be provided. For this reason, a port community system (PCS) can enhance efficiency of port operations, by providing a platform for data exchange between transport operators and public organizations –business to government or BtoG – and with other organizations in the transport chain (BtoB).

A PCS needs to be easy to use for all transport operators. This requires *interoperability* with the systems of specific companies. Furthermore, a PCS ideally should be an *open platform*. This allows firms to build applications that use the data available in the PCS. This enables further value creation and strengthens the position of the PCS. A PCS generally consists of some of the below mentioned services.

1. Notification of ship arrival. This service allows shipping lines and ship agents to electronically notify the port authority (e.g., for the payment of port dues), harbourmaster and customs organization of the arrival of a ship. A PCS can ensure that information only needs to be provided once.
2. On top of ship arrival, a PCS can also accommodate related notifications. These services allow shipping lines and ship agents to electronically notify of waste disposal and hazardous materials aboard the ship.
3. Third, a PCS can accommodate customs-related information flows for import and export cargo. These services allow forwarding companies and importers/exporters to meet the data requirements of export and import control systems (ECS and ICS) through one platform. Various firms (shipping line, terminal operator and forwarder) provide relevant data for customs.
4. Partly based on the information for the above services, a PCS can streamline information exchange between shipping lines/ship agents and terminal operators. Services include sending a list of cargo to be (un)loaded through the PCS. Generally, these services re-use some of the information provided to customs.
5. Finally, a PCS can enable data exchange by truck, barge and rail operators (for instance order of train wagons, pre-arrival notification of trucks) and terminal operators (e.g., customs status of cargo – relevant as some cargoes are not cleared by customs and thus cannot leave the terminal).

Like all platforms, a PCS becomes stronger with increasing numbers of users. This can also hamper the development of a PCS. When firms see that once many firms are using the PCS, it will be costly to stop using it, they will hesitate to start using it in the first place. In economic terms: when firms foresee an exit barrier, this also becomes an entry barrier. This issue is especially relevant when a PCS is a for-profit venture. Thus, a not-for-profit initiative, possibly with some sort of joint governance structure, may be appropriate to develop a PCS. If the PCS is developed in a not-for-profit manner, other firms can develop commercial services on the open PCS. The cases from Valencia, Barcelona, Rotterdam and Singapore are all examples of a not-for-profit PCS.

data. Because of this autonomous decision-making, logistics managers no longer need to make a decision on the inland transport mode to use; instead, an intelligent planning system/agent suggests the best alternative, and unless a planner interferes, this suggestion is executed.

As an example, information derived from in-car communication devices (such as a GPS system or a telephone) can be used to calculate expected delays on specific roads. This information can be used to dynamically and automatically re-route vehicles. A second example is using the stock levels in retail or distribution locations (say, of furniture) to dynamically and automatically update the required delivery dates of containers with additional stock. The required delivery day would be shortened if stock levels are lower than initially forecasted, or lengthened when stock levels are higher than initially forecasted. This approach enables the use of slow, sustainable and cheap modes (such as barge transport) when possible, and fast and expensive modes when required. A third example is the use of up-to-date port arrival data to adapt the sailing speed of vessels so that they can reduce speed (and save fuel as well as emissions) to arrive on time instead of too early, as is currently often the case. The IMO is promoting such "just in time" arrival processes, see Just in Time Portal: GreenVoyage2050 (https://greenvoyage2050.imo.org/just-in-time-arrivals/). In shipping, dynamic planning also includes real-time route adjustments based on weather data to reduce operational costs.

Cooperative planning between transport operators

Next to the "vertical" cooperation in supply chains, ICT also enables (horizontal) cooperation between transport operators. For example, freight exchange between carriers is increasingly feasible given automated tools that identify mutually beneficial exchanges. As a second example, where different transport operators jointly use one terminal (for instance, a barge or rail terminal), they all benefit from cooperative planning that reduces overall waiting times. Here, ICT technologies that allow *planning apart together* are especially relevant. With such technologies, transport operators remain fully autonomous, provide information to a shared platform and in return receive information from this platform that allows them to optimize their planning.

Better use of transport infrastructure

New ICT also enables better utilization of infrastructure. For instance, ICT enables *slot planning systems*. Such systems, especially when fed with dynamic pre-arrival information, can help increase utilization of such assets as filling stations and container terminals. Truck appointment systems are relevant examples. As another example, automatically generated data on the occupancy of berths for barges prevent traffic of barges searching for free berths. This leads to fuel savings and environmental benefits as well as higher berth occupancy. Finally, real-time information on the number of vehicles on the highway may be used to manage the number of additional vehicles that enter the highway (e.g., by automatically adapting the intervals of traffic lights at highway access points).

4.8.2 Supply chains designed for agility and resilience

Supply chain agility is the ability of all supply chain partners to adapt quickly to rapid changes in business environments. Agility is especially valuable for products with short product life cycles and an uncertain demand (e.g., consumer electronics, cars and fashion). Agility requires coordination, communication and speed in procurement, inventory, assembly and delivery of products and services.

In agile supply chains, all supply chain partners are encouraged to collaborate and share accurate information, for instance, by offering incentives (such as price reductions) to customers that provide accurate and timely information. This allows much better insights and forecasts of sales and allows companies to adapt production, storage locations, and transport routes on a continuous basis.

Supplier relations beyond *arm's-length transactions* (simple and temporary contracts) are necessary for agility, to ensure continuous information exchange. Close supplier relations allow for responding quickly and in concert to changing business environments. In agile supply chains, different companies collaborate on forecasting to align production and inventory levels with sales forecasts.

Thinking in terms of agility is relevant as many supply chains are designed for minimum costs rather than agility. There is a trade-off between both. In an uncertain environment, company performance improves by investing in agility, for instance, by being able to speed up deliveries when required or postpone deliveries when possible. This does incur costs in logistics, but yields benefits through lower "lost sales", higher yields and fewer unsold products.

4.8.3 Actionable visibility in supply chains

The trend toward more agile supply chains implies a greater need for supply chain *visibility*. Unless companies have an accurate insight into where products are and whether there are deviations from planned operations, they cannot make informed decisions. Thus, continuous real-time control of freight transport, e.g., through RFID in containers, is required, just as is accurate "estimated time of arrival" information of transport operators, which feeds easily into information systems of other firms in the supply chain.

4.8.4 Circular supply chains

Companies traditionally think in terms of "forward supply chains" from raw materials to end users. This scope is broadened in a "circular supply chain" perspective. The closed-loop supply chain includes strategies of manufacturers to create and capture additional value for users at the end of the life cycle, through the re-purchase of their products for re-use, repair, recycle or disposal. Companies that "close loops" often move from offering *products* to offering *services*. A good example is in printing: companies can sell printers (a *product* with a forward chain) or sell a printing *service*. In this case, they sell the availability of functioning printers for a certain contract period. This implies they become responsible for maintenance, repair, replacement of printers and re-use of obsolete printers. The latter approach creates additional value for companies, but also requires the development of new capabilities. Such a change from products to services may also be relevant for cars, trucks, office electronics, household heating and even chemical products.

Thinking in terms of circularity has economic as well as ecological advantages. Legislation that requires companies to deal with products they have sold again at the end of their life cycle (as is the case in Europe, for e.g., dishwashers) increases the relevance of circularity. Until recently, much of the re-use was concentrated in high-value goods. However, companies now re-manufacture large volumes of low-value items, for example, mobile telephones and ink-jet printers. Finally, closed-loop supply chains lead companies to re-think product design, with more attention to modularity.

While the extent and speed of the transition toward circularity are highly uncertain, the direction is clear. Large numbers of companies have a business model focused on advancing the transition toward circularity.[16] Ports handle huge volumes of raw materials, intermediates and finished products. The associated supply chains may be deeply affected by the transition toward circular supply chains. Ports are ideal places to further develop the circular economy, or CE (Kyllönen, 2017). Indeed, an increasing number of large ports all over the world are taking on the concept and aim to occupy a leading role in the transition toward CE. In Chapter 8, the "best case" of the Port of Amsterdam is discussed in detail.

Figure 4.5 shows a quadrant to position supply chains of commodities on the dimensions of geographical scope and the circularity of materials.[17] In the period 1950s–2000, many supply chains transitioned from linear and mainly local to linear and mainly global. Examples include textiles, toys and cars. In fact, not just finished products are frequently traded internationally, but intermediate products as well. This so-called "vertical specialization" explains the huge trade growth since the 1990s (Yi, 2003). The ongoing transition (with the major developments still

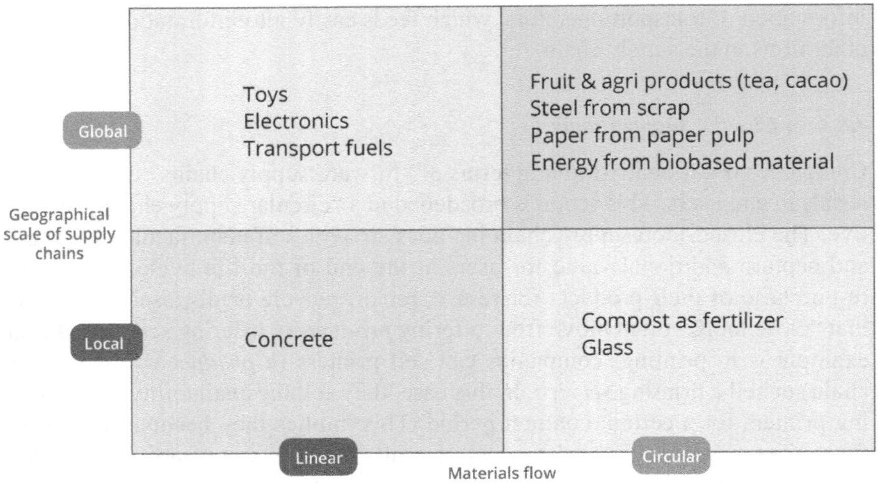

Figure 4.5 Circularity of supply chains – the positioning of some important commodities for ports

Source: adapted from de Langen and Sornn-Friese (2019).

to come) is from supply chains with a linear orientation to supply chains with a circular orientation. This may or may not affect the geographical scale of supply chains. For instance, both scrap and steel from scrap continue to be highly globalized supply chains where commodities are frequently traded and transported internationally.

Examples of global supply chains of "linear commodities" include toys, electronics and transport fuels. While for these commodities, a part of the consumption takes place locally, the majority of the global production is traded internationally. An example of a local and linear supply chain is concrete, which is produced for regional markets. Note that this is not the same for cement (a raw material needed for concrete), which is traded globally.

Examples of circular and global supply chains include many agricultural commodities such as coffee, tea, vanilla or fruit. While the expansion of the production of such commodities as palm oil, rubber or soybean is associated with dramatic deforestation, especially in tropical forest landscapes, many agricultural commodities are circular in the sense that they can be grown using only renewable, natural resources. Other examples of global and circular supply chains include steel, paper and energy from recycled materials.

The final part of the quadrant consists of circular supply chains at a local level. Examples of relevant products include compost. In addition, most recycled glass is re-used locally. The trend toward circularity has effects on volumes handled in ports and the opportunities for attracting new logistics and industrial activities to ports. Table 4.3 provides more details on circular commodities.

Table 4.3 Circular activities and location benefits of ports

Commodity/ value network	*Estimate of global waste generation*	*Trade of waste material*	*Benefit of locating recycling/ processing activities in a port*
Steel	~500 million tons	More than 100 million tons (e.g., France and Germany are large exporters, Italy and Spain are large importers)	Low inbound and outbound logistics costs for steel and scrap.
Plastics	~400 million tons	Less than 10 million tons of global plastics trade following China's import ban)	Low inbound and outbound logistics costs for plastics. Plastics can be converted into fuel, which can serve the fuel demand in ports.
E-waste	>60 million tons	Around 5 million tons of global trade, a substantial part of which is illegal trade	Low inbound and outbound logistics costs for waste and recycled material.
Car tires	~10 million tons	Limited	Low inbound and outbound logistics costs for tires and recycled material.
Building materials	~2 billion tons of global waste production. Important waste types include wood, cement, and metal scrap)	Very limited	Low inbound and outbound logistics costs for construction waste and recycled material.
Food waste	~900 million tons	Very limited	Low inbound and outbound logistics costs for food waste and recycled material.
Oils and fats	~40 million tons	Relatively large	Low inbound logistics cost for food waste, an important end-product, is transport fuel, which can serve the fuel demand in ports.
Batteries	~8 million tons	Limited	Low inbound and outbound logistics costs for batteries; the market for recycled materials in the port.
Ships and conventional offshore installations, offshore wind components	NA	Ships to be scrapped are traded globally, but offshore (wind) generally is not	Low inbound and outbound logistics costs; the market for recycled materials in the port.
Agricultural residues	~3000 million tons	Very limited, some trade of processed residues (e.g., wood pellets)	Low inbound and outbound logistics costs; the market for recycled materials (including fuel and gas) in the port.

4.8.5 Increased attention for sustainability and CO_2 accounting in supply chains

Many companies are increasingly aware of the need to substantially improve the sustainability of their operations from a "profit" perspective (new business opportunities, company image), from a "people" perspective (motivation of employees), as well as a "planet" perspective (to combat global warming). Many companies focus on reducing their carbon footprint, as this is widely regarded as the most pressing global environmental concern. For most companies, over 50% of an average corporation's carbon emissions are from the supply chain rather than in operations. Managing supply chain emissions is therefore critical to address climate change effectively.

Leading manufacturing companies, especially those with a strong consumer brand name (e.g., Nike and Heineken), increasingly use their influence to drive improved sustainability of supply chains by designing more carbon-friendly products, working collaboratively with suppliers to cut emissions and making effective carbon management a *supplier selection criterion.* Most companies either have "carbon criteria" in place or are committed to developing these. As a consequence, freight transport service providers have developed tools to precisely calculate the carbon emissions of specific shipments.

4.8.6 Increased horizontal supply chain collaboration

Many companies cooperate with customers and suppliers; this is termed "vertical collaboration" as the partners all play a role in one supply chain from raw material to end user. Many "next steps" can be taken, as many companies are still far removed from supply chain visibility.

Next to these initiatives, *horizontal* collaboration is increasing. Horizontal integration occurs when two or more companies at the *same level of the supply chain* cooperate, for instance by sharing resources such as warehouse space, transport equipment and manufacturing capacity. Contrary to vertical cooperation, horizontal cooperation generally involves *competing companies.* This is a significant barrier to horizontal cooperation, but the best cases from a number of industries show the benefits involved.

Industry examples of horizontal cooperation include:

- Suppliers: farmers who cooperate to sell and deliver their products (milk, cattle) to manufacturers.
- Transport companies: shipping lines cooperate by setting up joint services in alliances. Trucking companies cooperate to exchange cargoes to optimize utilization of equipment.
- Manufacturers: oil companies that jointly invest in oil pipelines and oil terminals to ensure a cheap and reliable supply of crude oil.
- Retailers: joint investments in collective last mile delivery in city centers.

Horizontal cooperation in liner shipping – alliances

Alliances in liner shipping are widely analysed. While the positive effects of larger scale are clearly established, there are legitimate concerns about the effect of alliances on competition. The OECD argues alliances between container shipping companies may have negative impacts on users and society at large (OECD, 2018). OECD argues alliances have helped create overcapacity, made maritime transport services more uniform and contributed to lower service frequencies, fewer direct port-to-port connections, declining schedule reliability and longer waiting times. The resulting policy advice is broadly sensible: make sure competition law applies.

One point is insufficiently addressed in the report: the potential of the ports industry to adapt in innovative ways to the new reality of megaships and alliances. This adaptation is under way and will soften or eliminate most potential negative effects of alliances and megaships.

Adaptation takes various different forms, operational and strategic. For instance, terminals and the port authority can increase the efficiency of exchange of containers between terminals, for instance through dedicated infrastructure (potentially coupled with autonomous vehicles), and improve planning of barge, train and feeder handling given the megaship and alliance reality. This may result in new value creation for port users. For instance, ship stowage based on hinterland destinations may become feasible with the huge call sizes, so that terminals may be able to unload containers for specific destinations at once and make loading trains or barges faster and more efficient. Container storage may further shift inland, enabling much higher terminal productivity. As a wild prediction, why could not, say, 30% of all containers directly leave the terminal without touching the yard? New terminal lay-outs, especially regarding hinterland modes, feeder berths and container yards, will arise as terminal operators adapt.

Pricing also may adapt to the new realities; both terminal operators and port authorities may benefit from pricing structures that incentivize on-time arrival and penalize late arrivals. Joint ventures between shipping lines and terminal operators will become even more common, as does the approach with a "launching customer" as precondition for port infrastructure investments and efforts to increase the flexibility in port planning and development.

Considered in combination, in my view this potential to adapt justifies a more positive assessment of alliances and megaships: sufficient competition – at the level of specific origin-destination pairs – must be maintained, but beyond that, alliances and megaships over time will make port users better off.

4.8.7 Location choices based on sustainability and energy consumption

Many companies have started to address the sustainability challenge, for instance, by changing from road to barge and train (more environmentally friendly transport modes), by aiming to reduce empty truck movements, by redesigning products and so on. For most of these companies, the current *location* of transport as well as logistics facilities is given. Companies periodically also make new (re-)location decisions, among others, for manufacturing plants and storage locations. Given the above-discussed increased importance of reducing the carbon footprint, the influence of a location on carbon footprint is expected to be of increasing relevance in location decisions. This favors locations with intermodal connections and locations with opportunities for energy-efficient production, for instance, because of opportunities to re-use heat and CO_2.

4.9 International freight transport

Below, the nine changes in freight transport systems that are the most relevant from a port development perspective are discussed.

4.9.1 Larger ships and trains

Over the last few decades, the average size of ships and trains has increased dramatically. Especially noteworthy is the growth in scale of container ships. At various moments, it was argued that the maximum economic size had been reached, but the industry has kept ordering larger ships. As of the end of 2025, MSC vessels of over 24,000 TEU are the largest. Further scale increases are not expected, as the scale economies are no longer substantial and the large ships also have disadvantages, as operations take more time and port infrastructure imposes limits. Nevertheless, designs for 25,000 TEU capacity ships have been approved, and various designs for ships of around 27,000–30,000 TEU have been presented.

Larger vessels call at a more limited number of ports. Ship sizes have increased on most shipping routes. The smaller vessels that were no longer competitive on the main trades (Europe–Asia and Asia–North America) replace smaller vessels in other trades, such as the US–South America. The increasing scale of vessels also leads to much larger feeder vessels. The increase in ship size is expected to lead to different container shipping networks, with a more limited number of "mega-hubs" that handle the largest ships.

The scale increase is also relevant in other markets, such as iron ore, where Vale, the Brazilian mining company, has developed a fleet of *Chinamax* vessels to shuttle between Brazil and a few Chinese ports. Furthermore, the scale of cruise ships has also increased rapidly in the past decades. Like in shipping, scale economies have also led to increasing sizes of trains. China has set a record for a train carrying more than 30,000 tons of dry bulk. Various countries are increasing the size of container trains, in the US, to trains with a train length of up to 2 km, with "double stacked" containers.

The effect of larger container ships – hotly debated

The effects of increasing container ship sizes are hotly debated, with some experts/institutions arguing that larger ships overall have a detrimental effect on overall supply chain costs. The main argument for negative effects of larger ships is that larger ships force other players in the supply chain to make investments (e.g., larger cranes and deeper port basins), thereby increasing the overall costs for users and society. While this is a relevant concern, it would be wrong to argue that megaships "impose" infrastructure costs on the public sector, as done by the OECD (OECD, 2015). Governments as well as government-owned port managing bodies have a choice about making investments in infrastructure. There is no innate need to deepen entry channels, raising bridges and widening basins. When the costs of such investments are prohibitive, governments and port authorities can decide not to make investments. However, they seldom do so, and in some cases for the wrong reasons.

Ports with good access to hinterlands will continue to receive ships and handle significant volumes, even if they do not invest in accommodating the largest ship sizes. Take as an example the ports in the Black Sea as well as the Great Lakes. They continue to be served directly with the maximum size of ships that can pass the Bosporus and the Saint Lawrence Seaway, respectively. The most efficient global port system is a system with a relatively limited number of ports capable of handling the megaships and a larger number of ports that handle smaller size classes.

4.9.2 Reducing transaction costs through online platforms and derivatives

Cost reductions equally relevant as those due to scale increases can be achieved by reducing *transaction costs* through online platforms to plan and book freight transport (similar to those existing for, e.g., car rental or passenger flights). Especially for shippers with small volumes, such platforms can substantially reduce transaction costs. Additionally, a "container freight derivative" has been introduced. While trade volumes are still low, this derivative is expected to become a viable tool to reduce risks for various types of companies. For instance, importing and exporting companies that want to make sure their transport costs do not fluctuate may use derivatives to "hedge" against maritime transport price increases. In a similar fashion, ship owners/operators can hedge against price decreases. Such developments will further reduce trade costs.

4.9.3 New or expanded shipping routes and shipping networks

Two main changes to shipping routes are to be expected. First, the expansion of the Panama Canal affects shipping routes between Asia and the US. The maximum ship size of ships that can use the locks has increased substantially from around 4500 TEU to around 13,000 TEU. The Panama Canal can also accommodate much larger dry bulk and liquid bulk vessels, roughly from the current maximum of around 85,000 DWT (dead weight tonnage, a standard for ship sizes) to 175,000 DWT.

A second development is shipping in Arctic waters. This has become feasible due to global warming. The "Nordic route" that connects north-east Asia with Europe is around 3000 nautical miles shorter than the alternative through the Suez Canal. This route was used for the first time in 2009 for commercial shipping between Asia and Europe. The time window during which the route can be used (currently only the summer months) will increase. Current estimates suggest the Nordic route may be accessible year-round in three decades. The Russian government is investing in making the route more attractive, because this would clearly improve the connectivity of many parts of Russia with the rest of the world. This would substantially alter trade flows between Asia and Europe, e.g., reduce the prospects of the ports in the Mediterranean to serve central European markets, while improving the prospects for ports in Northern Europe.

Gemini's network design: a new step in the evolution towards hub and spoke networks?

Shipping lines have always relied on hub-and-spoke networks to deploy large vessels and connect large numbers of ports. For this reason, the share of transhipment in the total container handling volumes has gradually increased over time, and currently is around 25–30% of total container volumes in ports. The Gemini network, launched in February 2025, relies to an even larger extent on hub-and-spoke networks, as the number of ports included in the core network has been reduced. This shift goes hand-in-hand with a stronger commitment to schedule reliability. This approach may over time be copied by other shipping lines, leading to a re-drawn map of direct and indirect services.

4.9.4 Increasing vertical integration in freight logistics

Container shipping lines continue to expand vertically, not just in terminal operations, but also in intermodal transport and integrated door-to-door transport. There are three main drivers of vertical integration with terminal services: synergies between the different activities, a more differentiated service offering and a reduced dependence on third-party terminal operators, especially in "must call ports". All major shipping lines have developed terminal activities.

Given the clear vertical integration strategies, terminal transactions including a vertically integrated partner are very common globally. Even though vertical integration is common, it may raise competition concerns. When the terminal

An overview of the container terminal activities of the top 7 shipping lines

All top 7 shipping lines have stakes in container terminals; only Evergreen has a limited portfolio (see Table 4.4). This overview demonstrates that the strategy of vertical integration into terminal operations is widespread among shipping lines.

Table 4.4 The terminal activities of the top seven global container shipping lines

Shipping line	*Terminal activities*
Maersk	Sister company APMT is one of the largest global terminal operators.
MSC	Sister company TIL is one of the largest global terminal operators.
COSCO	COSCO SHIPPING Ports (CSP) operates 35 container terminals, of which 12 outside China. Cosco Shipping is the main shareholder of CSP.
CMA CGM	CMA CGM operates 50 terminals worldwide, either through TERMINAL LINK or CMA TERMINALS
Hapag-Lloyd	Hapag Lloyd has decided relatively late, in 2023, to develop a portfolio of container terminals and has grown rapidly to more than 20 terminals.
ONE	The container terminal participations are held by ONE's shareholders. MOL, NYK and K-Line. In total these operate around 30 terminals.
Evergreen	Evergreen has a limited number of participations, mostly in terminals focused on transhipment.

ownership provides the integrated firm with exclusive access, this position may be carried over to other parts of the chain. In such a case, the vertically integrated entity may have an incentive to discriminate against other shipping companies so that they face competitive disadvantages. This threat is termed "foreclosure" and discussed in more detail in the regulatory chapter.

4.9.5 More sustainable transport infrastructure[18]

In addition to transport vehicles, transport infrastructure can also be made more sustainable. For instance, the sustainability of roads can be improved by using recycled material, by generating energy from roads (with solar technologies or by re-using the energy from vibrations of vehicles that use the road[19]), by reducing the energy use of lightning and by more sustainable maintenance. Initiatives to rate the sustainability of roads have emerged, while in some countries (especially France), an agreement between the state and road construction companies sets clear sustainability objectives, such as 100% use of recycled materials.

4.9.6 New fuels for road freight, maritime shipping and barge shipping

As transport accounts for over 20% of all CO_2 emissions, various ways to improve the sustainability of transport are underway. The transition toward more sustainable fuels for cars, trucks, ships and inland barges is very important in this respect. For cars, the required transition away from petrol and diesel is huge. Thus, it is most likely that in the long run these fuels will be replaced by a number of alternative primary energies. The most important ones are expected to be electric cars (with a range extender using a combustion engine or fuel cells), fuel cells powered by hydrogen (for onboard electricity production) and biofuel (diesel from palm oil, or soybeans or other natural resources). One main advantage of biofuels is that no new distribution infrastructure (gas stations) is required, as the existing infrastructure can be used. For fuel cells and electric cars, a completely new distribution infrastructure needs to be developed. However, the capacity to produce biofuels is limited, especially given the increasing demand for food. These three new fuel options are likely to become widely available. Additionally, LPG and LNG may be used as fuel for cars. Specifically for trucks, LPG/LNG (and in the long run biofuels) are the most likely fuel option, given the high energy density of these fuels and the long truck travel distances (which prohibit the use of electricity).

For seagoing vessels, fuels in the "post-oil era" include LNG, biofuels,[20] ammonia, hydrogen and even nuclear. This requires an adapted bunker infrastructure. For inland barges, electricity, LNG and hydrogen are regarded as the most feasible options.

4.9.7 More integrated planning of transport operations

Advances in information technology, as well as increasing recognition of the need for cooperation to further improve transport efficiency, are expected to enable further collaborative planning in transport chains. One "virtual arrival initiative"[21] for liquid bulk shipping aims at using arrival information to adapt sailing speeds. This is expected to reduce fuel consumption and CO_2 emissions at no cost. A related initiative is that of container shipping companies to substantially increase "schedule integrity". Currently, around 50% of all container vessels do not call at a port on the day they were supposed to. This unreliability is unwelcome, from an operational point of view (for terminals and shipping lines) as well as from a customer point of view. Maersk, leading in improving schedule integrity, aims to move toward 95% schedule integrity. This both requires more information exchange and collaborative planning, and also provides opportunities for substantially improved planning of intermodal services. Finally, advances in information technology increasingly allow for "planning apart together" systems. In such systems, intelligent agent technology is used to ensure that individual companies continue to do their planning independently, but based on relevant information from other companies. Such systems may be especially relevant for hinterland transport, where barges, trains and trucks currently perform planning unaware of each other's plans, even though these impact each other, mainly through congestion when they all intend to arrive at the port terminal more or less at the same time. A final development in this respect is interfirm empty container repositioning systems. Currently, import containers that are delivered inland are often returned empty to the seaport, while empty containers are also brought from the seaport to export locations inland!

4.9.8 Toward sustainable freight transport

In this section, we discuss in more detail the challenge faced by the freight transport industry to reduce greenhouse gas (GHG) emissions. This has such important consequences for port operations that it merits specific attention.

Transport systems have significant impacts on climate change, accounting for between 20 and 25% of world energy consumption and CO_2 emissions. Greenhouse gas emissions from transport are increasing at a faster rate than in any other energy-using sector. Given the widely expected future growth of transport, both for passengers and for freight, there is an urgent need for a transition away from fossil fuels and toward more sustainable transport, both to combat global warming and because of the increased scarcity of oil. For freight, this issue is particularly relevant in the container sector, where fuel consumption is highest (due to the relatively high speed of container vessels), and the share of road transport for the hinterland leg is also relatively high. In comparison, many liquid bulk flows are transported by pipeline, a much more sustainable hinterland mode, while bulk flows are transported inland by train or barge, also more environmentally friendly than road transport.

The drive toward more sustainable supply chains is led by shippers. Various large shippers have announced ambitious sustainability goals. However, the precise calculation of the carbon footprint for a specific shipment is still difficult. While some shipping companies provide carbon calculators, these are often not based on specific information about a specific shipment. Furthermore, such calculators are mostly limited to port-to-port transport and do not include all emissions in the door-to-door chain.

Shipping

For intercontinental transport, emissions in shipping are dominant (generally >70% of the total door-to-door emissions), even though shipping is environmentally friendly per ton/km. For shipping, a key driver of improved environmental performance is renewal of the fleet. The Sustainable Shipping Initiative analysis suggests a potential for over 50% reduction for newbuilds with existing technologies. IMO also developed a set of recommendations for newbuilds. For existing ships, emissions can be reduced by "retrofitting" the ships with new engines, and improving operational efficiencies, for instance by aligning terminal planning and vessel speed (so that speeds can be reduced when terminal capacity is not available). In bulk shipping, such initiatives can reduce emissions by as much as 10–15%. New technologies to use wind power, for instance, through sails, have an additional potential of 20%.

On top of these, in the long run a transition of bunker fuel from mineral oil to LNG is widely expected. This transition would be especially beneficial for air quality (reduced particles, NO_x and SO_2), also reducing CO_2 emissions by about 15–20%.

Greening shortsea shipping and inland waterway transport

Both shortsea shipping and inland waterways transport (IWT) are "hard-to-abate" forms of transport, as ships have large energy requirements, complicating the transition to battery-powered ships, compared to cars and light trucks. The low energy density of zero-carbon fuels has an important effect on fuel costs, because of the need to store relatively large volumes of fuel onboard.

Because of the low energy density of electricity and hydrogen (the latter in volume rather than mass), ships would have to either stop often for re-fueling or use large amounts of space for fuel storage, thereby lowering the amount of freight that can be carried.[22] Thus, the *sailing distance* is an important determinant of the feasibility of "all-electric shipping" (AES) and hydrogen. Above a certain distance, the most attractive (near-)zero-emission options are green ammonia or methanol. For medium ranges, hydrogen has more favorable characteristics, while for relatively short distances full electrification is most sensible (see Figure 4.6). The competitive balance between these alternatives depends mainly on the prices of energy as well as the cost of *storing* energy.

In the container swapping approach for providing electricity for IWT, a "pay-per-use model" has emerged. In this model, the operator of an inland barge pays for electricity and the use of the battery container. In this model, the ownership of this container remains with the battery and energy service provider. This is sensible as this company can benefit from scale economies, charge the containers

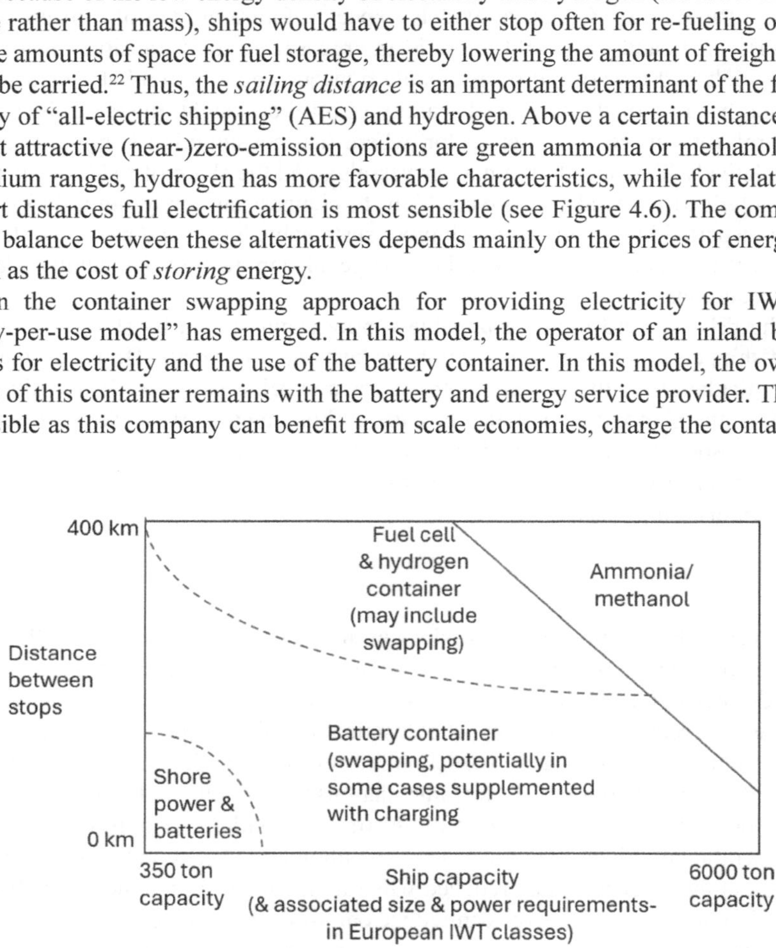

Figure 4.6 A stylized overview of best suited zero-carbon options for IWT

optimally under fluctuating energy prices and utilize the containers when not onboard of ships.

The costs of swapping a battery container are substantial (around US$50 to US$100 per move). Additional costs are incurred when a container has to be moved to a charging station, especially when this is not located on the terminal. Thus, in the swapping model, the charging station has to be placed at the terminal, else the costs of transporting the container become prohibitive.

A model with flexibility to swap containers in some cases and charge containers onboard in other cases may be most efficient. Broadly speaking, swapping containers, rather than recharging them onboard, makes sense if the revenue potential through higher utilization of the battery container outweighs the costs of unloading and reloading the container, instead of charging the container onboard. This revenue potential from "stationary storage" is around US$200– US$300 per day. Thus, unloading containers becomes attractive if containers are not used (either full or empty) for at least one day. Thus, a model in which a ship would carry a large number of battery containers (some full and some empty) generally is not optimal. In such cases, it makes more sense to minimize the number of containers onboard and generate revenue with these containers on the electricity "spot market".

Carbon markets in shipping

Carbon markets are fundamental to achieving the Net-Zero greenhouse gas emissions target. Their key benefit is that they help secure the most cost-efficient methods for reducing GHG emissions that are deployed. There are two different carbon markets: the compliance market and the voluntary market. Compliance markets are regulated by mandatory national, regional, or international carbon reduction regimes. These are generally aimed at large emitters. One example is Europe's ETS. Voluntary markets function outside of compliance markets, without direct government or regulatory oversight.

For shipping and logistics, both the mandatory and voluntary carbon markets are relevant. Since January 2024, the EU's Emissions Trading System (EU ETS) has been extended to cover CO_2 emissions from large ships (of 5000 gross tonnage and above) entering EU ports, regardless of the flag they fly. On a global level, the IMO has introduced a form of emission trading.

The voluntary carbon offset market is currently widely regarded as insufficiently transparent and trustworthy. Initiatives such as those of the Integrity Council for the Voluntary Carbon Market (ICVM, funded by a coalition of NGOs and companies, which aims to provide labels which allow customers to select high-quality carbon capture programs) aim to change that.

Port operations

Port operations generally only have a minor contribution to CO_2 emissions. In ports, the terminal operations are the most relevant. Emissions at terminals can be reduced by improved terminal efficiency, as well as cleaner equipment. Most

Carbon "insetting" in maritime transport

Another relevant initiative that has emerged is termed "insetting". Contrary to "offsetting", carbon "insetting" focuses on improving the value chain in which a company operates. Thus, whereas offsetting can be done through activities wholly unrelated to the own activities of the company that offsets emissions, for insetting, companies aim to reduce emissions in *their value chains*. The similarity with offsetting is the focus on creating projects that generate *tradable carbon credits* within a company's value chain. Thus, in this approach, companies still can benefit from a "market" for carbon credits to secure resources are allocated efficiently. In maritime transport, insetting could lead to tradable carbon credits for zero carbon transport. Thus, similarly to the "pooling approach" in the ETS for maritime transport (in which a company can meet emission standards even if some specific operations to not meet these standards, a shipping company can purchase "maritime transport credits" to decarbonize maritime transport, even if some of its freight flows continue to be shipped with vessels that generate emissions. They key difference is that in this approach companies can only purchase "maritime transport credits" from projects that decarbonize maritime transport (and not from for instance plantation projects for trees). Insetting would thus require accurate carbon emission data across (maritime) supply chains. One example of a transport insetting "platform" covering maritime/IWT is 123Carbon.com.

large container operators have already reduced emissions in the last few years, and further reductions are feasible. For roll-on–roll-off (RoRo), leading operator Wallenius Wilhelmsen has even designed a *zero-emission terminal*. The emissions of nautical services (pilotage, mooring, towage, patrol vessels) can be reduced by newer vessels and in more sustainable fuels.

4.9.9 More integrated global freight transport offerings

While a substantial share of maritime transport is purchased as "port-to-port" service, it is important to note that for the vast majority of shipments, the port is only an intermediary stop in a larger transport trajectory. Partly driven by vertical integration of shipping lines and partly by expanded digital capabilities, various players broaden their offerings, in some cases to "door-to-door" transport. However, especially in the container segment, new offerings also often start or end in inland terminals.

The container storage area of inland terminals (ILTs) often functions as an "extended storage area" of the importer/manufacturer. A transport order to deliver the container from the ILT to the distribution center can be met within hours, often even less than one hour. Thus, many manufacturing/warehousing operations use an ILT to buffer stock which is not immediately required. This practice leads to a close

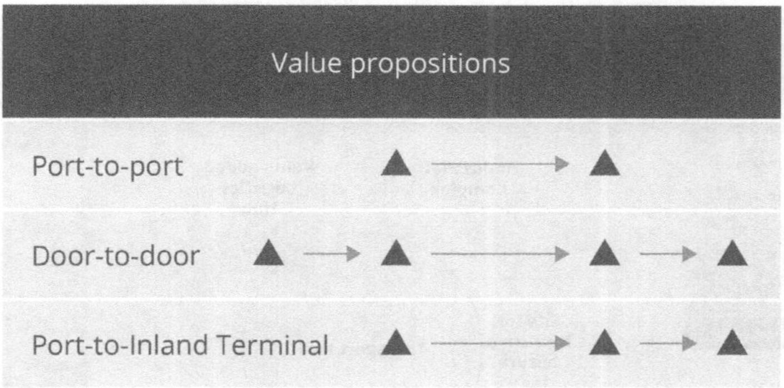

Figure 4.7 Three value propositions in intercontinental container freight transport

Source: Adapted from Van den Berg and De Langen (2015).

integration between the ILT operator and shippers. Because of this close integration, ILT operators often have direct contracts with shippers.

Figure 4.7 shows the three possible value propositions that shipping lines can offer: port-to-port, door-to-door and "port-to-ILT". In the ILT value proposition, at least one "landside leg" to an *inland terminal*, but without the "last mile" to the final destination, is provided.

Shipping lines have for decades aimed to provide integrated "door-to-door" services. This is understandable, as the port-to-port product is not attractive as the main product of shipping lines, as they have no control over the return flows of empty containers and have virtually no ways to differentiate their services from those of other shipping lines, especially since various shipping lines cooperate in alliances. While in some markets, shipping lines have been successful, other third parties, mainly forwarders, including "digital forwarders" such as Flexport, also position themselves as providers of door-to-door services. In the ILT proposition, shipping lines continue to focus on "scheduled services" (operating a transport network that includes barge and rail services), without moving into the last mile, which requires tight integration with shippers. In this proposition, shipping lines arrange bills of lading for and customs clearance in (a selected number of) inland terminals. Shipping lines increasingly provide such ILT services,[23] while terminal operating companies also increasingly develop a network of inland terminals, so that their customers – the shipping lines – can offer this network to their customers.

4.10 The impact of the changing landscape on ports; outlook of activities in the PBE

Based on the overview of trends and developments described above, Figure 4.8 shows a qualitative assessment of the growth potential of selected segments in the port business ecosystem.

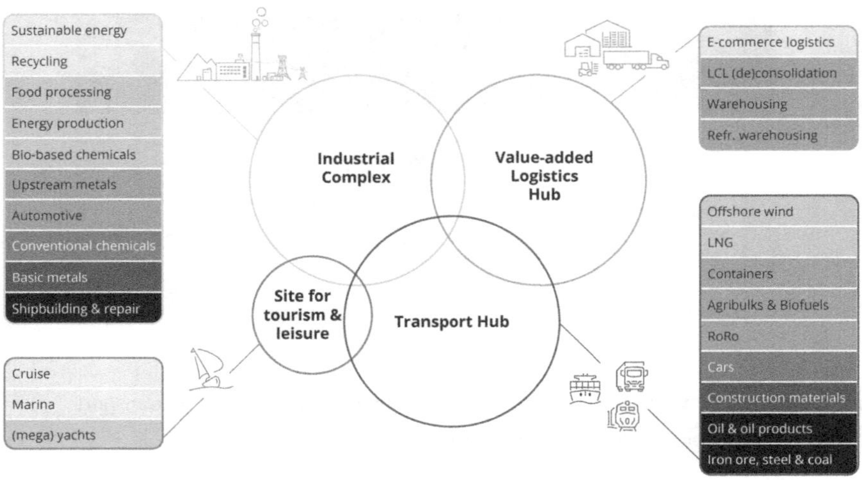

Figure 4.8 Growth prospects of activities in the port business ecosystem

Figure 4.8 shows that the largest growth potential may be in activities related to producing sustainable energies, new and cleaner feeds for fuel and chemicals, recycling, e-commerce logistics, and logistics services to offshore wind. This is a general "global outlook"; for each specific port, foresight is needed to understand the growth potential of activities in the PBE. Chapter 8 discusses relevant lessons learned regarding scenario analysis and forecasting and their role in port development.

Partly based on the growth prospects indicated in Figure 4.8, the ten *opportunity spaces* in the ports industry are discussed below.

4.11 The impact of the changing landscape on ports; ten opportunity spaces for ports

The trends and developments described above identify ten *opportunity spaces*[24] in the ports industry. Trends and developments lead to opportunities for creating value for port users. And as a general rule, *someone will come along and grasp these opportunities*: the opportunity space will be filled. The key question is who will do so. Clearly, the challenge for companies in the ports industry is to become early movers, since such early movers can develop competitive advantages. Based on the preceding overview of trends and developments, I identify ten broadly defined *opportunity spaces*. These ten apply to the ports industry[25] in general; some Port Managing Bodies (PMBs) are actively working on the opportunities, others are not. The ten opportunity spaces discussed below are:

1. Improve coordination in transport chains.
2. Develop port hinterland networks and intermodal platforms.
3. Gain a competitive advantage through reliable shipping and reliable port turnarounds.

4. Develop hubs for new energy/fuel types.
5. Green (trans)port operations.
6. Re-balance trade and transport flows.
7. Develop active infrastructure management.
8. Attract new activities to ports, including circular manufacturing and the blue economy.
9. Develop leisure activities.
10. Transition urban port areas to attractive and mixed areas.

In most of these opportunity spaces, initiatives for *digitalization* have a central place; I do not consider digitalization as a specific opportunity space.

For individual companies, strategies to deal with opportunity spaces take different forms. Often, the key to filling these opportunity spaces is taking *initiatives* to develop new concepts, creating *partnerships* with other companies to develop these concepts and translate them in *business cases*. *Chapter 9* discusses some examples of PMBs that have successfully developed strategies to grasp opportunities.

4.11.1 Improve coordination in transport chains

Transport operators have realized and will continue to realize important improvements in the *operational efficiency* of their own operations; the major challenge is improving efficiencies, beyond their organizational boundaries, for the transport chain as a whole. Information technology (e.g., blockchain) enables next steps in easy, cheap and reliable data exchange as well as tools to translate such information into better planning. The increasing focus on sustainable transport further drives initiatives to reduce inefficiencies in transport, such as empty container flows, unused container slots on trains and barges and inefficient routing of vehicles. The best cases of coordination across different companies show clear results. All of this leads to increased recognition that improved coordination in transport/supply chains creates value for customers. New ICT technology provides opportunities for better planning of infrastructure use. This means that both maritime access and road and rail access may be managed actively to secure efficient use of the infrastructure and port facilities. This implies systems need to be developed for arrival notification and planning of access to infrastructure. Huge potential for further efficiency gains in transport and port operations with the use of ICT. There is a large gap between the state-of-the-art and current practices, especially of small and medium-sized transport operators.

In some ports, this opportunity space was identified decades ago, and early movers have started port community system (PCS) initiatives long ago. The "next step" for many of these PCSs is to evolve to *chain* community systems.

In other ports, these opportunities are still there for the taking. There are two principal ways to "fill" this opportunity space. First, firms can form alliances in which they cooperate intensely to increase transport efficiency. Examples of cooperation between trucking companies (horizontal cooperation), or transport operators and terminal operating companies (vertical cooperation), lead to results. Second, new firms can develop business models that create as well as capture value through enhanced coordination. Examples include firms that develop cross-chain coordination software, firms that develop cooperative initiatives on a fee basis and internet-based cargo exchange platforms. Currently, there is a whole range of new start-ups active in this "space", including Arinto, Avikus and Harbor Lab.

4.11.2 Develop port hinterland networks and intermodal platforms

The trends discussed in this chapter (sustainability, coordination across end-to-end transport chains, improved information availability and tools to translate this in better operations across the chain), combined with the trend of increasing societal pressure to reduce road congestion in port regions and the trend to use inland nodes (dry ports) for functions previously carried out in seaports (such as empty depots and customs clearing), create an *opportunity space* for developing *port hinterland networks*. In some ports, such as Shanghai (where SIPC has developed a strong inland network) and Hamburg (where HHLA – partially together with Eurogate – have developed a strong rail network in the hinterland) and Barcelona (where the port authority is developing a network of inland terminals), companies and PMBs have developed an integrated port hinterland network, as a means to achieve competitive advantage. In many other ports, the development of inland ports (also called dry ports, or satellites or logistics zones) is still an opportunity.

This opportunity space is especially attractive, because of the *early mover advantage*: given scale economies, a strong inland port network can lead to a lasting competitive advantage (this issue is addressed in more detail in Chapter 5).

This opportunity space also includes the development of logistics clusters in the port hinterland. In many "gateway regions", areas outside the port and closer to consumer centers have become increasingly attractive for warehousing. Whereas many distribution centers traditionally focus on road transport, developing sites for distribution facilities with a strong *intermodal connectivity* creates value, especially for a specific segment of distribution centers (see Figure 4.9).

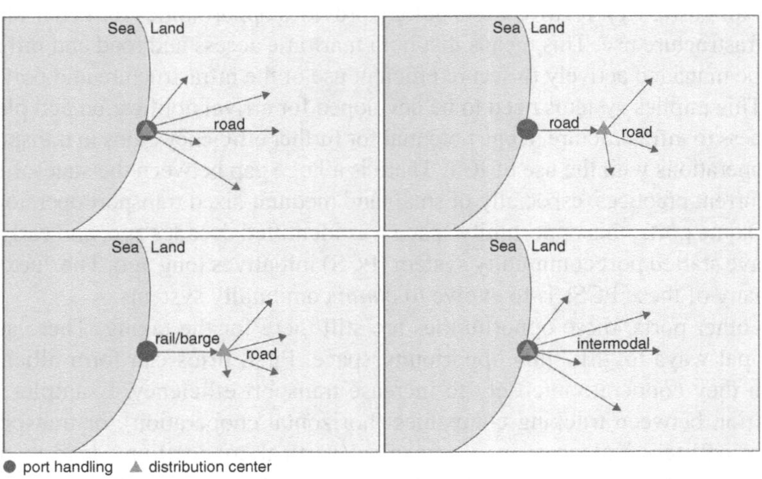

Figure 4.9 Distribution patterns for inbound maritime logistics

The different distribution patterns depicted in Figure 4.9 have always co-existed and will continue to co-exist. But the fourth pattern (left lower corner) is relatively new and (still) an opportunity space in ports, especially in developing economies.

Examples of PMBs that have invested in inland logistics zones

One recent example of a port becoming active in inland zone development is Reijka, that developed an inland terminal close to the port, with direct connections with the railway and highway and a substantial surface area of around 44 hectares. A second example concerns the port of Trieste, which has developed various inland terminals together with other partners (the port is a shareholder in "Interporto di Trieste" as well as "Interporto Cervignano del Friuli". Trieste also is a shareholder in the multimodal transport operators hat provide intermodal (rail) services to these inland terminals. In China, most of the port companies also have invested in inland networks.

4.11.3 Gain competitive advantage through reliable shipping and reliable port turnarounds

The focus on reliability in shipping is likely to increase further in the coming years. Reliability is a key issue for shippers. The current weak "on-time performance" record of most, if not all, shipping lines, with generally >25% of ships delayed more than one day. Shippers generally aim for stock levels >99.5% to prevent lost sales because they are out-of-stock. Thus, shippers are cautious regarding reducing the inventory in transport. Given the lack of reliability, less inventory translates to higher risks of out-of-stock.

However, the full costs of these high inventory levels are increasingly clear. For shipping lines, moving away from a focus on direct costs and toward a focus on more reliability is likely to lead to a value proposition that reduces total supply chain costs. What's more, *a focus on reliability may also translate to lower costs for shipping lines*, as better planning cuts out waste (for instance, terminals being idle as ships arrive late). The opportunity space is there for shipping lines to offer shipping services with far better reliability for a similar price. The Gemini alliance of Maersk Line and Hapag Lloyd have explicitly announced their intent to improve reliability.

This opportunity space is based on the idea that the costs of reliable operations ought to be as low as the costs of less reliable operations. While there are certainly costs involved in improving on-time performance, for instance, by increasing the vessel speed in case of a delay, thereby increasing fuel costs, there are also operational advantages that enable lower costs, especially in three areas:

1. Port operations. The current lack of reliability translates to less efficient terminal operations, since the planning of gangs as well as berths is often modified, with additional costs.

2. Feeder operations. The unreliable arrival of the mother vessels incurs high costs for feeder operators. In the case of a delayed mother vessel, the feeder either waits – thus incurring extra costs – or sticks to the planned schedule, with lower utilization.
3. Operations of inland transport services. If train operators can be sure that ships arrive on time, they can use their equipment more efficiently by avoiding either waits for late containers in the port or empty slots because containers were supposed to be on the train but did not make it, due to the vessel delay. Furthermore, a better on-time performance of the ships enables a higher use of intermodal transport that may be less fast, but is cheaper than road transport.

This opportunity space is not limited to shipping but also involves inland operations and port operations. The value created through enhanced reliability is substantial, so terminals that distinguish themselves with more reliable ship turnarounds create value: the challenge for them is to capture that value. The same applies to pilotage and towage service providers, as they also influence the reliability and speed of ship turnarounds. As discussed previously, higher standards in terms of efficiency and reliability of "ship turnarounds" require a more coordinated approach between shipping lines, terminal operators, towage, pilotage, lashing companies and the PMB.

4.11.4 Develop hubs for new energy/fuel types

The trends discussed previously clearly indicate that the *energy mix* will change and that new fuel types will increase their share in this energy mix. New fuel types include LNG, ethanol, other *biofuels* and dry biomass (e.g., wood pellets). And for the introduction of new energy sources, *distribution is the key*. It may be relatively easy to generate energy sources; the key issue is to get them to energy users in a cost-effective manner.

The huge investments in energy/fuel distribution infrastructure are fixed and make distribution patterns *path dependent*. Given the fact that over 30% of the worldwide shipping volumes consist of energy carriers such as oil, coal and LNG, combined with a fast-growing demand for energy and a changing energy mix, *new distribution patterns* for new energy/fuel types will need to be developed – and present four broad types of opportunities for ports:

- Develop a position as a *gateway* for new energy/fuel flows. Such a gateway position crucially depends on the quality of transport corridors from the port to inland locations. The port becomes a gateway through the development of superior inland connections.
- Develop a position as a *hub* for new energy/fuel flows. In this position, the port attracts cargo flows that are later distributed by ship to other ports. Like in other markets, the competition for this position is fierce, and few ports can truly become hub ports. Key challenges are secure and efficient ship turnarounds and a captive cargo base that provides the basis for developing hub flows.

- Develop a position as a *production center* for fuels/energy. Ports are often attractive locations for production plants; this also applies to energy/fuel plants. Key challenges include the quality of utility infrastructure (water, heat, electricity, industrial gases, CO_2) and cheap availability of (alternative) resources.
- Develop a position as a *bunker port* for ships. As ships only bunker once per 10 to 20 port calls, ports compete for this position.

These four broad opportunities mutually strengthen each other. And history matters: some ports already have a strong basis for grasping these opportunities, while others do not; the further development of distribution patterns continues to be path dependent.

Investments in green fuel production

Investments in green fuel production have been rising rapidly in the past decade and will continue to grow rapidly in the coming decades. According to IRENA (https://www.irena.org/), tens of trillions of investments are needed to move toward a sustainable energy system. A substantial part of these investments is in the production of green fuels, such as SAF (sustainable aviation fuel), biofuels, methanol and hydrogen.

Investments in green fuel production; the case of the Dutch ports

In all major Dutch seaports, investments have been made in the production of sustainable (transport) fuels. Many of these investments can partly be explained by the presence of existing industrial activities in the Dutch seaports.

In addition, all major Dutch seaports are committed to attracting additional investments in the production of sustainable (transport) fuels, because of their importance in the transition to a sustainable energy system and more specifically sustainable transport. All ports have a substantial "pipeline" with projects in the development phase. This pipeline includes various types of sustainable fuels, hydrogen and biogas occupy a prominent place, as well as projects for the production of e-methanol and bio-kerosene.

The spatial impact of the investments in sustainable (transport) fuels is significant. In some cases, existing facilities will be transformed, in other cases the use of space of existing sites will be intensified, and in addition, the Dutch PDCs will develop new port land to attract investors in sustainable (transport) fuel production. Partly due to the lower energy content of sustainable fuels, a relatively large amount of space is required. The amount of port land in the Netherlands on which sustainable fuel production will take place is expected to exceed 1000 hectares before 2030. However, in 2025 these developments faced a strong backlash: two large scale biofuels investments were stopped, mainly because of deteriorating demand forecasts.

Nuclear power plants in ports?

Nuclear power plants are often located in or near ports due to the need for a large supply of cooling water, which is essential for the operation of the reactors, as well as the large energy demand in ports and the planning regime, in which ports often are "islands" where industrial activities are accommodated. Examples include the nuclear power plants in the Dutch part of North Sea Port, in Antwerp, and near Port Gibson, Mississippi. In addition, as nuclear power plants become smaller, floating nuclear power plants become an option. The so-called Advanced Small Modular Reactors (A-SMRs) are suitable for maritime applications. Floating reactors can provide power in ports where the grid capacity is constrained. In the longer run, A-SMR-powered ships could be introduced. Such vessels could be faster and have lower propulsion costs than the current fleet. Such vessels could operate for years without needing to refuel.

Energy-intensive production

Because of their large (potential) role as energy hubs, in which various sources of energy are available at competitive prices, ports are also attractive locations for energy-intensive industries. Examples of such industries include steel, cement, chemicals, aluminum, ceramics, glass, paper, bitumen and fertilizers. Many industrial ports have already attracted huge investments in such energy-intensive industries. A good example is the port of Sohar (Oman), which has attracted a bitumen plant, steel plants, a refinery, a plastics plant and an iron ore pelletizing plant, chiefly because of the availability of competitively priced energy. Another example is Groningen Seaports, which has also attracted similar industries, and in addition various datacenters, which are also very energy-intensive. Ports that develop into hubs for new energy and fuel types become attractive locations for a large range of energy-intensive activities.

Challenging times for ports as energy hubs – the case of Bilbao

Bilbao is an excellent case to show the impact of the energy transition on the port business ecosystem. The port, which historically was an important element in the region's steel industry, and which was used to import and export coal, iron ore and steel, was redeveloped following the decline of the steel and related industries in the 1970 and 1980s. Currently, the port consists of a variety of terminals, logistics, manufacturing and leisure companies, all of which are impacted by the gradual transition towards a sustainable "net-zero" economy.

In recent years, the role of Bilbao's port as energy hub has expanded. The port is home of a large offshore wind manufacturer (Haizea Wind Group), a terminal for biofuels (sustainable fuels produced from biomass) a LNG terminal, developed amongst others to serve LNG fueled RoRo vessels, as well as a Petronor synthetic fuels demo plant, aimed at developing technologies for efficient and competitive large-scale production of e-fuels. These different initiatives are complementary and interdependent and all of them have emerged through partnerships between the port, the regional government and energy companies.

All these initiatives take place in a constantly evolving energy landscape, with some recent indications suggesting the energy transition may take longer and may need more policies to make sure it goes hand in hand with competitive energy prices. For instance, various countries and oil companies have rolled back initiatives to move away from fossil fuels, while some sustainable energy producers have downscaled investment plans and shipping companies have moved away from a fast transition to net-zero fuels and towards the use of LNG as a transition fuel. In this landscape, the path to develop ports as energy hubs requires both a bold sustainability roadmap and the flexibility to adjust and adapt along the way.

4.11.5 Green (trans)port operations

The opportunity space of green transport and port operations is still wide open. The number of port/shipping users willing to pay a premium for more sustainable transport is very limited (around 2% of the total market). Thus, it is still a challenge to turn being more sustainable into commercial value. However, the societal value that is created by greener operations is clear and will translate into economic value, through pricing mechanisms for CO_2, through reputation effects for green companies, through higher employee commitment for green companies and through shareholder pressure on the sustainability performance of the companies they have invested in.

Insetting initiatives

Carbon emission reductions can be turned into commercial value through carbon markets. These are fundamental to secure the most cost-efficient methods for reducing GHG emissions are deployed. A voluntary market develops as firms develop greening projects to generate tradable carbon credits. In this approach, companies benefit from a "market" for carbon credits to secure resources are allocated efficiently. However, contrary to offsetting, which has become less popular, in an insetting approach companies aim to buy carbon credits only from emission reducing activities that are related to *their* supply chain. In the domain of maritime transport, insetting could lead to tradable carbon credits for zero carbon transport. Thus, similarly to the "pooling approach" in the ETS for maritime transport (in which a company can meet emission standards even if some specific operations to not meet these standards, a shipping company can purchase "maritime transport credits" to decarbonize maritime transport, even if some of its freight flows continue to be shipped with vessels that generate emissions. They key difference is that in this approach companies can only purchase "maritime transport credits" from projects that decarbonize maritime transport (and not from for instance plantation projects for trees). Insetting requires accurate carbon emission data across (maritime) supply chains.

Port operations are a minor part of total emissions in the door-to-door chain. Generally, emissions from port operations are less than 2% of total door-to-door emissions. This suggests that initiatives in ports to help reduce emissions in shipping and hinterland transport are at least equally important as emission reductions in port operations.

Path-dependent distribution infrastructure and windows of opportunity

A clear example of the path dependence of distribution infrastructure of energy sources are the pipelines for crude oil and gas. Rotterdam, for instance, is connected by pipeline to refineries in Antwerp, Flushing, Gelsenkirchen (Germany) and four other refineries in the German state of North Rhine-Westphalia. This pipeline infrastructure was developed in the 1950s and 1960s; since then, the distribution patterns virtually *have not changed.* Rotterdam has a stable market share of >50% in north-west Europe.

For LNG, many ports are actively seeking a position as a bunker port, especially with the LNG-fuelled container vessels on order. Early movers most likely will consolidate their position as the demand for LNG as bunker fuel increases.

This path dependence creates a *window of opportunity* (a small period in which an opportunity manifests itself) when distribution patterns for new energy sources are developed. In some cases, the final consumption points are given (as is the case for oil refineries), in other cases not. For instance, LNG-fuelled ships need to bunker LNG in a few ports, but not all. Once some ports have invested in attractive LNG facilities for ships, the window of opportunity has disappeared. Similarly, when electricity plants start to use substantial volumes of biomass in addition to coal, this may need to be imported overseas – and new distribution patterns may need to be designed.

A key challenge for ports is to attract new "green" activities to the port. Examples include biofuel terminals, clean fuel production and wind activities (production, logistics, related services, e.g., maintenance). This opportunity space includes improvements of the sustainability of current port operations, for instance through more intermodal transport, smart electricity grids, and infrastructure to exchange heat and CO_2. This opportunity space is also very relevant for suppliers to the transport and ports industry, as it creates a market for new products such as foldable containers and electric terminal equipment.

The opportunity space for batteries in ports and shipping

Given the huge increase in sustainable energy generation (with its uneven generation over time), the battery market is rapidly evolving, and the costs of electricity storage are declining rapidly. The battery market is rapidly growing; investments in batteries in 2023 were >US$30 billion, higher than investments in wind and solar combined. The innovation intensity is also very high. As a consequence, battery technology is evolving in three different directions: first, the costs of energy storage are falling. Second, innovations increase the energy density of batteries, and third, larger batteries become economically viable. The dimensions of a 20/40-foot shipping container have become a standard size for a "battery container", even if it is used for "stationary" applications, because of the ease of transport of such a large battery container. Battery containers are increasingly used in barge and shortsea shipping, even if they stay on board permanently. The use of battery containers allows for the "*swapping*" of empty for full battery containers.

Batteries /battery containers can be charged in two ways: through traditional "shore power" installations, in which they remain on the ship, or through "swapping" empty battery containers with full ones. Charging a battery container in a charging station can currently be done in about 2.5 to three hours (but improvements are plausible). Charging times for a container onboard are similar. A charging station requires a "transformer" and an "inverter" (from alternating to direct current). Costs for a loading station may be in the range of US$500,000 to US$1 million. The annual capacity of such a loading station would be >2000 battery containers per year. However, in practice, loading may be mostly done when electricity prices are low.

In the container swapping business model for providing electricity, a "pay-per-use model" has emerged. In this model, the operator pays for electricity through:

1. A fee per kW used. This fee is linked to the general electricity price, and includes a mark-up for the services of the battery provider.
2. A time-related fee for the use of the battery container.

In this model, the ownership of the battery container remains with the battery/energy service provider. This is sensible as this company can benefit from scale economies, charge the containers optimally under fluctuating energy prices and utilize the containers when not onboard ships.

The costs of swapping a battery container are substantial (around US$50 to US$100 per move). Additional costs are incurred when the charging station is not located at a terminal, leading to a need to transport the battery container by truck. Thus, in the swapping model, the charging station has to be placed at the terminal, else the costs of transporting the container become prohibitive.

A *flexible charging approach*, with swapping of containers in some situations and onboard charging of containers in other situations, may be most efficient. Broadly speaking, swapping containers, rather than recharging them onboard, makes sense if the revenue potential through higher utilization of the battery container outweighs the costs of unloading and reloading. As this revenue potential is around US$200–US$300 per day (see below), swapping becomes attractive if containers are not used (either full or empty) for at least a couple of days. Thus, ships carrying a large number of battery containers (some full, some empty and some in use) are unlikely to be optimal, as it makes more sense to minimize the number of containers onboard and generate revenue with otherwise unused containers onboard on the electricity "spot markets". In other battery transport segments, especially buses, batteries are used that way when the buses are not being driven.

The use of battery containers in shipping is a niche market. Battery containers are more widely used for housing cooperatives and industrial users, and for reducing the grid requirements and trading on the various spot markets for power, through charging when prices are low and providing electricity when prices are high. Various trading instruments and places have been developed for this. The daily revenue potential in such services per battery container is currently around US$200–US$300 per day. Because the revenue potential of battery containers depends on the energy markets in general and the value of energy storage at a specific location, the location decisions for battery charging facilities are not only driven by "logistical considerations", but also by "energy market considerations".

Because of the high costs of the energy container, an efficient container battery system needs to allow a high utilization of battery containers, either onboard ships, at the terminal (for instance, by loading electric trucks and/or yard equipment) or for energy services. A model in which such containers are not utilized for long periods is economically not viable. In view of the above, the loading stations where containers are charged ideally need to be attractive both from a logistical (at a terminal that is located on a busy canal/river) and an energy (close to renewable generation, value added for local grid) perspective. *Developing loading stations at such strategic locations gives energy providers (and terminals) a competitive advantage that is durable, in the sense that it cannot be easily replicated by other battery container service providers.*

4.11.6 Re-balance trade and transport flows

Imbalances are a fact of life in supply chains. Imbalances also provide an opportunity for *re-balancing*. A number of trends expand this opportunity space: sustainability makes projects to re-balance very marketable, while better information provision and cooperation across supply chains enable re-balancing. Re-balancing can take many shapes, including:

- Sending paper pulp and scrap in huge quantities from consumer areas to producer areas, for upgrading and subsequent return to the consumer areas. This way, empty containers from consumer areas to producer areas are filled.
- Building vessels that can carry distinct commodities. Return cargo is often impossible for ships that can carry only one commodity. Especially ships that are designed for a specific route (e.g., wood from Scandinavia to Central Europe, or iron ore from Brazil to China) can be designed to carry specific return loads.
- Developing sea-air propositions from airports with a large empty leg (such as airports in the Gulf area). In such a proposition, a part of the journey is by sea, the other part by air. Given the imbalanced air transport, the overall price can be just a bit more than for an all-sea journey, while the transit time can be substantially shorter.
- Making commodity swaps between producers of homogeneous products (such as oil, chemicals, steel) in different locations, so that both reduce transport costs. In the swap, they exchange the ownership of the commodity in place A for the ownership of the same commodity in place B.
- Initiatives of shipping lines and forwarders to match shippers with import flows to shippers with export flows. Such initiatives can take many shapes. One promising avenue is to combine shipments of suppliers to large retail companies.
- Combining maritime flows with continental flows. The imbalances of maritime flows can potentially be re-balanced with imbalances of continental flows. For instance, the imbalance from Asia to the US leads to many empty containers that need to return from places like Chicago to the US West Coast ports. These may be filled with continental cargo from the Midwest to California.
- Locating products of export-oriented industries in excess import areas of containers to secure cheap connectivity to export markets. Producing chemicals in the Gulf area may be attractive given the low container rates for exports from the Gulf to areas such as India, other parts of Asia or Europe.

All these examples show how companies can create value by re-balancing cargo flows. Many such initiatives have been successfully taken, but there certainly are *next steps* to be taken.

4.11.7 Develop active infrastructure management

Currently, too often infrastructure is not actively managed. Infrastructure is often not used efficiently because coordination between users is limited or nonexistent. For example, on highways all users freely use it without coordination. This leads to congestion in rush hours. The lack of coordination between infrastructure users is, in general, explained because coordination is costly, and costs and benefits are not distributed equally. Without coordination, peaks arise and congestion, long waiting times (for instance, trucks waiting at terminals), and deviations from schedules will result.

Table 4.5 Cases of insufficient coordination that reduce utilization of infrastructure

Sources of inefficient use of infrastructure	*Potential solution through infrastructure access rules*
Too many calls of barges with small call sizes per terminal.	Only allow barges in the port when they call at a limited number of terminals.
Peak load on rail terminals in ports.	Only allow trains on rail tracks when the rail terminal operator confirms capacity to handle these trains in their allocated slots (real time).
Unused rail tracks because of insufficient planning.	Penalize train operators (substantially) for not using a track.
Peak loads in the arrival and departure of trucks at the deep-sea terminal.	Only allow trucks on port access routes when they have reserved a "slot" at the terminal.
Congestion on the road infrastructure in the port region.	Only allow (empty) trucks on port access roads outside rush hours.

Source: Adapted from Van Der Horst and de Langen (2008).

Efficient utilization of road, rail, inland waterways and maritime access channels cannot be achieved without active infrastructure management. Developing organizational structures focused on developing and setting *infrastructure access rules* that improve the utilization of this infrastructure, thus enhancing port competitiveness. In some ports, such access rules have been developed; for instance, in LA/Long Beach only environmentally friendly trucks are allowed in the port area. And there are many opportunities to develop access rules further to create value.

Table 4.5 shows a number of cases where insufficient coordination leads to a sub-optimal utilization of infrastructure and tentative infrastructure access rules that may enhance efficiency. These infrastructure access rules would only allow trucks, trains and barges to use the infrastructure if they meet certain criteria.[26] Alternatively, tariff structures can be devised that provide discounts when these criteria are met, or penalties when these criteria are not met. All these are forms of infrastructure access rules.

These examples of infrastructure access rules that improve the utilization of infrastructure are general and may not be required or effective in all cases. But given the trends described above, active infrastructure management is an important opportunity space for ports.

Given the central role of the PMB in the port (e.g., contracts with terminal operators, investments in a port community system, communication with all relevant stakeholders), partnerships between the PMB and the owners of the infrastructure to design and implement infrastructure access rules seem appropriate.

Active infrastructure management in Valparaiso (Chile)

Because of the specific lay-out of the port, Valparaiso is a frontrunner in active infrastructure management. The container terminal is located right next to the city centre, and the only access route that by-passes the centre is a steep two-lane access road, partly tunnelled, that ends outside the urban area at a plateau where the "gate area" is located. This "ZEAL" (translated broadly as "extended logistics zone") functions as entry and exit gate, both physical and virtual for Valparaíso. From this point on, the entry and exit of cargo to and from the terminals is coordinated. All document checks and inspections of public services are carried out in the ZEAL combined operations are planned to minimize empty truck movements. This requires coordinated planning, which is done through Silogport, the PCS in Valparaiso. The end result is a road corridor that is actively managed to secure minimum congestion and efficient utilization. This system was relatively easy to implement in Valparaiso, given the special lay-out of the port, but may also be attractive in other ports in which road access is provided by one highway.

4.11.8 Attract new activities to ports, including circular manufacturing and blue economy

The trends toward circularity lead to increasing flows of end-of-lifecycle products and to investments in new manufacturing processes, based on re-use of materials. Ports, especially ports in urban areas, are attractive locations for such activities, as they benefit from the availability of EOL materials. Thus, companies may aim to develop recycling processes for car tires, food waste, scrap, electronics, plastics and the like, and find that ports, especially those with established industrial and energy production, are attractive locations. While many of these circular recycling activities are on a large scale (e.g., electric arc steelmaking), some of them may be rather on a small scale. For such activities, locations in the vicinity of urban functions may be viable, and a potentially interesting way to revitalize waterfront areas adjacent to urban centers.

4.11.9 Develop and expand leisure activities in ports

The most "robust" growth segment in many ports is cruise and "maritime leisure" (large and small yachts, hotels in old port facilities, marina facilities including restaurants, facilities for excursions and so on). Leisure activities form a part of the overall port business ecosystem, and synergies between the leisure activities and other activities in the PBE can be developed. For instance, the cruise segment can be an important "lead user" with a demand for sustainable fuel. Leisure activities also generate demand for repair and maintenance facilities in the PBE. Given the limited and declining societal support for cruise and more broadly leisure activities, active approaches to reduce the negative externalities of these activities need to be developed, focused on two areas:

- Reducing negative environmental externalities through OPS facilities and policies to incentivize the use of green fuels at sea.
- Reducing the overcrowding of specific areas by cruise tourists. This can be done through allocating cruise slots with specific time windows, to avoid simultaneous arrivals of multiple cruise vessels and through actions to spread cruise visitors over different attractions.

In the same way that other parts of the port business ecosystem can be strengthened by attracting additional activities (often "downstream" in value chains), ports can also strengthen their leisure component by adding additional activities, such as hotels, restaurants, shops, and attractions. Cruise visitors can also increase the viability of port heritage/experience centers or museums, which many PMBs develop, in view of increasing stakeholder support for port activities. Examples of ports with such port experience/heritage centers include Rotterdam, Huelva, Marseille, Genoa and Los Angeles.

Amsterdam's ban on cruise may be a missed opportunity to promote sustainable cruise tourism

Amsterdam's city council has approved a plan to ban cruise from Amsterdam's city center. Another bold move from a port that some years ago took the decision to phase out the handling of coal by 2030. While I am positive about the decision on coal, in my view the ban on cruise is shortsighted. For very understandable reasons, Amsterdam aims to reduce the negative impacts associated with tourism. But negative effects from tourism are not a given, and they certainly are not similar across all tourist types. Amsterdam's core tourism problem is that it attracts large numbers of tourists attracted by the prospect of "drugs and drinking". Banning cruise does not help addressing that problem at all. Furthermore, banning cruise ships will certainly result in cruise calls in other cities (mainly Rotterdam and IJmuiden) with bus excursions from there to Amsterdam, while a mere 3% of all Amsterdam's tourists arrive with a cruise, so the decision is hardly material in reducing tourism numbers in Amsterdam.

Amsterdam's decision was also justified by rightly pointing out that the cruise tourism industry is not environmentally sustainable. This is where in my view the missed opportunity kicks in. Why not ban polluting ships only, while welcoming environmentally sustainable cruise calls if they submit a realistic plan to make sure the cruise activity in Amsterdam in environmentally and socially sustainable, for instance through zero-emission daytrips spread out over the city, to avoid overcrowding of tourism hotspots? And why not seek alliances with other in-demand ports in the same destination market, like Oslo, Copenhagen or Hamburg, to establish a coalition of port cities leading the transition towards sustainable cruise tourism? In such an approach, cruise would not be "labelled" as intrinsically "bad", but instead, Amsterdam would use its attractiveness as cruise destination to drive change in the right direction. Of course, more work would have to be done on the feasibility and spatial implications of such an approach, but an outright ban without much consideration of potential alternatives is in my view shortsighted.

4.11.10 Transition urban port areas to attractive and mixed areas

The urbanization trend leads to pressure on port land, and waterfront areas are potentially very attractive areas for a variety of functions. The redevelopment of the most central port areas can be a major opportunity for space. Redevelopment can imply that port activities completely disappear, but also lead to mixed "urban port areas". In such areas, a mix of various functions, including cruise, marinas, hotels, urban distribution, leisure, office spaces for port-related services, small-scale manufacturing, as well as housing, can be realized. Such urban port areas may be attractive for port developers, as the land value may be high compared to that for traditional port functions. In various ports, the PMB generates substantial revenue streams from urban port areas, including in ports such as Barcelona and Manchester.

4.12 The changing landscape of the need for "port innovation systems"

The overview provided in the preceding paragraphs shows a radically changing landscape in which ports operate. Ports need to become more *reliable* and *flexible*, offering different users different services and to adjust to volatility. Ports also need to embrace *digitalization* while controlling (cyber)security risks, and ports need to become *green* and *circular* and attract new economic activities.

This implies ports need to have sufficient capacity to adapt to this changing landscape. This is a huge challenge, especially because port development initiatives often require various years of planning and construction, in part because port development projects often are *contested projects*, with the subsequent need to involve all stakeholders and create sufficient stakeholder support for port development initiatives.

Because of the need to adapt and increase flexibility to deal with unforeseen events, *innovation* is critical. To understand how innovation in ports can be fostered, three characteristics of ports need to be kept in mind.

First, port ecosystems consist of a diverse set of mainly *operational* activities. Port activities include terminal operations, transport operations, warehousing, and processing activities across numerous supply chains (such as food, energy, automotive, steel and so on).

Second, given the international nature of the abovementioned activities in ports, *subsidiaries* of multi-national corporations (MNCs) make up the vast majority of firms active and are increasingly dominant in port clusters. These MNCs have operations in various countries, and very few of the involved firms (or sometimes none at all) are headquartered in the port. The MNCs generally have one central R&D department, often located in their home country and thus, no local R&D departments, and often not even an allocated "budget" for innovation in most ports.

Third, given the strong interdependencies of the activities in value chains, cooperation between different companies active in the port is often required to achieve the successful implementation of innovative technologies. Innovation does not thrive through isolated actions of individual companies, but rather depends on the joint actions of a broad array of interrelated actors (firms, research institutes, incubators, governments, industry associations).

Because of these three characteristics, ports are radically different from the widely studied "high-tech clusters". The main distinguishing characteristic of innovation in ports is that the central challenge is *absorptive capacity*. R&D activities in ports are limited, and the dominant innovation challenge is the (early) application of new knowledge and technologies developed outside the port. Examples of relevant technologies include digital technologies, recycling technologies, autonomous freight transport, biobased chemicals, smart grids, new energy generation technologies and so on. The absorptive capacity of a PBE can be defined as the capacity to absorb, enhance, diffuse and exploit knowledge from sources outside the PBE.[27] This requires a *port innovation system*.

The focus on absorbing (and in the process enhancing) knowledge and technologies rather than creating knowledge and technologies implies that measures of the innovation performance of a port differ from the indicators commonly used for innovation clusters, such as R&D spending and the number of patents. For ports, the most relevant indicators are 1) investments to apply new technologies in new or established operations and 2) the number and growth of start-ups with products and services, based on new technologies targeted to ports, maritime and energy industries. Figure 4.10 shows the components of such an innovation system.

More detail regarding the port innovation system (PIS) and the role of the PMB in fostering a PIS is provided in Chapter 8.

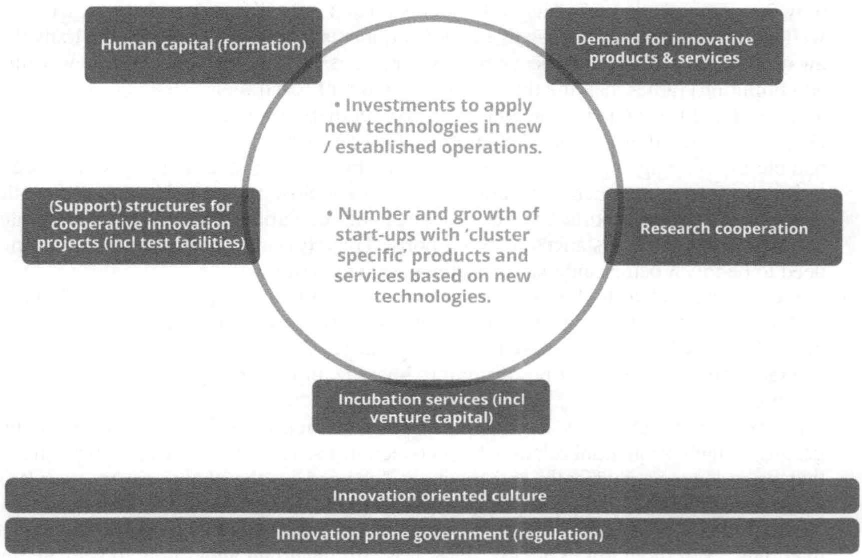

Figure 4.10 The components of the "port innovation system"

Source: Adapted from Mendes Constante et al. (2023).

Notes

1 For at least two reasons, a claim of such a comprehensive overview is problematic. First, the time gap between writing and publication/the moment of reading is such that new developments have emerged and the trends are outdated. Second, due to my own mental map, some potentially disruptive developments may be ignored in this book.
2 The four categories of external developments also affect each other: the societal trend of aging is partly caused by new technologies and affects developments in politics.
3 Specific trends that impact ports are discussed in more detail than general trends that affect a variety of industries. Specific ports operate in specific environments, where specific trends are relevant, and in specific ways. Nevertheless, the general trends we describe here impact the ports industry worldwide.
4 How to deal with such opportunity spaces is discussed in Chapter 5.
5 The EU has a formal set of energy intensive industries; see https://single-market-economy.ec.europa.eu/industry/strategy/energy-intensive-industries_en
6 See Contents_WR_2024_Industrial_Robots.pdf
7 An interactive map of the (BRI related) Chinese activities in ports is available at https://www.cfr.org/tracker/china-overseas-ports
8 See https://population.un.org/wpp/
9 The UN and the World Bank publish different figures.
10 Based on data from World Maritime Review 2018.
11 The scarcity argument is certainly relevant, but to be handled with care: already in 1865, scholars predicted that the UK would soon run out of coal, in 1939 it was predicted oil would run out in 13 years and the famous Club of Rome foresaw in 1972 th\t there was

only 20 years of oil stock. They all underestimated both discovery of new reserves as well as technological advances that enable an increase in fossil fuels. So the transition away from fossil fuels may occur for other reasons (mainly to reduce global warming and pollution) rather than the threat of running out of fossil fuels.

12 The non-tariff trade barriers include excessive regulations on, e.g., standards.

13 Distances have often been used as a proxy for transport costs. This is increasingly debatable as shipping lines have developed elaborate international networks, and ocean tariffs are related as much to locations of countries close to main shipping routes, the connectivity between ports, market structures and regulations on different trade routes and port costs, as to distances between ports. Thus, transport costs between countries need to be much better understood, as they drive trade flows.

14 Some factors, such as higher fuel prices and a switch to more expensive and sustainable fuel, may lead to higher transport costs. However, we argue that these will be more than offset by the effects of increased reliability, larger ship sizes, better information exchange, improved container repositioning, liberalization of transport markets and other factors.

15 The term "supply chain" is commonplace but nevertheless has been criticized for suggesting a stable sequential relationship between firms. This may have as a consequence that firms become physically and mentally "chained by the chain" (in the words of Richard Normann). A supply network is suggested as a better term.

16 As examples, Apple announced its aim to produce electronics based on 100% recycled materials, even though it explicitly states it is still uncertain about how to achieve that objective. Companies like TerraCycle and e-Cycle organize the collection of waste from households and upcycle such waste into more valuable products.

17 We recognize there are important differences between supply chains that handle the same type of commodities. Some fruit supply chains have a clear international orientation, while others may be regionally oriented, even for the handling of a single commodity. The classification in the figure gives the dominant scope of the supply chain.

18 See www.sciencedaily.com/releases/2010/01/100113091646.htm

19 See http://inhabitat.com/energy-generating-roads-by-innowattech/

20 Nuclear ships have been built and this technology remains an option, but is unlikely to become widely used in shipping, for both cost and safety reasons.

21 www.seaat.org/Article.aspx?articleid=59

22 However, an ICE (Internal Combustion Engine) requires more space than an all-electric propulsion system.

23 The ILT proposition has operational advantages over the port-to-port proposition: it enables triangulation of empty containers, leveraging of scale economies in intermodal transport and better planning of intermodal operations.

24 This term was introduced by Richard Normann (2001), in his book *Reframing Business*. At center stage in this book is the need for companies to re-frame their value propositions. And an important tool for this is a thorough analysis of trends and developments.

25 In addition, port-specific opportunity spaces may be present in specific ports, but these are not discussed here.

26 Governments obviously have general infrastructure access rules, e.g., a driving license and a sufficiently safe vehicle. The argument here is for additional rules aimed to improve efficiency of the utilization of infrastructure, sustainability and more coordination in hinterland chains.

27 This definition is adapted from Cohen and Levinthal (1990).

5 Getting port governance right

As discussed in the introductory chapter, ports in many countries are not performing well. Indicators of waiting times and handling times of ships in ports, as well as other indicators of the overall logistics performance (see World Bank, 2025a), show a huge gap between well-functioning and non-performing ports. The same applies to rankings of container terminal efficiency. Finally, some ports succeed in attracting large volumes of FDI, while others do not.

Governments are deeply involved in the ports industry, as regulators, policy makers and often as owners of port assets and/or the state-owned port development company (SO-PDC) or port authority (PA). Government involvement differs substantially per country. In Britain, ports are run as fully private companies (following port reform in the Thatcher era); in South Africa, a large government-owned entity (Transnet) is responsible for port development and provides most terminal services as well as freight rail transport. In most Scandinavian countries, local government owns corporatized independently operating PDCs, and in Brazil and India, some ports are state-owned, others are privately owned, and terminal services are both provided by state-owned companies and private operators based on concession contracts.

These large differences between countries – and between ports within a country – show that there is no consensus on the best model for government involvement in the ports industry. Too often, the existing model for public involvement is taken for granted. There are strong indications that ineffective port governance is the root cause of many hurdles to better port performance.[1] Thus, this chapter provides a detailed discussion on the appropriate port governance model. Governments face other policy decisions in ports, including decisions concerning port planning, port regulation and port financing; these are discussed in Chapter 6.

"Getting port governance right" is complicated, as there is no "one size fits all" governance model that is the most suitable in all contexts. However, there are clear indications that some governance models work better than others, and that specific governance models are appropriate in specific contexts. This chapter provides tools to rigorously analyze port governance and identify the most appropriate governance model. Appendix 1 contains a summary of the case studies (two best cases and

DOI: 10.4324/9781003630784-5

two worst cases) on port governance. The conclusions from these cases are in line with the arguments brought forward in this chapter.

5.1 A paradigm shift: from Port Authority to Port Development Company

The treatment of port governance in this chapter entails a paradigm shift, away from the conventional public sector-driven port development paradigm to an approach in which port development is treated first and foremost as a commercial activity.[2]

In the traditional perspective, port development is about the provision of port infrastructure. This infrastructure is regarded as a "quasi-public good", like other basic infrastructure that is provided by government (Goss, 1990). In addition, the provision of port infrastructure is important to regional economic development. Thus, in the same way that government has provided road infrastructure, the provision of port infrastructure is in this paradigm a responsibility of national and/or regional government. Often, this approach takes shape through a public sector embedded port authority tasked with developing and maintaining the port infrastructure.

In the paradigm I put forward in this book, I argue port development is *by nature* a commercial activity, as the central challenge is to develop a *vital and diverse port business ecosystem*, in which third parties invest, create value for port users and make a profit. The commercial nature of port development requires a governance structure focused on effective commercial operations.

Two arguments sustain the commercial nature of port development. First, port managing bodies (PMBs) compete fiercely for attracting ships, cargo volumes and investments in their complex. Many ports have contestable hinterlands, meaning that there is competition with other ports for vessel calls and cargo. PMBs also compete with other industrial and logistical sites for attracting investments in their ports, for instance, in manufacturing, warehousing and other logistics services. Port land and services are provided to specific port users, and charges can reflect their commercial value.

Second, as argued in Chapter 1, ports are business ecosystems. Port development is more than "just" signing land lease agreements with tenants and providing access to ships. In land lease choices, creating *synergies* between companies is crucial for the attractiveness of the port. In addition, port development includes developing (digital) infrastructure for intra-port connections, for instance, through open access pipelines, port community systems and utility infrastructures. Thus, port development requires a deep understanding of the PBE, opportunities to strengthen this ecosystem and the current and future infrastructure and services needs of the firms in this ecosystem. This requires commercial capabilities and routines. As port development is a commercial activity, it follows that it should be carried out by a *commercial undertaking*, either government-owned or private, that has advanced "market-based" capabilities allowing it to do well in a competitive environment. A focus on and a deep understanding of the value creation of investments is needed to make the best investment decisions. That explains why almost all PMBs have established commercial departments.[3]

5.1.1 The use of the term port authority

Notwithstanding the increasingly commercial attitude of PMBs, the term "port authority" continues to be widely used in the ports industry, even in cases where the PMB is a SO-PDC. For instance, the SO-PDC tasked with developing the port of Rotterdam uses the term "Port of Rotterdam Authority". In my view, the use of the term authority is not appropriate. In the case of Rotterdam, it is notable that while in Dutch the term port company (*havenbedrijf*) is used, in English this is replaced by "port authority". The same occurs with the German PMBs.

Marketing-wise, the PMBs increasingly do not mention "authority" and simply refer to themselves, for instance, the "Port of Barcelona". That is, in my view, not appropriate, as the Port of Barcelona *is the entire PBE*. It does not make sense for the state-owned entity developing this PBE to refer to itself as the "Port of Barcelona". In my view, the correct name would be the "Port of Barcelona Development Company".

The term *authority* is often used for an agency or body created by a government to perform a specific function, such as environmental management, tax collection or monetary policies. Its mandate includes the *authority* to impose actions on others, such as fines and obligations. Likewise, local governments are also often termed "local authorities". These authorities do not provide commercial services in competitive environments, even if some authorities may charge users for services (for instance, inspection authorities). However, they operate based on formally delegated power in a legal framework that grants them authority.

In contrast, "port authorities" operate in a competitive environment. They cannot force users to use the port or investors to invest in it. PMBs have limited authority, outside a potential role as a competent harbor master. The presence of formal authority (except as harbor master) is often not warranted. For instance, in countries such as Spain and Oman, the port authority establishes maximum tariffs for port services provided by third parties. In my view, an independent *competition agency* is much better placed to regulate and monitor the pricing of service providers in ports than the PMB, which also has its own commercial interests, given that the price a third party can charge directly determines the value of the right to provide that service. Thus, a PMB that regulates or sets prices of port service providers needs to make a choice between more revenue and more competitive prices for port users.

The PMB is often mandated to act as a competent harbor master. However, this mandated activity is not a convincing reason for using the term "port authority": in the UK, the authority of the harbor master is mandated to individual employees of private port companies. Some PMBs have police staff on their payroll (e.g., Spanish PAs) or execute ship inspections (as is the case in the Dutch ports). This combination of policing/inspection activities and commercial port development activities is problematic in the sense that commercial objectives and law-enforcement objectives may not always be aligned. In addition, it is questionable whether combining both activities in one PMB creates synergies or requires a delicate balance between a commercial culture and an "oversight" culture. In my view, the port authority "paradigm" is outdated and positioning a PMB as a Port Development Company (PDC) is a better approach.

5.1.2 Three types of port managing bodies

The advocated paradigm shift does *not* imply a free market approach. Governments need to develop adequate mechanisms to secure public interests, through *regulation* and, in many cases, in addition, through *government ownership* of the PDC.

In line with the European Seaports Organisation (ESPO), the industry association of the European ports, I use the term "port managing body" (PMB) for all organizations tasked with developing and managing ports. I distinguish three types of governance models for port managing bodies:

1. State-owned corporatized port development companies (SO-PDCs). The term PDC is detailed by De Langen and Van der Lugt (2017).
2. Privately owned port development companies (PO-PDCs).
3. Public administration embedded port authorities (PAs).

The distinction between privately and government owned companies

As long as the corporate governance is effective, public ownership does not necessarily have a huge effect on day-to-day operations and performance. There is no reason why government owned companies in the ports industry could not be commercially operating in similar ways as privately owned companies. The key is that SOEs need to be run as companies, without political interference in decision-making. The cases of DB World, PSA and COSCO illustrate this point: all three are state owned but have developed advanced "market-based" capabilities. Even though SOEs can be commercial in similar ways as private companies, there are two important differences between both:

1. States as owners of the PDC need and often do provide a direction to the SOE, in which not profits but the SOEs contribution to "value for society" is the ultimate goal. A more detailed analysis of this aspect, focused on the question how SOEs create value for society what should be included in a shareholder policy of a SO-PDC is discussed later in this chapter.

2. Foreign states may use the activities of their SOEs to advance their interests. Thus, the ownership of port companies can give a foreign state leverage over the country in which these companies are active, even if exercising this leverage goes against the commercial interest of the SOE involved. This threat of leverage is a relevant concern for the "host country" and may lead to policies limiting the activities of foreign SOEs. This issue is further addressed in Chapter 6.

In addition to the distinction of PMBs based on three governance models, a distinction can be made between two different *business models*: an integrator model, in which the PMB provides terminal and nautical services "in-house", and the landlord business model, in which specific port services are provided by third parties. In practice, some PMBs have somewhat *mixed models*, with some services provided in-house (for instance, towage) and others (container terminal operations) by third parties.

A business model

A business model can be defined as: "a firm's underlying core logic for creating and capturing value within a value network" (Shafer et al., 2005). The concept "core logic" hints at the fact that a business model needs to be coherent. For instance, a business model generally does ensure that customers are not simultaneously competitors. A business model also needs a pricing structure to capture value. Finally, the term "value network" emphasizes the importance of taking the overall value network into account. The "landlord" and "integrator" business models are widely used across different industries.

The three governance models and two stylized business models (see Figure 5.1) enable a classification of PMBs in one of six types.

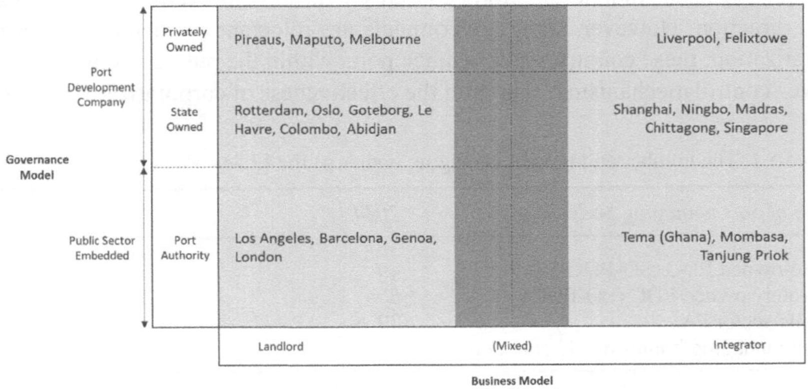

Figure 5.1 A typology of PMBs according to governance model and business model

5.1.3 The different port governance models of the EU core ports

Europe has designated 89 EU "core ports", which together account for the vast majority (>95%) of cargo handled in the EU and are central in the port policies and corridor development plans of the EU. All of these ports, except for the ports in Malta,[4] are developed by a PMB. Table 5.1 shows the governance model of the port managing bodies of the EU core ports in 2024, with the distinction discussed above. The PMB is classified as a PDC when it has a formal corporate structure (i.e., it is registered as a company) *and* it operates autonomously in the sense that there is no direct government involvement in aspects such as hiring, internal organization and price setting. I use the term state-owned irrespective of where in the public sector the ownership resides. Thus, municipally owned ports also fall in the "state-owned" category.

The PMB is in 78 out of 83 (around 94%) of all EU core ports, a government-owned entity, either a PA or a SO-PDC. In an increasing number of EU countries, following corporatization, the port managing body is organized as a PDC, with autonomous decision-making. The 49 independent state-owned PDCs include SO-PDCs in Portugal, Bulgaria, Croatia and Cyprus that were corporatized in the last decade. The majority of the SO-PDCs are responsible for one EU core port; in some cases (including Copenhagen Malmo Ports and Nort Sea Port) they are responsible for two EU core ports. The SO-PDC can be owned by the state, the port city or the province (see ESPO, 2022).[5] The 29 PMBs that are embedded in the public sector and have limited autonomy (the PAs) are in Spain and Italy.[6] The five private PDCs operate in Greece.[7]

The most common business model for the PMBs in Europe is a "landlord" business model, in which the PDC makes investments to attract private sector third parties (such as terminal operators and logistics companies) to invest in the port. The PMBs in Greece, Denmark and Slovenia operate as "integrator ports" with in-house provision of terminal services.

As in Europe, the global experience reveals a clear transition from the public administration embedded PA toward a government-owned yet autonomously and commercially operating SO-PDC.[8] Port reform efforts in countries such as Taiwan, Canada, Indonesia, Morocco and Oman have moved or are moving in this direction. However, some governments are reluctant to advance to full corporatization; these countries still manage ports within the public administration or have "control mechanisms" that limit the effectiveness of corporatization. A strong

Table 5.1 The number and type of managing bodies of the EU's core ports

Type of port managing body	*2024*
State-owned PDC (SO-PDC)	49
Privately owned PDC (PO-PDC)	5
Public sector PA	29
Total managing bodies of EU core ports	83

Source: own elaboration based on websites of PMBs.

argument in favor of corporatized SO-PDCs is the successful experience derived from the airport sector, to which the port sector is highly comparable. Virtually all airport companies operate as autonomous corporate entities, while most of them are state-owned enterprises.

Reference industries for the ports industry: airports, chemical complexes, shopping malls

Port development is similar to the development of a shopping mall, a chemical complex, and an airport complex – all commercial activities carried out by companies (that may be privately or government owned). Port development, like the development of airport complexes, chemical complexes and shopping malls, is by nature commercial. Consequently, PDCs may be able to learn from airport companies, for instance in relation to generating revenue streams outside charges to passengers and airlines (most large airports generate most revenues in retail and real estate), attracting new activities to the airport business ecosystem (airports have attracted activities ranging from hotels, museums, hospitals and housing) and partnerships with third parties (airports generally have a centralized payment system that is used by all retail concessionaires).

The fact that port development is a commercial activity implies that the best organizational structure is a corporation. However, there is *no implication that this corporation is best privately owned.* In many port reform processes around the world, port authorities are transformed from state-embedded PAs into state-owned enterprises (the SO-PDC model).

5.1.4 The content of this chapter

While all countries can take incremental steps to improve port governance, I distinguish three major "port reform" initiatives that can have a huge and positive impact on the ports industry:

i.) Transitioning from a PA-model to a SO-PDC model.
ii.) Improving the corporate governance of the SO-PDC model.
iii.) Transitioning the business model of the PA or the SO-PDC from the integrator model to a landlord model. This leads to an increased *private sector participation* in the ports industry.

In all these three port reform steps, governments retain the ownership of the SO-PDC. I do not consider the fully private port as the appropriate governance model for large and diverse ports. However, for specific ports in specific contexts, the PO-PDC model may be appropriate.

As the choice between state ownership and private ownership is the foundation for the logic of the three port reform steps discussed above, the framework to assess the case for state ownership of a commercially operating port development company is presented first. Next, the appropriate geographical scope of the (state-owned) port development company is discussed, followed by an analysis of key issues in achieving effective corporatization, i.e., moving from a public sector embedded PA-model to a SO-PDC model. Next, attention is given to the increasing internationalization of port development companies. Finally, major port reform challenges are discussed.

5.2 A framework to assess the case for state ownership of corporatized PDCs

State-owned enterprises (SOEs) engage in commercial activities in competitive environments and are extensively used by virtually all countries in a range of sectors, from mining to housing and infrastructure provision.

State ownership is considered to be appropriate when regulatory or other subsidy mechanisms to secure public interests are not effective (Shirley & Walsh, 2001). Thus, state ownership of enterprises is a "*second best*" method to secure public interests. This is because less effective governance hampers the efficiency of SOEs[9] compared to fully private companies.

In line with Sappington and Stiglitz (1987), I argue that there is a trade-off between the welfare effects of (potential) reduced efficiency of the SOE because of government ownership and the welfare effects of the imperfections of a regulatory/contractual approach by government to secure public interests.

In industries in which public interests require a substantial government involvement in a regulatory/contractual approach, the negative welfare effect of this approach is larger, because regulations are imperfect and costly. Thus, in such industries (for instance, water and energy distribution), government involvement through SOEs is more appropriate than in industries where the need for government involvement is more limited[10] (for instance, retail).

A case-by-case analysis with different results per industry and country is needed to assess whether there is a case for government involvement through SOEs. Industry characteristics that favor SOEs include:

i. Imperfections in drafting, monitoring and enforcing a contract between the government and a private firm; (more imperfections favor using the SOE to promote public interests). This is the root cause of the imperfections of a regulatory and contractual approach. While contracts can in theory be used to incentivize private companies to take public interests into account, problems in drafting, monitoring and enforcing contracts due to opportunism, uncertainty and imperfect information need to be acknowledged. The more difficult it is to develop and monitor specific contracts aimed at aligning the public interests with the interests of private companies, the more attractive is the option to use SOEs as an instrument to promote public interests.
ii. Competition in the industry (less competition favors SOEs, as limited competition increases risks of abuse of dominant market positions; regulation to prevent

this is not perfect). Competition regulation is an imperfect way to tackle the disadvantages associated with market power. Competition regulation is imperfect, as the regulator has incomplete information. Thus, for natural monopolies the trade-off is more likely to tilt in favor of SOEs. This argument in isolation is an insufficient argument for state ownership, but it is a relevant consideration in the trade-off between state ownership and a regulatory and contractual approach.

iii. The importance of continuous improvement and innovation. As SOEs are generally weak when it comes to innovation (see Shleifer, 1998), the higher the importance of continuous innovation, the stronger the case for private companies. The disadvantages of state ownership are not similar across industries *but depend on the "innovation intensity"* (see Sappington & Stiglitz, 1987; Peng et al., 2016). SOEs are, in general, not as innovative and agile as their private sector counterparts (Shleifer, 1998) because state ownership reduces the risks of bankruptcy (Sheng et al., 2013). Thus, SOEs are more likely to have a low innovation performance (Lerner, 2009). Thus, in industries with a high innovation intensity, the imperfections resulting from state ownership are larger than in industries with a low innovation intensity, and the trade-off is more likely to tilt toward regulation, even if such regulation is imperfect.

In this trade-off approach, for most industries (such as retail, car manufacturing, all kinds of services for producers and so on) the common free market model of private companies with government regulation is the best model. There is a limited set of industries, with some or all of the characteristics above, where government ownership may be appropriate. Figure 5.2 gives a stylized overview of the regulation/contracts vs state ownership trade-off, with some industries including port development as illustration.

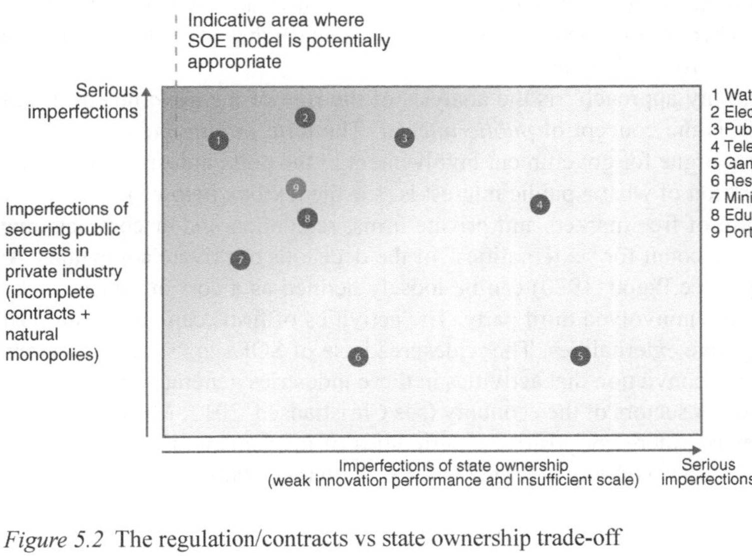

Figure 5.2 The regulation/contracts vs state ownership trade-off

Public transport constitutes a good example of a sector where some of the characteristics mentioned above are relevant, especially in cases where governments have policies in place to subsidize public transport (which is the case in most countries, either directly or indirectly, for instance by public funding of public transport infrastructure such as rails; dedicated bus lanes, bus stops or railway stations). In such a situation:

i. Contracts between governments and private companies are complex, as governments specify service levels and prices.
ii. Competition with other public transport providers is absent or limited.
iii. The service is fairly stable over time, so the innovation intensity is relatively low.[11]

In line with the logic above, SOEs provide public transport services in most developed countries as well as many developing countries (South Africa, Brazil, India). However, there is debate about the best approach. A model with government subsidies for private companies that provide public transport services (e.g., in remote areas and/or public transport for elderly or school children) is often argued to be more effective than government-owned public transport companies. A country like Brazil has privatized many state-owned public transport companies. However, in the UK the opposite is taking place: passenger rail companies that were privatized are being re-nationalized and turned into SOEs. This description only aims to show that public transport is one of the sectors where state ownership is considered as a credible alternative to private companies. Other sectors where SOEs may be[12] appropriate include mining, education and *port development*.

The distinction between port development and port operations is relevant. Port development is the development of a port business ecosystem, which consists of activities including *terminal operations* (as well as trucking operations, warehousing operations and others), which can very well and often are carried out by private companies. There is a strong case for government ownership of the PMB, based on the arguments provided below.

Central to my approach[13] is the analysis of the role of the government in seaports, which is the concept of *public interest*. The term *public interest* is widely used, often to argue for government involvement in the ports industry, but without a strict definition of what a public interest is (see the textbox below[14]).

In the case of free markets and private firms, regulation and/or contracts may be needed to account for "externalities" of the decisions of private companies. An "externality" (see Pigou, 1920) can be loosely defined as a cost or benefit that is imposed on an uninvolved third party. The activities of firms can have both positive and negative externalities. The widespread use of SOEs in "strategic sectors" is based on the conviction that activities in these industries generate positive externalities for other sectors of the economy (see Christiansen, 2013; Musacchio et al., 2015). Likewise, there are positive externalities of investments in R&D on other companies and the economy at large (Jones & Williams, 2000).

Public interests and government involvement

Mainstream economics starts with the premise that under a strict set of conditions, markets are "Pareto-efficient": there are no alternative outcomes where all parties are better off than in the market equilibrium. This is a widely accepted starting point.

The key to justifying government involvement is the analysis of whether or not these conditions are in place. If these conditions are *not* in place, government intervention may be in the public interest. A huge body of economic research has led to detailed knowledge of these conditions and potential roles of governments when the conditions for Pareto-efficiency are not in place. There are three important cases where the conditions for efficient markets are not in place, and government intervention is called for:

- Imperfect competition. Abuse of market power, by monopolists or cartels, is clearly not in the public interest. Imperfect competition requires government involvement, for instance through competition law.
- Externalities. Externalities exist when there is "interdependence among economic actors for which a market or some other compensatory device does not exist". This is the case in well-known examples such as environmental damage, labour safety and noise as well as with "spill-overs" of technology between firms. Externalities justify government intervention, e.g., through environmental regulation and – an example that recently was widely debated – regulation of the banking industry.
- Imperfect information and bounded rationality. Unless firms and consumers have access to relevant information and make rational decisions, market outcomes are not efficient. This is for instance the case in health care, where people acting on the basis of free choice do not sufficiently insure themselves.

Note that in this approach "employment", a widely used argument for investments in port infrastructure, is not regarded as a public interest, as it is too open: precise arguments as to why conditions for employment creation through markets are not in place are needed. There may be valid arguments, for instance in regions with structurally high unemployment, but "creating employment" in general does not provide a sound basis for government involvement.

Adverse environmental effects of economic activities are important negative externalities. Regulation can be used to "internalize" externalities or to increase environmental standards. However, *environmental regulation cannot secure companies to go beyond compliance and lead in the transition toward sustainability*. In cases where specific companies play a key role in the national/regional transition toward sustainability, a regulatory approach may not be effective. In such cases, state ownership may be instrumental in speeding up the transition toward sustainability (see Haney & Pollitt, 2013).

The considerations for the policy choice to use SOEs as described above suggest there is only a rationale for SOEs in specific sectors, in which a regulatory/contractual approach to securing public interests is not effective. This is in line with empirical observations showing that across different countries with market economies, SOEs are mainly deployed in a few specific sectors (OECD, 2017), including transport and port development.

Port governance is often shaped by a tradition of public provision of common infrastructure

Governments can be involved in different ways, through regulation, contracts, SOEs and public provision of services (e.g., the police force). The last two options are generally considered as "second best options" i.e., only suitable when alternatives are not effective. In the ports industry, historically *service provision* by government, often through "port authorities" deeply embedded in the public administration, has been the dominant approach to ensure public interests. This often resulted from considering port infrastructure as public infrastructure in the same way as road and rail. This probably was the case in the early days of port development, when "common user" public berths were built in port cities. However, that approach is in my view outdated, large scale port development currently involves massive investments for specific users that operate vast areas of land, for either terminal, logistics or other activities. In this context, port development needs to be undertaken on a commercial basis, and by an entity that has developed market-based capabilities. Thus, if there is a case for government ownership, the SO-PDC model is better suited than the public administration embedded PA model. However, *institutional inertia* often results in the continuation of the port authority model and the treatment of port facilities as public infrastructure.

5.2.1 The case for state ownership of the PMB – public interests in ports

In the case of port development, four externalities are relevant (see De Langen & Van der Lugt, 2017).

Indirect economic effects of port development

First, investments in port development generate national and regional economic effects (see Musso et al., 2006; Wang & Wang, 2019), including indirect effects on trade-intensive sectors. Better ports lead to a better logistics performance, resulting in growth of seaborne trade and economic growth overall; the impact of ports is especially large for developing countries (Munim & Schramm, 2018). While a

PDC (publicly or privately owned) aims to "capture" that value creation through charging port dues and land lease fees, fully capturing the value arising from port development is impossible. For instance, land prices of privately owned land adjacent to newly developed terminals may rise,[15] and new port infrastructure may lead to new investments in manufacturing and logistics, which generate employment as well as benefits for established firms through positive effects from agglomeration. In addition to the imperfect value capture, port development projects are often contested projects in the sense that there is serious opposition from one or more interest groups. The PDC faces uncertainty regarding approval of investment plans and substantial costs for developing port plans.[16] Both the imperfect value capture and the huge uncertainty and planning costs may lead to *lower* private investments in port development than desirable from a societal welfare perspective.

Regulation or contracts are ineffective policy tools to take these externalities into account. Providing state funding to private port development initiatives is complicated as it distorts the "playing field", i.e., it leads to unfair competition between ports. In addition, state funding increases risks of politically motivated choices, e.g., for investments in ports in underdeveloped regions, which in various cases have not achieved the expected results, see European Court of Auditors (2016). State funding often goes hand in hand with overly optimistic demand projections and cost underestimates (Flyvberg, 2007).

These considerations suggest a contractual approach, in which a private port developer would invest in port infrastructure, based on an agreement with the government, which does not guarantee a sufficiently high level of investments in ports, nor that these investments create the most value for money. The risk of underinvestment is especially high in countries in which the "country risks" are considered to be high.

The risk of insufficient private investments; the case of Georgia

The theoretical argument that "the private sector model may not lead to an investment level in port development that is desirable from a societal perspective" may sound abstract and hard to grasp; there are various clear cases that clearly show the relevance of this issue, including Georgia.

In Georgia the state-owned port companies were sold, land including. The private operators have made (incremental) investments in the ports. However, none of the ports is capable of handling container vessels larger than 2500 TEU. This severely restricts Georgia's connectivity to international markets. The government as well as importing and exporting companies are very vocal about this shortcoming, as well as the relatively high prices charged by APMT, the operator of Georgia's main port Poti. The government has launched a tender for the development of a new deepwater port in Anaklia, and has created quite favourable conditions for a private consortium, but even under these conditions, so far the private consortium has not committed to making these investments, at least in part because they would have to compete fiercely with the existing ports of Poti and Batumi and the market in Georgia is limited. The result is a stalemate in which investments are limited, with adverse effects for the Georgian Economy. Of course one can only speculate about how the industry would have developed in a port model with a state-owned landlord PDC, but it seems plausible that in such a scenario government would not have had to try and develop a new greenfield port, but could have pursued an expansion in Poti instead.

Thus, state ownership of the PDC may often be more effective in securing sufficient commitment to port development than private port development in a contractual approach. State ownership of the PDC leads to a "business case-driven" approach to port development/expansion projects, but with a more long-term orientation and higher risk tolerance levels than would be expected from a private PDC. This risk tolerance dimension is important given the uncertainty of demand and the long payback period of investments in port infrastructure.

Reducing negative externalities

Second, reducing negative environmental externalities is a relevant public interest in port development. As argued above, commitment "beyond compliance" cannot

Incorporating environmental effects in land use decisions

In a substantial number of ports, especially those in metropolitan areas and those with large industrial clusters, there may be a case for a central place for environmental considerations in land use decisions, which are core decisions of PDCs. The decision to which company and activity to lease the land, and under what conditions, deeply affects negative externalities from port activities, especially CO2 emissions, noise and stench. For instance, granting an energy company a land lease to construct a coal fired power plant directly affects CO2 emissions. Or the decision to grant an LNG terminal a lease directly affects (positively) the transition towards LNG as (relatively clean) ship fuel. Regulation creates a minimum environmental standard (uniformly for a country or region), but anything beyond such minimum standards cannot be regulated. In addition, once companies have an environmental permit, regulation to ensure that the latest technologies are used to reduce negative externalities is problematic (Ashford, 2002). Thus, regulation can set minimum standards, but is not suited for ensuring additional emphasis on environmental effects "on top of compliance". Given the importance of ports in energy production (Acciaro et al., 2014) and CO2 emissions, the limitations of a regulatory approach to ensure sustainability in specific cases provide an argument for state ownership of the PDC: only through state ownership can environmental attention on top of compliance be ensured.

be secured through regulation. If a PDC plays a key role in the transition toward sustainability, this strengthens the rationale for state ownership of the PDC. Indeed, a port complex may be an important source of environmental pollution in a region/ country (Damman & Steen, 2021).

Smooth land transitions

Third, port development in metropolitan areas often requires port expansion and enables the transfer of land from port functions to urban functions in old port areas. There are many examples of re-development of port areas into urban waterfronts (see Brown, 2009, for examples from the US), such as Port Vell in Barcelona and Hafencity in Hamburg. In many port cities, waterfront re-development creates public space for the city residents. Such a land use transition is difficult in the private sector port model. In this private model, a contract between the government and the private operator would have to specify under which conditions land was to be transferred from the private port company that either operates based on a concession or owns the land (as is the case in the UK) to a government entity. Such a legal/ contractual approach to enable land transfers is problematic, given the uncertainty of future developments. The case for land transfer depends on many uncertain factors, such as re-location decisions of port users, port expansion prospects and industry trends such as increasing ship sizes, that may reduce the viability of terminals with draft limitations, which often are close to city centers. Given all these uncertainties, land transfer from the port to urban functions cannot be effectively regulated or included in a concession contract.[17]

Instruments to influence the use of land for port activities

It is hard to optimize the land use from a "value for society perspective". In some cases, building apartments may be commercially more attractive but have negative external effects. However, the SO-PDC or the PA may also stick to port land use of areas that have much higher societal value if transformed in urban waterfront areas. There are many examples of redevelopment of port areas into urban waterfronts (see Brown, 2009 for examples in the US). In many port cities, waterfront redevelopment creates public space for the city residents.

Land use transitions taking into account the value for society cannot be achieved based on a "for profit" model. When it is important to keep a port facility open, while commercially non-port uses are more attractive, a subsidy would need to be provided to a private operator to keep the port open. Or alternatively regulation would have to be developed to prevent land use transitions. For instance, the New Zealand port act obliges ports to "act as ports", which limits the freedom to transform docks in real estate, and in Canada ports have to make land use plans publicly available, and third parties can file complaints that are to be handled by the Transportation Agency. However, a contractual approach is problematic, as many uncertain factors such as re-location decisions of port users, port expansion and technological developments are relevant. For instance, larger ship sizes may reduce the viability of terminals with draft limitations, which often are close to city centres. A regulatory approach, banning the use of port land for non-port activities on the other hand carries an important risk as it is too rigid. Thus, in ports where these issues are important (local) government ownership of the PDC is the best model. This applies especially to ports located in metropolitan areas.

Innovation externalities

Fourth, externalities from a "port innovation system" (Rohrbeck et al., 2009) are relevant. A well-functioning port innovation system has positive effects for firms active in the port and port users, but investments in the port innovation system do not have a direct positive financial return. Private port companies would be expected to invest in research and capacity development within the boundaries of their own enterprise, not for third parties active in the port.

On the contrary, a SO-PDC is well positioned to play a leading role in developing partnerships to make investments in training, education and innovation. Most SO-PDCs contribute substantially to investments with collective benefits – as such investments are directly in line with their mission. This role of the SO-PDC provides continuity and resources for investments with cluster benefits. In the case of private port development, PO-PDCs also play a role in investments with collective benefits, but often rely on the support of government agencies and industry associations.

On top of these four imperfections of private port development, the competition intensity is relevant, as discussed previously. In case of limited competition with other ports, the trade-off would more easily tilt toward state ownership, as a private PDC would enjoy a dominant market position, and regulation is a necessary but imperfect instrument to prevent abuse of this dominant position.

Figure 5.3 shows the five imperfections of private ownership that can be diminished through regulation, and the four imperfections of state ownership, which can be diminished through good shareholder policies and corporate governance of the PO-PDC. The choice between the SO-PDC model and the PO-PDC model requires an analysis of which imperfections carry more weight. This requires a case-by-case analysis. An important factor that influences the best model is the *fit* of both models in the national institutional context, i.e., whether the national institutional context is conducive to the PO-PDC model or is better suited for the private port development model. As an illustration, the SO-PDC is more likely to be preferred in Scandinavian countries, which regularly use SOEs and where SOEs are generally well

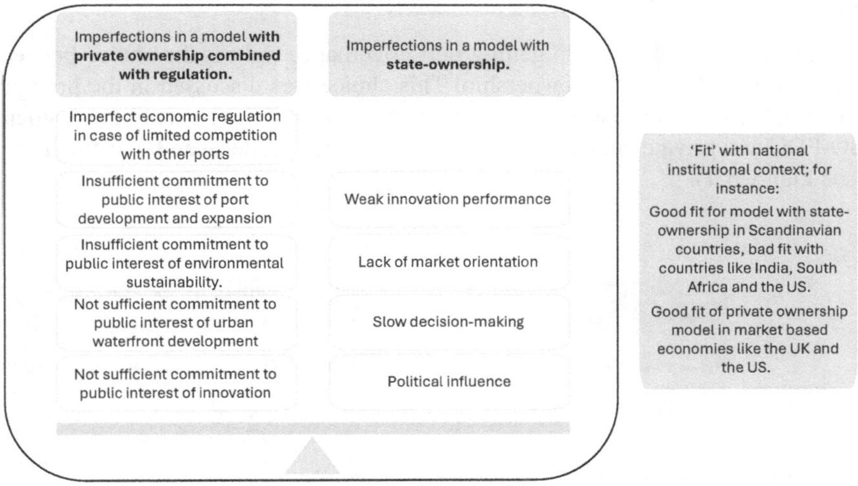

Figure 5.3 The trade-off between state-owned or privately owned PDCs

run, while in the UK, a fully private model with regulation fits better in the national institutional model.

Furthermore, the port characteristics influence the best model: specialized ports (or in extreme cases "single user ports", for instance export ports for mining products) outside metropolitan areas are well suited for private sector ownership, whereas for diverse ports in metropolitan areas the SO-PDC model may be better.

The exceptional nature of Singapore's SOE model

Often, the case of Singapore is brought up in discussions about state ownership. Singapore has two state-owned port companies (PSA and Jurong Port) with an integrator model. This is not aligned with international best practices, in which a landlord model is often advocated for state-owned companies. Furthermore, both port companies are not tasked with port development, this responsibility sits with the Maritime & Port Authority of Singapore (MPA). The Singapore model works very well for Singapore, which has developed into the leading hub in South-East Asia. In addition, both SOEs are profitable and active overseas. However, part of the success of this model is that it has a perfect fit with Singapore's institutional characteristics: a business-oriented city-state with a development-oriented government with a strong performance orientation. As a result, all SOEs in Singapore are well run and the "SOE model" is a part of Singapore's economic development approach (see Huat, 2016).

5.2.2 Risk allocation in different port models

The most principal choice in getting port governance right is the choice between private ownership or state ownership. This choice was discussed in the previous paragraphs. This choice leads to a division of responsibilities between government, SO-PDC and private entities, for which four stylized models can be distinguished (see Figure 5.4).

	Large government role ← 4 stylized port models → Large private role			
	Public service port State-owned PDC with in-house service provision	**Landlord PDC** State-owned Landlord PDC; third party operators	**BOT type concession** Build-Operate-Transfer Agreement (BOT)	**Private port development initiative**
Government role	Regulator & planner	Regulator & planner	Regulator & planner	Regulator & planner (of transport infrastructure)
	Shareholder, with a shareholder policy	Shareholder, with a shareholder policy	Concession granting agency	
Role of Role of state-owned PDC	State-owned PDC with service port business model	State-owned PDC with landlord port business model	No role	No role
Role of private sector	Engineering, construction, maintenance	Private operator (based on lease contract)	Private PDC (based on concession)	Private PDC (based on land ownership)
		Engineering, construction, maintenance	Engineering, construction, maintenance	Engineering, construction, maintenance
			In case of landlord BM: Private third-party service providers	In case of landlord BM: Private third-party service providers

Figure 5.4 Public and private sector responsibilities in four port models

My distinction of port models differs from the distinction used by the World Bank (2025d) in two ways.

1. I do not consider the "toolport" as a specific model. Leasing specific equipment is generally inefficient, as private concessionaires are best positioned for these investment decisions. On top of that, a "toolport" contract is in my view an option for a contract between the landlord and a third party. No port development company is likely to use it "across the board", i.e., for all customers. In some specific cases, especially when there are pre-existing assets, it may be deployed. But in that case it is a specific contractual arrangement, not a distinct "port model".
2. I also do not make a distinction between a model in which a concessionaire gets the right to build and operate a port and a model in which a concessionaire gets the right to operate an existing port complex based on a master concession. In both cases, the model is based on a concession agreement between the state and a private party in which the latter has a responsibility for developing the port.

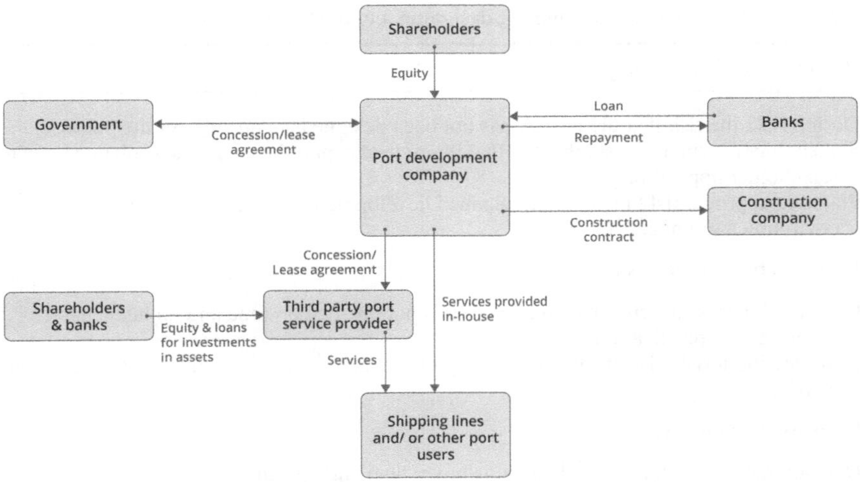

Figure 5.5 A stylized overview of important (contractual) relations of the landlord PDC

In practice, there are various "grey areas" between these four models. For instance, in countries like Oman, Mozambique and Brazil, a part of the shares of the PDC is owned by the government and a part by a third party. Likewise, in countries like Indonesia and Ghana, the state-owned PDC has developed subsidiaries, partly owned by third parties, that operate one or more terminals. These four stylized models are the most widely used and the basis for assessing what works best in which environment. A stylized overview of important relations in the "landlord PDC model" is provided in Figure 5.5.

The allocation of risks

The allocation of risks in these four models differs. Table 5.2 summarizes the main risks in planning and design, construction and operation of port infrastructure. The allocation of the most relevant risks to either the public or the private sector in each of the models is provided in Figure 5.6.

Figure 5.6 shows the huge differences in risk allocation between these four models. In the landlord model, most risks associated with investments in *port infrastructure* are borne by the SO-PDC. The demand risk is generally shared by the private operator and the SO-PDC, as both have revenue streams related to the volumes/number of ships handled at the terminal. The private operator bears the risk that regulatory/legal changes negatively affect their expected operational/financial performance. However, lease contracts generally include clauses to increase the legal certainty of the private investor. The *force majeure* risk is shared, with the lion's share generally borne by the public sector.[19]

In the BOT model (model 3), most risks are borne by the private investor; the public sector still carries the risks associated with planning approval and

Table 5.2 The main risks in planning, designing, building and operating port infrastructure

Planning and Design Stage Risk

Design risk: the risk that the project has not been designed adequately for the purpose.

Stakeholder acceptance risk: the risk that the project cannot be executed as planned due to stakeholder opposition.

Planning approval risk: the risk that planned development is not approved (e.g., due to environmental impact[18]).

Construction Stage Risk

Construction risk: the risk that construction is not finished on time and on budget and according to specifications.

Resource/input risk: the risk that the supply of inputs or resources is interrupted or the cost increases.

Operation Stage Risks

Demand risk: the risk that the demand is lower than anticipated.

Maintenance risk: the risk that maintenance costs are higher than foreseen. These risks are related to the port infrastructure, not the superstructure.

Force majeure risk: the risk that unexpected external events (e.g., earthquake, war) negatively affect financial and/or operational performance.

Regulatory/legal risk: the risk of changing laws/regulations that negatively affect financial and/or operational performance.

Public investments risk: the risk that promised/planned government investments, for instance, in hinterland connections, do not materialize.

Allocation of risks

	Public service port State-owned PDC with in-house service provision	**Landlord PDC** State-owned Landlord PDC; third party operators	**BOT type concession** Build-Operate-Transfer Agreement (BOT)	**Private port development initiative**
Planning & Design Stage				
Design risk	SOPDC	SOPDC	Private sector	Private sector
Stakeholder acceptance risk	SOPDC	SOPDC	Government	Private sector
Planning approval risk	Government	Government	Government	Private sector
Construction Stage				
Construction risk	SOPDC Private sector	SOPDC Private sector	Private sector	Private sector
Resource or input risk	SOPDC Private sector	SOPDC Private sector	Government Private sector	Private sector
Operation Stage				
Demand risk	SOPDC	SOPDC Private sector	Private sector	Private sector
Infra. maintenance risk	SOPDC	SOPDC	Private sector	Private sector
Force majeure risk	Government SOPDC	SOPDC Private sector	Government Private sector	Private sector
Regulatory/legal risk	Government	Private sector	Private sector	Private sector
Public investments risk	Government SOPDC	Government SOPDC	Government Private sector	Private sector

Figure 5.6 The allocation of the most relevant risks in different port development models

stakeholder acceptance, as the public sector takes the planning initiative and provides legal certainty to the private sector investor. BOT clauses generally place part of the risk associated with inputs/resources (e.g., availability of electricity) with the government. The same applies to *force majeure* risks. In addition, the government generally guarantees some public investments that are critical for the viability of the BOT project, such as investments in hinterland infrastructure.

Different scopes of BOT agreements

While in all BOT agreements a private third party is responsible for building and operations, there are differences between BOT agreements, with at the one extreme a "full BOT" in which the private operator is responsible for the design of the expansion, as well as the environmental compensation, and the full development, including the construction of a breakwater, and dredging works. At the other extreme is the "BOT light" in which the private operator is building the land and quay (and all terminal equipment), but dredging, the breakwater and environmental compensation are outside the scope of responsibilities of the private partner. In this BOT light model, dredging, a breakwater and environmental compensation are provided by a government entity (either the government directly or a SO-PDC).

Regardless of the scope of the BOT agreement, an important characteristic of investments in port infrastructure and suprastructure (cranes, warehouses, etc.) is that the pay-back period is long, and consequently huge sums of capital, through both equity and loans, are required. Figure 5.7 shows a stylized overview of the cash flows associated with an investment in port infrastructure and suprastructure.

In this hypothetical example, *the cumulative cash flows are negative until year 13*. So even if a project is profitable in a 30-year period, it may be difficult to finance. This is a secondary argument for loans of state-owned or multilateral

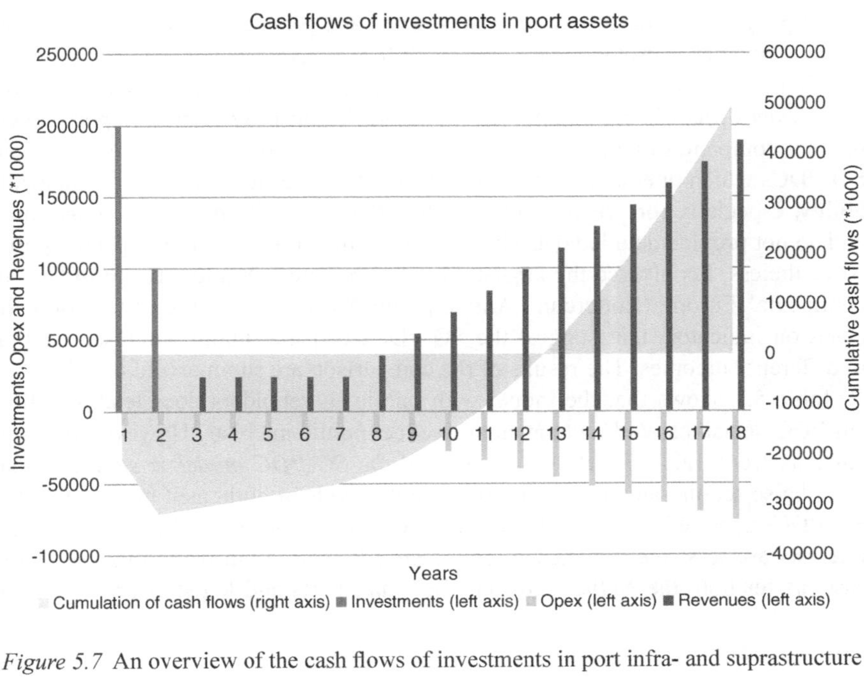

Figure 5.7 An overview of the cash flows of investments in port infra- and suprastructure

development banks for investments in ports, on top of the core argument that such investments often generate "value for society" in addition to value for users.

5.3 Experiences with private PDCs in the UK

In the UK, most port companies were privatized in the Thatcher era, often through management buy-outs and in some cases through listings on the stock market. A process of mergers and take-overs led to the consolidation of the ownership of UK ports in different port groups. The ownership of the UK port companies changed various times, often with large increases in transaction prices. Currently, the UK ports are mainly owned by international investors, attracted to the prospects of a good return on investment and relatively limited risks.

The UK experience shows that the port companies often have changed their business model, from an integrator model to a mixed model, with a larger role for port industrial users in operations. The private port companies provide some terminal services in-house and sign land lease agreements with third parties for other activities. For instance, Peel Ports, the second largest port operator in the UK, describes its business model as follows: Peel Ports' business model can be considered a "value added model" where it acts as both a landlord and an operator … Peel Ports will lease port estate, acting as landlord where such an arrangement ties users sufficiently into ancillary port services (https://www.peelports.com/investor-relations).

5.3.1 Comparing the outcome of private and state-owned port development companies

A comparative approach between state-owned and privately owned port development companies is problematic in the sense that a "like-for-like" comparison with a fully private port developer is not possible. First, because the structure of port complexes differs in important ways, second, because most private port development companies operate with a "mixed business model" in contrast with most SO-PDCs which operate as landlord ports and third because of limited data availability, especially for private port operators that generally operate various ports, and do not provide detailed data (like e.g., investment levels) on the specific ports. Nevertheless, I compared the largest three UK private PDCs to three SO-PDCs in continental Europe (Rotterdam, Antwerp and Amsterdam). This comparison focuses on indicators that suggest the SO-PDCs consider public interests, leading to different outcomes. The results of the comparison are summarized in Table 5.3.

Table 5.3 shows that the model with public shareholders does lead to different PDC decisions, with outcomes that reflect public interests. However, the conclusions from Table 5.3 *do not imply that the SO-PDC model is superior*; that would also require an analysis of productivity levels of both, as it may be that the SO-PDCs operate less efficiently. Furthermore, it may be that in the UK, the public interests are less relevant than in continental Europe. Intuitively, this seems the case, as for both the Netherlands and Belgium, ports and logistics are important

Table 5.3 Indications that SO-PDCs focus more on public interests than private UK ports

Indications public interests	*Conclusion*
High investment level in port infrastructure	There is no proven difference in investment levels between the SO-PDCs and their private peers.
Moderate tariff/rate increases	There is strong evidence for a more moderate price development of the SO-PDCs compared to private peers.
Resources for "not-for-profit" services that benefit all firms in the port.	There is strong evidence for more investments in "not-for-profit" services, aimed at improving efficiency/productivity in the port ecosystem of the SO-PDCs.
High investment levels to reduce negative environmental externalities.	Due to lack of data, it is not possible to assess differences in investments to reduce negative externalities.
Focus on attracting "green" activities to the port.	Due to lack of data, it is not possible to assess differences in attracting green activities. The private UK ports are as active as the continental ones in offshore wind; it appears the continental ones are more active in attracting other clean energy generation, but that may also be explained because they are more industrial ports.
Transfer/re-development of underutilized port land.	The continental SO-PDCs take an approach to (co-) developing port areas into mixed use area that differs from a private PDC in similar circumstances in terms of attention for "value for society".
High investment levels in the "port innovation system".	The SO-PDCs invest substantially in port innovation systems; their approach differs from a private PDC in similar circumstances.

drivers of overall economic development, whereas the UK has evolved into a service economy, in which the overall port volumes have declined since the 1980s and are not expected to grow significantly.

5.3.2 *Committed port development in the UK?*

In the UK, one of the few countries with fully private ports, port development plans need to meet various legal requirements (e.g., the Coast Protection Act), and for major expansion projects, a *public inquiry* is held to assess whether or not port expansion is in the public interest. Private operators do take such initiatives, for instance, with Dibden Bay and Felixstowe South. The largest port development in the UK, London Gateway, is also a private initiative, but the Port of London Authority – a government entity tasked with promoting port development in London has played an important role in realizing this project.

The private port operators do stress that regulatory burdens and uncertainty are complicating port development. Thus, a "National Policy Statement for Ports" is being developed to protect port areas and streamline port expansion projects. The proposed statement argues that additional port infrastructure is needed in the next few decades. The framework and procedures are pro-port development. Positive external effects of port infrastructure are taken into account in planning decisions. It may well be that the UK will develop a new public funding instrument for port development, to replace the EU funding options that were available prior to Brexit. For instance, Peel Port financed a new container terminal with a £150 million loan from the European Investment Bank and a Regional Growth Fund grant of £35 million. Nevertheless, an applicant has to address a broad range of issues, including biodiversity, visual impact, and effects on woodlands, placing a substantial burden on private port development initiatives. My assessment is that this policy framework will be conducive for relatively modest port expansion projects with a clear market demand, but may not be sufficiently accommodating for private initiatives for large-scale port (re-)development, for instance, for new facilities to serve offshore wind, especially in densely populated areas.

The gradual private development of a port business ecosystem: London Gateway

DP World, the developer of London Gateway, continues to invest step by step in developing London gateway as *port business ecosystem*. It invested around £350 million in a fourth berth project (opened November 2024) to increase London Gateway's capacity by a third. In also announced investments for a fifth and sixth berth and a second rail terminal. DP World also announced further investments in the logistics park adjacent to the terminal, stating that demand for premium warehousing space in the South East of England reached "unprecedented" levels. Various new tenants have taken leases at London Gateway's Logistics Park (around 400 hectares), increasing revenues as well as employment.

These investments demonstrate 1) DP really is developing a "port business ecosystem" not just a container terminal 2) developing such an ecosystem is a long-term endeavour and 3) in specific cases, a commercial developer is willing to take the risks associated with building a port business ecosystem from scratch, even in a fairly mature market like the UK.

Other countries may be interested in replicating this approach. However, this success case may be fairly unique in the sense that the development took place in a privileged location (which became available after the closing down of a refinery) in a competitive private market and a stable regulatory environment. These characteristics may not replicated in most markets.

5.3.3 The UK freeport initiative

There are no indications that the UK ports industry is underperforming by international standards in terms of terminal productivity or ship waiting times. However, UK ports have arguably lagged behind some European peers when it comes to diversifying their ecosystems, especially with logistics and manufacturing activities.

The UK freeport initiative was aimed at increasing international investments in such areas. Local public–private partnerships were invited to submit initial bids to government, articulating why a Freeport is the best solution for economic growth in the area. In the next stages, these ideas were developed into detailed business cases that show how the tax advantages and public were to be used. Based on these, over ten freeport sites were established, with substantial tax benefits for investors in these sites. The tax relief period was extended to ten years. The initiative has led, according to UK government documents, to 2671 hectares of land rehabilitated and the attraction of £6.4 billion of private investment, almost 90% FDI, in sectors such as clean energy (£2.6 billion), ports and maritime (£1.56 billion) and advanced manufacturing, engineering, and construction (£839 million).

The transition of industrial activity in the Teesside Freeport

Teesside Freeport used the Freeport public funding to accelerate the redevelopment of 130 hectares of contaminated land on Teesworks, a large brownfield site that used to be a steel plant. It was closed in 2015 (ending 170 years of steelmaking in Teesside), resulting in the loss of 3000 jobs. Teesside Freeport has attracted £1.5 billion in investment, including an offshore wind manufacturing facility that will create around 2250 jobs.

In conclusion, the UK's Freeport initiative (with public funding and tax incentives) is an instrument that fills the void of not having a SO-PDC focused on developing and transitioning the port business ecosystem. In this approach, the downside of the UK's private port development model is mitigated, while its strengths remain. However, the freeports were also explicitly used to spur economic development of weak regions (leveling up), justifying a policy approach in which specific zones are prioritized through special tax regimes. Thus, implementing such an approach in another policy context carries large risks of promoting uneven development.

5.3.4 Collective goods in a privately owned port?

The second largest port operator in the UK, Peel Ports, operates Liverpool's port, which includes a large number of port-related firms, some of which lease land from Peel Ports. The central organization in promoting and investing in collective goods is Mersey Maritime. This organization is private sector-led, but supported by various regional development agencies. The organization, with over 1700 members, is mainly engaged in promoting innovation and improving the quality of maritime education. This shows how mechanisms of cooperation and collective action emerge. Similarly, various large private (air)port companies cooperated in a public–private partnership termed Superport, which aimed to attract publicly funded strategic investments, among others, to invest in hinterland infrastructure.

This case shows that a fully private port operator will seek partnerships with the public sector for investments in collective goods. However, in comparison with a model with a state-owned PDC securing leadership, capabilities and resources for investments with collective benefits may be more challenging.

5.3.5 Conclusions regarding the private sector model in the UK

In conclusion, unlike with British Rail, where initiatives to re-nationalize operations are underway, the private UK ports industry has delivered connectivity and port performance levels in line with international benchmarks. However, for various reasons, fully privatizing the ports industry in other countries is not advisable for a number of reasons.

- First, the UKs privatization took place when the ports were mature activities; since the privatization, the total volume handled in the UK has not grown. As a consequence, with the exception of London Gateway, investments in port development have been incremental.
- Second, the UK ports industry is characterized by the co-existence of a relatively large number of ports of a limited size (in terms of volumes handled and hectares of port area), with relatively fierce competition between these ports. This is a favorable characteristic for privatization.
- Third, the limited role of port companies in developing land for industrial/logistics activities is partially remedied through other policy instruments, most importantly the Freeport initiative, which do involve public funding (partially indirectly through tax holidays).
- Fourth, while most port companies were privatized, others continue to operate under state ownership, including London and Dover, both important UK ports.

5.4 The business model of the port managing body and business model reform

As discussed in the previous paragraph, four public interests cannot be effectively secured through regulation/subsidies alone and thus provide an argument for state ownership of the PDC. To recapitulate the arguments, first, negative externalities from port activities cannot be effectively secured through regulation. One of the core decisions of PDCs is the land lease agreement. Thus, regulation can set minimum requirements, and state ownership of a PDC is required for commitment to sustainable development beyond regulatory requirements. Given the importance of ports in energy production and the large share of CO_2 emissions in port areas, in various ports this is a valid argument for state ownership of the PDC.

Second, a fully private ports industry may not in all cases generate the desirable investment level in port development from a societal perspective. A SO-PDC generally will be specifically tasked with developing certain ports and while it must have a solid financial performance, it does not strive for profit maximization.

Third, the model with a private sector ports industry and associated regulatory framework has serious shortcomings with respect to enabling effective transitions of land use that often result from port expansion and the re-location of port activities close to city centers. Like the previous arguments, the argument does not apply across the board but only for ports located (partly) in urban centers.

Finally, the private sector port model does not secure investments with positive externalities, such as investments in education and R&D. While R&D and education and training strengthen the port cluster as a whole, collective action from all companies in the cluster to invest in R&D, and training and education is problematic. While a private PDC may invest in research and capacity development within the boundaries of its own enterprise, it lacks incentives to fund and/or coordinate R&D activities for the entire cluster of logistics services adjacent to the port. This provides a fourth argument for SO-PDCs, as governments as shareholders can specifically task the SO-PDC with developing a "port innovation system" (discussed in more detail in Chapter 8).

Given the serious regulatory imperfections and the low/medium innovation intensity (while innovation clearly is important in port business ecosystems, but it does not disrupt the business model of the PDC, which can continue to function with a landlord business model, which provides financial stability over the long run), government ownership of the PDC is a viable policy option. This does not imply that the SO-PDC is the "best" model for all ports regardless of their characteristics, the location and the governance culture in the country. Figure 5.8 shows a stylized decision tree which aims at assisting government in deciding on the appropriate governance model for their ports.

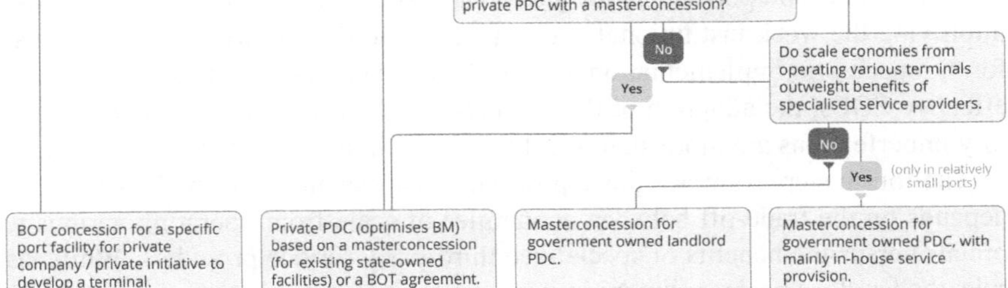

Figure 5.8 A stylized decision chart for port governance

Source: adapted from de Langen and Saragiotis (2018)

Four considerations are relevant for selecting the appropriate port model:

1. Is the port an integrated port complex?
2. Are the imperfections of the private model critical?
3. Is the institutional structure and culture of the country suitable for SOEs?
4. Is there stakeholder support for a privately owned PDC?

The arguments developed above apply to integrated port complexes, not to specific terminals. We define an integrated port complex as a port designated area comprising an entry channel, breakwater structures, various terminals and adjacent logistics and industrial activities. Such an integrated port complex is very common because of the scale economies involved.

For the above-mentioned reasons, in most port development projects, there is a need for an *integrated development* of a port complex.[20] In some cases, individual terminals are developed, for instance, for dedicated terminals for the export of mining commodities, import terminals of large plants or transhipment terminals. In such cases, there is no need for the establishment of a PDC, since a government entity can be tasked with granting the right to build and operate a terminal.

The second step in the decision chart deals with the regulatory imperfections. These are important in some cases, for instance, in large-scale ports in urban regions with limited competition from other ports. In case regulatory imperfections are of limited relevance, for instance, with a small port outside an urban area, a fully private port company is appropriate. The private PDC can freely choose the business model, i.e., in-house provision of terminal services or land lease agreements with third parties. In this case, the appropriate model for greenfields (newly developed ports) is a BOT/BOO concession for a private PDC. In cases of divestiture, such a port may be completely sold to a private operator.

The third step takes into account experiences with the SOE model in the country of focus. The relative efficiency of a SO-PDC, compared to a private port company depends to a large extent on the institutional framework and the political culture in the country. In countries with weak institutions, the regulatory imperfections for private companies may carry less weight than the disadvantages of government ownership, provided that there is sufficient stakeholder support (from port users, residents and port labor) for the private port company model. In such cases, improving the weak institutional and regulatory SOE framework is a prerequisite for the successful implementation of a SO-PDC. In countries with a track record of effective SOEs, the adoption of the SO-PDC model is appropriate in case regulatory imperfections are more significant than SOE imperfections (see Figure 5.3).

The fourth step examines the appropriate business model of the SO-PDC. This depends on the trade-off between economies of scale from operating various terminals versus the benefits of specialized third-party service providers. While, as a rule, the landlord business model is most appropriate, especially in view of the risk of limited operational efficiency of SOEs, in small ports, the scale economies from an integrated operational model may justify a SO-PDC that provides all or some terminal services (the so-called *integrator model*).

In conclusion, we have argued that port development is intrinsically commercial and is therefore best executed by a commercially focused organization. The model with a SO-PDC is appropriate under specific conditions that were detailed above; if these conditions are not met, fully private port companies are appropriate.

The rationale for concessions/contracts to promote private port development

In case the trade-off tips in favor of private port development, often the best approach to implement that is through concession or other contractual agreements with private companies. In the case of pre-existing ports, the most widely used form is a master concession for the whole port area, often including sub-concessions or sub-leases with third parties. Such a concession can be temporary, but there are considerable contractual complexities, which generally lead to extensions of such periods. For instance, the concessionaire can only agree sub-leases or other contracts with third parties until the duration of the master concession; meaning that in the last 20 years of the master concession, its ability to attract third parties is constrained.

In the case of newly developed ports, a BOO agreement, in which a concessionaire gets the right (and obligation) to build, own and operate the port facilities is widely used. However, this model is seldom used for large scale port development initiatives, as the risks for the concessionaire are substantial.

5.5 The appropriate geographical scope of PMBs

While in the context of private port development, mergers between PO-PDCs that develop ports in proximity have occurred,[21] to achieve the right geographical scale for port development, such a market mechanism resulting in an efficient geographical scope is lacking for SO-PDCs and PAs. Consequently, the geographical scope of both is often not optimal and can be either too large or too small.

A national SO-PDC (PA) is generally not effective (too large) for three reasons. First, the principal-agent problem is relevant: local port branches compete for investments and develop overly optimistic business cases. Furthermore, investment decisions are more likely to become subject to political considerations. Finally, a nationally operating SO-PDC (PA) generally sets national tariffs, even though these do not promote an efficient allocation of resources, as some ports are cross-subsidized by others. This will lead to under- or overinvestment, both with adverse welfare-economic effects.

Too much decentralization is also not effective, for three reasons: a too small jurisdiction of a SO-PDC will prevent investments in new port facilities outside this jurisdiction, even if locations outside this jurisdiction are superior. Second, a too small jurisdiction of a SO-PDC prevents the creation of scale economies, since different SO-PDCs will invest in similar facilities, such as container terminals, vessel tracking systems, hinterland infrastructure, and a port community ICT system. Third, small SO-PDCs may hardly be able to develop commercial capabilities. One larger entity that manages a number of ports in the same region is better positioned to develop better commercial capabilities.

Thus, the appropriate geographical scope is *one port development company for one port cluster*. In this case, overinvestment in similar facilities is prevented, while the SO-PDC is still focused on the development of one integrated port cluster.[22]

EU investment in ports: centralization leads to bureaucracy and wasted public money

In the EU, the court of auditors looks at the results of EU funded port development projects. The findings are sobering: many projects were delayed, changed and/or under-utilized. The picture that emerges from the report is a picture of opportunistic use of EU funding to create economic growth, but without well-developed monitoring to assess the impact on growth. Instead, in many cases available funding was used to develop port facilities without sound analysis of the benefits of such facilities. Some facilities remain under-utilized. In many cases, regional governments tracked progress of *spending*, but not *utilization*! Many of the projects had ineffective links to the hinterland, and a substantial number required additional investments. So from an effectiveness perspective, centralized funding for port development does not seem attractive. On top of that, the EU funding distorts the level playing field. EU funds were used to fund warehouses in Italy. This clearly leads to distorted competition with private warehousing companies/retailers. The funding also distorts the playing field between ports. For instance, the funding for Le Havre puts the ports of Antwerp and Zeebrugge at a disadvantage. It is hard to see compelling arguments why this would be justified. Furthermore, it may provoke further public funding for the Belgian ports, to prevent loss of traffic!

In many ports, port governance structures evolve in the direction of one PMB for one port cluster: in most cases through mergers (cases include North Sea Ports, Stockholm Ports, and Vancouver) and in some cases through devolution of a central PMB.

5.6 Effective corporatization

In many parts of the world, SOEs are not autonomous but instead subject to political decision-making. That also holds true for SO-PDCs. Applying lessons learning for effective corporate governance of SOEs to the SO-PDC is an important port reform challenge.

5.6.1 *The case for explicit shareholder policies for government-owned PDCs*

In an analysis of previous empirical literature, Boardman and Vining (1989) as well as Megginson and Netter (2001) conclude that there is strong evidence of superior performance of private corporations compared to SOEs. As state ownership in general is likely to negatively impact performance, the argument for state ownership needs to be based upon the fact that such different behavior of SOEs is in the public interest: SOEs "are expected to act, at least in some respects, differently from private companies in like circumstances" (an OECD paper by Christiansen, 2013, p. 6). This raises the question of *how* the government owner can induce the SOE to act in the public interest. Rentsch and Finger (2015) point out that government shareholders of SOEs (local and national) often behave *ad hoc* instead of based on a clear policy framework. In line with the OECD approach, I argue that effective state ownership requires a *shareholder policy*. Important elements of such an ownership policy include identifying the public interests served through the state ownership, detailing the (executive and supervisory) board nomination process and defining the targets (including the dividend policy) and risk tolerance levels (OECD, 2015).

If the PDC is a SOE, who should own the shares?

The question of the appropriate shareholder is relevant, as different government entities have different interests. The right shareholder is conditional on the most important reason for state ownership, from the four potential reasons identified above. If problems with land use decisions or *externalities from education and R&D* are the core reason for state ownership, *local/regional* government shareholding is appropriate, as these public interests are mostly relevant regionally.

If the core reason is the policy aim to make sustainability a core port development goal (instead of a "compliance approach") or the need to secure sufficient investments in ports from the (regional) economic development perspective, there is a case for national as well as local/regional ownership. The national ownership can be justified based on the effects of the port on economic development and sustainability *nationally*.

In addition to these arguments, capabilities in managing SOEs may also be relevant; one could assume national governments generally have stronger capabilities. Finally, on top of the question of which administrative layer (municipal, regional or national) is most appropriate, the issue of which ministry or department is relevant. Generally, the best approach would be to combine all SOE activities in one department/ministry, and not place the shareholder role at a specific ministry (such as a Ministry of Transport/Ports). However, such a ministry/department would have an important role in drafting a shareholder policy document.

As argued previously, regulation is not an effective policy instrument to secure four public interests. These four public interests may provide an argument for government ownership of the PDC *and consequently need to be addressed in a shareholder policy.*

1. Insufficient commitment to port development.
2. Securing positive externalities.
3. Reducing negative externalities.
4. Changes in land use.

Table 5.4 shows these issues and the desired effect of state ownership that needs to be reflected in the shareholder policy.

Table 5.4 Issues to be addressed in shareholder policies

Issue	Expected/desired differences: state-owned port development company compared to a fully private port development company.
Societal value of port development	Stronger commitment to the development of ("home") port from a wider societal perspective (creating social value next to private value).
Positive externalities	Stronger commitment to investments with positive externalities.
Negative externalities	Stronger commitment to prevent/limit negative externalities.
Land use planning and transfer	More cooperative approach to transferring land; a shared approach to/with other state agencies in case of changing land use to urban functions.

Source: Adapted from de Langen and van der Lugt (2017).

Retaining public ownership of land; an additional method for securing public interests

The government ownership of the PDC is in principle sufficient to secure public interests, through a clear shareholder policy. Nevertheless, in many ports governments have introduced an additional mechanism, by retaining the ownership of the port land, and granting the SO-PDC a concession, that may be either "eternal" or renewable, to develop that port land. Examples of concessions for state-owned PDCs for the development and management of a port complex include Rotterdam, Copenhagen Malmo Port and Goteborg Port, which all operate based on a lease agreement with the state/municipality, which retains the ownership of the port land. The most significant advantage of this model is that it enables more smooth transfer of land from the PDC to the municipality or regional/national government.

5.6.2 The risks of additional "government control mechanisms"

Notwithstanding the case for explicit shareholder policies, international experience shows that, instead of the development of long-term explicit shareholder policies, in combination with the establishment of autonomous supervisory boards, governments often develop other control mechanisms that reduce the independence of the port company and thereby the effectiveness of corporate governance. Common control mechanisms include:

- Supervisory boards with members based on their administrative function (i.e. the mayor of the port city or minister of transport), instead of independent professionals selected based on irrefutable experience and expertise.
- Selection and appointment of the PDC CEO by the government (as shareholder), instead of selection by the supervisory board and formal appointment by the shareholder based on the proposal of the supervisory board.
- Government approval of port pricing decisions or precise pricing regulations (instead of autonomous pricing decisions with checks and balances through competition law and/or an independent ports regulator).
- A tight regulatory framework, government approval, or even a direct role of government in negotiating concession agreements with tenants.[23]
- Government-led initiatives for, or a strong directive role of government in, port expansion projects.

Such "control mechanisms" reduce the effectiveness of corporatization, as they reduce autonomy levels and eradicate a supervisory board's performance incentives, thus paving the ground for political control over decision-making. For instance, in cases where politicians have decided on the career advancement of port managers based on criteria other than performance criteria, these managers did not have incentives to focus on the company's performance improvement and instead favored certain interest groups, such as employees or important port users (Vickers& Yarrow, 1991). Furthermore, independent supervisory board members may be selected based on personal relations with political decision-makers instead of on qualifications. This will also affect the way the board executes its monitoring role.[24]

Shareholder mechanisms to make sure the SO-PDC takes public interests into account

An in-depth case study of the Port of Rotterdam (PoR; see de Langen, 2023b) provides a number of relevant insights for other SO-PDCs. First, the two public shareholders of PoR have made an explicit choice to "permanently" use state ownership to achieve public interests. This choice was based on an analysis which concluded that alternative ways of securing public interests (i.e., through regulations and/or contracts) are not sufficiently effective. This approach and resulting policy choice is in line with the arguments provided in this book.

Second, the shareholders of PoR have identified specific public interests that PoR should take into account in their decision-making. These public interests are broadly in line with the public interests identified in this book.

Third, the shareholders of PoR have developed specific mechanisms to secure that PoR takes the public interests into account in decision-making. This suggests that providing direction through specifying the relevant public interests and monitoring progress at the shareholder meetings is not enough. In addition, the shareholders provide input for the development of a "port vision" (a long-term vision for the development of the port complex) and the "corporate strategy" (the measurable goals PoR sets for a period of five years). These mechanisms to turn the public interests into tangible objectives may also be relevant for other state-owned PDCs.

This analysis suggests that the "SOE model" requires a well-functioning public sector that is focused on using the SOE to secure public interests and has the capabilities to design mechanisms to make sure public interests are incorporated in the SOE decision-making.

5.6.3 International partners as tools for effective corporate governance?

There is a limited number of cases in which an international partner, sometimes from the private sector and sometimes a foreign SO-PDC, holds a minority share of a SO-PDC. Such a partnership can have two benefits:

- It can be an effective method to enhance SO-PDC capabilities. A commercially operating SO-PDC needs a set of capabilities that include commercial capabilities to attract customers as well as developing partnership agreements (such as concession/lease contracts), port planning capabilities (to ensure synergies in the port cluster are maximized), and engineering and maintenance capabilities for port infrastructure. While such capabilities can be developed without partners, international partnerships may be an effective way to quickly upgrade capabilities.
- A *partnership with an international partner may also be a good method to secure good governance of the SO-PDC*. In such an arrangement, a limited political influence on decision-making and *de facto* autonomy are more likely, as the corporate governance standards of the international partner would have to be applied. This may be an important argument in countries where SOE governance in general is problematic.

In case a partnership model is appropriate, a competitive process for partner selection is in the public interest. The best competitive process may be a "*beauty contest*", where, in addition to financial bids, a bid is evaluated on the expected impact on improving the capabilities of the "host" SO-PDC.

Such international partnerships in PDCs are slowly emerging. The country that has adopted this model most structurally is Oman;[25] countries with some emerging partnerships include Brazil and Benin.

Oman's partnership model for port development

Oman's port policies are somewhat different from most emerging economies, in that it has allowed foreign companies a central role in port development, within a well-developed port policy framework.

Salalah has grown consistently over the last decade, to become an important and efficient transhipment hub, with a throughput of over 3.5 million TEU. Salalah Port Services Company has 30% foreign (APM Terminals) and 70% local ownership, predominantly public.

Likewise, the port of Sohar is a 50/50 joint venture between the government of Oman and the Port of Rotterdam Authority. Volumes at this port have grown in seven years from about 6 million tons to 44 million ton. Finally, port development in Duqm is through a 50/50 joint venture between the Omani government and Antwerp Port Authority.

These arrangements secure the inflow of world class port development capabilities, while securing competition between the ports in Oman as well as a strong government influence in major decision making.

5.7 Port reform: effective corporatization and more private sector involvement

The sections above provide a clear direction for "getting port governance right" in terms of ownership of the PDC and corporate governance of the SO-PDC, including the role of public shareholders. A comparison between the insights presented in this chapter and port governance practices is sobering. Many ports and countries are far removed from the effective port governance practices as described above. Unless port governance is effectively organized, investments in port infrastructure are unlikely to create value for society. Often, when governance is ineffective, there are huge, untapped opportunities for better use of existing facilities and assets. In many countries, the port governance shortcomings are recognized, at least by most private sector stakeholders. Thus, many countries have embarked on port reform processes. As indicated in the introduction to this chapter, three broad reform steps can have a huge impact on the ports industry:

1. Transitioning from a PA-model to a SO-PDC model.
2. Improving the corporate governance of the SO-PDC

3. Transitioning the business model of the PA or the SO-PDC from the integrator model to a landlord model. This leads to an increased private sector participation in the ports industry.

Each of these reform steps requires adjustments to the regulatory framework for the ports. This regulatory framework is discussed in more detail in the next chapter.

Figure 5.9 shows a framework with the previously used port governance and business model distinctions, with, as an addition, a port governance model with ineffective corporatization, as this is common in the ports industry. Figure 5.9 also shows important reform processes.

Public sector embedded port authorities with an integrator model are found in Kenya and Ghana. In these ports, the reform trajectory consists of increasing the private sector participation through leasing terminal sites to commercial third parties (reform arrow 1). Public sector port authorities with a landlord business model are found in Spain, Italy and the US. For these countries, corporatization in such a way that the newly established SO-PDC will develop market-based capabilities is the main reform step (arrow 2). Arrow 2 is a follow-up step for the public sector embedded port authorities with an integrator model. Cases of landlord ports with ineffective corporatization include Lome and Constanza. While there is a corporatized entity, its autonomy is limited and market-based capabilities are weakly developed. In these cases, a reform process aims to move up by effective corporatization of the SO-PDC (arrow 3). In cases of integrator PDCs that are not effectively corporatized, reform should increase private sector participation as well as improve the corporate governance of the PDC (arrow 4). In the upper two layers, the reform challenges are much less: landlord ports generally can still make incremental steps to improve corporate governance (for instance, making explicit the hiring practices and profiles of supervisory board members as well as evaluation processes for the board). For integrator ports, reform initiatives may entail a switch to more private sector participation, as has, for instance, happened in Denmark and Sweden, where well-run SO-PDCs have switched to a mixed model.

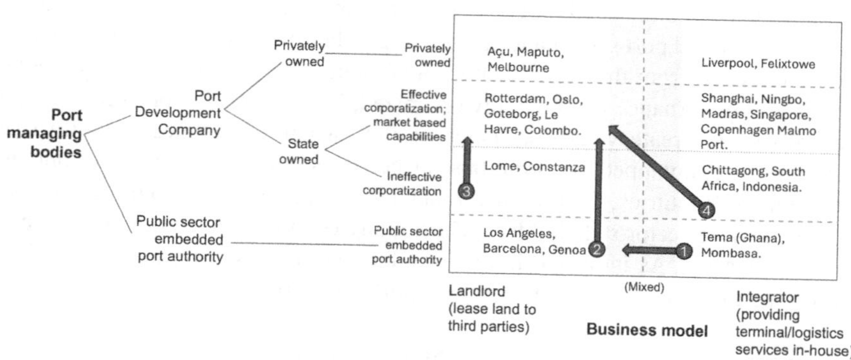

Figure 5.9 Visualizing port reform processes for PMBs

5.7.1 Corporatization of state-embedded entities, establishing an independent SO-PDC

In most reform processes, governments are reluctant to let go of control. This often leads to a strong government influence on the key decisions of the SO-PDC. The most important reform processes to secure effective corporatization are:

- Securing the SO-PDC is a normal enterprise to which general corporate laws apply, meaning it is obliged to pay taxes and is subject to economic regulation.
- Give the SO-PDC freedom to set tariffs and sign commercial agreements.
- Increasing the autonomy of the SO-PDC. There is a clear trend toward increased autonomy, but in countries such as Spain, Italy and Brazil the port authority is still deeply embedded in the public administration. Reform processes are aimed at increasing autonomy. For instance, the SO-PDC should be responsible for the design and execution of competitive bidding processes for its parties.

5.7.2 Improving the corporate governance of the SO-PDC

Corporatization is often used as a method to secure more autonomy, but many PDCs are not *effectively* corporatized. Many corporatized PDCs are strongly subject to political influence. Issues such as the composition of the supervisory board and the appointment procedures of senior executives are critical for effective corporatization.

While many PDCs are organized as corporatized entities, in practice they are not fully autonomous and commercially driven. As argued in this chapter, government generally can achieve policy aims better through regulation and a government shareholder policy than through direct control mechanisms. Reform items include:

- Set the supervisory board composition and develop clear merit-based processes to select supervisory board members.
- Develop a shareholder policy that provides direction but gives the supervisory and executive board freedom to develop a strategy on *how to achieve* the goals in the shareholder policy.
- Give the SO-PDC freedom regarding hiring and firing decisions and variable/bonus salary components.
- Give the SO-PDC freedom regarding purchasing (no overly strict obligations regarding selection of service providers) and commercial agreements.

Table 5.5 summarizes guidelines of international organizations (which were based on academic research) with respect to board size, gender balance and independence of board members.

However, in many countries/ports, these guidelines are not adhered to. Table 5.6 shows the board composition by member type for the years 2018 and 2023 of a sample of 32 European Core Ports (see de Langen, 2025, for more details).

The role of the board of the SO-PDC

The transition to the SO-PDC model increases the relevance of effective corporate governance. Nevertheless, attention to the decision-making of the port authority and more specifically the role of the board of directors has been very limited.

The body of research on boards has clearly established the influence of the board of directors on the performance of the corporation as well as generated insights on board effectiveness.

In contrast to these insights, in ports, politicians and public sector representatives account for a large share of the board members. In addition, especially boards with large shares of politicians and/or public sector representatives tend to be larger than has been found to be effective. Finally, even though most corporate governance codes stress the need for independent board members, with no "material interests", some boards of PDCs have members from the port business community. This is at odds with corporate governance codes. Thus, the governance of many SO-PDCs can be improved substantially, and may be expected to result in better port development capabilities.

Table 5.5 Board guidelines with respect to size, gender balance and independence

Item	*OECD guideline/ recommendation*	*IMF*	*World Bank*
Board composition	The state SOE boards need to exercise their responsibilities in a professional and independent manner. Individual board members do not act as representatives of different constituencies.	Selection of independent, nonpolitical and competent supervisory board members.	Appointing independent members enables SOE boards to operate at greater arm's length and address issues with unbiased judgment for the benefit of the SOE. Independent representation could be increased, eventually to a majority.
Board diversity (focused on gender)	The state should improve the gender balance in leadership positions in the public sector.	No specific recommendation.	WB stresses the need for a "sound gender balance of the board".
Board size	Board size should be limited, comprising only the number of directors necessary to ensure their effective functioning.	IMF alludes to the risk of excessive sizes of supervisory boards.	"Adopting a board size somewhere between 6 and 12 members seems prudent". The precise size should be determined by the SOE's needs and resources.

Source: Own analysis based on World Bank (2014), IMF (2016) and OECD (2015).

Table 5.6 Prevalence of board member types in the EU's core ports; 2018 and 2023

Board member types	*total 2018*	*total 2023*	*share 2018*	*share 2023*
Politician	40	61	13%	20%
Independent	118	135	39%	44%
public sector professional	97	58	32%	19%
ports industry stakeholder	7	3	2%	1%
employee representative	36	45	12%	15%
CEO	5	5	2%	2%

Source: Own analysis based on annual reports/corporate information of the SO-PDCs.

Table 5.6 allows the following conclusions. First, "independents" are the largest category of board members. The share of independents in the boards of SO-PDCs is increasing, from 39 to 44% between 2018 and 2023.[26] However, independents account for less than half of the total number of board members in the sample, even though guidelines stress that the best practice is an "all independents board".

Second, in 2023, a total of around 39% of board members were appointed because of their public sector affiliation. This group consists of both active politicians (around 20%) and public sector representatives (around 19%). This is surprising, given that research suggests such members do not contribute to board effectiveness. The corporate governance of SO-PDCs would improve when such public sector members are replaced with independents – some of whom should have public sector experience.

Third, the model with "ports industry stakeholders" on the board is only used in a small minority of ports, and this practice is declining. This implies an increasing alignment with board best practices, advocating that board members have no "material interests" as this is likely to lead to conflicts of interest. Fourth, around 15% of board members are employees who represent employee interests on the board. This model is widespread in Scandinavian and German SO-PDCs.

Overall, the data on the board composition shows convergence to best practices, but significant scope for improvement.

5.7.3 *A SO-PDC supervisory board quality indicator*

The board composition analysis and lessons learned allow the development of an indicator of the board quality of SO-PDCs (see, for more details, de Langen, 2026). The quality of SO-PDCs indicator developed is based on three components, in line with the best practices discussed in Chapter 2: the share of female board members (as % of total), the share of independent members (as % of total), and the board size.[27] Table 5.7 shows the quality of the SO-PDC boards indicator for 2018 and 2023.

Table 5.7 shows that five of the 32 SO-PDCs included in the sample have a maximum score in 2023, especially SO-PDCs in Finland and the Netherlands, which are well aligned with board best practices, while France is not. This indicator has a practical relevance as a benchmark for SO-PDCs as well as the governments that own them.

Table 5.7 The quality of SO-PDC boards indicator for 2018 and 2023

Port	*Country*	*Quality of Board 2018*	*Quality of Board 2023*
Amsterdam	Netherlands	1.00	1.00
Helsinki	Finland	0.94	1.00
Limerick	Ireland	0.67	1.00
Naantali	Finland	0.88	1.00
Stockholm	Sweden	1.00	1.00
Gdansk	Poland	1.00	0.98
Rotterdam	Netherlands	0.93	0.93
Dublin	Ireland	0.88	0.88
Ventspils	Latvia	0.33	0.84
Moerdijk	Netherlands	0.81	0.81
Tallin	Estonia	0.81	0.79
Aarhus	Denmark	0.66	0.78
Cork	Ireland	0.81	0.77
Wilhelmshafen	Germany	0.64	0.75
Koper	Slovenia	0.83	0.74
Patras	Greece	0.50	0.73
Hamburg	Germany	0.72	0.72
Riga	Latvia	0.44	0.71
Gdynia	Poland	0.67	0.67
Lulea	Sweden	0.57	0.66
Klaipeda	Lithuania	0.50	0.62
Copenhagen/Malmo	Denmark	0.58	0.57
Trelleborg	Sweden	0.77	0.54
Galati	Romania	0.33	0.54
Sczecin, Swinoujscie	Poland	0.52	0.52
Nantes	France	0.43	0.41
HAROPA	France	0.31	0.36
Marseille	France	0.29	0.36
Bordeaux	France	0.30	0.36
Bremen and Bremenhaven	Germany	0.31	0.31
Gothenburg	Sweden	0.50	0.28
Dunkerque	France	0.17	0.27

Source: Own calculations based on boards' data from the SO-PDCs.

5.7.4 More private sector participation

A comparison between the insights presented in this chapter and port governance practices suggests that in many countries, an increase in the role of the private sector is in the public interest and can be achieved through two related reform processes.

First, the transition from in-house government service provision to third-party service provision. This applies to activities such as training, maintenance, warehousing services, waste collection, catering services, and conference facilities. In a substantial number of countries, the SO-PDC or public PA provide some of these services in-house; this transition is often ongoing (examples include the Philippines, Indonesia, Bangladesh, Pakistan, Iran and Sudan).

Second, in a number of countries, including South Africa, Indonesia and Germany, some terminal operating companies are SOEs. In general, full privatization of terminal operating companies is in the public interest.

Is there a rationale for state ownership of terminal companies?

In general, terminal services are provided by private often internationally operating companies, with well-developed market-based capabilities. There is no rationale for state owned terminal companies, with the exception of small-scale terminals in metropolitan areas. The value creation for local users and the need for an excellent environmental performance (dust, noise, emissions) of the terminal may be a rationale for state ownership. Limited local negative externalities may be in the public interest, for instance due to huge numbers of residents in the immediate vicinity of the terminal. A regulatory and contractual approach to secure a top environmental performance is imperfect, as best available technologies cannot be predicted, nor enforced contractually or through regulation. Furthermore, the market appetite for running a small terminal may be limited. However, cases where there really is a specific need to secure a top environmental performance specifically for a small terminal may be relatively scarce and limited to terminals in central locations of metropolitan regions.

The geographical scope of state-owned entities

As discussed above, in many countries it is in the public interest to merge SO-PDCs of ports in close proximity. Such reform processes are relevant in countries such as Canada, Italy, Spain, Portugal, the Netherlands and New Zealand.

In addition, merging state entities involved in port development and those involved in industrial development is relevant. Given the fact that ports are *integrated ecosystems*, port development needs to cover the entire ecosystem, not just one part of it. However, in various countries, a split is made between the development of the port (understood as the cargo handling facilities) and nearby industrial and logistics zones. This is for instance the case in Brazil, where the port of Suape does not manage the nearby industrial zone, Oman, where various industrial parks are developed close to the port, Portugal, where the industrial park in the immediate proximity of the port of Sines is developed by another entity and South Africa, where the logistics park/freezone area right next to the port of Ngqura (Coega) is developed by a separate entity. Such an unintegrated approach is problematic, as users in the industrial/logistics zone rely on the port, often even through dedicated infrastructure, such as pipelines and conveyor belts.

Empirical evidence on effective port governance

This chapter has provided a deductive approach to getting port governance right. For various methodological reasons, there is empirical evidence on the effect of governance on port performance. But all available evidence is in line with the conclusions in this chapter. For instance, Bolevics (2017) finds a corporate structure contributes to port efficiency, in a comparison of four Baltic ports. De Langen and Heij (2014) show positive effects of corporatization. Cheon et al. (2010) show the positive effect of third-party operations (i.e., a shift to the landlord model) on efficiency, a result also demonstrated by Tongzon and Heng (2005). A World Bank study by Dappe and Suárez-Alemán (2016) also finds that the public sector service port model reduces port performance. Bichou (2021) finds that container terminals of state-owned ports with an integrator business model are less efficient as private sector peers.

5.8 Good practices for port governance

In the final five chapters of this book, I summarize the main ideas as presented in the chapter in the form of "good practices".

1. Retain state ownership of the port development company-bar exceptional cases.
2. Give the SO-PDC responsibility for the development of the integrated port business ecosystem, including manufacturing sites and logistics zones.
3. For state-owned PMBs with integrator models: transition to a landlord/mixed model, thereby increasing private sector participation in the ports industry.
4. Effectively corporatize the SO-PDC so it can develop market-based capabilities.
5. Give SO-PDCs sufficient freedom to optimize financial management, to set tariffs and sign commercial agreements.
6. Enable and provide direction for the evolving role of the SO-PDC, with an explicit shareholder policy.
7. Do not establish additional "government control mechanisms" regarding concessions, pricing, purchasing and hiring and firing practices.
8. Install a merit-based supervisory board of the SO-PDC consisting of independents.
9. In countries with weak institutions: consider attracting a foreign minority partner for the SO-PDC to secure good governance practices.
10. Merge small regional SO-PDCs to increase their investment capacity and enhance specialization.
11. In countries with centralized PMBs: decentralize (and where needed corporatize) and establish regional SO-PDCs.

Notes

1 However, conclusive empirical analysis is lacking. Relevant studies include Suárez-Alemán et al. (2016), Suárez-Alemán et al. (2017) and Barros et al. (2012) for the Brazilian case.
2 This paradigm shift is about port development, not port operations. Following a large wave of port reform, port operations are now done by specialized private companies in virtually all countries. In addition, this paradigm shift is under way: there is a (slow) transition in port governance, away from the public sector embedded "authority" model, and towards the commercial and self-sustaining "corporation" model (see, for instance, Verhoeven, 2010; Van der Lugt et al., 2015).
3 Even in countries where governments fund part of the port expansion, port expansion projects are increasingly developed with a "business case" and a "value case". For instance, in Belgium, the SO-PDC takes the initiative for port development and assesses the financial feasibility and economic impact. A substantial part of the investments in port infrastructure is funded with government grants. This approach applies for most port development projects. The rationale for public funding of port infrastructure is further discussed in the next chapter.
4 In Malta, the organization responsible for port development is Transport Malta, but its role is limited; they provide concessions for private operators, but do not charge port dues or private harbor master services. The ports in Malta are locations where a small number of operators have developed a terminal based on a concession agreement directly agreed with Transport Malta as Government agency.
5 In a small number of cases, a minority of the shares is privately owned, as is for instance the case for Copenhagen Malmo Ports.
6 In Italy and Spain the port managing body has limited freedom to engage in organizational reform, limited say over pricing decisions and no corporatized governance structure.
7 For completeness, we note that a Chinese SOE owns the Port Development Company of Piraeus. This is a contentious issue (see an edited book by Blanchard, 2023), that I do not discuss in this paper. We treat this as a private company.
8 See, for instance Verhoeven (2010), Debrie et al. (2013) and Van der Lugt at al. (2015).
9 Galal et al. (1994) show for a number of cases that there are no positive external effects that make up for greater inefficiency.
10 Note that this approach requires not an argument that governance of private firms is perfect (which is clearly not the case), but only that governance of private firms is better than that of SOEs. There is a strong theoretical and empirical case for this argument (see Shirley & Walsh, 2001).
11 That is not to say that there is no need for innovation in public transport; public transport companies do (need to) innovate in terms of payment systems, information provision, and equipment. There are obvious cases where state-owned bus companies clearly show the validity of the argument that SOEs are not very good in introducing innovations. However, compared to industries like telecom, the service is rather stable.
12 there is no clear-cut approach to identify industries where the conditions for government ownership of enterprises are in place. The "best model" also depends on country characteristics, such as the political culture and institutions, the quality of the legal system and the development stage of the economy.
13 This approach does not start descriptions of different "port models" but goes back to the "core question" why is there a case for government involvement and how can that involvement best be shaped? In my view, most literature on port governance (including the World Bank's recently updated Port Reform Toolkit) is too descriptive and without sufficient attention for the core questions regarding government involvement.
14 The definition of externalities is from Baumol (1964).

15 In general, the positive relation between transport infrastructure and land value has been well established; see Rietveld and Bruinsma (2012).
16 See Asteris and Collins (2010), who show this is the case for the fully private port development initiatives in the UK.
17 Stipulations that give government the right to cease land from the operator "when the time is right" are obviously not acceptable for a private operator that needs to make investments with long pay-back periods.
18 This risk often also is relevant in the construction phase, as construction works may give rise to additional procedures (e.g., discovery of artefacts of historical interest).
19 *Force majeure* can be insured against, and development banks may play a role in reducing *force majeure* risks.
20 However, in some cases there are no, or limited, scale economies, and individual terminals are developed. Some examples of this model are dedicated terminals for the export of mining commodities, import terminals of large plants (see, e.g., for the import of iron ore to a steel mill), container transhipment terminals or specialized roll-on–roll-off (RoRo) ports. In all these cases, the port consists of facilities for one segment only.
21 The experience from the UK indeed shows increasing concentration of ownership of ports in proximity, especially in the Liverpool/Manchester area.
22 The issue of market power of such a PDC that administers one port cluster must be assessed case by case. In some cases, competition from competing ports will be sufficiently strong (thus, the PDC has no market power), while in other cases, regulation to prevent abuse of market power is necessary.
23 It is important to recognize that negotiating a concession is a commercial activity. Not only the price is relevant; various clauses, such as investment levels, service levels and the use of a shared ICT system, can deeply impact port development. Furthermore, in some cases, especially when the port authority has sound reasons for developing partnerships with end users (such as steel companies and trading companies), regulations that require competitive bidding may be counterproductive.
24 The case of The Port Authority of New York and New Jersey (PANYNJ) is insightful. The governor of each state appoints six members of the Board of Commissioners, a non-paid function. Each governor retains the right to veto the actions of the Commissioners from his or her own state. In this set-up, board member are not fully autonomous. In the case of PANYNJ, the board virtually always votes in "blocks" (the six commissioners appointed by the same governor vote the same).
25 A formal evaluation of Oman's approach is lacking. The score of Oman on the WEF "quality of port infrastructure indicator" suggests this approach has worked; between 2007 and 2013, Oman consistently improved its ranking, but since 2013 the ranking declined a bit.
26 The selection of independent board members differs widely between country. In Ireland, the board member selection is all SOEs is carried out by a specialized public agency, that announces job listings and invites interested candidates to apply. In most other countries, the procedure is less transparent. In the Dutch ports, there is a publicly available profile for the board as a whole, and the shareholders select board members in line with this profile.
27 Each component has an equal weight and a score between 0 and 1. For the share of female board members, the score is higher for a higher percentage until 40% is reached. This number is taken because given the limited size of boards, for uneven board sizes an equal number of male and female board members is impossible, and therefore one can argue that a board with say 40% (two out of five) or 45% (four out of nine) is sufficiently diverse. For the share of independent board members, the score is higher for a higher percentage until 70% is reached. This threshold is taken as best practices clearly indicate independents should be the majority. For size, based on the guidelines we take five to nine board members to be the appropriate range, with increasingly lower scores for larger deviations from this range.

6 Port policies

As discussed in the introductory chapter, ports in many countries are not performing well. Indicators of waiting times and cargo handling times of ships in ports (for instance, the World Bank's CPPI report and UNCTAD's data on time spent by ships in ports) show a huge gap between well-functioning and non-performing ports. Often, the root cause of such differences relates to government policies. Governments are deeply involved in the ports industry, as regulators, policymakers and often as owners of port assets and/or the state-owned port development company (SO-PDC) or port authority (PA). The preceding chapter detailed steps to improve port governance; this chapter details important port policy choices and initiatives.

Governments inevitably need to develop policies for port development. I discuss four interrelated themes that need to be included in a comprehensive port policy (at national, regional/local and in some cases also supra-national level).

1. A national port development strategy that informs infrastructure planning decisions. Such a framework is needed as port development has externalities, both positive ones (economic development, trade facilitation, jobs) and negative ones (i.e., pollution and emissions).
2. Regulation of the ports sector. Policy choices are needed with regard to regulation, for instance, with regard to nautical safety, fair competition and environmental impacts of port activity.
3. The funding of investments in port development.
4. Policies to promote training, education and innovation in ports. Governments generally play a large role in shaping innovation and education activities. These are generally important success factors for port development. Thus, a national ports strategy needs to consist of policy choices in these areas.

6.1 National strategies for port development

Port development has a positive impact on economic development (Fugazza & Hoffmann, 2017; Herrera Dappe et al., 2024). Given the impact of ports on an economy, governments generally develop national strategies for port development, which cover at least spatial planning and financing (discussed in paragraph 6.3).

DOI: 10.4324/9781003630784-6

A planning framework within which ports can be developed is required. Government infrastructure planning decisions and activities influence port development. For instance, government decisions about planning and investment in rail, road and inland waterway infrastructure deeply affect the development of ports. The same applies to investments in electricity grids and hydrogen infrastructure. A national port strategy may include the items below, most of which are further detailed in this chapter.

- The value creation of ports.
- Planning of port development and hinterland corridors, focused on improving intermodal access.
- Identification of ports of national interest.
- Initiatives/policies to promote complementarity, specialization and cooperation of the ports.
- A framework for financing port development.
- Initiatives/policies to enhance data exchange, for instance, in maritime single windows.
- Initiatives/policies to transition toward green ports.
- Initiatives/policies to promote education and innovation in the ports industry.

6.1.1 How ports create value for society

I distinguish five mechanisms by which ports (as business ecosystems) create value for society:

1. Contributing to the *future earning capacity* of the economy, through vital port ecosystems and international connectivity. Port development can contribute to the future-proof earning capacity through the development of vital "port ecosystems" that are a source of current and future employment and added value, and through the creation of *connectivity* that contributes to the competitiveness of Dutch importing and exporting companies. Innovation, synergies in the port business ecosystem and a transition to sustainable activities contribute greatly to future earning capacity. Future earning capacity is also associated with high productivity, because high productivity is associated with employment with high wage levels. Port development contributes to the earning capacity of importing and exporting companies if the port development leads to better "connectivity", i.e., reliable, frequent, safe, sustainable and competitively priced international supply chains.
2. Contributing to the strategic autonomy of the country, for instance, by increasing the availability of critical raw materials. Port development can contribute to strategic autonomy by attracting investments in sustainable energy generation (including nuclear energy), storage and distribution. In addition, ports can increase strategic autonomy by attracting activities in the value chains of critical raw materials as well as critical goods such as batteries and semiconductors.
3. Contributing to the transition to climate-neutral and (more) circular value chains. Port development can create societal value by contributing to the transition to

a climate-neutral and circular economy. This element is very relevant in countries, such as the Netherlands and Belgium, in which port ecosystems account for a large share of the nation's emissions. In addition, ports often play a role in facilitating the transition of the country as a whole, for instance, through the import of sustainable energy.

4. Contributing to intensive and adequate use of port land. Port development can contribute to more intensive use of scarce port (industrial) land. Port land is needed for industry, energy generation and logistics. The efficient use of port land results in a lower land use footprint outside the port.
5. Contributing to efficient (multimodal) freight corridors. Attracting industrial and logistics activities to the PBE increases the possibilities for intermodal transport, due to the good intermodal connectivity of port areas. Increasing multimodality leads to more rail, water and pipeline transport and reduces the pressure on the heavily congested road network.

The value creation of the ports by these five mechanisms cannot be fully quantified, but Table 6.1 shows relevant data or questions to get a better understanding of the value creation of ports.

Table 6.1 Relevant data/questions to map societal value creation of ports

Form of value creation	*Relevant data/questions*
Future earning capacity	Value added and employment generated by port activities Productivity and wage levels of port activities Investment levels in port activities Synergies in the port business ecosystem Connectivity and the contribution to efficient global logistics chains
Strategic autonomy	Does the port reduce energy dependence? Does the port contribute to the availability of critical raw materials? Does the port reduce dependencies on specific trading partners or corridors?
Transition to climate-neutral and circular	Does the port generate or enable the generation/use of clean energy? Do the activities in the port enable the reduction of CO_2 emissions outside the ports? Do the activities in the port contribute to the circularity of value chains?
Intensive and adequate use of scarce space	Does the PBE offer synergy benefits that cannot be achieved elsewhere? Is the "spatial efficiency" of activities in the PBE higher than elsewhere?
Commitment to multimodal transport and efficient freight corridors	Does the PBE contribute to a favorable modal split of transport flows? Does the concentration of economic activity in the PBE contribute to a reduction in transport movements?

6.1.2 Land use planning

Given the positive societal effects of port development, policymakers often should consider making *spatial reservations for future port development.* Government can *secure port development options* in their spatial planning. In such an approach, governments reduce the burden for port expansion through identifying sites that should remain available for future development, and ensure that PDCs can develop these sites when the societal value case is positive – of course, given the relevant environmental regulation.

The use of spatial reservations implies that plots of land can only be used temporarily for purposes that are compatible with their future use for port activities. Such uses may include nature, agriculture and other temporary activities not requiring large investments (from storage space to karting care tracks). While spatial reservations have a cost, the lack of spatial reservations may often have a much higher cost, as future port development can only be executed when residents of such areas are relocated. Furthermore, the lack of a spatial reservation may impede port development.

Cases of costly relocations to enable port development

In Sohar (Oman), the lack of a spatial reservation of land for future port development has meant housing settlements have emerged in the direct vicinity of the port area. The Omani government has had to provide alternative housing for the residents involved, with substantial costs. In the Netherlands, ambiguity regarding the development of the port of Moerdijk forced local government to commit to purchasing houses of all residents that want to sell their house, for 95% of the valuation of the house in question. This policy measure has been in place for more than ten years and residents claim it needs to be continued given ongoing uncertainty regarding the long-term viability of the village (around 1150 inhabitants). Relocating residents is also common in developing countries, cases include Kingstown (Saint Vincent and The Grenadines) and Laem Chabang (Thailand). Spatial reservations can be a useful instrument to enable port development without high additional costs. However, adherence to the policy is critical. In the case of Lome (Togo), even land in the port area was utilized for non port-related activities to such an extent that this impedes the further development of the port.

The policy framework for port development needs to strike a balance between protecting the environment and the livelihood of citizens near the port and, on the other hand, enabling the development of new port facilities. Given the complex stakeholder environment, the uncertainty and time and costs involved in getting approval for investments may be prohibitive. Approval procedures for port development plans often take years. Approval is further complicated if private developers count on governments to manage and finance “compensation measures” for the loss of environmental quality.[1]

In metropolitan areas, port land may be more valuable for other uses, even though the port function may have positive externalities. Different possible uses of land (terminals, industrial activities, housing or real estate development) have different "external effects". These external effects can be negative (stench, noise, pollution) but also positive. For instance, a terminal in a metropolitan area may reduce congestion as cargo can be shifted from roads. Relocating a terminal can lead to a reduction of noise and stench in urban port areas. A cruise terminal may lead to an increased land value in the surrounding area. Thus, planning initiatives often need to ensure there is sufficient land for (developing new) port activities.

In this context, the changes in land use in ports is relevant. Three developments may drive a transition in metropolitan ports of land from port to urban functions. First, changing user needs (for instance, larger ships) may reduce the value of port land for port functions. Second, increasing urbanization may increase the value of port land for urban functions. Third, negative externalities of port activities may be increasingly relevant, for instance, because the role of ports in creating employment in local communities has decreased and/or because the effects of noise, exhaust of particles and stench become more relevant concerns with rising welfare and growing numbers of residents living in the direct vicinity of the port. For these reasons, a transition of port facilities to urban functions may be in the general interest. However, such a transition may not emerge "spontaneously" given unaligned interests. Often, residents want public space in waterfront areas. Thus, such a transition may create a huge value "for society" but not have a positive business case.[2] While in some cases there is a rationale for maintaining port facilities even when more revenue-generating urban functions can be developed, the opposite case is also possible: transitioning a port area to an open waterfront may be desirable from a societal value perspective. However, such a transition may not be initiated as the SO-PDC does not have commercial incentives to do so. Both cases demonstrate the public interests at stake in port land use decisions[3] and thus the need for policies that enable smooth port (re)development processes. Such policies generally need to depart from a "pro port development" stance. For instance, in Germany, the federal port policy explicitly aims to:

> Permanently ensure that the ports sector and the businesses established in the port area can fully use the port areas defined as special areas under the Federal Land Utilization Regulations (BauNVO) without being prevented from doing so by closer residential property development and the requirements this entails, e.g., under emissions law.
>
> (Government of Germany, 2025, p. 38)

In addition to this policy action, other policy actions also focus on securing land that is available for port development, i.e., creating sufficient port development options.

6.1.3 Ports of national interest

In various countries, as well as in the EU, an explicit policy decision is made to identify ports that are of national interest. In the Netherlands, five ports of national interest are identified, in Spain, 46 "ports of general interest" are identified, and in the EU, 89 core ports are identified. In Oman, the port policy identifies three main ports (Sohar, Salalah and Duqm). Such a decision can be useful as it enables focusing the development of freight transport corridors on these ports of national interest. The EU port policy explicitly links the EU core ports to EU core corridors, which are partially funded by the EU.

Criteria for selecting ports of national interest

In most countries, the selection of ports of national interests in done by policymakers, and often guided by various criteria. Political considerations can also play a role. The most relevant criteria are the volumes handled in the port. In some cases, especially container and RoRo volumes are considered, as these generate the largest volumes of landside flows (as bulk flows may be processed in the port business ecosystem). The size of cruise activities generally is only a secondary consideration, as these also do not generate inland flows. The size of logistics and manufacturing activities in ports generally is also a secondary consideration.

6.1.4 The rationale for policies for specialization, complementarity and cooperation

Some national governments have developed explicit policies to promote specialization, complementarity and cooperation. The rationale of such policies lies in the positive effect of those policies on the benefits of public investments in ports. If all ports develop container terminals, residents will demand rail and road connections from these ports to the hinterlands. Such connections generally have to be funded by the state. In the case of more specialization, the public funding is more limited. This also applies to other types of activities. For instance, if all ports aim to attract energy-intensive industries, this leads to demands for publicly funded pipeline and electricity infrastructure. Specialization can also lower costs associated with dredging and nautical access, as only a limited number of ports specialize in activities for which a deep draft is needed.

The cases of mergers between ports generally show the benefits of specialization. The merger of the SO-PDCs of Copenhagen and Malmo led to an integrated development of the entire Copenhagen–Malmo port complex, in which automotive was concentrated in Malmo, while for cruise a combined offering was developed to maximize utilization of the cruise facilities. In the case of North Sea Port (a merger of the SO-PDCs of the port of Ghent and two Dutch ports, Vlissingen and Terneuzen), the integration also allowed more specialization. In various other regions, the lack of cooperation hampers specialization. The nearby ports of Seville, Huelva and Cadiz compete fiercely in the container and ferry segments, often with partly publicly funded investments.

6.2 Regulating ports

Government intervention is needed to secure public interests in ports. As argued previously, any form of government intervention needs to be reconciled with the fact that PDCs need to be able to operate as *commercial undertakings*, even if they are government-owned.[4]

For this reason, governments need to develop a regulatory framework in which PDCs, even when they are government-owned, are treated as companies. State ownership provides the government with a mechanism to influence the SO-PDC beyond what can be done through regulation or a contract between the government and a private PDC. As argued in Chapter 5, if public interests are important in a certain port, but cannot be secured through regulation/contracts, government ownership of the PDC is a viable policy choice. But even if that is the case, regulation is needed, both for the SO-PDC and all other players in the ports industry. Below, the most relevant regulations are discussed, with a focus on economic regulation. Various economic regulations are highly relevant in the ports industry. The most relevant items are:

- Competition regulation.
- Regulation of access to port markets.
- Regulation of access to essential port facilities.
- Regulation to secure fair competition.
- Regulation to prevent bankruptcy of the SO-PDC.

Applying economic regulation to state-owned entities

Economic regulation also needs to be applied to government owned organizations, such as a SO-PDC or state-owned pilotage organization). This is the case in most but not all countries, exceptions include Brazil and Dubai. That has considerable risks, as state-owned monopolies may be even worse for port users than privately owned monopolies. Cases where competition law has been applied to SO-PDCs point out their market power.

In the Netherlands, the competition agency concluded that Port of Rotterdam Authority has market power in some segments. This has led to a "soft law" approach, where the competition agency stipulates that the SO-PDC and port users annually have to formally agree on port tariff changes. In Finland, a SO-PDC in the 1990s raised prices for passenger vessels by about 400% but had to reduce price increases after an investigation of the competition agency. Finally, in New Zealand, Northport Ltd, a majority publicly owned port company, was found to have abused monopoly power by not allowing access to the port facilities to a third party. These three cases of breaches of competition law by government owned PDCs show the benefits for port users of competition regulation that applies to these entities.

6.2.1 Competition regulation

Competition between firms in ports is in the public interest, but often missing or weak. When competition is insufficient (or even completely absent), prices are raised, leading to higher costs for consumers and producers. If *inter-port competition* is fierce enough, *intra-port competition* between terminal operators in the same port is not required to ensure sufficient competitive pressure. Inter-port competition is fierce *except in cases where the captive hinterland is substantial*. This is not the case in port ranges with many competing ports (e.g., transhipment ports in the Mediterranean), but it is the case in many ports that serve large hinterlands without competition from nearby ports. Examples include New York, Reykjavik, Durban, Casablanca, Abidjan and St Petersburg.[5] In such ports, without intra-port competition, port service providers do have dominant market positions. A similar logic applies to competition between PDCs. These PDCs mainly compete for attracting investments from third parties. PDCs often have some degree of market power, as the competition from other ports generally is imperfect.

Competition law is required to ensure sufficient competition or prevent abuse of market power. The most straightforward regulatory approach is to apply general competition law to the port sector. In most countries, this is the case. There are different approaches with regard to the organization of monitoring to ensure that competition law is not breached. In some countries, for instance, in the UK, a competition agency that oversees all sectors is responsible for monitoring the ports industry. This agency has assessed (and approved) take-overs and mergers. In other countries, such as Canada, New Zealand, Greece and Australia, an *independent institution* (often called "ports regulator") has been set up to actively monitor the ports industry.

Assessing market power

Dominant market positions arise when competition with service providers in other ports is imperfect, and there is no competition between service providers operating in the same port (intra-port competition). For the analysis of market power of port service providers, a distinction between three port services is useful:

1. Terminal handling services. For terminal handling, competition between ports is generally speaking imperfect, as at least for a part of the cargo flows, different ports are not perfect substitutes (since a part of the volumes handled in a port, and in most ports a substantial part, have a final destination in the vicinity of the port). As an example, take the case of a large island with only one terminal operator. Only in rather exceptional cases, in port ranges with fierce inter-port competition, are ports sufficiently good substitutes to argue that a single terminal operator does not have a dominant market position.
2. Port services that are a necessary part of a port visit, such as towage and pilotage. For these services, there is no competition from service providers in other ports. If there is no intra-port competition, there is no competition at all.

However, there may be competition *for the market*, in case the service provider is selected through a competitive process. In addition, depending on the regulatory framework, entry may be possible, making the market *contestable*.

3. Port services that are provided only in some ports (bunkering or port supplies). For these services, competition is fierce, and a dominant position in one port is not a threat to a competitive market, as shipping lines can use service providers in other ports.

Captive and contestable hinterlands for terminal operators

The first category (terminal services) is the most relevant for port users. For terminal services, the distinction between *captive* and *contestable* hinterlands is useful. Captive hinterlands are all those regions where a port has such a competitive advantage, because of lower generalized transport costs to those regions, that it handles the vast majority of all cargoes. Contestable hinterlands consist of all those regions where there is no single port with a clear cost advantage over competing ports. If the vast majority of cargo is originating from or destined to a contestable hinterland, a single provider in a port may not have a dominant position.

If parts of the hinterland are captive, opportunities for capturing economic rents by the port service provider exist if the service provider can differentiate prices (high for port users in the captive hinterland, low for port users in the contestable hinterland) *or* the captive hinterland is large compared to the contestable hinterland. In the latter case, high prices will lead to a shift of some contestable cargo to a competing port, but the resulting reduction in revenue will be smaller than the additional revenue from high prices.

When the captive hinterland is not sufficiently large to make rent extraction through high prices attractive, it may be possible to charge higher prices from port users in the captive hinterland (since these port users can hardly shift to other ports). Whether this is feasible depends on who the customer is: shipper (cargo owners), shipping line or forwarder. Generally speaking, shippers have the *worst* bargaining position, because for shippers located in the captive hinterland, switching to a second-best port does lead to higher transport costs. Therefore, port service providers can charge high prices for "captive shippers" and lower prices for "contestable shippers".[6]

The bargaining position of port service providers *vis-à-vis* forwarders and shipping lines is weaker, because forwarders and shipping lines *consolidate* cargo with different origins/destinations, and price differentiation related to the origin/destination of cargo is not viable. Thus, port service providers do not have market power *vis-à-vis* shipping lines and forwarders in ports where the contestable hinterland is substantial.[7]

Port services that are a necessary part of a port visit, such as towage and pilotage (the second category), have market power in the absence of intra-port competition. This market power will be larger the smaller the share of their service in the overall port costs: they will hardly lose business when they raise prices, because port users are sensitive to total port costs, not to individual components of these overall port costs. In various countries (the UK, Australia), court rulings confirm that for necessary port services, the relevant market is within the port.

When it is not feasible to have competition *in* the market, it is especially important to ensure competition *in* the market. Port service providers that do not face competitors in the same port do not have market power if entry and exit to these markets are costless. In such a case, the threat of potential entrants prevents excessive pricing. However, entry and exit to the market for port services is generally not costless (port-specific non-movable investments need to be made, e.g., cranes, trained crews for towage operations) and often not feasible. Entry and exit barriers can be legal/institutional (no permit is given to start a new firm), related to the availability of physical space (there is no attractive site in the port for an entrant) or economic (entry is not attractive due to scale advantages of the incumbent). Given the relevance of these entry and exit barriers, most markets for port services are not contestable.

The threat of monopoly pricing by port service providers may lead to *vertical integration*. Port users can invest in dedicated terminals "in-house" to prevent abuse of market power by a third-party terminal operator. Both shippers and shipping lines frequently own and operate dedicated facilities. Especially large shippers mainly operate terminals to prevent exposure to market power. This explains why many shippers in liquid and dry bulk (such as Shell, Exxon, Tata Steel and Vale) own terminal facilities. Investments in dedicated terminals of shipping lines may be partially explained by the above considerations.

Such user-owned port facilities prevent rent extraction *if the end products of these vertically integrated firms are sold in a competitive market*, which is generally the case.[8] Figure 6.1 summarizes the conditions under which port service providers have dominant market positions and can extract economic rents.

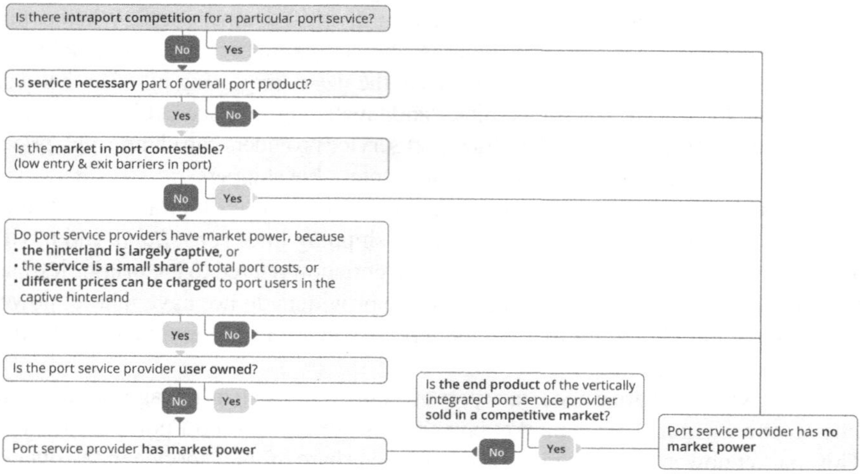

Figure 6.1 Conditions for dominant market positions of port service providers

Source: Adapted from de Langen and Pallis (2006).

Table 6.2 Number of terminal operators in ports of three size classes; 2019 and 2024

Year	*Port size*	*Number of ports*	*average number of competing terminals*	*Lowest number of operators*	*Highest number of operators*
2019	<1 million TEU	15	1.07	1	2
	1 to 3 million TEU	10	1.90	1	4
	>3 million TEU	10	2.30	1	4
2024	<1 million TEU	12	1.17	1	1
	1 to 3 million TEU	12	1.40	1	2
	>3 million TEU	12	2.46	1	4

Source: Own analysis based on publicly available data.

An overview of competition levels in ports worldwide

Data for the largest ports in 35 randomly selected countries[9] shed light on the number of competing container terminal operators in relation to the total volume handled in the port (see Table 6.2).

Table 6.2 clearly shows that the number of different operators per port is limited. In virtually all ports with a volume below 1 million TEU, there is only one operator. In the larger ports, the average is somewhat higher, while some of these larger ports also have just one operator, and the maximum number of operators is four.

Furthermore, the average number of terminal operators per port is relatively stable. Only in Le Havre did the number of operators decrease (from four to three), following take-overs, while in Haifa the number of operators increased (from one to two), following a new terminal development, and in JNPT the number of operators increased (from three to four), following the entry of a new operator (PSA) as winner of a bidding process for the newly developed terminal.

In conclusion, in all ports in the sample, the number of different terminal operating companies is limited. In 19 ports, there was just one operator (down from 21 in 2019). In nine ports, there were two operators, in five ports there were three operators, and in only two ports (Antwerp–Bruges and JNPT), there were four different operators. There is no intra-port competition in the case of one operator, while in the case of two operators, intra-port competition may be considered as weak.

Intra-port competition – the case from Buenos Aires

One of the best-known cases of a port reform process aimed to create intra-port competition is that of Buenos Aires, the largest port of Argentina (more information is available from various World Bank publications). In the early 1990s, Buenos Aires was widely considered as an inefficient state-run port. Cargo volumes fell between 1970 and 1990. The port tariffs grew, in some cases by over 250% in real terms in a decade.

The Argentine government decided to reform the ports industry, and privatise port operations, while securing sufficient competition between ports and a deregulated environment for private operators. Five terminal plots in the port of Buenos Aires were tendered, with one important condition: the new operators must employ workers from a labour pool. The concessions (a right to operate the terminal for 25 years) were granted to the highest bidders. The regulatory framework at the time explicitly prohibited mergers between terminals. The bidding process worked well and led to five different operators, mostly global terminal operators, that competed for attracting containers. The concessioned terminals are small; the largest was smaller than 30 hectares, with a maximum capacity of below 1 million TEU. The intra-port competition between the terminals was fierce, as illustrated by the bankruptcy of terminal 6 in 1996. The operator of terminals 1 and 2 (combined from the start) placed a bid to take over terminal 3. After an investigation, the competition agency argued that even after the merger intra-port competition would be sufficient and approved the merger. In hindsight, aiming for five different operators was too much, as there are substantial scale economies in terminal operations.

For a substantial period, terminals 1, 2 and 3 were majority owned by DP World, terminal 4 by APMT and terminal 5 by HPH (both after a successful takeover bid). After the privatization, port users experienced important benefits: the capacity increased, the productivity increased (the number of employees declined) and the prices decreased. From one of the most expensive ports in South America, Buenos Aires became one of the cheapest. As a result of these changes, volumes have grown, from roughly 450,000 TEU in 1995 to 570,000 in 2003 and 1 million in 2012.

However, the volume has stalled since 2012, while ship sizes increased and shipping alliances became stronger. As a result, the government decided to tender a 50-year concession to redevelop the Puerto Nuevo area of Buenos Aires, including consolidating three terminals into one. Several of the major players in international port operations are expected to bid for the project, including the current operators Hutchison Port Holdings, DP World, and APM Terminals. While there are serious competition concerns, there is still intra-port competition with a PSA-operated container terminal in Dock Sud, an adjacent terminal in Buenos Aires, as well as with smaller newly developed terminals in the vicinity.

This case demonstrates the large initial benefits of intra-port competition. The case also the need to continue to adapt port regulations and port development plans to changes in the ports industry, such as scale increases. As a result, larger terminals are needed and a too fragmented terminal market in a port can lead to operators that are too small to operate efficiently.

Regulating port companies with dominant market positions

The central challenge for competition regulation is to prevent abuse of a dominant position, without hampering investments.[10] One type of regulation is "rate-of-return regulation", which sets a fixed rate of return for the service provider. This type of regulation is applied, for instance, in South Africa (where it is applied to the tariffs of TNPA – the National Ports Authority) and the Netherlands (where it is applied to the single pilotage provider in Rotterdam). The main disadvantage of rate-of-return regulation is that it provides little incentive for efficiency, since it allows firms to pass increased costs on to users via higher tariffs. As a result, economic rents may accrue to employees, customers and suppliers of the regulated entity (but not the regulated entity itself, as its rate of return is fixed). In the rate-of-return approach, the regulated entity has an incentive to push for approval of high price increases. In addition, the regulator is forced to evaluate and approve the operators' investment decisions, since these investments increase cost levels and thus tariffs. The service provider has no incentive to minimize investment risks, since it has a guaranteed rate of return.

Regulation in airports: a relevant benchmark

There is a similarity between airports and seaports. Both generate revenues from port dues as well as from renting/leasing land and facilities to providers of additional services. In airports, prices are frequently regulated. The two main approaches are the *single till* approach, that considers all costs and revenues at an airport when considering the level of airport charges. Costs associated with non-aeronautical activities are included in the cost base for calculating airport charges, while associated revenues subtracted before airport charges are calculated. The prices of non-aeronautical activities are not regulated, but the revenues generated are considered when setting the charges for the aeronautical services. This means that when an airport increases its "landside" revenues, fees for passengers and airlines will decline.

In the dual till approach only costs associated with aeronautical activities are considered when setting airport charges. Thus, airport operators can increase their profitability by generating additional "landside" revenues. For seaports, the "dual till" approach is more sensible: it gives PDCs freedom to invest in the attractiveness of their land, and generate revenues from that, without repercussions on the port dues.

An alternative approach to the rate-of-return regulation, which provides incentives for controlling operating costs, is "price-cap regulation". Such price-cap regulation specifies the maximum allowed price increase related to an inflation index. Generally, the allowed increase is (and should be) below inflation. price-cap regulation provides incentives for cost-cutting and maximizing revenue given tariffs. A price cap needs to be periodically – but not too often – reviewed. price-cap regulation provides incentives for cost-cutting and maximizing revenue given tariffs, as these increase profits and thus the investment capacity. In a price-cap regulatory approach, concession prices and revenues would *not* be subject to a price cap.

6.2.2 Regulating market access in ports

Many ports have insufficient land to accommodate (all) new entrants. Especially in these cases, open procedures to gain access to the market are in the public interest. Incumbents often operate in a port based on a concession or land lease contract. In other cases, incumbents only implicitly (they have always been the only service provider in the port; this is sometimes termed "grandfather rights") have been awarded the "right" to operate in a port. Examples of port services with limited market access in many ports include terminal services, towage, pilotage and mooring. An open market for providing such services is in the public interest, as it puts pressure on incumbent firms to charge reasonable prices and secure sufficient productivity.[11]

In the ports industry, obtaining a *concession* to provide services is the dominant entry mode (see Pallis et al., 2008 for a detailed analysis). Regulations that ensure open and transparent processes for granting concessions to operate in a port are required to ensure the public interest of access to markets. This may be achieved through regulation specific to the ports industry, similar to the regulation that has been developed for industries such as the airports industry. As one example, in Canada, the Canada Marine Act obliges port authorities to use open and transparent procedures for granting concessions. We argue that competitive bidding processes to grant concessions should be the rule, but PDCs (regardless of whether they are state-owned or private) *should have some scope to deviate from this rule*. Regulation that establishes open and transparent procedures as the rule, with some scope for the PDC to deviate from this rule, is appropriate. Such a regulation needs to allow disadvantaged parties to appeal on the grounds that they have not had a chance to compete for the contract. Such an approach gives PDCs scope for developing strategic deals with customers but places the burden of justifying this approach on the PDC.

Arguments for not using open competitive bidding processes for concessions

Direct negotiations with incumbents may be needed for effective port development in at least these cases:

- A re-location deal whereby an incumbent gets a concession for a new site and vacates an old site for the PDC to redevelop.
- A deal with an end user that wants to develop a terminal in a port to handle its own cargo. For instance, a large fruit producer wants to invest in a terminal and storage facility in the port to export its fruit. In such a case, competitive bidding is not as effective as direct negotiation with the end user, as this company controls the volumes for the terminal. As another example, if a large manufacturer in a port (say BASF, Shell, Petrobras) wants to partner with the PDC to develop a common user rail terminal, partly with the aim of transporting their goods to the hinterland, direct negotiations are better suited than competitive bidding.

In such cases, a PDC has sound arguments for direct negotiations; regulation should recognize the option for direct negotiations; such a regulatory framework would also have to allow a potential competing entrant to file a complaint.

Regulating concessions without placing too many constraints on the PDC

A central insight from this book is that port development is a commercial activity, not a public sector activity. For this reason, the model with a port authority embedded in the public sector is not appropriate. Acknowledging the commercial nature of port development – and the need for commercially operating PDCs (state-owned or privately owned) has implications for the perspective on concessions. In this perspective, a concession contract between a PDC and a private operator is *not* a partnership agreement between the public and the private sector (PPP) in the same way as a BOT.

In the PDC perspective, a concession is and agreement between the PDC and a third party. The PDC may often use competitive bidding processes to select a third party as this makes commercial sense. However, the PDC may also use other partnerships forms in case these are better suited to reach its objectives and directly negotiating a contract with a third party does not breach competition law. The partnership agreements of the PDC and a third party are often not "concessions" in the legal sense of agreements between the public and private sector. Regulation that obliges the port authority/PDC to select third parties under all circumstances through open, competitive tenders is not appropriate, as there can be good reasons for direct negotiations with third parties. In Spain, with a public sector embedded PA model, developing agreements with third parties without competitive process is hard to justify and time-consuming. This negatively affects the ability of the Spanish PAs to attract third parties to their port ecosystems.

6.2.3 The rationale for excluding interested parties in competitive bidding processes

In competitive bidding processes, *financial and legal* requirements and requirements concerning *industry experience* are often used. These ensure that prospective bidders are administratively and legally in order. The financial strength of the bidder is relevant to ensure it is capable of financing the required investments, both the initial investments and the additional investments over the concession's lifetime. With regard to industry experience, requirements are more disputable. Arguably, terminal handling capabilities can be developed relatively rapidly (mainly through hiring qualified professionals and partnerships with equipment/specialist service providers).[12] Thus, it may be sensible to define industry experience broadly.

The risks of excluding newcomers through criteria regarding specific industry experience

Industry experience requirements specifically for container terminal operations (for instance a requirement to operate at least *x* different terminals with a combined volume of at least *x* million TEU) create entry barriers for firms active in freight logistics but not yet in container terminal operations. Potential new entrants could include large international freight logistics firms that so far have operated a business model not involving container terminal operations (examples could include Flexport, Amazon, DHL and DSV) as well as large freight logistics operators that may want to expand from other segments into the container terminal segment (examples include Grindrod, an African company traditionally active in bulk, Seatrade, active in fresh logistics or a freight train operator that may be interested in expanding into container terminals).

On top of the above grounds for exclusion, various countries have considered exclusion of interested candidates because 1) they are foreign state-owned entities, 2) they are incumbent operators already active in the port, and 3) they are vertically integrated shipping lines.

However, excluding interested parties has three adverse effects.

- First, policies to exclude qualified interested parties go directly against the interests of these parties and are thus prone to legal proceedings.[13] This is likely to delay concession-granting processes, which may have an important negative impact on the country. This is, for instance, the case in an ongoing legal case for the main container terminal in South Africa.
- Second, excluding interested bidders reduces the competition for the concession. This implies the expected bids are likely to be less attractive, financially but also in terms of other criteria that may be included in the bid evaluation, including a commitment to handle a certain minimum amount of volumes, investment volumes, operational performance levels or the sustainability performance of the terminal.
- Third, excluding interested candidates also impedes maintaining good relationships with large multinational companies that may play an important role in freight logistics in the country. In the case of excluding incumbents, this approach also impedes accommodating established operators that want to expand. This may have a detrimental effect on the utilization of the port infrastructure, as incumbents may be better positioned to achieve higher utilization, especially if they migrate from another smaller terminal in the same port.

Cases where incumbents are seen as partners of a PMB

The PMB (PA or SO-PDC) as concession granting entity is likely to look at concession granting processes through the lens of "customer relations". In such a perspective, the PMB regards the terminal operators active in the port as partners. This does not imply favoring incumbents, but it does mean an open eye for opportunities for win–win agreements that are in the mutual interest of the PMB and the terminal operators. As examples, Fremantle Ports (the port authority of port of Freemantle, Australia) has simultaneously negotiated 10+11 year lease extensions for the current operators Patrick and DP World for new leases of the two existing container terminals in Fremantle.

As a second example, Port of Montreal has decided to turn to its existing two container terminal operators to develop a new container facility at Contrecour. The two incumbents were asked to indicate whether they opt to work together or to compete on the planned new terminal (capacity of around 1.15 million TEU) and have agreed on an operating partnership. Operation of the new terminal is expected in 2026. There are various other examples of partnership type agreements with incumbents for expanding their terminal, migrating to a new one or extending/re-awarding the concession.

This, customer/partnership approach of a PMB is different from a concession granting process managed by a specific state entity (generally under the ministry of Finance). In my opinion, generally, the PMB is better positioned to make the right choices in concession granting processes.

Policies to exclude bidders on the grounds that they are owned by a foreign state

Various countries have developed instruments that may lead to the exclusion of foreign state-owned bidders. The potential negative effects of foreign state ownership of a terminal operator have recently gained prominence. This is relevant: while there are many private multinational terminal operators, various large international terminal operating companies, including COSCO Ports and PSA, are state-owned.

This may give a foreign state the ability to utilize the capacity of its SOEs to affect the "host country". This creates "leverage" that the foreign state may use to achieve security, economic and strategic interests, for instance, by influencing voting in international institutions such as the United Nations.[14]

Given that leverage can cause harm, states are better off without the activities of foreign SOEs that give foreign states leverage.[15] SOE activities do not give the home country leverage per se; if the SOE activities could instantaneously and without significant disruptions be replaced by another (privately owned) company, there is no leverage. In the container terminal industry, there are three ways in which foreign SOEs may give a foreign state leverage.

- First, if a foreign SOE is able to seriously affect a country's maritime connectivity, it can impact the host country's trade dynamics.
- Second, A foreign SOE can have control over critical links or nodes, i.e., links or nodes which cannot be replaced.
- Third, a foreign SOE may influence strategic supply chains to/from the host country. Examples of strategic supply chains include energy commodities like oil, gas, and hydrogen, semiconductors, raw materials like lithium or phosphate or specific agricultural products if these constitute a notable share of the host country's exports.

Figure 6.2 shows the conditions under which a foreign terminal operating SOE would give a foreign state leverage.

The absence of substitutes is a critical condition for leverage. This would, for instance, be the case if a foreign SOE operated the only terminal in a port that is important for a country's trade.

Various countries have policies in place to constrain the activities of foreign state-owned enterprises. The EU has denoted ports as *critical infrastructures*, which provides a basis for limiting ownership by foreign SOEs. This applies both to the port managing body and to terminal operators in ports. For terminal activities, the EU has developed a mechanism of *investment screening*, which is deployed in the case of proposed large-scale FDI in container terminals. The screening can result in blocking investments of foreign SOEs. Various EU countries also have national regulations to prevent the influence of foreign states over critical infrastructure.[16] The US also has policies to prevent the leverage of foreign states, which limit the activities of foreign SOEs as terminal operators. The US also implemented policies to hinder the emergence of international information platforms in logistics owned by Chinese state-owned companies.[17] In South America, Argentina has implemented policies to exclude foreign state-owned enterprises from bidding processes for infrastructure construction and maintenance contracts.

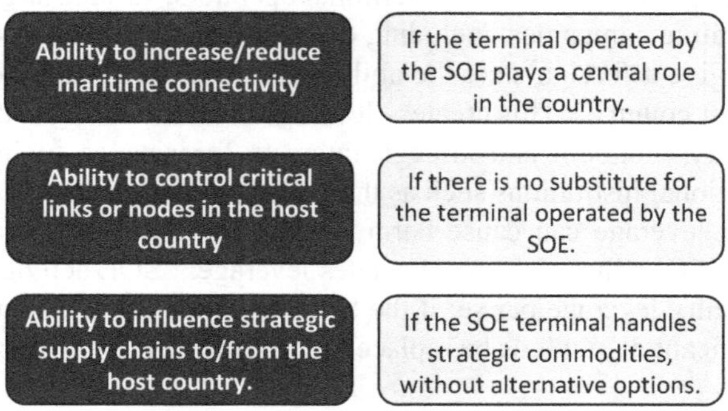

Figure 6.2 Conditions for leverage of a foreign state through its terminal operating SOE

Alternatives for the exclusion of foreign state-owned bidders

The use of policy alternatives to the exclusion of foreign state-owned bidders is not straightforward, given that leverage derives from the *potential* to act. Such leverage may be exercised implicitly, without explicit reference to potential actions of the foreign SOE. Generally, deploying leverage does not require explicit actions of the foreign SOE. Nevertheless, three alternative policies can be identified.

First, a regulation specifically aimed at enabling the expropriation of a foreign state-owned enterprise (SOE). This would be permissible if it is for a public purpose, non-discriminatory, conducted with due process, and involves compensation. An additional stipulation in a concession contract of an operator that is controlled by a foreign state may also be considered.

Second, as the EU has done, a country may develop an Anti-Coercion Instrument (ACI) designed to counter economic coercion by third countries. However, such a policy is only credible in case a country has credible potential countermeasures. Third, a country may actively supervise the operations of a terminal operated by a state-controlled entity, on the grounds that it is a "critical entity".

The rationale for excluding bidders because of their vertically integrated nature

Container shipping lines continue to expand vertically, not just in terminal operations, but also in intermodal transport and integrated door-to-door transport. The operation of a container terminal is a modest degree of vertical integration. There are three main drivers of vertical integration with terminal services: synergies between the different activities, a more differentiated service offering and a reduced dependence on third-party terminal operators, especially in "must call ports". All major shipping lines have developed terminal activities, as discussed in Chapter 4.

Given the clear vertical integration strategies of the leading terminal operators, terminal transactions including a vertically integrated partner are very common globally. Even though vertical integration is common, it may raise competition concerns. When the terminal business of the integrated business dominates the market and provides the integrated firm with exclusive access, the dominant market position may be carried over to other parts of the chain. In such a case, the vertically integrated entity may have an incentive to discriminate against other shipping companies so that they face competitive disadvantages. This threat is termed "foreclosure".

One of the areas with structured processes to prevent foreclosure is Europe. All transactions of a certain size need to be notified to the European Commission, and their effects on competition, including through foreclosure, are assessed. However, none of the transactions that were notified were ruled out by the competition agencies. Even in the single case in which the EU concluded that the transaction led to a vertically integrated firm with high market shares (the case of the Deurganckdok terminal owned by MSC entity TIL and PSA), no competition concerns were raised. Furthermore, no complaints have triggered an "ex-post assessment" (a tool available based on articles 101 and/or 102 of the EU Treaty), in which the

Commission assesses whether there is evidence of anticompetitive behavior. Thus, in Europe, the threat of foreclosure is generally deemed to be not material in the container terminal market. As another case, the economic regulator of Ecuador also assessed the effects of vertical integration in a takeover of Hapag Lloyd and decided to allow it without conditions.

Another country in which the potential negative effects of vertical integration have been assessed is Chile. In Chile, the competition agency is especially concerned about the effects of vertical integration in a scenario where capacity utilization is very high. In such a scenario, the competition agency points out the risks of unjustifiable tariff discrimination. The competition agency also considers the effect of the strategy of the vertically integrated terminal on the competition intensity of shipping services to and from Chile. It is of the view that a vertically integrated terminal could deter the entry of competing shipping services. In view of the above risks, the competition agency decided to limit the share of a shipping line (or shipping line-controlled operator) to 40%. In addition, the competition agency requires a terminal with shipping line involvement to disclose tariff structures to secure non-discrimination. Over the years, the regulator has become less concerned about vertical integration, and in specific cases the maximum allowed share of a vertically integrated player has been increased to 50 or 60%.

The different treatment of vertical integration in Chile and Europe is explained by the much denser service network to/from Europe compared to Chile. In shipping markets with limited numbers of services on specific routes, the risks of adverse effects of vertically integrated terminal operators are higher.

Policy alternatives to excluding vertically integrated terminal operators

The most straightforward policy tool is to include non-discrimination clauses in concession contracts. Including non-discrimination clauses in concession contracts for container terminals is deemed appropriate by the World Bank (Juhel, 2017).

Reference Clause on Price from the World Bank Port Reform Toolkit

The World Bank has developed a series of reference clauses to assist concession granting agencies. The reference clause dealing with discrimination is as follows:

> The Operator agrees that the charges for his services rendered in connection with his operations on the concessioned premises shall be competitive within the port and with other competing ports having such facilities and services. The Operator shall, however, at all times have the right to increase or decrease such charges and modify the

relevant rules and regulations, in accordance with sound business practices. In the event the Port Authority (or port regulator, if applicable) receives a complaint or complaints of discrimination on the part of the Operator of the concessioned premises and the Port Authority (port regulator) concludes after thorough investigation that there are reasonable grounds to believe that discrimination has been practiced by the Operator, then the Operator, upon written notice to him by the Port Authority (port regulator) shall cease and desist from such practices.

Such clauses may go hand in hand with a formalized process to submit and handle complaints. In addition to a general non-discrimination clause, the port authority or regulator may oblige an operator to provide 1) specific services on tariffs for different services, 2) the berthing priority rules it applies to the terminal, and 3) service quality indicators such as the moves per hour per ship. The competent agency in Chile has instructed the state-owned landlord port company to ensure that a newly selected operator – in case a shipping line is involved – will provide such data. This "lighter" approach is generally more appropriate than excluding shipping lines (and related companies) from participating in bidding processes.

The rationale for excluding incumbents

The rationale of excluding incumbents is to increase the competition levels in the market for terminal services. A necessary condition for this argument to be valid is that an incumbent would have a dominant market position when awarded the concession. Policies to ban incumbents are rare; some cases are given in Table 6.3.[18]

Policy alternatives

As discussed previously, the instrument of the exclusion of an incumbent has serious disadvantages and therefore an analysis of "lighter alternatives" is needed. The four most relevant ones are discussed below.

1. Application of competition law. The main regulatory approach for preventing potential adverse effects of concentration in the container terminal market is competition law. The most straightforward regulatory approach is to apply general competition law to the port sector. In most countries, this is the case, and generally a cross-industry competition agency oversees all sectors and is also responsible for monitoring the ports industry.
2. Proactive initiatives to strengthen the effects of competition law. In countries such as Canada, New Zealand, Greece and Australia, an independent institution has been set up specifically for monitoring the ports industry. Such a port-specific agency actively monitors the ports industry, which has an important advantage: the competition agency not only acts based on signals (like complaints)

Table 6.3 Cases with policies to exclude or disadvantage incumbents

Case	*Description*
JNPT	JNPT launched a tender for a second terminal and excluded the operator of the first concession from bidding. This decision was challenged in court. Subsequently, an explicit policy for bidding was developed, aiming for at least two operators in large ports. Under this policy, an operator can only have a concession for two terminals in the port and an awardee was excluded from bidding for the next terminal in the same port. The policy was later modified to explicitly exclude an incumbent in a port with only one private operator.
San Antonio	Incumbents in the "greater Valparaiso region" were only allowed to bid under the condition that they would divest their current concession in the case of winning the new concession (Tribunal de defensa de la libre competencia, Republica de Chile, 2020).
Valparaiso	A bidding procedure with "two boxes" was used. Under this method, the best entrant and one of the best incumbents were selected. The entrant was granted the *right to match* the incumbent bid. The bidding process was carried out, but the contract was canceled later due to environmental concerns. In a modified approach, the incumbent is allowed to bid, as the regulator has acknowledged the increased competition with terminal operators in San Antonio.
Vancouver	The incumbent GCT was excluded from the bidding process for a newly developed container terminal when GCT argued an expansion of its terminal would be more sensible and filed a court case alleging bias of the PA. Following a change in the leadership of the PA, it decided to allow GCT to bid for future terminals.
Callao	Peru's concession-granting agency decided to exclude the incumbent, DP World, from the bidding process for a second large container terminal. DP challenged this decision in court, but lost, and the concession was awarded to another operator.

that there are competition issues, but proactively and permanently monitors compliance of all stakeholders in the ports industry with the relevant regulations. In a similar fashion, regulation can stipulate that in case an incumbent wins a concession, approval by the national competition agency is required.

3. One terminal per operator. This policy is in place in Chile and India. When implementing such a policy, attention is needed for what qualifies as a "terminal", keeping open the option to exclude small terminals. Second, it may be sensible to accommodate for the possible exclusion of terminals that over time will be converted to different uses (e.g., urban functions in city ports). That may lead to a scenario in which an incumbent operates a new terminal as well as an old one until it is converted to a non-port use. Finally, a maximum period for an incumbent to divest from the current terminal in case of a successful bid for a new terminal needs to be stipulated. The most sensible approach is to allow the incumbent to "migrate" its operation to a newly awarded concession, while not allowing the simultaneous operation of two terminals to be more than necessary. In Chile, the port managing body proposed a period of 18 months, starting from the "milestone" of the start of operations (even though the milestone was not

precisely defined), but the regulator suggested reducing this to nine months. A secondary consideration that is relevant is the remaining lifetime of the terminal to be divested by the incumbent. A very short remaining lifetime (indicatively less than a couple of years) will make it practically impossible for the incumbent to sell the terminal. In such a case, an agreement to return the concession after volumes have "migrated" to the new terminal is more sensible.[19]

4. Favoring entrants in bid evaluation. Favoring an entrant in bid evaluation is a strong instrument and may only be a sound option in very specific cases. This alternative is a "lighter" alternative to the full exclusion of an incumbent, but most likely it has the same effect, and thus should be considered only when there are proven and serious competitive concerns. The approach was taken by the Port of Rotterdam, which evaluated bids with various criteria and sub-criteria, including competition effects. The incumbent (ECT) participated unsuccessfully, challenged the outcome in court, but lost. To our knowledge, the approach has not been replicated and may not be feasible in countries in which the PMB has more limited freedom in designing competitive bidding processes. In such cases, the "right to match" mechanism may be an option to favor entrants. Under this mechanism, bids are classified in two "boxes" (entrants and incumbents) with a winner for each box. Under this mechanism, the winning entrant has the option to match the bid of the winning incumbent, in case the latter has a higher financial offer. While this policy option has an intuitive appeal, it may alter the bidding strategies and therefore impact outcomes in unforeseen ways. Furthermore, it may increase the risks of renegotiation as it drives up the price for an entrant.

A "ladder" of policy options to prevent (abuse of) dominant market positions

Based on the overview above, the policy options can be regarded as a "ladder", in which a step up the ladder only is justified when there are good reasons to dismiss the "lighter" policy option as insufficient for achieving the policy goal of healthy competition between terminal operators.[20] The five policy options ordered from "light" to "heavy" are:

1. Application of competition law.
2. Proactive initiatives to strengthen the effects of competition law.
3. Stipulate that no operator is allowed to operate more than one container terminal in the same port.
4. Favoring entrant in bid evaluation, including a "right to match".
5. Excluding an incumbent from a bidding process

6.2.4 Regulation of access to essential facilities

Next to open procedures for granting contracts to service providers, *essential facility regulation* is relevant in the ports industry. Such regulation allows third parties access to an essential facility that is owned/operated by a competitor. Port facilities

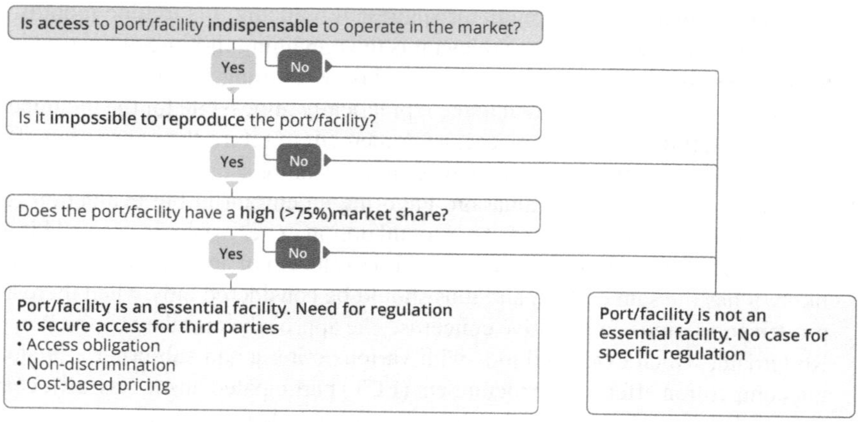

Figure 6.3 An essential facilities test for a port facility

are often essential facilities, as access to the port facility is essential for providing shipping services, while developing competing facilities is not feasible, for planning or economic reasons. Essential facility regulation in general applies in Europe and many other countries. In court cases, port facilities have been considered as essential facilities, with beneficial effects for firms seeking access to port services. The case of Port of Helsingor in Sweden is illustrative; in this case, the ferry port, owned by a ferry operator, had to allow another operator access against the same conditions as the incumbent operator and at a reasonable price. Figure 6.3 contains an essential facilities test for a port facility (see OECD, 2011).

6.2.5 *Regulation to reduce the risks of financial distress of the SO-PDC*

The risk of bankruptcy of the SO-PDC can have major consequences for the port and the economy at large (recall the opening chapter with the economic effect of a port being closed for a period of one to two weeks).[21]

Bankruptcy of a PDC – the case of Frederikshavn (Denmark)

In May 2024, Frederikshavn Harbor an independent municipally owned company in North Jutland, Denmark, was placed under municipal control, after it became clear that it could no longer make repayments on its debt of close to 1.7 billion Danish kroner (around 230 million euro). This debt led obligations of around 35 million Danish kroner per year, while the total turnover of the port was no more than around 85 million kroner. The large debt arose because of a major expansion of Frederikshavn Harbor, which turned out to be riskier than anticipated. Because the port company was owned by the municipality, the transition was relatively smooth, and it was made clear from the outset that the harbor is not closing and continues to operate as a business. The debt has been transferred to the municipality and ultimately to the taxpayers. The municipality has not received a financial contribution from the state. The city council unanimously voted in favor of retaining control of the port. The board in place before the bankruptcy consisted of seven members, of which two town councilors and one employee representative.

While in the Frederikshavn case, investments in expansion without return caused bankruptcy, external disruptions may also cause problems. In the case of Eilat Port, ship traffic at the port has completely stopped in 2024 after the Houthi attacks began. The port's primary import was cars from the Far East, the prime export was millions of tons of potash to India and China. This flow was rerouted through the Mediterranean Sea and via the Cape of Good Hope – with significantly higher costs. The port has continued to pay wages and other expenses, but without income but is in financial distress, which increases uncertainty.

The most straightforward regulation to secure continuity of the port developer (whether public or private) is a requirement for a minimum risk rating (by risk rating agencies such as Moody's). Alternatively, the introduction of borrowing limits is an option.[22] Both principles have been introduced in Canada. A similar approach has been taken in the Netherlands, where the SAO-PDC (like all state-owned companies) need to meet strict financial ratios. Thus, regulation is an effective method to secure this public interest.

6.2.6 *Regulations to secure nautical safety*

Accidents have "negative externalities": stakeholders that have not caused the accident are negatively impacted and do not (automatically) receive compensation. For instance, accidents can cause substantial environmental damage and/or delays in shipments. These negative externalities explain the existence of international agreements between governments to regulate quality standards for seagoing vessels as well as crews. In ports, *safe maneuvering* is a public interest. In ports, vessel traffic management is needed to prevent accidents. Furthermore, the complex navigating environment in ports often requires the use of specialized pilots that assist the captain when entering the port, as well as regulations concerning the use of towage services.

Regulation to secure nautical safety is prevalent internationally. Such regulation generally addresses two issues: the competent nautical safety authority and the use of pilots. A competent nautical safety authority (harbor master) is accountable for safe maneuvering in the port. In some countries (such as Australia and New Zealand), a public harbor master operates independently from the PDC; in other countries (Belgium, the Netherlands, Germany), this function is integrated into the SO-PDC, so that it also acts as harbor master. In the UK, a private port acts as harbor master. All these arrangements work well in terms of securing nautical safety. Thus, a clear regulatory framework can ensure this public interest regardless of the ownership and governance structure of the competent nautical safety authority.

All ports/countries also regulate the conditions under which pilotage services are mandatory. In some ports/countries, pilotage services are provided by private companies, while in other cases these services are provided by a government-owned organization. The key regulatory challenge is to secure nautical safety while minimizing pilotage costs for port users. That requires an open eye for technological improvements that reduce the need for or costs of pilotage. Ships have much better maneuvering capabilities than a decade ago, while information on drafts nowadays is more reliable and readily available. Thus, pilotage requirements may be lowered, and productivity of pilotage processes may be improved.

Pilotage is often (if not always) a monopoly. This means that *economic regulation* should apply to the pilots, whether public or private. In the absence of such regulation, pilots will abuse their dominant market position. In many countries, the wage levels of pilots are hotly debated (for instance, in Brazil, where pilotage is an unregulated monopoly, and on the US West Coast, where pilots reportedly earn a yearly salary of US$250,000 to US$500,000).[23] A widely used regulatory approach is to make the pilotage tariff increase subject to approval by an economic regulator.

6.2.7 Regulation for environmental protection in ports

The activities in ports (potentially) have negative effects on the environment. Some important harmful effects are:

- Noise effects of port activities for nearby residents.
- A detrimental effect of port activities on the air quality in the port area.
- Carbon emissions of port activities.
- Waste generation and waste dumping in ports and by ships at sea.
- Destruction or damage to valuable environmental resources through port development.

These negative environmental effects are "external effects" in the sense that (private) port companies do not automatically take these effects into account in their decision-making. Therefore, as with economic activities in general, environmental regulation is required to ensure sufficient protection of the environment. Some environmental effects, especially carbon emissions and regulation to prevent the dumping of waste at sea, require regulation by international bodies such as the IMO. For others, environmental regulation is a local issue. The tightness of environmental regulation is a political decision. Harmonized regulation would be ideal, as it secures a level playing field. However, regulation also needs to be responsive to concerns of local stakeholders.

Table 6.4 The regulatory framework for the ports industry

Public interest	*Regulations of international bodies and agencies (including the EU).*	*Regulations of national/regional governments.*
Nautical safety	International safety standards (among others: ship safety, crew requirements).	Clear legal framework for responsibilities and requirements of harbor master and pilots.
Environmental protection	International environmental standards (among others: carbon emissions, waste reception, protection of ecological assets).	Environmental regulation regarding noise, stench, air quality.
Sufficient competition	Legal framework with competition law applicable to the ports industry.	Competition law applicable to the ports industry, active monitoring of port pricing when required (i.e., when market power is likely – countries where ports have captive hinterlands).
Market access	Legal framework to ensure non-discriminatory granting of concessions and entry to essential facilities.	Legal framework to ensure non-discriminatory granting of concessions and entry to essential facilities.
Level playing field	Legal framework that prohibits state aid to port infrastructure, suprastructure and operations.	Legal framework that prohibits local subsidies to port infrastructure, suprastructure and operations.
Port development options	Planning regulations concerning the protection of valuable ecological assets.	Planning regulations that enable business case-driven port development initiatives. Conditions in the land lease to commercially operating landlord.
Continuity of port operations	–	Regulation that limits risk profile of port authority.
Training, education and innovation	–	No port-specific regulation required; general regulation to promote/enforce investments in education.

Source: Adapted from de Langen and van der Lugt (2017).

6.2.8 *The appropriate regulatory framework for the ports industry*

Based on the discussion in the previous paragraphs, Table 6.4 summarizes the appropriate regulatory framework for the ports industry. Such a regulatory framework enables the development of a commercially focused ports industry. This framework can be applied to all countries.[24]

6.3 Financing investments in port development

The investment needs in ports are huge, both in emerging and advanced economies, in part driven by the implications of the energy and sustainability transition for ports. Table 6.5 shows some important types of investments.

Table 6.5 Examples of investments in the PBE

Investments for the Port as Transport Node	*Investments for the Port as an Energy Hub*
• New sites for terminals • Terminal equipment and superstructure like warehouses • Landside port infrastructure (in the port area)[25] • Onshore power supply and electricity infrastructure	• Land for ports industries, such as fuel production • Production of electricity (e.g., solar, wind) and fuels • Pipelines for fuels, steam, CO_2 or heat

The availability of financial resources for investments in ports is critical for port development. As argued previously, a substantial part of funding sources is non-commercial, as a part of the value creation is partly "value for society". However, the rationale for public funding inevitably leads to concerns about the playing field.

6.3.1 An equal playing field for competition between ports and port companies

Port competition is healthy when this competition takes place on a *level playing field.* This is the case when firms/ports compete on the same basis, in the sense that differences in government funding or regulations do not distort the competition.[26] As port infrastructure is not a public good (see the textbox below), it is sensible to apply the "*user pays principle*". Limits to public funding for port infrastructure are the key to realizing a level playing field.

A seaport contributes to the overall attractiveness of a region or country. Thus, regional and national governments consider ports as strategic assets and develop policies to enhance the competitiveness of their ports. Governments often provide public funding or other support mechanisms for port development. However, public funding inevitably leads to a distorted playing field, where some ports receive more public support than others. This can have negative economic consequences; heavily supported ports attract cargo at the expense of ports that receive less support. "Policy competition" between countries occurs when neighboring countries aim to advance the development of their economy through large-scale public funding for ports. Such policy competition leads to an inefficient allocation of resources.

Regions with policy competition between ports

Policy competition between countries through large scale public funding for ports is especially prevalent in regions with relatively small countries competing for the same traffic. This is for instance the case in the Middle East, where virtually all countries (Dubai, Abu Dhabi, Qatar, Oman, Saudi Arabia) pour substantial public funding in port development, leading to overcapacity and unhealthy competition. According to media reports, this even led to subsidies for shipping lines that were willing to bring containers to Middle East ports. Other regions with policy competition through port development include the Mediterranean, where North African countries invest massively, as especially in the case of Morocco successfully, to gain a larger share of transhipment business, West-Africa with various large scale investments were made, in some cases hand-in-hand with tax breaks for port operators, South East Asia and the Caribbean, where countries aim to develop as shipping hubs.

In Europe, ports are one of the few industries where distortions of the playing field between member states persist. The public interest of an equal playing field is also relevant *within countries*, especially large federal countries like the US and Brazil. Regional governments are often deeply involved in port development as an instrument for regional economic development. This involvement also potentially distorts the playing field.

The implementation of the user pays approach is straightforward on paper: the PDC should be self-sustaining, with separate and transparent financial accounts and without (implicit) subsidies. In practice, differences in financing and regulation can and do continue to distort the playing field. Some important issues include:

- Funding of port development. In some countries, large-scale public funding is available, in other countries not.
- Taxes. In some countries, the SO-PDC pays corporate tax, while in other countries, it is considered part of the public administration and thus exempted from such a tax. Such a tax exemption is an implicit subsidy.
- Dividend payments. In some countries (Ireland, New Zealand, the Netherlands, Australia), the SO-PDC pays dividends to their public shareholders, but in other countries (Belgium, Spain, Portugal) not. Not paying dividends can be justified in fast-growing ports, but as a principle, unless the government receives a dividend at some point, it is implicitly subsidizing the SO-PDC by providing equity without financial return.
- Fees for the provision of public services. In some ports, the SO-PDC receives a fee for providing public services, such as operating locks (Belgium) and environmental monitoring. In other countries (Spain), this is not the case. Differences in such arrangements are also distortions to the playing field.
- Pensions. In some countries, pensions of the staff of the SO-PDC are financed not by the SO-PDC but by the state (as the SO-PDC is a state entity). This is an implicit subsidy.

Distortions from the level playing field: an issue of serious money!

The most important distortions from the level playing field arise because of subsidies to port access channels, port infrastructure, port suprastructure, port services (e.g., navigational aid provided free of charge) and port labor (through subsidies on port labor, mainly through partial unemployment schemes such as in Belgium). It is relevant to understand how these subsidies affect an economy at large: they lead to "subsidized" imports and exports, because these flows do not bear the real costs of the use of seaports. Subsidized exports are a clear income transfer from taxpayers to foreign companies and consumers. The subsidized imports may make imports cheaper for consumers but also reduce the competitiveness of domestic producers.

Thus, while subsidizing ports to promote economic development may seem a good idea on for small countries of regions, from a national or supranational perspective they do not make sense. Efficient ports are important for an integrated global economy, but in general that does *not* require subsidies.

As a rough indication of the order of magnitude of these subsidies, the average overall costs per ton handled in a port are roughly somewhere in the range of €5–€15. Assuming cautiously that in Europe, on average 20% of costs are not passed on to port users, annual implicit subsidies in Europe for imports and exports (often accumulated through past investments that are not recovered) are in the order of magnitude of €5–€15 billion!

A regulatory complication: "from now on"

Legislation that bans public funding to port infrastructure "from now on" would place "incumbent ports" that received substantial public funding for past port development projects at an unfair advantage *vis-à-vis* new ports. Thus, the best way forward would be a nationwide (in the case of Europe, a European-wide) independent audit of the value of port infrastructure. This audit would be used to determine the asset value, and the owner of this infrastructure would be forced by law to pass on the associated costs (depreciation, maintenance) to the port users. While conceptually, this is the best approach to ensure that the "user pays principle" is applied, such a policy has not been implemented anywhere, precisely because countries are keen to continue to support their ports.

Intra-port competition and the level playing field

The playing field within the port is a delicate issue for regulators and PMBs. Competing firms operating in the same port generally demand an equal treatment. That also is in the interest of port users and the PMB. However, it often is hard or even impossible to achieve. As concessions are conceded at different moments in time, in different market environments and with different types of terminal operators (e.g., shipping lines that want dedicated terminals vs independent terminal operators), it is close to impossible to always have the same conditions (especially lease/concession fees) for the different operators. In various cases this has led to court cases against the PMB. One case involved the terminal operator Ceres, which complained about being discriminated against. The Federal Maritime Commission ruled in 1997 that the Maryland Port Administration indeed violated the Shipping Act by discriminating against Ceres. This led to other court cases of operators, most of these cases were settled with good terms for the operators. The regulation and the court ruling gave the operators leverage in re-negotiating with the PMB.

The case of *Maher vs the Port Authority of New York & New Jersey* (PANYNJ) is another important example. Maher claims that PANYNJ gave preferential treatment to a rival terminal, operated by APMT. The rental differences are indeed substantial, with Maher paying around $10 per m2 compared to about $5 for APMT. PANYNJ decided to sign a deal with APMT to ensure that Maersk would continue to use the port instead of shifting volumes to the competing port of Baltimore. PANYNJ argues that the difference is (at least partly) justified because the Maersk/APMT deal guarantees traffic for the port, something Maher does not guarantee. The case was settled in 2016, without significant compensation to Maher, as the owner sold the terminal to a new investor – and PANYNJ had to approve the sale.

While PMBs clearly need some freedom in striking deals with customers, even if such a deal differs from existing agreements, discrimination and unfair treatment of specific third parties needs to be prevented. In my view, regulation in which the PMB carries the burden of demonstrating a clear rationale for different contracts with different customers is appropriate. An explicit effort to introduce intra-port competition, as well as adapting to changed market environments, would qualify as justifications for treating different companies differently.

6.3.2 Financing investments in port infrastructure; combining a level playing field with partial public funding

Even though the differences between financing of port development as discussed above impact the playing field, there is a trend toward more autonomy and financial self-sufficiency of the PMB (whether a PA, a SO-PDC or a PO-PDC). The core concern for an equal playing field is the widespread use of public funding for port infrastructure.

Such public funding is justified for investments that create value for society. Port investments generally create value for users. Three types of users can be identified: shipping lines that use the port and pay port dues, terminal operating companies and other service providers that occupy land in the port area and pay lease/concession charges, and finally import–export companies that use transport service providers for their trade flows. The last of these generally pay indirectly for the use of port infrastructure (i.e., they pay the shipping line, the terminal operator or both). Thus, the PMB captures part of the value it creates.[27]

Why port infrastructure is not a public good

A public good is a good that is both non-excludable and non-rivalrous: individuals cannot be effectively excluded from use, and use by one individual does not reduce availability to others. Examples of public goods include fresh air, knowledge, lighthouses and national defence. Public goods cannot be effectively provided by the market. Thus, public investments in port infrastructure would be justified if port infrastructure were a public good. However, users can be excluded from the use of port infrastructure, and the use is rivalrous as the capacity of port infrastructure is constrained. Thus, the "user pays principle" can be applied to port infrastructure, and subsidies to port infrastructure are not in the public interest.

This conclusion is controversial, as many countries heavily subsidize port infrastructure (and in some cases also port operations). These subsidies are often justified with (local) economic impact of ports. However, there is increasing recognition that these arguments are not valid from a national or supra-national perspective. In Europe, the European Commission has expressed its ambition to apply the "user pays principle" to the ports industry.

This broad conclusion may be increasingly agreed upon, yet specific discussions on what exactly qualifies as port infrastructure are still unanswered. While we do not go into detail into these issues, the overarching rationale is to also apply the "user pays principle" to maritime access to a port (e.g., dredging costs), mitigation of environmental effects of port activity, and the use of locks and canals. However, in many countries that is at odds with existing practices and regulations.

In addition, investments in port infrastructure also create societal value, through benefits for society at large. The societal value creation is based on externalities, i.e., effects of the investments that reach beyond the users. The most prevalent forms of societal value creation through port investments are the following:[28]

- Improved maritime and hinterland connectivity, resulting in enhanced trade flows. A share of the benefits of enhanced trade, notably a stronger export competitiveness and positive effects for the economies in the port hinterland, can be considered as value for society.
- Local and regional economic development and associated employment creation,[29] especially in regions with a weaker economic basis (e.g., peripheral regions).
- Reduced road congestion. Making shortsea shipping more competitive and promoting modal shift reduces the costs for society generated by traffic congestion (such as increased travel times, unreliability, increased energy consumption and emissions).

- Reduced negative externalities for residents around the port and improved the attractiveness of public spaces in the port area (e.g., green zones). For instance, investments facilitating the use of clean fuels in ports, such as in cold ironing, lead to a better air quality.
- Reduced CO_2 emissions. The reduction of CO_2 emissions in the port industrial cluster[30] and beyond the port area contributes to the decarbonization of the economy and climate change mitigation. This form of value creation is especially relevant following the Paris Agreement to reduce CO_2 emissions.
- The transformation of port land for urban purposes. Urban waterfront development (including housing) is often enabled by the transfer of port facilities to locations elsewhere. Thus, investments in port infrastructure that enable a shift of port activities away from the city center create value for society.
- Increased safety and security, including flood protection and more resilience of coastal zones against extreme weather conditions caused by climate change. Locks, for instance, may protect the area behind them against flooding. Likewise, investments in ICT infrastructure may increase security due to better data and real-time availability.
- Innovation. Ports are active in all phases of innovation, from Research & Development (R&D) to testing and scaling-up, which have positive external effects for society.

Table 6.6 shows the potential value creation of various types of port infrastructures.

Viable port infrastructure investments from a societal perspective produce a high value (for users and/or society at large) relative to their costs. However, not all viable investments generate the necessary financial return on investment to make them financially feasible for the PDC. The core reason is the fact that the societal value creation (which is often substantial) cannot be (fully) captured through user charges.

Conceptually, a distinction can be made between the "business case" of an investment in port infrastructure for the PDC and the "value case" of the investment for society at large. The business case only includes the value that is captured by the PDC through charges and lease fees, while the "value case" also includes the value creation and the costs for society, which include its positive and negative externalities (see Figure 6.4). Examples of value for society of port investments, on top of the ones mentioned in Table 6.6, include a more resilient overall freight transport system as well as a contribution to military logistics capabilities.

Public funding is legitimate for "type 2" projects, which have a positive value case, but a negative business case. There may also be a case for public involvement and even funding for "type 4 projects". The combination of considerable development costs, lengthy and uncertain approval processes and high risks (risks associated with stakeholder acceptance of port development, political risks associated with uncertain political support and infrastructure policies and commercial risks because of long pay-back period and associated uncertainty) may lead to a low private investor "appetite" in port projects, even in those with a positive financial business case.

Table 6.6 Value creation of investment in selected types of port infrastructure

Type of port infrastructure	*Potential economic value creation*[31]	*Potential societal value creation*
Maritime access	Reduced shipping costs per ton in case of improved maritime access.	Increased trade as a result of reduced import/export costs; increased safety (and possibly flood protection).
Reduced environmental footprint if investments enable the deployment of larger ships and/or a shift of cargo flows to the port closest to the cargo destination.		
Basic port infrastructure	Reduced costs for port users (shipping lines, tenants and shippers).	Reduced environmental footprint if investments enable a shift of cargo flows to the port closest to the cargo destination.
Energy-related infrastructure	Value for port users through lower production costs.	Reduced emissions. Increased energy efficiency and energy independence.
Road transport connection	Lower generalized transport costs.	Increased trade, reduced emissions (e.g., due to reduced congestion) or local pollution (through removing traffic from urban areas).
Inland waterway and rail infrastructure	Lower generalized transport costs.	Increase in trade due to the extension of the hinterland; reduction of the carbon footprint and road congestion.
ICT/digital infrastructure	Lower generalized transport costs.	Reduction of emissions (due to better utilization of assets such as trucks).
Infrastructure for reducing environmental footprint	No direct economic value creation for port users, unless infrastructure reduces the costs of users to meet their environmental requirements (SECA, LNG, etc.).	Reduced (local) pollution and CO_2 emissions.
Sites for logistics and manufacturing activities	Value for (future) port tenants that benefit from a location in a port ecosystem.	Support regional development through facilitation of investments in manufacturing and logistics.

Source: Adapted from de Langen et al. (2018).

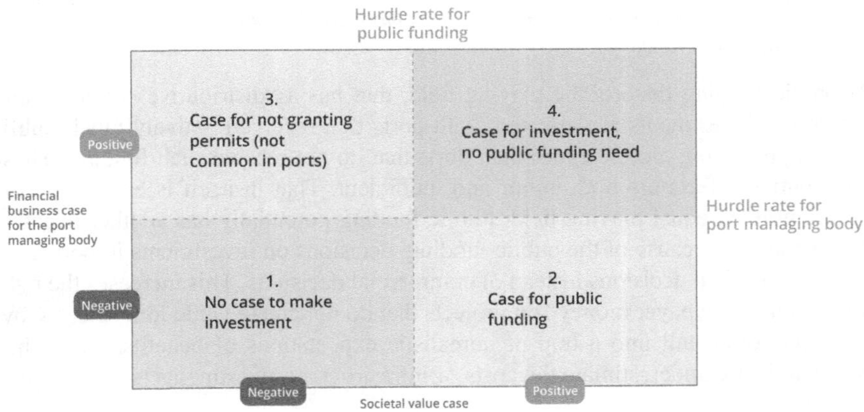

Figure 6.4 A framework for public funding for port investment projects

Source: Adapted from de Langen et al. (2018).

Each PMB will have specific minimum financial return requirements for investment projects. In line with their societal goals, SO-PDCs are likely to have lower "hurdle rates" (i.e., minimum rate-of-return requirements) than PO-PDCs. For the "type 2 investments", financing would be problematic for all PDCs as the business case is negative. Thus, public funding for such projects is legitimate.

However, public funding, especially for projects that predominantly create value for users, distorts the playing field, unless the allocation of grants to port investments is done in a competitive process in which all competing ports can participate. While large countries can develop such a policy nationally, in other cases, such as Western Europe, the Malacca Strait and the Gulf region, it would require supra-national policy coordination.

Marginal cost pricing

Port infrastructure is characterized by substantial fixed costs and economies of scale. Thus, marginal costs are rather low and "simple" marginal cost pricing does not lead to full cost recovery. Instead, long-run marginal cost pricing is required. The long-run marginal costs can be split into two elements:

1. marginal operating costs (MOC), which in the case of infrastructure mainly consist of maintenance costs;
2. marginal capacity costs (MCC). These would have to include the costs of future investments to cater for the expected future demand. Thus, these costs are related to future expansion needs.

These elements taken together form the total long-run marginal costs. In this approach, ports that have received huge past subsidies would at least have to charge port users for maintenance and future expansion needs. Even though there are no standards to calculate the long-run marginal costs, the approach is increasingly accepted.

6.3.3 Public funding: not distributive effects but wasted public money as key concern

If public funding distorts the playing field, that has a "distributive" effect: cargo flows and investments are affected, with ports that receive relatively much public funding receiving more cargoes than ports that do not receive such funding. These distributive effects are both unfair and inefficient. That in itself is enough reason to promote an equal playing field. Public funding potentially has another negative consequence: because of the public funding, decisions on investments in ports may become political decisions instead of commercial decisions. This increases the risks of spending "taxpayer money" on projects that do not create value for society. Governments often fall into a trap of unrealistic expectations of benefits, while they systematically underestimate the costs of infrastructure investments (see Flyvbjerg, 2007).

Thus, government spending on port infrastructure involves risks, because governments do not have the incentives nor the capabilities to assess the market potential of development projects and select the most attractive options from a user perspective. Governments may, for instance, intend to use port development as a tool to encourage growth in underdeveloped regions, even though success is unlikely. Given the politics involved in government decisions, it is no surprise that governments have invested in port development projects that, in hindsight, were not justified.

Some examples of inefficient use of public funding

Gwangyang Port (Korea)

The Korean government decided to develop a two-hub strategy and a major investment in a second large container port (next to Pusan). Gwangyang was selected based on geography: Gwangyang is closer to major trading partners. Furthermore, due to the closer proximity to Seoul, shifting some cargo to/from the greater Seoul area from Busan to Gwangyang was argued to reduce transport costs. However, the immediate hinterland of Gwangyang did not evolve as planned: in 2011, Gwangyang handled 2 million TEU instead of the foreseen 5 million. In 2017, the port handled no more than 2.2 million TEU. Even though Gwangyang does attract investments, the huge public funding of terminals was not creating value for society.

Eemshaven (Netherlands)

The Dutch government decided in the 1960s to develop port infrastructure in the north of the country, because port development would contribute to the economic development of the region as a whole. Thus, a port complex of 2600 hectares, roughly half of which would be port land, was developed. More than 35 years after the development, roughly 500 hectares are still not utilized. After it was realized that providing land was not enough to promote development, huge amounts of public funding were invested in a fruit terminal. This project also failed, and 14 years after completion, the terminal was dismantled. Eemshaven currently develops into an energy valley, but the initial public investments (land, quays and terminal facilities) were wasted.

Burgas (Bulgaria)

Public funding as well as a loan from the Japan Bank for International Cooperation were used to invest in a huge terminal mainly aimed to serve a steel mill about 400 km inland. However, the mill went bankrupt and the terminal had limited alternative uses. The terminal is now re-developed by the former state-owned shipping company Navibulgar. However, as in the other cases, public funding went awry.

These three examples are enough to illustrate the argument; other examples abound. A report of the European Court of Auditors concluded that in the majority of cases analyzed, the EU public funding was not well spent. Overall, the past experience is that public port development decisions are very likely to lead to a misallocation of resources.

The conclusion drawn above is that the risk of wasting public funding on investments in port infrastructure is huge. This implies that mechanisms to reduce this risk are needed. The following mechanisms (which may not be applicable in all cases) can be considered:

- Competitive funding schemes that are open for all competing ports. A supranational (or, in the case of the US and Australia, federal) set of funding instruments with a considerable budget is preferable to a variety of national/state-wide arrangements for funding investments in port infrastructure. This is because national/state-wide funding inevitably introduces an element of "policy competition" between countries/states aiming to increase the competitiveness of their ports. This is likely to lead to more state funding than needed, with a serious risk of overcapacity. In a competitive funding scheme, a key requirement is a uniform approach to assess competing grant requests, *with cost–benefit analysis according to established standards*.
- Next, a regulation that places a limit on the government's share of total funding is appropriate. Such a limit may differ between different types of port infrastructure (for instance, it could be higher for maritime access than for basic port infrastructure). Such regulation forces a business case approach to investments, even if part of the funding is public.

- Similarly, providing a funding mix in which loans are an important component has the same effect. This is because loans lead to financial scrutiny of the project by lenders (i.e., commercial or development banks) and place the risks with the PMB, reducing the risk of excessively optimistic assumptions in the business case.
- Splitting an investment project into various phases, potentially with loan commitments that are conditional on the achievement of demand-related performance criteria.
- Finally, and perhaps most importantly, a phased decision-making process is relevant. In such an approach, planning processes can be finalized so that a project is ready to be launched. This final investment decision can be tied to trustworthy information that corroborates the demand for the infrastructure, for instance, a contract with a "launching customer" that is willing to pay for the use of newly developed infrastructure.

EU's state aid regulation – clear principles and permissive practices

The EU regulation on public financing of investments in ports was concluded in 2017 with the regulation (EU) 2017/352. That regulation establishes a framework in which PMBs carry out both economic activities and non-economic activities (i.e., maritime traffic control or anti-pollution surveillance) that fall outside the scope of EU State aid control. For the economic activities, financial transparency is required and profits from these economic activities should be taxed by national governments, as is done with corporations in general. In addition, The EU regulation, more specifically the block exemption, allows Member States to invest in port development, for example to achieve EU transport objectives or to put in place necessary infrastructure investments which would not have been possible without public aid. Under the block exemption, Member States can invest up to €150 million in seaports and up to €50 million in inland ports with full legal certainty and without prior state aid assessment by the Commission.

6.3.4 Investment drivers and funding aspirations of EU ports

In this section, I present some data on investment needs of EU ports, which serve to demonstrate the relevance of getting funding policies right. Based on a survey in Europe with a good response rate (de Langen, 2025), Table 6.7 provides some insights regarding the investment drivers for the investments of PMBs in Europe, in 2018 and 2024.

Table 6.7 shows an important shift in what drives the investments of PMBs: while in 2018 the expected growth of volumes was by far the most important driver, in 2024, the "green transition" was almost equally important. This has led to shifts in the investment pipeline in 2024 compared to 2018 (see Table 6.8).

Table 6.7 Investment drivers in 2018 and 2024

Investment driver	**2018**	**2024**
Expected growth of trade flows and the resulting growth of volumes handled by ports	74%	52%
Increasing size of vessels (mega vessels as well as "cascading effect" leading to larger vessels in other trades)	34%	22%
Protection of the environment and ecological assets (e.g., biodiversity protection, nature restoration)	25%	17%
Decarbonization of the economy and the associated transition to zero-carbon energy sources	23%	48%
Societal pressure and policies to shift hinterland cargo away from road transport (Transport policy)	21%	15%
Expected growth of cruise/ferry passenger volumes	14%	11%
Increasing pressure on the use of port land close to city centers into pure urban functions	8%	9%
Increased digitalization digitalization of transport chains	7%	6%

Source: Based on ESPO (2018, 2024).

Table 6.8 The distribution of investment projects by investment category

Investment category	*Number of projects 2018*	*Number of projects 2024*
Expansion of port basins, quays, or terminals	148	123
Infra/services for the sustainability and energy transition of ports and shipping	32	118
Maritime access	33	45
Infra. for smooth transport flows in the port	32	39
Equipment and superstructure	29	32
Intermodal/multimodal terminals	19	19
ICT/digital infrastructure	14	19
Rail transport connections	27	18

Source: Based on ESPO (2018, 2024).

Table 6.8 shows that the major shift of investment projects is toward projects aimed at accommodating and advancing the transition toward sustainable energy and materials. Whereas the share of such projects was below 10% in 2018, it stood at 25% in 2024. Table 6.9 shows the most relevant bottleneck for investments.

Table 6.9 clearly highlights the importance of funding as a bottleneck for investment projects. An additional important bottleneck of a financial nature is the increase in costs of an investment due to inflation, and specifically higher material costs.

Table 6.10 shows for the seven investment categories with the highest number of investment projects, the value creation according to the PMB. Three types of value creation are distinguished: value for users, value for society through CO_2 emission reductions (i.e., at a global scale), and value for residents surrounding the port, for instance, through lower noise and stench levels.

Table 6.10 shows that not only do the "sustainability projects" contribute to decarbonization. The vast majority of all investment projects of the PMBs contribute

Table 6.9 The most relevant bottleneck for investments of EU PMBs; 2024

Bottleneck	*% of all projects*
Inability to secure funding for the investment project	45%
Increases in costs because of inflation and material costs	43%
Lengthy and complex permitting procedures	34%
Insufficient financing instruments to close the funding gap	31%
Complexity of agreement among all project partners	27%
Legal hurdles stemming from environmental regulations	12%
Insufficient societal support	4%

Source: Based on ESPO (2024).

Table 6.10 The distribution of investment projects over the seven largest categories

Investment type	*total projects*	*Value for users*	*Value through CO_2 emission reductions*	*value for residents (reduced nuisance)*
Expansion of port basins, quays, and terminal sites, including pavement of terminal sites.	108	99%	96%	25%
Infrastructure and facilities for reducing the environmental footprint of shipping.	50	92%	88%	82%
Infrastructure and services related to the energy transition of the economy.	45	93%	91%	38%
Maritime access (dredging, sea locks, breakwaters).	44	89%	89%	16%
Infrastructure for smooth transport flows within the port.	38	97%	97%	45%
ICT/digital infrastructure for efficient and safe port and hinterland operations.	19	100%	95%	26%
Intermodal/multimodal terminals in the port area and/or dry ports outside the port area.	17	94%	94%	53%

to decarbonization, in different ways, often through enabling more efficient maritime logistics (through better information exchange, larger vessels, more intermodality or reduced ship congestion). Overall, the creation of external "value for society" is common for investments of PMBs and reiterates the rationale for public funding – in case cost-benefit analysis shows that such projects are "type 2 projects" with a positive "value case" but a negative business case.

6.4 Port policy reform

Developing adequate port policies is a complicated challenge in many countries. New developments, such as increasing vertical integration of shipping and terminal operations, the energy transition, and a changing security environment, call for new port policies. While all countries face specific port policy challenges, many countries can improve with regard to the following three issues.

1. An integrated approach to promote port development in line with national policy goals in energy, industrial development and trade facilitation. For instance, ports often can be magnets for attracting FDI in the energy and manufacturing industries. But allowing ports to grow into large-scale economic complexes requires an integrated approach that cannot be developed by the Ministry of Transport alone.
2. A "port development-friendly" planning framework that incorporates environmental and residential interests, but does not give PMBs sufficient port expansion options, for instance, by making spatial reservations that constrain alternative development of logical sites for future port expansion.
3. The establishment of a clear policy framework regarding public funding (local, regional and national) for port infrastructure, suprastructure and operations. In such a framework, some public funding of port infrastructure should be possible, but clear limitations that prevent distortions of the playing field or excessive funding are called for. Investments in port development should primarily be market-driven and be financed to a large extent through future revenues of the PMB.
4. Improved economic regulation, potentially through the creation of a "ports regulator", which monitors competition and market access in the ports industry. Economic regulation should create legal certainty for private investors while protecting port users.

Lessons learned from China's port policies.

China has grown rapidly in the past decades and port development mostly was a growth driver rather than a constraint. That is remarkable in itself; as the ports had to accommodate annual growth rates of well over 10% for decades, leading to the current situation in which China's ports top the world rankings and world's two largest ports (Ningbo Zhoushan and Shanghai), both located in the Pearl River Delta, together account for around 8% of the volume handled worldwide. Important lessons learned from China's experience include (see Aritua et al., 2022, for more details):

1. Integrated economic development. The development of ports to support export-led economic growth occurred in tandem with the formation of special economic zones (SEZs). The foreign direct investment attracted by the SEZs boosted demand for cargo handling and resulted in a high rate of utilization of newly developed terminals. Predictable and strong demand growth facilitated the transition to a more commercial approach to port development.

2. Regionalization of state-owned port companies. Before 1978, China's port sector was very centralized, the Ministry of Transport owned the ports. Local government had no control and all revenues from port operations accrued to the central government. Stepwise port reform led to the emergence of decentralized port companies operating on a commercial basis. Later, state owned port companies in the same province were merged into one regional entity.
3. Strong public funding to develop corridors linking ports with hinterlands. China's experience shows that long-term competitiveness depends on good multimodal connectivity with the hinterlands. After the early stage in which cargo originated fromm nearby SEZs, intermodal connectivity became vital, in part because of financial incentives for locating manufacturing activities inland.
4. Relocation of port facilities in urban areas. Many of China's major ports have moved to new locations. In some cases, the new port areas were partly funded by redevelopment of the original city-center location for higher-value commercial and residential uses. Relocating port activities to areas with plenty of room for port, logistics, and manufacturing activities facilitated city-center regeneration.
5. Investment in human capital and innovation. Both were identified as drivers of productivity and efficiency. The need to develop advanced commercial capabilities and a performance culture required human capital and innovation, which government policies strongly promoted.

6.5 Good practices in developing port policies

In summary, the good practices listed below have helped ports in the countries involved in becoming attractive, diverse and competitive business ecosystems that create value for society.

Policy objectives

1. Develop a fact-based understanding of how ports create value for society
2. Identify ports of national interest as well as strategic freight corridors
3. Set clear, measurable long-term policy objectives for ports that align with stakeholders' objectives

Planning

1. Promote complementarity, specialization and cooperation of the ports
2. Make spatial reservations for future port development
3. Make sure that the planning framework allows for smooth adaptation of port development to changing environments

Regulation and markets

1. Promote intra- and inter-port competition
2. Develop regulation that encourages investments in port development as well as private investments in the PBE.
3. Create aligned regulation across geographical scales
4. Prevent dependence on activities of foreign SOEs in ports
5. In case of recurring regulatory dilemmas, establish an independent ports regulator or task a national economic regulator with proactive monitoring of the ports industry.
6. Acknowledge the presence of large vertically integrated players, monitor for abuse of dominant positions.

Funding instruments

1. Allow for public funding for port development based on fact-based impact assessment.
2. Develop competitive public funding schemes to maintain an equal playing field.
3. Align public funding instruments and regulatory measures.
4. Use public funding, especially in the early development stage of a port or port service.
5. Provide non-commercial loans (potentially through international development banks), especially for large capital projects with demand risks.
6. Take administrative burden and need for flexibility into account in designing public funding mechanisms.

Notes

1 Regional or national governments may be willing to partially fund such compensation measures, but this increases uncertainty and may complicate decision-making procedures.

2 In some ports the government owned port authority has a substantial revenue stream from the development of urban functions. In Spain, the port of Barcelona has developed hotels and a conference center, while in India MbPT (the former Bombay Port Trust) is one of the largest public land holders in Mumbai (and the owner of the Taj Mahal) and has recently announced a large scale urban development of about 500 hectares for a mix of port operations, businesses, offices, commercial, retail, entertainment, and convention centers.

3 See Pellegram (2001) and Frantzeskaki et al. (2014) for cases.

4 Note that port authorities may also engage in non-economic activities, such as firefighting and vessel traffic management. However, these are not the core activities of port authorities.

5 A more detailed discussion of the effects of intra-port competition is provided in the reader on port development.

6 This explains why large shippers in captive hinterlands frequently invest in user-owned port facilities. This issue is discussed later.

7 "Substantial" can be defined further as "so large that the loss of volume (volume effect) offsets the additional revenues from the price increase".

8 A fictitious example where it is not the case is a steel producer that owns the only steel terminal on an island. This means this company can charge monopoly prices to handle import flows of steel. As argued in Chapter 3, *essential facility regulation* is required to secure access to port facilities or services for port users with only a small volume of cargo.

9 As in the previous report, some data interpretation choices are inevitable. Only deep-sea terminals specialized in container handling are included, and minority shares of shipping lines in a specific (part of a) terminal are not treated as a separate terminal operator.

10 In Australia, price regulation was in hindsight too strict. Competition agencies did not agree on the price increase proposed by a private operator to recover investments. The operator then declined to invest, with adverse effects on the supply chain.

11 Both competition law and market access regulation may influence labor relations amongst port service providers. A lack of intra-port competition, especially when combined with entry barriers, may provide labor unions with a strong bargaining position. Port workers may end up receiving a substantial share of the "economic rents". That is not in the interest of port users.

12 The rapid emerge of new internationally active terminal and logistics companies (like QTerminals from Qatar and ASYAD from Oman) seem to confirm this.

13 In the cases of Santos and JNPT, excluded incumbents indeed filed court cases.

14 The relevant question in my opinion is whether a *foreign country* has leverage, not a foreign company. It may well be that if the state decides to deploy its leverage, this may be against the commercial interests of the SOE involved. Given the geopolitical uncertainty in my view assessing the likelihood that a foreign state would use its leverage is not advisable; it would be better to prevent leverage of foreign states *per se*.

15 In case a foreign SOE has unique capabilities or a unique "offering", countries may need to decide what carries more weight: the positive direct effects of foreign SOE investments or the negative consequences of the third nation's leverage capacities. In cases where there are private sector alternatives, it is easier to prevent leverage.

16 This includes Germany (see BMI – Protecting Critical Infrastructure) and France (see https://cyber.gouv.fr/en/french-ciip-framework). See www.transportation.gov/mission/office-secretary/office-chief-information-officer/prohibited-platforms.

17 In Europe, no such case was found, in the knowledge that incumbents were allowed to bid into large ports in which the incumbent had a large market share (Rotterdam, Valencia, Wilhelmshaven). In Morocco, all large concessions were granted without excluding incumbents and the same applies for the countries in the Middle East and North America.

18 The process of awarding a concession for the new terminal in Valparaiso is such a case. Due to the remaining lifetime of the concession of the incumbent tailor-made provisions for bids of incumbents are required and currently (August 2025) in development.

19 ANTAQ in its 2022 evaluation also applies a type of "ladder" approach, as shown by the statement "both authorities suggested less drastic solutions to the ban on the participation of certain companies, through behavioral remedies that should be included in the lease agreement and the bidding notice".

20 The effects of the bankruptcy of a firm in the port will generally be more limited. For instance, terminal operators have gone bankrupt in Buenos Aires and Port Everglades, in both cases with a limited effect on the port. In Everglades, the terminal concession was sold to the highest bidder, while in Buenos Aires cargo shifted to other terminal operators. Nevertheless, PDCs may need to address the event of bankruptcy in their concession contracts.

21 As in the banking industry, the alternative, to "bail out" port organizations on the brink of bankruptcy, is more costly and sends the wrong signals.

22 See, for instance, www.cruiseindustrynews.com/cruise-news/3301–102109-study-reveals-pilot-compensation-tops-368000.html
23 This framework is high level; implementation of such a framework requires many detailed policy choices. A fully detailed description of all policy issues is beyond the scope of this book.
24 Landside infrastructure outside the port area generally is the responsibility of national or regional government; with limited involvement of the PMB.
25 The playing field is also distorted by differences in regulation. For instance, distortions also occur with tight regulation regarding fuel use in one port and loose regulations in another port. Again, such regulatory differences lead to an inefficient allocation of resources.
26 However, this value capture mechanism is imperfect. For instance, long-term lease contracts with tenants generally imply that port managing bodies cannot increase lease fees even if they make investments that improve the competitiveness of the port. Thus, the charges to users can be regarded as the minimum of the economic value creation of these infrastructures.
27 Investments in port infrastructure may also lead to negative externalities, such as the environmental impacts due to the construction works. In general, compensation of such negative effects is required.
28 In a strict approach to societal value creation, the economic development impact and positive impact on trade may not be regarded as such, because the economic impact of the investment arises mainly through the direct benefits of port operations for users. Thus, this impact is already considered under the economic value creation for port users. However, in the case where port development is essential to boost regional development in regions with a weak economic basis (e.g., peripheral regions and cohesion countries), notably through the enhancement of industrial and tourism potential, these effects can be considered as "value for society". Various studies show the substantial effect of port efficiency on trade and development (Clark et al., 2004; Portugal-Perez & Wilson, 2012).
29 The CO_2 emissions in the port area are often a substantial part of the industry related emissions in the country as a whole. For instance, in the Netherlands, over 50% of all CO_2 emissions by industry is emitted in port areas.
30 Even when investments in port infrastructure create value for port users, capturing that value may be problematic. For instance, investments to improve maritime access create value for tenants, but given the long-term lease contracts, this value creation cannot be perfectly captured. Likewise, given the fierce competition between ports, raising port fees to capture the value created by investment projects in ports may result in loss of traffic and thus not lead to an increase in revenue.

7 Developing collective initiatives in port business ecosystems

While port governance and port policies are central to improving the ports industry, an additional important issue is the need for *cooperation* among companies in the port business ecosystem (PBE), including the port managing body (PMB). The PBE consists of *independent* as well as *interdependent* companies (such as terminal operators, logistics service providers, manufacturing companies and others), with a range of shared interests.

Investments such as a port community system, training and education facilities and port marketing are in the interest of the port community as a whole. However, *collective action* is required to achieve joint initiatives and investment of firms in the port community. Such collective action does not emerge spontaneously because of free rider problems. For this reason, investments of private for-profit companies in training, education and innovation may be lower than is in their shared interest.

Thus, enhancing cooperation in a port community is a relevant challenge in ports. Cooperation often is difficult to achieve, as it cannot be achieved based on "authority" or "coercion" and only emerges when all stakeholders in the ports industry are sufficiently *cooperation-oriented.* Cooperation is increasingly not some "nice to have" element that is widely communicated, but a secondary interest only. Instead, for many of the largest challenges ports face, cooperation both within the port business ecosystem and beyond it is needed.

7.1 Collective goods and collective action

Collective goods are goods with benefits for all (or a large group of) firms in a PBE. The benefits of collective goods "spill over" to all firms in the PBE and cannot be "internalized" by specific firms. For the provision of collective goods, the *collective action problem* is relevant: even though collective benefits of investments in collective goods exceed collective costs (i.e., there is a positive *business case*), cooperation to invest in collective goods may not develop because (the threat of) *free riding* may prevent joint investments in collective goods.[1] At least six important collective goods in ports can be identified:

- Education and training: All firms in the port complex need well-trained staff. Thus, they all benefit from investments to enhance port-related education and

DOI: 10.4324/9781003630784-7

training. In virtually all sizable ports, some sort of public/private cooperation in this field develops.

- Marketing and promotion: Port users perceive one *port product*, which consists of nautical access, terminal handling, towage, pilotage, customs clearance, hinterland transport and so on. Thus, port marketing and promotion is also partially a collective good: all ports benefit from a stronger brand of the port.
- Data exchange: A port community system (PCS) that allows for efficient data exchange between the various firms in the port can substantially improve port efficiency. Such a system works best (or works only) when a large number of firms are willing to make such a PCS successful.[2] A for-profit PCS is problematic, mainly because of the reluctance of firms to become dependent on such a PCS. Thus, a PCS is often developed in partnership and can be considered a collective good.
- Optimizing the use of shared infrastructure: An individual firm will not have sufficient incentives to shift traffic away from congestion hours, but a collective effort to do so will improve overall accessibility of the port.
- A societal *license to operate* for port activities: A lack of societal support for port activities can substantially constrain port operations and port development. For instance, it may prevent port expansion and lead to policy measures that hurt port companies (e.g., tighter environmental regulation). Most residents and stakeholders look at "the port activities" and do not differentiate between companies, especially for such issues as noise and air quality. Thus, a societal *license to grow* is a collective good that requires commitment from all firms in the port ecosystem.
- A good *port innovation system.*

7.2 The role of the PMB in promoting cooperation

As argued in Chapter 5, the PMB has a large role in promoting collective efficiency and cooperative initiatives. This is one of the arguments for the state ownership of the PMB: the comparison between the SO-PDCs in northern Europe and the private port companies in the UK shows that the former are more engaged in collective initiatives. The PMB aims at strengthening the long-term vitality of the port and therefore is often involved in providing collective goods. However, the PMB cannot effectively provide these collective goods in isolation, for two reasons:

1. The PMB, especially if it operates with a landlord business model, is only indirectly involved in the collective goods identified above. Companies with operations in the port ecosystem *directly* feel the effects of scarce vocational labor, congestion on port access highways and delays due to unplanned ship visits. The landlord PMB has a limited staff and does not operate trucks, ships or other transport modes. Thus, both the urgency and most effective initiatives with collective benefits need to come from private firms.
2. Second, *effective* investments are only feasible with commitment from the firms in the port ecosystem. For instance, partnerships with firms in the port are required for making the right choices about collaborative planning based on shared data.

Thus, while the PMB is generally deeply involved in investments that have benefits for the PBE, in some cases with a leading role, effective collective action always requires an active role of private firms.

Convincing private firms, often branch offices of large multinationals, to contribute to collective initiatives is not straightforward. A sense of "community" with trust among all individuals active in that community is helpful. Furthermore, the PMB as well as public entities involved (for instance, schools, universities, etc.) need to be responsive; develop the ability to incorporate input from the private firms in the PBE in collaborative initiatives. The conditions need to be such that executives can make a positive impact with a limited involvement in terms of time and financing. This also implies public entities need to accept that they need to fund the lion's share of collaborative initiatives. This funding is justified if the private participation guarantees that collaborative initiatives create value for the PBE.

7.3 The role of a ports industry association

Given the shared interests of firms in the port, a "ports industry association" (sometimes termed "port community") in which all firms are represented is an important vehicle for collective action. An association enables coordination between firms. Associations are collective organizations of firms in similar or related industries that provide collective goods for the members of the association. Associations are set up to enable cooperation between large numbers of firms with shared interests. Most associations are *national* and *industry-specific* (for instance, the freight forwarders association in France, or the terminal operators association in Brazil). Such associations are mostly involved in influencing policymaking at a national level. For a port, a *ports industry association* brings additional value, especially if it unites all firms that operate in a port complex and thus has a membership base across different industries (e.g., shipping lines, terminal operators, forwarders, inland shipping companies and so on). Such a ports industry association is generally actively involved in *developing projects that help the port in the long run*. For instance, evidence from a comparison between Durban, the lower Mississippi and Rotterdam indicates that in Rotterdam, the only port with a ports industry association, collective action is widely regarded as a strength of the cluster. The value of this association is widely recognized among leaders from the ports industry (de Langen, 2004).

7.4 Analyzing collective action as a regime

The concept of collective action regimes can be used to understand collective investments in ports. A port may have a very effective *training and education regime* but an ineffective *marketing and promotion regime*, or vice versa. Each of these regimes differs, partly because such regimes are path dependent: once cooperation is established, this tends to reinforce itself. A collective action regime can be defined as *the set of collaborative initiatives taken by the relevant actors in the port ecosystem with the aim of improving the quality of a specific collective good.*

The relevant actors include the SO-PDC, the cluster association, private firms and public organizations. Central to creating effective regimes is the ability to commit resources to investments with shared benefits for firms in the cluster.

The value of a ports industry association

The six collective goods require collective efforts from all companies. As example: Rotterdam's investments in a network to transport excess heat from plants in the port to households can work only if all (or most) companies support the initiative. The following examples of ports industry association demonstrate their value:

- Deltalinqs in Rotterdam and AGHA in Antwerp, are also deeply involved in projects to strengthen synergies in the cluster (in areas such as training, innovation and re-use of heat, steam and waste).
- Mersey Maritime Knowledge Hub can only create value if all/most leading maritime companies cooperate to make this a success.

It is striking that in many ports, such associations have not emerged. As quoted in a report on the Norther Powerhouse "The existing ports industry associations have a mandate to represent their members throughout the UK but are constrained in the extent to which they can advocate specifically for the northern ports and those northern issues that affect them".

A crucial insight is that *cooperative regimes tend to be relatively stable over time*. Once collaborative efforts have emerged, these tend to reinforce themselves, while lack of cooperation tends to result in a *lock-in*, where none of the actors is willing or capable to develop cooperation. Firms do not necessarily have sufficient incentives to change a regime. *Consequently, regimes differ substantially between countries, industries and ecosystems, and such differences can persist over long periods of time*.

An effective regime generally requires a form of *regime management*. This involves no more (or less) than bringing all relevant stakeholders together to identify and develop projects. In some cases, this is done by a specific organization, in other cases by a steering group (or platform, or roundtable). Figures 7.1 and 7.2 show the general logic for analyzing a regime applied to training and education, and next a schematic visualization of the position of a regime manager.

To conclude, firms in ports have many collective interests, and are better off when they jointly (with other stakeholders) develop effective regimes. In all ports, some cooperative efforts are undertaken; some best practices are provided in Table 7.1.

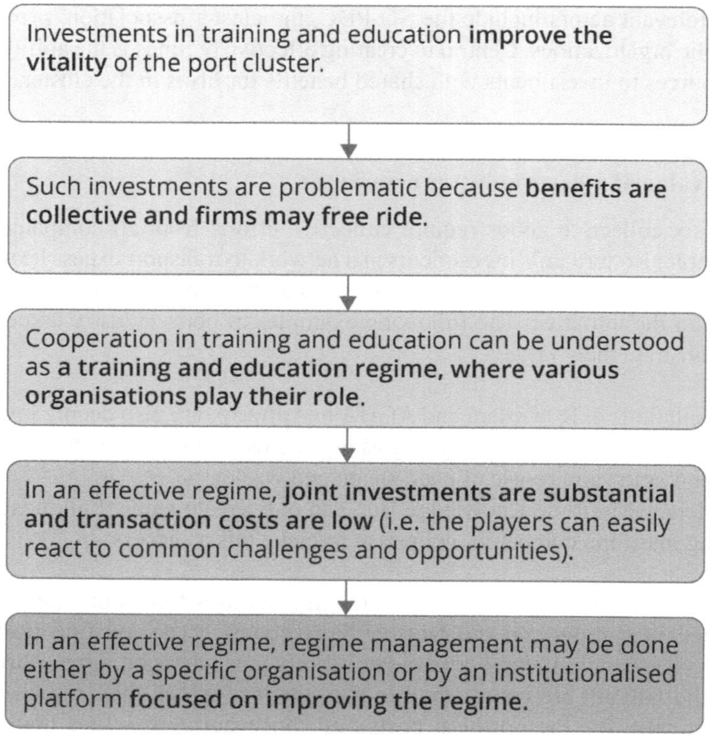

Figure 7.1 The logic of regimes in ports; example training and education

Source: Adapted from de Langen (2008).

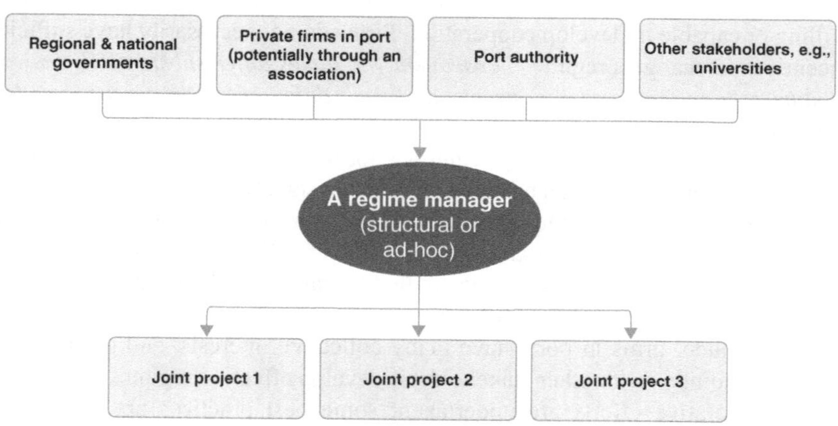

Figure 7.2 The position of a regime manager

Source: Adapted from de Langen (2008).

Table 7.1 Some best practices of cooperation in port business ecosystems

Collective good	*Example port*	*Description*	*Role of port cluster association*
Education and training	Rotterdam	Joint investments of petrochemical firms in an education facility for *process operators*.	Deltalinqs played a key role as a platform to bring together the main chemical companies.
	Hong Kong	The port community encourages the development of tailor-made education programs.	
Marketing and promotion	Mersey Maritime	Joint platform for promoting the Mersey cluster.	Mersey Maritime can be considered a port cluster association.
Information exchange	Antwerp	Joint investments in a port community system, partly funded by the regional government.	Deep involvement through providing key users for the port community system.
Congestion reduction	Rotterdam	Partner in the traffic management company aimed at reducing congestion on the main port access highway (A15).	An active role in encouraging the participation of large firms in the port.
A societal *license to operate* for port activities	Felixstowe	Fund for annual donations for community activities in communities in the vicinity of the port.	The fund is managed by an organization that can be considered a port cluster association.

7.5 Good practices in collective initiatives in the port business ecosystem

In summary, the good practices listed below have helped in successfully implementing collective initiatives that create value for the companies in the port business ecosystem.

1. Build trust among the companies in the PBE and a sense of a "port community".
2. Establish a "port cluster association" that unites the diverse firms that are active in the PBE, from logistics service providers to ship agents, terminal operators, and processing firms.
3. Invest in single-issue platforms (focused, for instance, on training and education, or innovation, or data exchange) with a capacity to follow up on agreed-upon actions.
4. Especially for the port authority (PA) or SO-PDC, and national/regional government, demonstrate the ability to incorporate input from the private firms in the PBE in collaborative initiatives and do not shy away from funding the lion's share of collaborative initiatives.
5. Set conditions that enable executives of (multi-national) firms active in the PBE to contribute to projects in the collective interest.

Notes

1 This tendency towards insufficient investments in collective goods is relevant in all clusters, and for various types of collective goods. The presence of "collective action problems" explains the emphasis placed on trust and "community involvement" in clusters.
2 Collective information systems become more valuable, the more firms use such a system. Thus, involvement and support of the port business community is crucial for developing a PCS that creates value for its users.

8 Port planning and development

All ports have port development challenges and opportunities, often huge ones. Additional cargo volumes and the newest generation of ships need to be accommodated; the terminal–hinterland interface needs to be effectively organized; well-performing terminal operators need to be attracted; logistics and manufacturing clusters can be developed, just as cruise and leisure activities and ports need to define their role as (sustainable) energy hubs. This chapter provides concepts and insights relevant to port planning and development.

As discussed in the Chapter 1, port complexes consist of four components (transport node, logistics cluster, industrial complex and site of cruise and leisure activities). Port development requires an *integrated approach* to each of these four components.

The need for a port development vision is discussed first. Next, I deal with port performance indicators, followed by an overview of the economic importance of ports, both for the port city/region and for the wider national economy. In the next paragraphs, the port innovation system and port development challenges in emerging economies are discussed.

8.1 The need for a port development vision

Port development benefits from a long-term port development plan. “Adaptive port planning” is needed, as unexpected events can deeply impact port development (Taneja et al., 2010). However, that does not imply that developing a long-term vision and masterplan is not needed. Such a vision and masterplan are valuable for at least three reasons.

First, due to the huge scale economies involved in port development, a port cannot be effectively developed “project by project”. A long-term development effort often involves land reclamation for multiple future uses and users. Such investments generally are indivisible, either for technical reasons (a complete breakwater is needed) or for economic reasons (one integrated construction project is much more cost-effective than a “patchwork approach”). This does not imply that a large-scale project cannot be phased; it generally can be phased, but still an integrated port development plan is needed.

DOI: 10.4324/9781003630784-8

The disadvantages of "project-by project" port development – cases

Examples of ports with too much of a project-by-project approach include:

- Valencia, a port in which a project-by-project approach has led to breakwaters not ideally located for additional expansions as well as too narrow infrastructure corridors, constraining the ability to connect all terminals in a cost effective way through the rail network and the suboptimal location of marinas, as these prevent large scale expansion.
- Santos, a port where terminals are scattered along the estuary, thereby not benefitting from scale economies in construction and incurring increased costs for hinterland infrastructure as well as reducing the competitiveness of intermodal services.

Second, as previously argued, port development is the development of an *integrated economic ecosystem*. The benefits of co-locating different port activities (terminals, warehousing, manufacturing – both upstream and downstream, leisure, maintenance, shipbuilding and repair) in this ecosystem depend to a large extent on the quality of port planning. For instance, making *reservations* for future transport infrastructure (road, rail and pipelines) is an important part of port planning. Likewise, planning sites adjacent to each other, to ensure close integration between logistics, manufacturing and terminals in the port leads to higher land values and more synergies in the port business ecosystem (PBE).

The invisible costs of not developing an integrated PBE

As highlighted in the introductory chapter, the non-performance of ports in terms of attracting investments often is *invisible*. Ports only thrive if they attract investments of private sector firms such as terminal operators and logistics service providers. The *development* of the port is the most challenge, not the *exploitation* of existing facilities. The lack of space or attractive investment conditions limits the inflow of investments and may have serious consequences for the regional and national economy. But these missed opportunities are invisible. While bad public transport services are immediately visible, and through user complaints put pressure on politicians, a dysfunctional PMB, that only exploits existing facilities but is not developing new ones can go unnoticed and persist for decades. As a very rough indication in my view it is healthy for a PMB to have around 10 to15% of existing port land available for new investors. For All PMBs that have close to zero land availability, an assessment of their development initiatives and capabilities may be healthy. It may well be that insufficient capabilities lead to land scarcity with high but largely invisible costs for the national and local economy.

Third, port development, regardless of the port model in place, is deeply affected by government investments. Governments generally (co-)invest in maritime access and hinterland infrastructure; they are also relevant as planners and regulators, for instance, regarding land use and labor conditions, and they are responsible for border processes (for cruise passengers), customs procedures, port-related education institutions and more. A port development plan is an important instrument for developing "stakeholder support". This also implies that in creating a port vision/development plan, stakeholder issues and concerns need to be addressed; stakeholder support is generally not achieved unless issues and concerns of stakeholders are taken seriously. While there are huge differences between countries in terms of stakeholder influence (in more autocratic regimes, stakeholder influence is less), there is a clear trend toward increasing stakeholder influence. In various cases, a conflictive stance between the PMB and other stakeholders results in last-minute modifications to port development plans; a more inclusive approach generally is more effective.

The strategic plan as inclusive process

Deep involvement of stakeholders in a port vision and masterplan is an effective way to create stakeholder support for such a plan. This may even lead to stakeholders signing a final vision document, as is the case, for instance, in Rotterdam, where the port community and the municipal, regional and national government sign the port vision document.

Nevertheless, some PMBs stick to an approach of first developing a vision, and afterwards communicating/selling it. However, that may lead to lukewarm support and limited "ownership" of the government actions required. Involving stakeholders does not imply the vision process is aimed at keeping everybody happy. Dialogue on strategic choices leads to better acceptance of the choices, even if stakeholders do not fully agree with those. Examples of planning processes where the lack of stakeholder support has had a deep negative impact include Antwerp, where stakeholder opposition to port development led to court cases won by the opposing stakeholders. As a consequence, the proposed spatial plan was nullified. Another example is Dubrovnik and various other cities where stakeholder opposition to cruise tourism has led or is likely to lead to limits to the number of cruise vessels.

8.1.1 The structure of a port development plan

While all port vision and development plans are different, they generally share a similar structure, which is provided in Figure 8.1.

Generally, a market outlook, trends and developments are addressed in the vision and development plan. Given the uncertainty of future developments, *scenarios* are a valuable instrument for developing a "robust" port development approach. These components, together with a description of the port complex "as is", provide

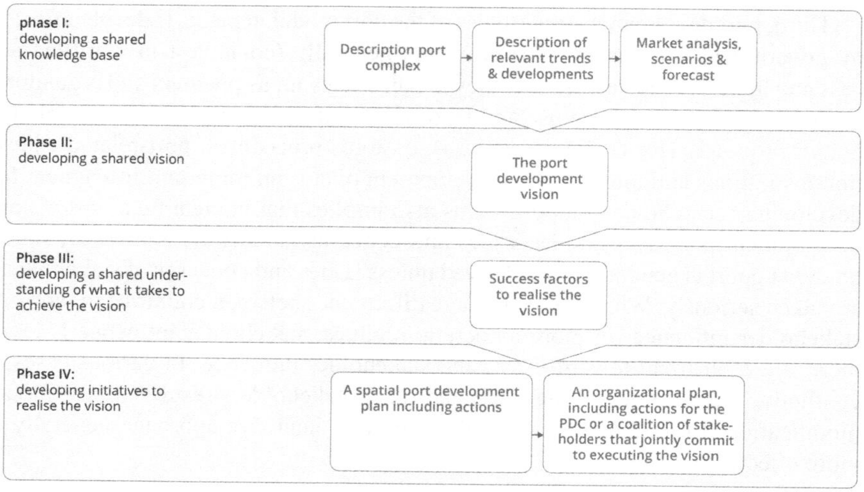

Figure 8.1 The structure of a port development plan

a basis for developing a vision, which is translated into an understanding of success factors as well as a spatial[1] and organizational action plan.

8.1.2 The value of a vision statement

A vision statement provides a clear, long-term direction for port development, helping to guide decisions, motivate employees and involve stakeholders. It acts as an inspirational and aspirational guide for the future, showing what the port complex will look like when development goals are achieved.

While all port vision statements are different, they share a number of characteristics. Based on an overview of vision statements, four components that are often used are listed below. Thinking through these components is useful for developing a port vision.

1. *Important functions of the port complex*: This first component describes in general what the important functions are: hub, gateway, industrial complex, a logistics zone, or a combination of some of these.
2. *Strengths of the port*: This component contains a (claim of a) distinctive feature or various distinctive features that set the port apart from other (competing) ports.
3. *Positioning in clusters and networks*: This component addresses the position of the port in wider transport/supply chain networks. Often this includes a spatial element.
4. *Value for society*: The last component shows how the port creates value for society. This can be in various ways, such as attracting foreign direct investment (FDI), facilitating trade and/or supporting the growth of strategic industries/clusters.

Examples of vision statements

- Aveiro (Portugal): Give competitive access of goods to the regional, national and international markets, in order to promote the region's economic development.
- Los Angeles (US): We are America's Port – the nation's #1 container port and the global model for sustainability, security and social responsibility.
- Miami (US): To operate and further develop the world's leading cruise port and the largest container port in the State of Florida; to maximize its assets and strengthen its advantage for future growth; promote international trade and commerce as a vital link between North and South America and a growing center for global trade; support sustainability and operate in an environmentally responsible manner.
- Halifax (Canada): To be an economic catalyst for regional and national growth.
- Singapore: To develop and promote Singapore as a premier global hub port and an international maritime centre, and to advance and safeguard Singapore's strategic maritime interests.

A port vision that embraces change – the case of Hamburg

In 2023, the government of the city state of Hamburg published Hamburg's port vision until 2040. The vision clearly describes the changing environment and discusses the initiatives to succeed in this new environment, with a strong focus on sustainability and digitalization. This approach clearly embraces transitions as the "new normal" in the ports industry. The following five observations are especially noteworthy:

First, while other ports also indicated that they shift away from a "volume focus", in which the tons handled are central to a port's success, Hamburg probably does so in the most explicit way. The vision suggests Hamburg can cater for eventual growth of demand for cargo handling through improving productivity of existing facilities and assets; no large-scale new port development initiatives are explored.

Second, the vision emphasizes Hamburg's strength and growth potential as a port industrial-logistics ecosystem, with opportunities for attracting new activities in energy production, circular manufacturing and maritime technology. The vision also suggests that the port authority (HPA) aims to take new steps in "designing" this ecosystem, for instance through maximizing the use of rail and barge by companies located in the port and by promoting intensive land use.

Third, the vision shows Hamburg aims to benefit from growth opportunities in the cruise segment. This contrasts with other attractive port-cities like

Amsterdam, Valencia and Barcelona, that explicitly or implicitly take an approach focused on improving cruise sustainability.

Fourth – though this was not a recent decision – the "Hafencity" redevelopment of older port areas will cross the river Elbe with the development of the Grasbrook Neighborhood. As initially with the development of Hafencity, sceptics may rightly point out the increasing pressure this puts on the adjacent port activities, but this redevelopment undoubtedly creates value for residents and visitors alike.

Perhaps the best way to assess foresight is to look at past vision documents. In 2012 Hamburg published its plan for 2025. Then, it handled more than 130 million tons (compared to 112 in 2024) and forecasted a (staggering) volume of 296 million tons in 2025. Hamburg remained a thriving port industrial-logistics ecosystem, but did not come close to the forecasted volumes. Many of the actions included in the 2012 vision relate to IT and sustainability and have borne fruit ten years later. Totally absent in 2012 but prominent in the latest vision: efforts to secure the availability of well-trained labour. Indeed, it may well be labour which will be most radically transformed 15 years from now.

8.2 The case for flexibility in port development

As argued in Chapter 4, while many ports look into new trends and developments in the planning process, this too often consists of *extrapolations of past developments* (larger ship sizes, more concentration of shipping lines, growth of trade flows) while potential disruptive developments (closing down of coal-fired power plants, containerization of bulk and automotive flows, supply chain redesign following "strategic uncoupling" of economies of China and the US) are insufficiently considered.

As a result, the huge uncertainty is downplayed, and consequently, the value of flexible port development is underrated. Looking back on port plans from 15 or 20 years ago is eye-opening: most of them turned out in hindsight to have been wrong in most aspects (volume of flows, type of cargo flows, required terminal dimensions, land use). Thus, I advocate a planning approach focused on *adaptation*. In this approach, a port development plan is mainly about identifying development *options* and ensuring that such options can be accommodated. In such an approach, a periodic review of the strategic plan is called for; it may even be sensible to (briefly) review progress yearly to assess development as well as issues that require attention.

The risks of a port expansion mindset

In an "ideal world" stakeholders involved in making a port development plan (or port vision) have an open mind about the outcome at the start. However, often that is not the case. Central stakeholders, especially the PMB, the port business community and often also government, have a "port expansion mindset": they are convinced upfront that port expansion is good as it will allow the port to grow. It is empirically demonstrated that demand estimates of public infrastructure investments are generally too optimistic, while costs are generally underestimated (see Flyvbjerg, 2007). In some cases this is because stakeholders translate their port expansion mindset into very positive outlooks. This may be a pragmatic strategy when lobbying for government investments, but it can lead to (government) investments without the expected value creation.

Table 8.1 shows the differences between a stylized "traditional approach" and an adaptive port development approach.

Table 8.1 Differences between a "traditional" and adaptive port planning approach

Traditional approach to port development	*Adaptive port development approach*
One decision moment	Staged decision-making
Uncertainties not emphasized, nor quantified	Quantification of business and value case under different scenarios
No continuous updates based on latest data	Continuous updating of business case and value case
Reliance on reports from third parties, such as forecasts or economic impact studies	Acknowledging third-party forecasts are not a sound basis for major investments
No active search for instruments to increase flexibility	Focus on using instruments that increase flexibility and/or lower risks (such as phasing, designing expansion projects for multiple potential uses and making development conditional on a "launching customer")

Can we do away with planning altogether and do "responsive" port development?

If the future is uncertain, can we do away with planning altogether and instead just develop the port solely in a "responsive" way, i.e., by responding to events as they occur? That has serious disadvantages. In a responsive port development approach, there is a long time-lag between market interest and investments. This often does not work as investors want to be able to start with their investments quickly. Public approval procedures are required for major new developments, such as land reclamation, and the deepening of entry channels. Such processes are time consuming and lead to a huge time lag between start of a development project and start of operations. In a responsive approach, huge societal costs are incurred in this period, as capacity shortages lead to congestion.

In addition, the long pay-back period of fixed and immovable assets implies that both the PMB and companies in the port need to take a long time horizon into account. For instance, in port development, assumptions about the evolution of ship sizes are needed, as investments need to create value for decades. Various cases show how lack of foresight can be costly. For instance, New Orleans developed a container terminal with insufficient draft and the Port of Rotterdam designed port basins that turned out to be to narrow. Finally, a responsive approach also is too passive for a PMB: it can create value (financial value and value for society) through "entrepreneurial" port development, i.e., actively seeking to attract new investments to the port complex. An entrepreneurial approach implies making upfront investments without committed customers and thus requires foresight.

8.2.1 Incorporating emergent strategies

Mintzberg's classical distinction between emergent and deliberate strategy (Mintzberg & Waters, 1985) is highly relevant for port development. Mintzberg and various scholars afterward have argued convincingly that generally a portion of a firm's intended strategy will not come to fruition, while, on the other hand, some of the "realized strategy" will not derive from intentions as stated in a vision or strategy document and will instead *emerge* through projects. This is considered as a healthy process: emergent strategies evolve out of projects because there is demand, and then gradually become formalized in a strategy. Thus, an approach to port development that acknowledges that the realized development generally differs substantially from the planned and forecasted development is healthy.

Adaptive port planning and emergent strategy

In 2016, a lease agreement was signed between Feadship, a leading builder of mega-yachts, and the Port of Amsterdam (PoA). Yet, Amsterdam's vision document, officially launched a year earlier did not mention mega-yachts as a potentially relevant market segment. The lease agreement is interesting as yacht-building does not generate substantial cargo volumes. Thus, it is not well aligned with PoA's (traditional) business model in which revenues from ships have a central place.

The market segment was not actively targeted but once an opportunity presented itself, PoA decided to grasp it, even though it did not align well with its traditional business model.

This may be an example of an "emergent strategy". In my view, this example points to a wider transition of port complexes, in which the cargo handling activities are gradually less important, while logistics, manufacturing, tourism and real estate activities are gaining in importance. I would not be surprised if ten years from now Feadship is no longer a single client but a yacht cluster has evolved, with substantial value creation for Feadship, as well as for PoA and the regional economy at large.

Groningen Seaports is a similar example of an emergent development that was eventually embraced in the deliberate strategy. Groningen Seaports made an agreement for the establishment of a Google datacenter in the port area, even though it had never included datacenters in its formal strategy and vision documents. Now, Groningen seaports embraces datacenters as a promising market segment and promotes a part of the port area as Green Dataport Eemshaven.

8.2.2 Mechanisms to increase flexibility in port development

Figure 8.2 lists the most important mechanisms to increase flexibility in port development.

The instruments in Figure 8.2 are divided into four categories. The first category deals with instruments related to decision-making. The first instrument deals with the length of approval processes. If such processes are fast, companies, and especially the port development company, can react more flexibly to disruptions. For instance, by switching the land use from as an example a container terminal to a site for circular manufacturing. Regulatory processes may be lengthy, especially when such a switch would require new economic and environmental impact studies. A situation in which a port area as a whole is given a certain environmental constraint, in terms of noise and emissions, allows for fast decision-making.

The second relevant "process-related" instrument is making port development conditional on a launching customer. In this approach, the risk of under-utilization and associated low revenues is lower than when an investment in port expansion is made in the hope that customers can be attracted. In some cases, this approach can be extended: in response to a customer demand, a port development initiative that accommodates this demand while at the same time providing space for other

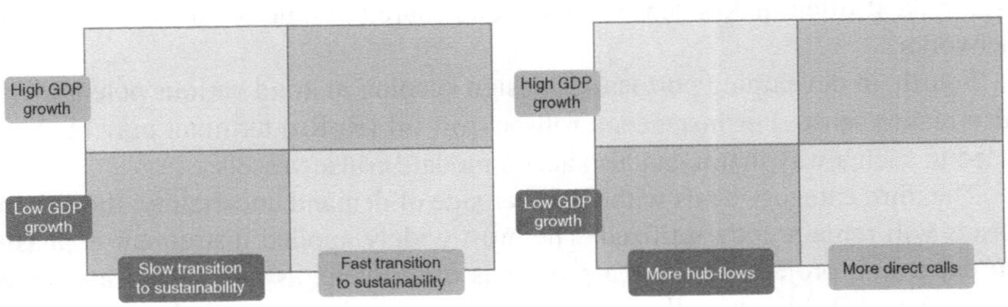

Figure 8.2 Mechanisms to increase flexibility in port development

investments can be developed. This approach is very common in many industries. For instance, companies investing in logistics (or office or housing) real estate often develop new facilities based on contracts for around 60% of the newly developed surface.

The third process-related instrument is the decoupling of the legal approval, as well as the approval of loans, for instance, with development banks, from the final investment decisions. In such an approach, the final "push on the button" for the investment can be postponed once legal approval and financial closure have been achieved. This creates valuable flexibility, as projects can be postponed or canceled in case of unforeseen development affecting demand. Especially development banks, such as the World Bank, Asian Development Bank and the European bank for Reconstruction and Development, are used to such decoupling of financial closure and the final investment decisions.

The second group of instruments aims to create flexibility so that unforeseen new activities or cargo flows can be accommodated. As previously discussed, many ports are rather diverse ecosystems and may be attractive locations for a wide variety of activities, such as shipbuilding, ship-repair, warehousing, datacenters, hotels and more. Thus, accommodating unforeseen activities is critical to develop the ecosystem. Likewise, unforeseen cargo flows may emerge; ports with sufficient flexibility to accommodate these generate more activities and value. Thus, as a first instrument, ports benefit from having land available to accommodate new activities. A percentage of around 5 to 15% of total land available for new activities is healthy; more than that probably means past investments were too high (as there obviously is a cost associated with having land available), less than that may mean the port has insufficient flexibility to accommodate new activities.

A second instrument is to have plans ready to increase the spatial productivity of land that is already utilized. For example, by investing in additional equipment, throughput can be increased. Likewise, through "co-siting", additional activities can be placed on sites already in use. Such co-siting often leads to a higher spatial productivity.

The third instrument is to make spatial reservations for (bundles of) critical infrastructure. Rail, road and pipeline infrastructures need space. Without spatial reservations for such infrastructure, the long-term development of the port is at risk. It often makes sense to have one shared bundle for different transport networks.

Fourth, in developing port land, a design keeping in mind various potential uses also makes sense. For instance, a roll-on–roll-off (RoRo) terminal may be developed in such a way that it can also accommodate cruise vessels.

The third category deals with the other side of demand uncertainty: the risk that assets will remain under-utilized. The most widely applied instrument is phasing an expansion project. Phasing a project is often done, as part of the investment is postponed. While overall construction costs may increase, the benefits, mainly lower capital costs often outweigh these.

The fourth category of instruments to increase flexibility relates to the flexibility of port operations. Given the fluctuations of demand and the changes in technology, flexibility in operations is valuable. Three relevant instruments are:

- Investing in the availability of different transport modes to serve the hinterland, so that in case of disruptions in one mode an alternative is available.
- Developing intra-port competition where possible, so that port users have switching options in the same port.
- Promote decentralized decision-making to the extent possible. While companies in ports benefit from shared services, decentralized systems are more flexible than centralized ones. Incidents with cyber-related disruptions show the vulnerability of ports; more centralized systems are especially vulnerable. Another area where decentralized systems are more flexible concerns labor relations. Centralized systems with a port-wide labor pool and collective bargaining agreements are less flexible than decentralized ones.

Flexibility and designing port infrastructure

A long-term perspective is needed when making design choices of port infrastructure. For instance, there is a choice between a cheap structure with a relatively short technical lifetime or a more expensive structure with a longer technical lifetime. In case of a foreseen relatively short-term boost of cargo flows and associated storage, it may be wise to opt for floating storage structures (for cars, liquid or dry bulk). In case of flows that are tied to the port for the long term (for instance because of a new car plant has started operating in the immediate hinterland of the port) structures with a long technical lifetime are more appropriate.

In addition, it is worth considering if infrastructures with a long technical life can be designed, so that they can create value for different "use cycles". For instance, many terminal sites in ports were initially used for general cargo and later modified for containers. Other well-known cases are old warehouses that later are turned into apartments. These examples demonstrate that a long-term perspective is required for making the right investments in port infrastructure. Investments in flexibility of infrastructures may pay off.

8.3 Five iterative steps in port development

Adaptive port development can be structured in five (iterative) steps (see also Taneja et al., 2010). In this approach, the key result of port planning efforts is that they allow the PMB to take specific investment decisions, taking into consideration potential future port developments.

1 Develop scenarios and forecasts

Scenarios help imagine plausible alternative environments in which ports operate. Developing scenarios allows considering a range of plausible futures in making investment decisions. Scenarios are therefore indispensable for port planning under uncertainty. More details on how to develop scenarios are discussed in the next module.

2 Identify "port development options" in each of the scenarios

A scenario is a plausible future environment in which the port operates. In each scenario, development options can be identified. Examples of such options can include:

- Developing a marina
- Developing an (additional) container terminal
- Attracting investments in logistics
- Building an (additional) rail terminal
- Building a new (sustainable) powerplant
- Building a hotel in the port area

Some of these development options can be realized in all scenarios, but others are likely to materialize in only one or two scenarios. For each of the development options, estimates of some key characteristics, including land use, environmental footprint and effect on transport infrastructure, need to be made to be able to assess what investments are needed to accommodate all these options.

3 Identify risks and uncertainties of each of the port development options as well as mechanisms to reduce risks

As a next step, for all options, key risks and determinants are identified. For instance, the development of a biomass energy plant may depend on national regulation. Next, the value of each of the mechanisms discussed above to increase flexibility and reduce risks needs to be assessed. For instance, for a new container terminal, a partnership model can be designed in which the PMB only invests based on a contract with a launching customer. For a new logistics zone, a phased approach may be feasible.

4 Develop a "high-level" port development plan for each of the scenarios

As a fourth step, for each scenario a high-level port development plan can be created. In this plan, all expected investments and new activities in one specific scenario are described. Thus, such a plan contains the main investments for the coming 15- to 20-year period for one scenario. In this phase, there is no need for very detailed numbers, as figures are indicative and the "real development" will almost certainly deviate from the scenarios. This step requires input from port engineers about the technical feasibility of solutions to accommodate the development options. Some pragmatic choices are needed to differentiate between scenarios (e.g., in one scenario, an additional container terminal, in another scenario not). The end result is a high-level idea of what the port may look like in each scenario in 15–20 years and the relevant investments that are needed to achieve such growth. All of this serves to allow decision-making on specific projects with a long-term view. For instance, if a container terminal is developed, this development may need to take into account other options such as logistics zones and rail terminals.

5 Define decision moments and develop a system of monitoring and trigger points

The final step in the adaptive planning approach is developing a monitoring system, including trigger points to start new projects. In this phase, the key decision moments for the PMB are identified, the alternative decisions (e.g., extend lease or terminate contract and change land use) are mapped together with signals that favor one of the conditions. Key decision moments often relate to expiry dates of land lease/concession contracts, as at these moments the PMB (together with other stakeholders) can decide to change the land use of plots. For instance, trigger points may be defined for transitioning land from a port function to an urban function. For instance, if the scale of vessels exceeds a certain size, draft limitations of terminals in urban areas may become so severe that relocation and re-development projects need to be initiated. Likewise, when a terminal reaches a certain utilization level (say 70%), projects focused on increasing capacity may be worthwhile.

In the high-level port development plans for the different scenarios, some plots of land (or areas where land can be developed) are likely to have different uses (e.g., a marina versus a container terminal). For these plots, investor interests for all potential uses need to be monitored continuously, either informally or formally to a request for proposals. Moving through these five steps allows for making informed long-term investment decisions in an uncertain environment.

Flexibility and financing port development

An important aspect of flexible port development relates to financing. If loans are required for the investments in port development, especially loans of national or international development banks such as the World Bank and Asian Development Bank, approval procedures of these financing institutions are generally lengthy (they may require impact studies, environmental studies and the like). Thus, ideally these procedures are set in motion, prior to the final investment decision. Agreements can be made that loans become available once the final investment decision is taken. This increases the flexibility of the port development company. However, achieving this ideal is complex and requires constant alignment between the "commercial track" aimed at finding customers for (future plots) and the "financial track" aimed at securing funding for these investments.

8.4 Scenarios

As argued in Chapter 4, the risk of relying on past trends and assuming too much *business as usual* is huge. A tool to reduce that risk is using scenarios. Scenarios invite identifying *un*certainties surrounding economic development, trade flows and logistics patterns. Scenarios allow for identifying possible futures. A scenario consists of a number of (coherent) assumptions about future developments. By using a number of scenarios and assessing how port development can be adapted in these scenarios, a port development plan that is robust, i.e., provides a sound direction in all scenarios, can be developed. It is not warranted (and impossible) to assess the *likelihood* of scenarios, or to select a "best scenario". For cargo throughput, some important uncertain factors for which assumptions in scenarios need to be made are:

1. Economic development of the hinterland.
2. The development of *industrial production*. Many commodities handled in ports are raw materials or intermediates; these are closely related to industrial production.
3. The speed of a shift toward a sustainable economy. Many commodities handled in ports (crude oil, oil products, coal, liquid natural gas) are energy-related, and one of the main challenges in the transition toward sustainability is to increase the share of renewable energy in the energy mix.

In addition, specifically for containers, the balance between transhipment and direct calls is a relevant uncertainty. This has a huge impact on future transhipment (T/S) volumes, which account for a large part of total container volumes in most large ports. For instance, a large part of the transhipment flows of the ports of Algeciras and Tangier-Med are related to West Africa. However, growing volumes and improved port infrastructure may lead to more direct calls in West Africa and, as a result, declining T/S volumes in Algeciras and Tangier-Med. Figure 8.3 shows possible scenarios that have been used by ports.

8.4.1 Energy mix scenarios

For many ports, the future energy mix in their hinterlands is an important uncertainty. With regard to energy, various institutions make energy scenarios, including the International Energy Agency and some major oil companies.

Figure 8.4 shows the energy mix in 2050 forecasts of ExxonMobil, which foresees a majority of fossil fuels in the energy mix in 2050, and two scenarios of the International Energy Agency, the first STEP, on the basis of stated national energy policies (in 2024) and the second a net-zero 2050 scenario. The net-zero scenario also assumes a total energy use that is 22% lower than in the stated policies scenario. ExxonMobil assumes an even higher total energy use. These figures show the uncertainty regarding the future transport of energy commodities. This translates directly to uncertainty for volumes handled in ports.

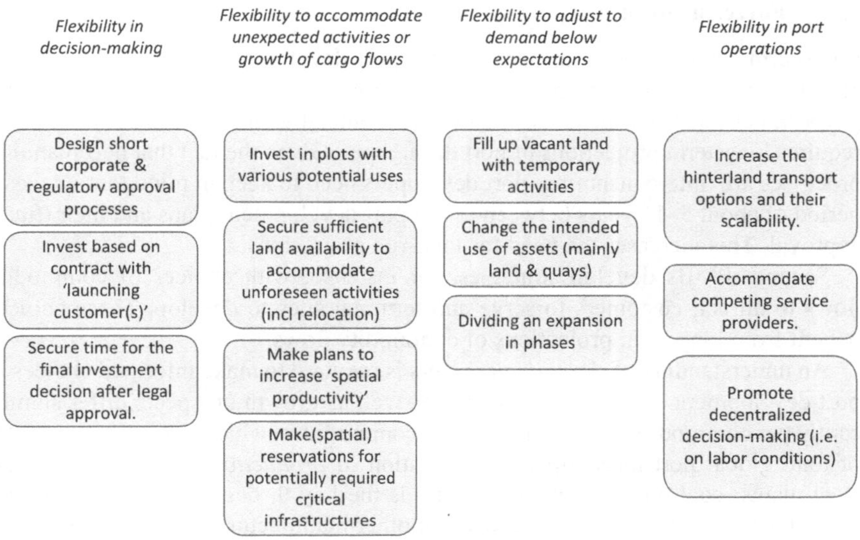

Figure 8.3 Two examples of scenarios

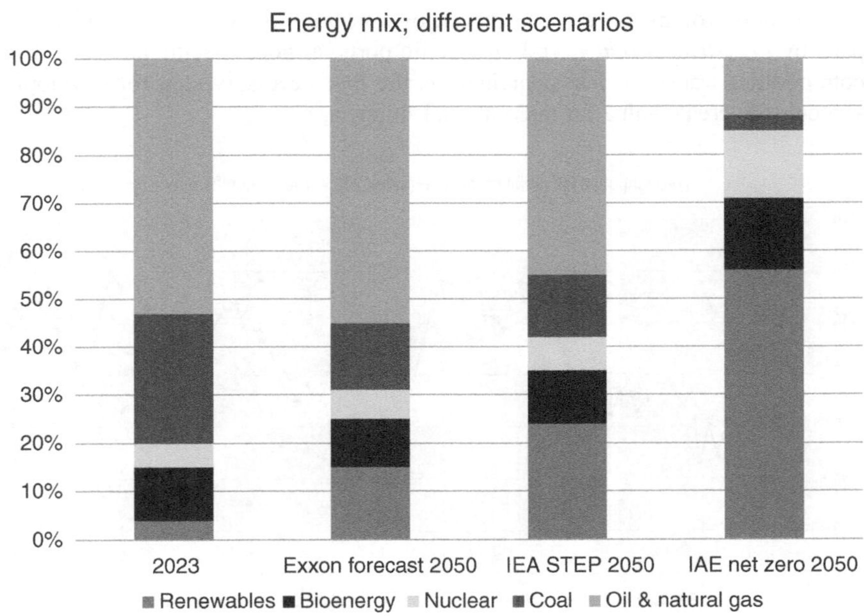

Figure 8.4 The energy mix according to different energy scenarios

Source: Own analysis based on ExxonMobil (2025) and IEA (2025).

8.5 Forecasts of future port volumes

Long-term forecasts are indispensable for port development plans, for two main reasons. First, investments in port infrastructure are fixed investments, with a long payback period. Thus, an assessment of the financial viability of such investments requires long-term projections of port throughput. Given the fact that port planning processes are time-consuming, port developers need to keep in mind that it takes a period of about 5–15 years between initial port development plans and their (final) approval. This increases the need for long-run projections.

Second, PMBs develop strategies, for instance, with choices of commodity flows to attract, customers to serve and terminal sites to develop. These choices benefit from long-term projections of commodity flows.

An understanding of *throughput drivers* is required to make informed choices in port development. Past growth patterns as well as growth prospects differ significantly per commodity. For the major bulk commodities, which constitute over 50% of total global port throughput, the evolution of *production capacity* (refineries, steel plants, coal-powered energy plants) is the key throughput driver. This production capacity is, in turn, dependent on other manufacturing sectors. The future energy consumption and energy mix deeply influence the throughput of major bulk commodities. Appendix 2 provides a detailed analysis of the throughput drivers of coal, iron ore and crude oil.

Container volumes are partly driven by consumption and also, in substantial part, by *industrial production.* For specific ports, a more specific analysis of the commodities transported in containers is the first necessary step for developing strategies to create value for international shippers.

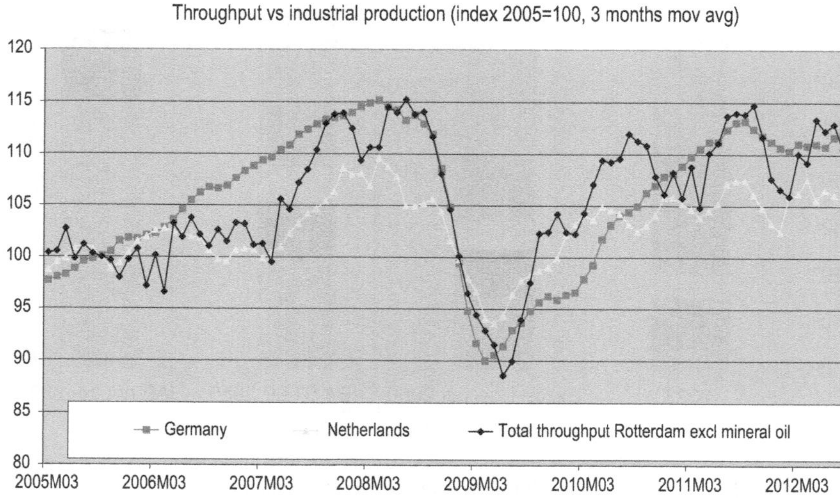

Figure 8.5 Industrial production (NL + GER) and Rotterdam's throughput

Source: Own calculations, based on Eurostat data (2025b) and Port of Rotterdam Authority data.

Figure 8.5 shows the relation between industrial production in the Netherlands and Germany, related to the monthly throughput in Rotterdam during the period of the financial crisis.[2] The data show a strong correlation between throughput and industrial production, confirming that it is a main driver for many commodity flows.

Forecasting is not the same as extrapolating past growth patterns

There are often huge differences between forecasts and realized volumes. Four examples illustrate this. First, the Port of Rotterdam Authority (PoR) made projections shortly before the oil crisis in 1973. The projections foresee a crude oil throughput of more than 200 million tons in 1980 and more than 300 million tons in 1990. The realized throughput of crude oil peaked in 1976, with almost 150 million tons, and declined to slightly less than 100 million tons in 1990. Second, when PoR made forecasts after the 1979 oil crisis the overall forecasted volume for 2010 was between 270 and 330 million tons, compared to a realized throughput of over 420 million tons.

Third, in 2004, conventional breakbulk volumes in Antwerp were around 20 million ton. The forecasts for 2015 were roughly between 17 million (low growth scenario) and 22 million (high growth scenario). However, partly due to rapid containerization of flows, breakbulk throughput declined to about 11 million ton in 2010.

Fourth, many port authorities and TOCs underestimated the surge in container volumes between 2000 and 2008, when global container volumes more than doubled, with an average annual growth of more than 10%, higher than most firms in the industry expected, as demonstrated by capacity shortages in various parts of the world.

All major ports use projections when drafting long-term development plans, but generally do not report how the realized volumes compare to the forecasts. In general, real throughput has differed substantially from the forecasts.

8.5.1 A forecasting model is helpful, but requires verification/modification based on deep industry insights

Long-term port flow projections benefit from a systematic treatment of the effect of global economic developments on world trade and port throughput, a key capability of models. The standard scientific freight model is based on a description of regional production and consumption patterns (in a first layer of the model) and trade modeling through GDP-based regression functions or spatial equilibrium modeling (a second layer). The choices of transport mode (third layer) and transportation route (fourth layer) are also modeled. These models have been improved substantially over the last few decades and have been applied to many long-term freight forecasts.[3]

The use of GDP/trade multipliers

Multipliers to develop a traffic forecast based on a GDP forecast are often used, for both total cargo volumes and container volumes. Such multipliers are an "*ad hoc* approach", in the sense that they are not based on a solid (econometric) model, but popular due to their simplicity. The risk of "extrapolation" is very relevant with a multiplier approach, as often a constant multiplier is used – and often based on past experience. The evolution of the multiplier of port/transport volumes to GDP multiplier shows it is far from constant. Over the past decades, the multiplier has fallen substantially. For total cargo volumes in advanced economies, the multiplier is below one, i.e., economic growth has been faster than growth of port volumes. In some countries, such as the UK, there is a complete so-called "decoupling": while GDP continues to grow, that does not apply for total cargo volumes. In the container segment, the multiplier has decreased from levels of more than 3 (three times more container volume growth than GDP growth) to slightly above 1. There are reasons to assume that it will continue to fall, some of them discussed in Chapter 3; a multiplier below 1 for containers may well become the new normal in the coming decades.

However, these models had limited capabilities to incorporate *disruptive developments*. Large-scale freight modeling approaches rely on publicly available statistics of production and trade and are insufficiently detailed to capture developments in production networks, hub formation, technological innovation and so on. As these models provide insufficient detail for specific markets, analysis of industry trends and implications for projections is needed to check and modify the model results. Combining a freight transport model with industry analysis and expert judgment leads to better projections and also improves the stakeholders' acceptance of the results. A systematic overview of the steps in this approach is given in Figure 8.6.

8.5.2 TEU throughput per capita

A metric that is relevant for understanding trade flows and can be a useful first clue for the growth potential of container volumes is *TEU per capita.* This metric has to be interpreted with care (for instance, it may be distorted by transhipment movements) but provides information on the growth potential of trade and container flows (see Table 8.2).

Table 8.2 shows that Iceland and New Zealand have very high TEU per capita ratios. This is mainly because both islands are small in population terms. As the scale of the market is insufficient for domestic production, most products are imported. Furthermore, both countries have a few strong exporting sectors (e.g., fruit, ores and fish). The large, advanced, open economies (the UK, Japan, the US, Canada) also have relatively high TEU/capita ratios. China stands out, as it has a

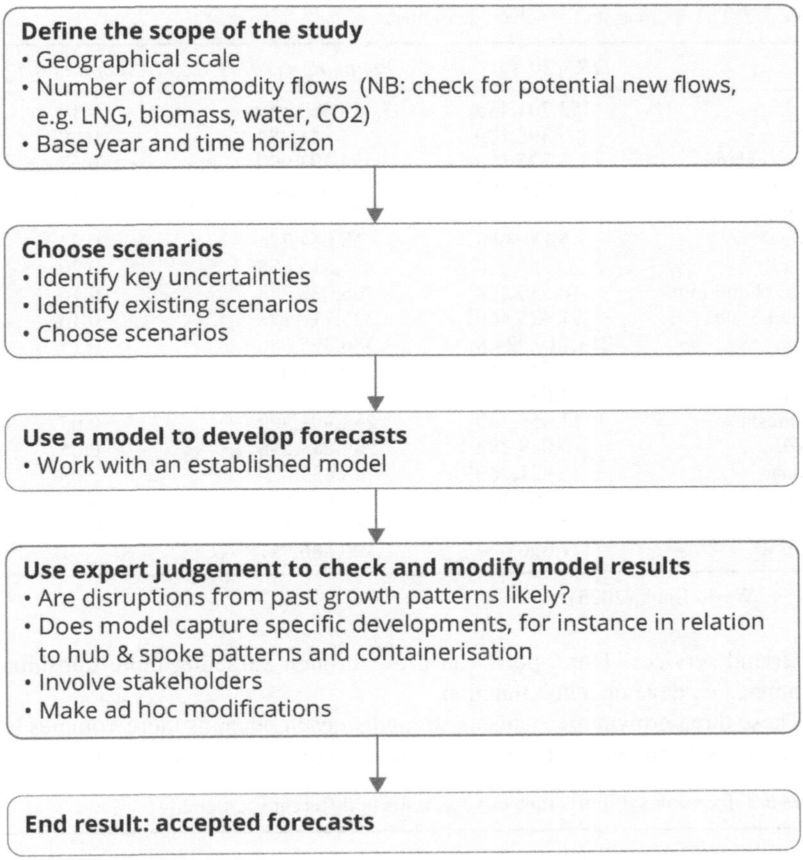

Figure 8.6 Schematic overview of the forecasting approach

Source: Adapted from de Langen et al. (2012).

ratio similar to those of the advanced open economies. These data suggest that the potential for additional growth of container volumes in China is more limited than one may think based on the GDP growth potential of China. On the other hand, this table hints at a huge growth potential for Brazil, Mexico, and especially India and Nigeria.

8.5.3 Growth mechanisms for container ports

Three growth mechanisms for container volumes in ports can be distinguished. First, growth through expanding the local cargo base (for instance, through the development of logistics, processing or freezones in the port region). Second, growth through expanding the hinterland, for instance, by new infrastructure or new

Table 8.2 TEU per capita for selected countries

	TEU (2017)	*Population (2017)*	*TEU/capita (2017)*
World	752,704,435	7,530,360,149	0.10
Iceland	308,100	341,284	0.90
New Zealand	3,227,100	4,793,900	0.67
Finland	1,920,800	5,511,303	0.35
Australia	7,693,643	24,598,933	0.31
Chile	4,189,669	18,054,726	0.23
Ireland	955,000	4,813,608	0.20
United Kingdom	10,530,328	66,022,273	0.16
United States	51,425,466	325,719,178	0.16
China	213,719,924.8	1,386,395,000	0.15
France	6,714,551	67,118,648	0.10
South Africa	4,634,900	56,717,156	0.08
Indonesia	13,859,500	263,991,379	0.05
Brazil	10,049,282	209,288,278	0.05
Ghana	921,000	28,833,629	0.03
Kenya	1,200,100	49,699,862	0.02
India	13,259,000	1,339,180,127	0.01
Nigeria	1,656,000	190,886,311	0.01

Source: World Bank (2025).

hinterland services. Third, ports can grow through attracting more transhipment volumes, i.e., develop a hub function.

These three growth mechanisms strengthen each other, as more volumes translate into scale economies that increase the attractiveness of the port. These growth

Table 8.3 Examples of ports that serve as hubs in different segments

Commodity	*Hub function*
Containers	Various ports have developed a hub function, including Singapore, Colombo, Aden, Port Said and Tangier-Med.
LNG	There is a market for "small-scale" LNG vessels that serve small ports with limited volumes. This creates a demand for hub operations. For example, the port of Zeebrugge (Belgium) has developed into an LNG hub.
Fruit	Fruit is in some cases transported in dedicated containerized reefer services. These call one hub port, from which the fruit is further distributed to other ports. North Sea Ports (the Netherlands/Belgium) is a hub port for fruit.
Cars	Like container carriers, car carriers have established shipping networks, in which some ports serve as hubs. For instance, the port of Sohar (Oman) is used as a hub for cars in the trade between Asia and East Africa.
Crude oil	Crude oil is frequently commercially stored (i.e., awaiting favorable market conditions) in oil hubs. Some main oil hubs are Fujayrah, Houston, Singapore, Rotterdam and Tenerife.
Coal	Even though coal is mostly directly shipped between the origin and destination port, even in this segment ports do aspire to attract hub flows. For example, both Rotterdam (the Netherlands) and Krishnapatnam (India) serve as hubs from where coal is "feedered" in smaller facilities in other ports.

mechanisms apply across all commodities, as well as beyond containers; ports can develop a hub function (see Table 8.3).

In virtually all these cases, the three growth mechanisms – grow the captive cargo base, expand the hinterland and attract hub flows – have worked hand in hand.

8.6 Investments in port development

The forecasting and scenario analysis allow for the identification of activities that can be attracted to the PBE, such as a marina, a hotel, an (additional) container terminal, warehousing facilities, and green energy production. All of these activities require available land. Furthermore, to attract these activities, *specific critical location factors* may need to be in place. For instance, a container terminal may only be feasible if road and/or rail connections are sufficiently well developed. A marina may only be feasible if the public space in the port area is attractive. Refrigerated warehousing activities may require efficient food inspection facilities in the PBE.

The analysis of the development potential thus leads to port development options, i.e., "investment projects to develop land and other facilities with the aim to attract third parties to the PBE". Some of these development options can be realized in all scenarios, but others are likely to materialize in specific conditions. A relevant distinction of port development projects is between "greenfield" and "brownfield" developments.

8.6.1 Greenfield

A greenfield project has no constraints imposed by prior activities carried out on the land to be developed. In ports, greenfield development mostly occurs by converting agricultural land or nature in port land. Greenfield development generally is less complicated as there are fewer constraints in terms of size, infrastructure connections, functions and future use. In advanced economies, Greenfield projects are also extra complex due to stakeholder opposition to converting agricultural land or nature in port land. Thus, the capabilities to re-develop brownfield areas become increasingly important.

8.6.2 Brownfield

Brownfield sites have previously been used, generally for industrial purposes (but potentially also other economic activities). Brownfield sites require investments in development before they can be re-used. Furthermore, the previous use often leads to constraints: the size and lay-out is fixed, and there are pre-existing connections to road and rail infrastructure. Furthermore, the previous use often has led to pollution or residues of the prior use in the soil. These may constrain future developments. Especially in large PBEs in advanced economies, brownfield development often is as important, or more important, than new greenfield development.

In Antwerp, the closure of the GM plant made a huge site (88 hectares) available for re-development. The land was bought, with support of the municipality, by Port of Antwerp and added to the port area. The land is re-developed as a circular-economy hotspot in Antwerp, where the Port of Antwerp aims to attract companies in the circular process and manufacturing. The site was bought in 2014, the first customer agreements were signed in 2022, and as of the end of 2025 the site is still virtually empty. This demonstrates the long time-horizon of brownfield projects.

In brownfield re-development, the PMB generally is an important partner, but it may not always be in a position where it can attract new investors to vacant land. For instance, in the Port of Rotterdam, Gunvor bought a refinery in 2016 and thus became the new tenant. Gunvor announced a "transition strategy" and aims to re-develop the site from a traditional "gray" oil refinery to a green energy producer. One of the main initiatives is to import ammonia and produce hydrogen. Another project involves the production of SAF. In this project, Gunvor (so not the Port of Rotterdam as the PDC) has reached an agreement with a third party to establish a joint venture at the Gunvor site.

Similar closures of large-scale sites in ports have occurred in many other ports, including Groningen (the Netherlands), Teesside (the UK), Wilhelmshafen (Germany) and Port of Newcastle (Australia). These closures create re-development challenges for ports. Compared with new greenfield developments, re-development at the end of the life cycle is more complicated. Outdated infrastructure or industrial sites often remain underused and/or derelict for long periods of time. The creation of value for new types of users – and society at large – is often hampered by legal and institutional complexities. Issues include responsibilities for soil pollution and the complex business case for re-development. In specific cases, instead of waiting until plants close down, a more proactive approach of the PMB may be appropriate. Perhaps infrastructure investments are needed to create new development options? These generally have to be planned well in advance – certainly if government entities are expected to financially contribute. In other cases (as in Rotterdam), co-siting may be attractive, and the PMB can help attract new investors. For PMBs in mature economies, acknowledging the inevitability that some activities will close down sooner or later and developing scenarios on how to re-develop large sites currently occupied by mature industries is worth the effort.

8.6.3 Risk tolerance of the PMB

The PMB needs to decide how much risk it is willing to take in development projects. At the high-risk extreme is the development of land without agreed contracts with tenants (I use the term *speculative*). At the low-risk extreme is full commitment of tenants prior to the PMB investment decision, effectively reducing the PMB risk to construction cost overruns, since the third-party tenant runs all commercial risks. This can be termed "*secured*". Somewhere in between these two is an approach that is appealing, especially for SO-PDCs, which have a strong commitment to port development. This approach consists of a larger project supported by a *launching customer*. An important characteristic of this approach is that it is not a one-off deal for one customer but uses one launching customer to develop a bigger project aimed at attracting various companies, generally with synergies between them.

Three examples illustrate this approach:

- North Sea Port (NSP) and ArcelorMittal Belgium's joint North-C-Circular initiative for the development of a port area specifically designated for circular business activities. This 150-hectare area, located next to the ArcelorMittal site, will be re-developed for circular activities, of which only ArcelorMittal's facility to produce bio-coal from wood waste is guaranteed. NSP aims to attract at least ten still unknown circular activities to the North-C-Circular site.
- The Rotterdam food hub development, which used Innocent's willingness to invest in a fruit processing facility to develop a larger area (of around 60 hectares) as a food hub, with the aim of attracting other food companies and creating synergies. Five years after the signing of Innocent, no additional clients have been attracted, so it is still too early to regard this as a successful case. Rotterdam also used the launching customer approach for its 1000-hectare expansion project Maasvlakte II".
- RAK Ports (UAE) Saqr 2.0 deep water port development project, focused on the liquid bulk, project cargo and break-bulk segments, and ship-repair and recycling. RAK uses part of this area for in-house terminal services and aims to attract third parties, especially to the freezone area.

8.6.4 The need to envisage a desired "end state" for some characteristics of the PBE

For some characteristics of the PBE, the PMB needs to define a desired "end state". This is necessary because it guides both the investments of the PMB and those of the third parties that will be active in the PBE. Careful analysis of the desired "end state" helps create clear, appealing goals. The desired end state needs to be driven by productivity and efficiency considerations and consists of elements such as:

- Should there be various competing terminal operators or one single terminal operator?
- Should all different container terminals have rail access, or should the port operate with one common rail terminal?
- Should nautical service providers be obliged to adhere to service levels set by the PMB or operate as free commercial ventures?
- Should there be a target for intermodal volumes for the PBE or not?
- Should companies in the PBE be obliged to provide data to a port community platform?
- Should companies in the PBE commit to a path to a net-zero PBE?

Often, the end state is "aspirational", and the PMB does not have instruments to enforce decisions of third parties in the PBE to achieve the desired endstate and various transitory steps may be required. However, the PMB also needs to have clarity on the desired end state and the transition path, to make sound investment decisions and allow third parties to make such decisions. For instance, in all ports with substantial volumes and one (container) terminal operator, the issue of whether and if so how to bring in a competing terminal operator requires careful analysis.

Hong Kong's cooperative competition model – a desirable endstate?

To enhancing the overall competitiveness of Hong Kong Port, in 2019, four terminal operators formed the "Hong Kong Seaport Alliance", in which they collaborate in their container terminal facilities in Kwai Tsing to deliver a more efficient service offering to customers. A fifth operator remains outside the alliance.

The alliance is a joint venture set up to create operational coordination (by pooling and sharing of terminal capacity), as well as commercial coordination, by offering equal pricing for all shipping lines and "terminal neutrality". In this model, while the shipping lines continue to contract with one terminal, the service levels are equal across all terminals and ships are allocated based on terminal capacity.

This clearly gives the terminals a dominant market position for gateway cargo. Thus, the alliance was only accepted by the competition agency after making the commitments that charges for gateway cargo are capped at the level that applied prior to the implementation of the Alliance (subject to indexation), and handling times for ships and trucks are below values prior to the alliance. In this model, utilization and productivity have increased while prices remained stable. From an "ecosystem perspective" this may be a desirable end state; other PMBs may be tempted to copy parts of this model.

8.6.5 Risk appetite and construction costs

As in all investment projects, construction costs are an important consideration in the business case. In the ports industry, construction costs fluctuate with the general economic cycle. Thus, in some cases, a PMB may be better off taking an "anti-cyclical approach" for those long-term investments that have a low risk profile. By contracting these when the construction market is good, costs can be substantially (>50%) cheaper than when construction is booming. This may be relevant for such aspects as capital dredging, capital maintenance and land reclamation for further port development.

8.7 Port performance indicators

Port performance indicators (PPIs) are indispensable for a well-functioning port industry. At the same time, the public availability of PPIs is very limited, which constrains informed decision-making in the ports industry. There is a long history of efforts to develop and publish PPIs.[4]

Notwithstanding the progress on PPIs, further initiatives continue to be relevant, given the key role of ports in facilitating trade, the huge investment needs in ports and increased stakeholder involvement in port development.

In addition, major changes in the ports industries create a need for different types of PPIs and also lead to better data availability. For instance, the ongoing transition toward the SO-PDC, leads to a greater need for PPIs regarding concessions, while digitalization enables the development of PPIs regarding ship turnaround times in ports.

8.7.1 The relevance of PPIs for the port stakeholders

PPIs are relevant for various types of stakeholders in the ports industry. *Policy makers*, at regional, national and supra-national levels, benefit from PPIs in developing policies for the ports industry. Such policies may include reform of port governance structures, regulations concerning concessions in ports, transport corridors and spatial plans for developing port-related industrial and logistics zones. All of these policy decisions benefit from good port performance indicators.

Second, PDCs benefit from insights into port performance for their investment decisions. For instance, understanding productivity levels at current facilities is critical for making informed port expansion decisions. PPIs are also required for good customer relations, for instance, with third-party terminal operators.

Third, PPIs are highly relevant for *port users*. These use PPIs for different purposes. Shipping lines benefit from good indicators on terminal productivity, cargo volumes and hinterlands served by the port. Terminal operators benefit from insights on port turnaround times, especially when these can be used to identify opportunities to reduce turnaround times among all relevant actors (terminals, PDCs, customs, towage companies, pilots and others). Shippers also benefit from PPIs, such as cargo dwell times, in the supply chain choices. Also, shippers directly benefit from information-based initiatives to improve port performance. Finally, various NGOs focused on the interests of specific communities also benefit from PPIs. For instance, residents living near the port benefit from environmental PPIs.

In conclusion, the challenge of PPIs is no longer mainly a challenge of PDCs but is of direct relevance for all stakeholders on the port.[5] Better availability of relevant PPIs will enable better use of PPIs to make informed policy and investment decisions. This would represent a major step forward compared to the current state-of-the-art in many countries, where the PPIs are mainly used for marketing and communication.

In the last few decades, efforts to develop PPIs have increased substantially. However, most initiatives to develop and report PPIs are local or national, with little standardization across ports and countries. Because of the lack of uniform definitions and methods of data collection, international comparison of PPIs is complicated. Recently, more international initiatives on PPIs have emerged.

The case for less focus on volumes as the measure of performance

Most ports, as well as governments, place much focus on the volumes handled in the port as an indicator of performance. While volumes are publicly available, widely reported internationally in the form of rankings and very intuitive indicators of performance, they also have serious and acknowledged disadvantages. Most importantly, the volumes handled in a port mainly reflect the economic development in the area served by the port. For instance, it would be clearly misguided to conclude that the UK's ports are not performing on no basis more substantial than that the total volumes handled by the UK ports have declined since the 1990s. The fall in volumes is mainly driven by the transition of the UK economy towards a service economy. A comparison between the user perception of the quality of the ports in a country (reported by the World Economic Forum's Global Competitiveness Report) and the growth of volumes handled in the country's ports shows there is virtually no relationship.

For port users, indicators such as costs, productivity, reliability and time are more relevant than volumes. Thus, better availability of such indicators will help in a more informed view of port performance.

This section presents an overview of relevant and widely used PPIs in the ports industry. The overview is not comprehensive; various PPIs are excluded, such as "socio-economic indicators", which are discussed in the next paragraph on the economic impact of ports. Furthermore, indicators specifically for the performance of the PDC, such as financial indicators, are also excluded. The PPIs included in this overview are grouped in six categories in Table 8.4.[6]

There is no such thing as the right set of port performance indicators. The relevance of indicators depends on the specifics of the port or port region in question[7] and data availability. Poor data availability often limits the options for developing a performance dashboard. For these two reasons, stakeholders need to select indicators case by case based on the longlist of potential indicators presented in the table above. Appendix 3 provides more details for each of these indicators.

In my view, the most important PPI from the PBE perspective is the investment level of third parties in the PBE. These investments are critical for a PBE that is vital in the long run. Investments show trust in the PBE, lead to enhanced productivity and tie the third parties to the PBE for longer. In addition, investments create jobs. In many countries, investments in ports are a very substantial share of FDI in the country.

Table 8.4 An overview of common Port Performance Indicators

Category	*Relevant Port Performance Indicators*
traffic volume indicators	Number of ship calls
	Total volume of goods handled in the port
	Containers: Share of transhipment of total cargo
	Share of transit cargo of total (container) cargo
connectivity indicators	Liner shipping connectivity
	Intermodal connectivity
	RoRo connectivity
productivity indicators	Containers: moves per hour per ship
	Bulk cargo: tons per (working) hour
	Tons per berth meter
environmental performance indicators	Containers: modal split (shares of rail, road and inland waterways)
	Containers: terminal CO_2 emissions per TEU
Governance indicators	Presence of third-party terminal operators
	Independent state-owned enterprise port development company
	Corridor governance
Transport chain indicators	Average ship waiting time
	Average truck waiting time
	Containers: dwell time
	Burden of customs procedures
	Quality of ports infrastructure (WEF)

Ballpark estimates for investments by the PMB and third parties

When making a "high level" port vision with private investments as indicator, the rules of the thump below may be useful. A landlord SO-PDC may be expected to have a yearly investment level of around 15–20% of turnover. Expressed in € per ton throughput, a yearly investment level of a SO-PDC is often around €0.20 to €0.40 per ton handled. In landlord ports, the private investments in the port (in terminals, warehousing, manufacturing and so forth) around often around three to five times higher than investments of the SO-PDC, while the public sector investments (excluding the SO-PDC, e.g., in transport infrastructure to/from the port) are often broadly similar in size to those of the SO-PDC. Thus, as indicative ballpark figures, for a port that handles 30 million ton, the SO-PDC would be expected to invest around €100 million in a ten-year period, with a similar investment level of other government entities. This should allow the PBE to attract around €400 million of private investments.

8.8 The economic impact of ports

Virtually all port development plans pay attention to the economic impact of port development. Most of these studies focus on employment, value added and in some cases tax income. Often, such studies use "input–output" analysis to estimate the (regional) economic impact of specific ports.[8] Even though employment and value added seem relevant for (local) policy makers, we argue that they do not truly show the economic impact of a port. Instead, they show the sectoral composition of a region/country. However, in the long run, the unemployment level in a country or region is mostly determined by characteristics of the labor market (flexibility, education level, mobility of labor), not by employment levels in specific industries.

Employment and value added: what to include as port activities?

Employment is perhaps the most widely used socio-economic indicator. The advantage of employment is that it is relatively easy to collect, as most countries have company registers with the number of employees per company. Two issues deserve attention.

First, the calculation of direct employment requires a definition of "port activities". In virtually all countries, companies are classified in a certain industry. The most widely used industry classifications are the Standard Industrial Classification (SIC) or the North American Industry Classification System (NAICS). Calculating direct port employment requires developing a list of port industries. Once certain industries are classified as "port activities", the employment in these industries can be included in the direct port employment data. However, there is no consensus on which industries to include. There is consensus on including industries that provide services needed to handle ships and cargoes, such as terminal operators, pilots, towage companies, ship agents, inland freight transport companies and others. Difficulties arise regarding such activities as warehousing, manufacturing activities of commodities handled in seaports (e.g., flour milling and oil refining), port-related services (e.g., banking, maintenance). In line with our definition of ports as clusters of activities, I argue for including warehousing and manufacturing.

Second, the geographical borders of the port area are relevant. The calculation of direct employment generated by ports requires a "spatial delimitation" of the port. Activities inside this area are included in employment data, others not. Often, state, regional or municipal borders are used. That may be pragmatic, but it is important to keep in mind that such "political boundaries" are not relevant when analyzing the relevant region of the port complex. For activities such as repair and maintenance, it is appropriate to include companies located next to terminals – but not those located elsewhere in the province. Thus, identifying the "relevant port region" is not trivial. In addition, some services are port related but often provided by companies that are not located in the port. The best example is trucking: ports generate cargo flows, and thus employment in trucking is part of the employment generated by the port. But trucking companies are often not located in the port area. Therefore, proxies are often used to estimate the jobs in trucking generated by the port.

We argue that impact studies should focus on the contribution of ports to enabling trade. As discussed previously, ports create connectivity. This allows firms to serve markets overseas more efficiently and allows firms as well as consumers cheaper access to imported products. These effects make firms more competitive and consumers better off. Therefore, for policymakers, PDC managers and company executives, a focus on improving port connectivity as well as explaining the benefits of such connectivity to the public at large may be advisable.

Economic impact of ports: not confined to the port region

While the impact from the connectivity perspective is relevant for all consumers and port users in the hinterland, the impact from the employment/value added approach is mostly confined to the port region. Most port activities – and thus employment – are located in the port region itself. Thus, too often, port regions are aware of the importance of their ports, but port users in the hinterland are not. Nevertheless, advantages of an efficient port are passed on to these users.

Note that there is even a "conflict" of interest between the economic value for port users and the value in terms of employment. For instance, a huge productivity increase is good news for port users but translates into lower employment and value added!

Selecting the right approach to measure the impact of a port may also be relevant for port development decisions. For instance, when one aims to increase connectivity with port users and consumers, investments that enhance the efficiency of the supply chain will have priority. When one aims to attract employment and value added, port development plans may be directed towards attracting economic activities to the port region. For instance, a port may aim to attract warehousing activities. We would be cautious about such kinds of ambitions: more warehousing activities in the port may go at the expense of warehousing activities at hinterland locations. Furthermore, hinterland locations may have some important advantages over port areas (more space, less congested road infrastructure and closer proximity to consumer markets).

As a final example, consider a port that only has one piece of land available, which can be leased either to a container terminal operator or to a chemical plant. The chemical plant will most likely generate more value added (more investments). However, the container terminal will most likely create more value for port users. We argue that the economic impact of developing the container terminal would (generally) be higher.

Economic impact studies should examine how port investments impact supply chain efficiency and consequently enable trade flows. Analytically, this can be done by analyzing how port development influences generalized transport costs for port users. In line with this approach, the economic impact of new port development will be higher the more it solves (capacity) bottlenecks in a port and/or the higher the difference in generalized port costs of the port in question compared to the "second best port".

8.8.1 Transport hubs and re-exports

Many people implicitly (and classical trade models explicitly) have a simplistic idea about international trade: goods are traded between an origin country and a destination country. In practice, a *third country* is often involved. This third country imports and then *re-exports* goods. Countries where re-exports constitute a very high percentage of total trade include Belgium and the Netherlands (in both, re-exports account for more than 50% of total exports), Singapore, with over 40% re-exports, Hong Kong and Dubai, each with over 60% re-exports and Panama. Not incidentally, these countries are important transport hubs, with very large ports. The presence of re-export activities partially explains the huge volumes in ports, while on the other hand, the port strengthens the attractiveness of a country for trading activities.

The position of a country as a trade hub, with many trading firms that import and re-export goods, provides a good basis for prosperity. For instance, in Hong Kong the average mark-up, the difference between import prices and export prices of the same commodity, is about 24%. Re-export activities account for over 12% of the Hong Kong GDP. The productivity of trading activities is also very high, and most jobs are high-wage jobs.

The position of a country as a trade hub is often stable over long periods of time: the re-export share of the Dutch economy was as high as 60% in the 16th century, while Hong Kong's position as a gateway to China has also already lasted centuries.

8.8.2 Ports and industrial development

Especially in developing economies, port development can also enable industrial development, as efficient and well-connected ports are attractive locations for export-oriented manufacturing. Thus, investments in ports can help in attracting "Foreign Direct Investment" in manufacturing.

However, investing in ports without a broader effort to increase export competitiveness (with attention to fiscal and legal factors, availability of utilities, political stability and the labor market) is unlikely to bring success, as is clear from the case of Port Said (Egypt), where despite huge investments in infrastructure, the inflow of FDI in manufacturing has been very limited.[9]

Port development and attracting FDI

In many countries, ports play an important role in attracting Foreign Direct Investments. Such investments are often critical for achieving economic development. In the Netherlands the share of ports in overall inward FDI volume is around 10 to 15%, three to four times higher than the value added generated in the ports as a share of the Dutch economy. In other countries, the relevance of ports for attracting FDI is even larger: For instance, in Oman, around 50% of all FDI takes place in ports.

8.9 The relevance of a "port innovation system"

Ports face huge transition challenges, given mega-trends discussed in Chapter 3, such as the energy transition, the transition toward a circular economy, urbanization that puts more pressure on land use in port areas, digitalization and the transition of manufacturing activities often summarized under the label "Industry 4.0". The core challenge for ports is to ensure that their clusters remain economically vital and future oriented. Success in (developing and) applying new innovations is central to this transition.

Innovation in ports is especially complicated as ports are clusters of interrelated activities, with a need for coordination and cooperation between firms. For instance, coordination and cooperation are preconditions for meeting innovation challenges such as autonomous transport, digitalization of the supply chain, the capture and use/storage of CO_2 from port-related industries, integrated port call processes (between all relevant service providers and government agencies), electrification of port processes, both at terminals and at port-related industries (e.g., the chemical industry).

The "value for society" of innovations in ports is huge, and ranges from higher safety levels, lower emissions and other negative externalities, to more publicly accessible waterfronts and the creation of job opportunities for local communities. This value for society justifies strong support for and involvement in efforts to promote innovation, both by government in general and by the SO-PDC, as was discussed in Chapter 5.

The concept of a "port innovation system" is useful for understanding the innovation performance of the port ecosystem. The core idea is that innovation does not thrive through isolated actions of individual companies, but rather depends on a broad array of interrelated actors (firms, research institutes, incubators, governments, industry associations) and institutions (risk-taking culture, regulation, cooperation).

8.9.1 The innovation challenge in ports: building a port innovation system

Various studies distinguish different components of an innovation (eco)system; based on a review of these studies, we developed the framework provided in Figure 8.7, which is specifically tailored to ports, as clusters where the main challenge is enhancing the absorptive capacity.[10] Each of the components is briefly discussed below.

Two components can be thought of as the institutional environment of a port innovation ecosystem, as they are mainly external to the port ecosystem and based on regional and national institutions. First, an innovation-oriented culture has been widely described as a relevant part of an innovation ecosystem. Second, governments influence innovative activity. The innovation-prone government (regulation) encompasses both the regulatory side of governments, in which the removal of regulatory obstacles to innovative products and services is central, and the potential role of government as a user of innovative products and services.

Given the institutional environment, five related components shape the port innovation ecosystem. These five components are, in substantial part, "port-specific", in the sense that they are shaped by the actions of the firms in the port cluster. The two items in the middle of the circle depict, in line with the previous section, the main outcome of the innovation ecosystem in the port: investments in new technologies and the growth of start-ups with port-specific products and services.

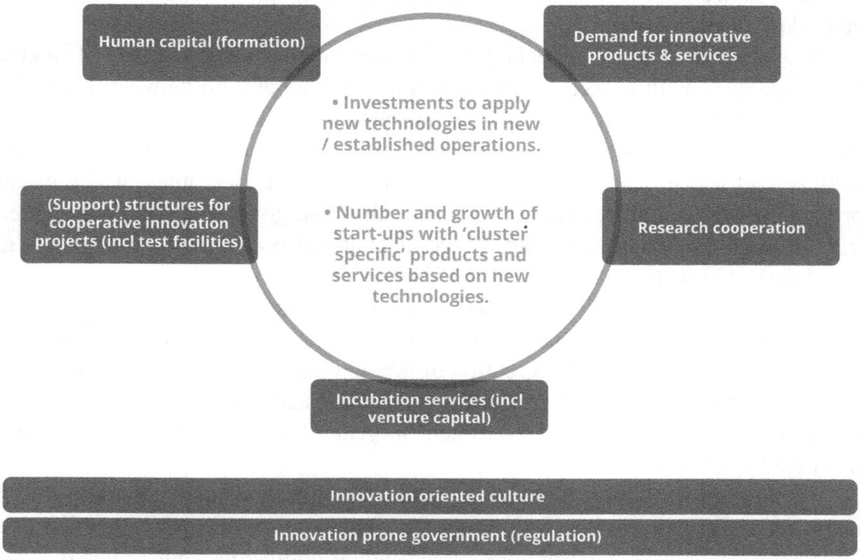

Figure 8.7 The components of the "port innovation system"

The first of the five components is human capital (formation), which is widely acknowledged as a relevant factor. Given the strong local effects of universities and other educational institutions (both in the quality of the local labor base and in attracting outside talent), the formation of human capital through education is highly relevant.

Second, innovative market demand is a relevant driver of innovative activities. This innovative demand is often exerted by a specific group of companies, called lead users, that have a sophisticated demand for innovative products and services. In the port context, the challenge is to connect to the innovative demand of MNCs active in the port.

Third, research cooperation is relevant. This component encompasses cooperation in research, as well as cluster-oriented initiatives to disseminate research results to companies.[11] University R&D has a proven impact on the innovation performance of regions.

Fourth, the availability of incubation services is relevant. These incubation services include financing and mentoring. Overall, incubation services enhance the survival and growth of new start-ups. One relevant aspect is the support for internationalization, as most opportunities are outside the ecosystem.

Fifth, support for innovative projects is relevant, especially for SMEs. Support for innovative projects goes beyond applied research and consists of financial and organizational support for realizing innovative projects. Test facilities for new products, services and technologies (in some cases referred to as "labs" or "living labs") are included in this component. Such labs can be regarded as places where various stakeholders collaborate for the creation, prototyping, validating, and testing of new technologies, services and products in real-life contexts.

The relevance of a well-functioning port innovation system is increasingly recognized, and various ports have taken initiatives to improve the port innovation system. Some best practices are summarized in Table 8.5.

Table 8.5 Best practices in developing the port innovation system

Component	*Best practices*
Innovation-oriented culture	An annual port innovation prize in the North Sea Ports (Netherlands/Belgium).
Innovation-prone regulation	Government support for a variety of initiatives to improve Singapore's maritime innovation.
Human capital (formation)	Valenciaport Foundation's focus on human capital formation of employees in the port.
	Rotterdam's efforts to enhance port-related education from vocational to university.
Demand for innovative products and services	Hamburg's efforts to work with leading technology companies such as Volkswagen and IBM on the digitalization of freight transport.
Research cooperation	Valparaiso's effort to establish cooperation with universities; Rotterdam's cooperation between the ports industry, the port authority and various universities and knowledge partners.
Incubation services	Rotterdam's PortXL program has expanded to include Singapore, Houston and Antwerp.
Support for innovative projects	Singapore's funding for innovative projects.

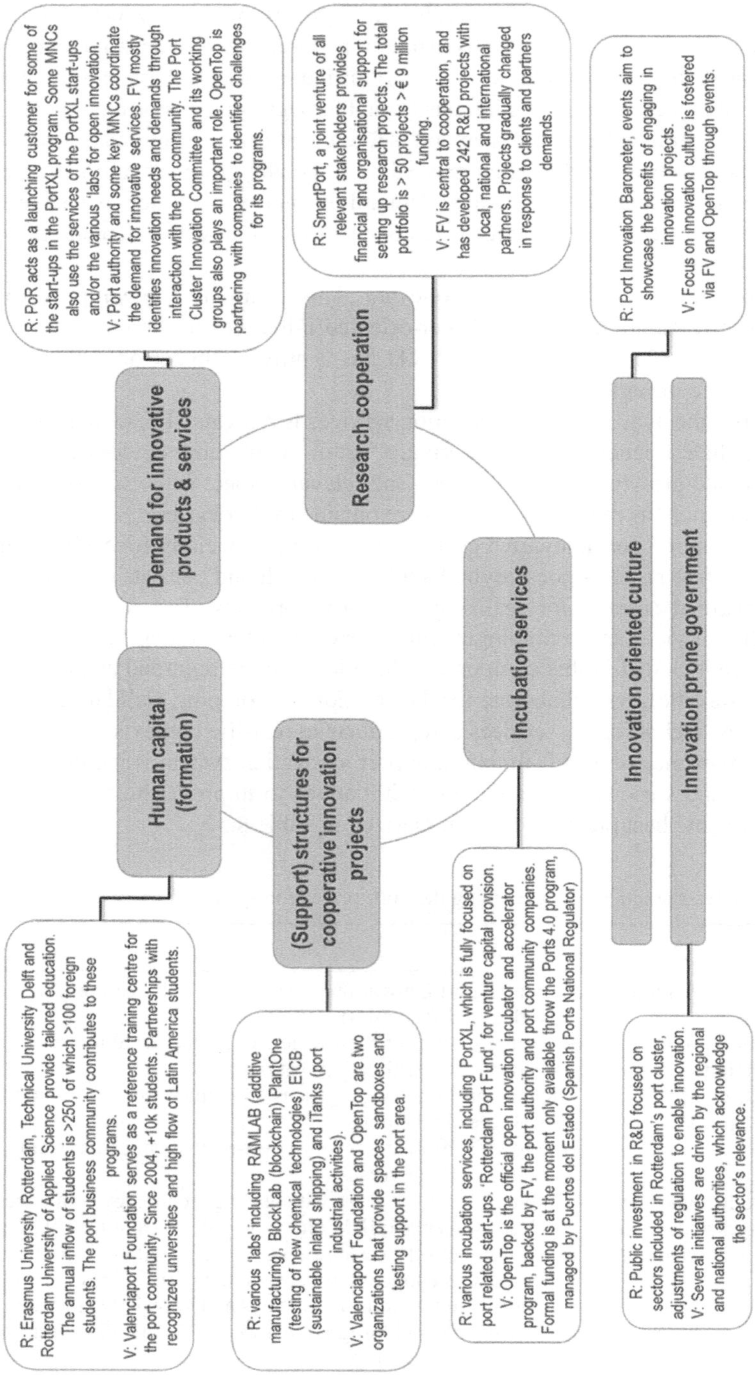

Figure 8.8 A description of the port innovation system in Valencia and Rotterdam

In the PBEs of Rotterdam and Valencia, various stakeholders invest substantially in creating a good port innovation system. A comparison of these initiatives is provided in Figure 8.8.

The role of accelerators in the port innovation system

Various venture funds have emerged in port cities over the last years. Some major other venture funds include Copenhagen-based Rainmaking Transport, PortXL, based in Rotterdam but with other locations in some other major ports, Hamburg-based Next Logistics Accelerator, and Marseille-based ZeBox. Singapore seems to be ahead of other maritime capitals, with accelerators Unboxed (by PSA International), and Pier 71 and Reefknot Investments, an accelerator of Singapore sovereign wealth fund Temasek (and owner of PSA) and the global freight forwarder Kuehne + Nagel.

While for most of the start-ups and some of the venture funds location is not top of their mind, this wave of venture capital initiatives is relevant for port cities. All port cities seek to find ways in which the port activities continue to create value for their regional economies, in the context of increasing automation and digitalization which transform port activities, as well as the increased competition between urban economies for attracting innovative minds and companies. In this context attracting start-ups is a key challenge for all port cities. Venture capital initiatives are a powerful and perhaps even indispensable element of the "port innovation system". There is obviously competition between start-ups as well as competition between the (port) innovation systems in which they are embedded.

8.10 Port development and emerging economies

One key characteristic of emerging economies is an increase in large-scale (local and foreign) investment. Moreover, (foreign) investment is a signal that the country will increasingly be incorporated in *global commodity chains*, leading generally to (potential for) rising trade flows. Thus, port development is a crucial condition for the growth of emerging economies.

8.10.1 Huge growth potential for ports in emerging economies

One key common characteristic of emerging economies is their huge growth potential, both economically and specifically for port throughput. Recall the TEU per capita in India, which is lagging over ten times that of the OECD average! Even though the growth potential differs between specific emerging economies, the BRIC countries, as well as the "next 11" (Bangladesh, Egypt, Indonesia, Iran, Mexico, Nigeria, Pakistan, Philippines, Turkey, South Korea and Vietnam, which were identified by Goldman Sachs as large countries with huge growth potential) have a huge growth potential.

8.10.2 Ports are important constraints to international trade

Next, in many emerging economies the port sector is a huge constraint for trade. Brazil, for instance, continues to struggle to develop world-class PBEs. This is a huge issue as Brazil has a vast potential for increased exports, imports and production. Important improvements in the port sector are required to enable the growth of the PBEs, including investments in infrastructure and port governance reform. Estimates of volume growth for Brazil suggest sustained container volume growth.

However, that requires huge infrastructure investments, roughly US$3– US$4 billion per year in the coming ten years. Currently, Brazil's infrastructure bottlenecks lead to inefficiencies that end up taking logistics costs to 12–15% of GDP compared to 5% in OECD countries. Economists at Goldman Sachs estimate that if Latin America, led by Brazil, doubled its infrastructure investment to 4–6% a year over the next 20 years, potential GDP growth would rise from below 4% to about 5.5%.[12] This need for huge investments in port development, often combined with a need for port reform, is not unique to Brazil but also applies to other emerging economies.

8.10.3 Scale increases of ships pose challenges

The trend of increasing ship sizes affects emerging economies. The deployment of the largest vessels (>20,000 TEU) in the trade between Europe and Asia and between the US West Coast and Asia leads to cascading: the ships currently deployed on both routes will be deployed elsewhere. Furthermore, the "Asia–Europe" route around Africa, due to the unrest close to the Suez Canal, led to port calls of unusually large ships in African ports.

Various ports have draft restrictions; hinterland connections are congested, and many ports in emerging economies do not provide sufficiently large cranes and gantries for the smooth handling of these vessels. Furthermore, there may not always be sufficient demand to fill the larger ships. Ensuring that ports can reap the benefits of the arrival of larger ships (lower slot costs and thus opportunities for increased trade) is a huge challenge.

8.10.4 Benefits of the entrance of global players

The growth prospects of emerging economies attract the interest of investors, mainly international terminal operators (ITOs). In Africa, ITOs are responsible for over 90% of privately handled containers (Drewry Shipping Consultants, 2025). The entrance of these global players generally brings substantial benefits to emerging economies: compared to local operators, global players have more financial resources, more expertise and technological skills in terminal operations. Next to higher productivity, this also leads to better safety records and environmental management at terminals. A study of the Nigerian ports after global players entered the market shows that operating hours have increased, and productivity, connectivity and container volumes have gone up (UNCTAD 2012).

8.10.5 Information exchange and customs procedures are crucial enablers for commodity flows

In many developing economies, in addition to port operations as a main bottleneck, information flows and administrative processes associated with port operations, especially of exports and imports, are a major bottleneck. The administrative processes may lead to very large dwell times at container terminals and high generalized transport costs. Thus, efforts to improve ports may work best when integrated into an overall effort to reduce trade costs.

8.10.6 Opportunities to expand and diversify the PBE

Ports in many emerging economies are located in capital cities and face huge land constraints, often without cost-effective solutions. Thus, there is an opportunity space for newly developed ports. These are best developed with an ecosystem perspective, i.e., with large stretches of vacant land to located trade-oriented activities. Various countries, including Kenya (Tema), Nigeria (Lekki) and South Africa (Nqura), aim to develop new port business ecosystems outside the capital city.

8.11 Good practices in port development

In summary, the good practices listed below have helped PMBs to successfully develop their ports.

8.11.1 Visioning

Use the value of attracted investments as a/the key performance indicator for the PBE.

Understand the changing landscape and its implications for the PBE.

Invest in open stakeholder dialogue to develop a shared vision.

Think carefully about the desired "endstate" of relevant characteristics of the PBE; adjust the market structure in the PBE if this enhances ecosystem productivity.

8.11.2 Port development approach

- Align third parties with overall ecosystem productivity.
- Aim to attract a wide range of activities to the PBE if these benefit from its unique features.
- Identify growth segments; make spatial reservations for sufficient options to accommodate investments in these.
- Develop a bold sustainability transition roadmap.
- Develop an active approach to transform unsustainable activities in the port business ecosystem.

8.11.3 Investments in port development

- Aim to enlarge expansion projects with/for individual third parties to accommodate other (future) customers.
- Invest in newly emerging opportunity spaces.

- Be flexible and agile to capture opportunities to reduce construction costs.
- Develop land for new industrial activities that strengthen the port business ecosystem.
- Attract public co-funding for investments, based on stakeholder support and demonstrable value for society.

Notes

1 Many PMBs, especially those run as government entities, have an "infrastructure DNA", which may lead to too much focus on building new infrastructure. Obviously, it is necessary to consider port infrastructure, but it is also important to consider other elements like institutional context and environmental aspects. Taking infrastructure as a starting point may best be avoided.

2 In this analysis, mineral oil products are excluded, as their behavior tends to be countercyclical in Rotterdam, because traders store these products in volatile market environments. Furthermore, a moving average is used, as the mere variation in working days per month leads to substantial computational variations per month. (These are smoothed with the moving average.)

3 Some consulting firms that forecast freight flows have developed less "scientific" but often more industry-smart models. However, such "models" are often partially based on "*ad hoc* assumptions". Conversations about these assumptions are key to truly understanding development prospects.

4 UNCTAD has a strong tradition in developing PPIs, starting in the 1970s, and continuing with the yearly publication of the Review of Maritime Transport, as well as the development of a Liner Shipping Connectivity Index. Other relevant stakeholders include the World Bank, which developed a series of indicators directly relevant for ports in the Logistics Performance Index, as well as individual ports, national and international port associations, governments and private sector organizations.

5 In addition, such stakeholders not only benefit from better PPIs but often can also add value in providing data and turning data into intelligence.

6 These categories are adapted from a classification made in the European Research Project PORTOPIA.

7 As one example, while dwell time (of transit containers) is a huge issue in Africa, it is far less of an issue in Europe, given the more harmonized and streamlined customs procedures.

8 An example of such a case is Santander (Castro & Coto Millan, 1998). Economic impact studies are also made for an entire port company, e.g., Associated British Ports (Brayn et al., 2006), and for specific port segments, such as cruise terminals (Chen et al 2019).

9 See a World Bank report by Arvis et al. (2018) for more details.

10 The above components are in line with established frameworks on innovation ecosystems. Isenberg (2014) took an approach focused on start-ups and listing six components. In comparison, our framework adds "research cooperation". In addition, we use "incubation services" while Isenberg uses "finance". Compared to the World Economic Forum's eight components (WEF, 2013), "human capital" and "education and training" are merged into one component. Overall, the frameworks are rather similar.

11 This factor is not included in Isenberg's framework, even though it is widely acknowledged as an important determinant of innovation and start-up success.

12 www.fusioninvestmentsltd.com/downloads/gs_research_africas_turn.pdf

9 Strategies of port managing bodies

This final chapter deals with strategies of port managing bodies (PMBs). The role of the PMB is center stage as it plays such a key role in port development. The mission and goals of the PMB are discussed first, followed by a discussion of the strategy and business model of the PMB. Relations with third-party service providers are the focus in the fourth section and include an overview of challenges related to competitive bidding processes. Sections 5, 6 and 7 discuss port pricing, hinterland strategies and business development in ports.

9.1 The mission and goals of the SO-PDC

As discussed in Chapter 5, PMBs are financially self-sustaining but generally do not aim to maximize profits unless they are privately owned. A PMB invests in port land and infrastructure based on a business case approach, in which risks are managed and controlled. For instance, for large-scale investments in expansion, *launching customers* are critical to reduce risks.

The key objective of the PMB is to attract commodity flows and investments of third parties to the port business ecosystem (PBE). Investments in new sites as well as in upgrading established facilities are relevant.

9.1.1 Suggestions for a strategy map with goals of the PDC

A strategy map is a tool to visualize the goals and associated key performance indicators (KPIs) of an organization. Figure 9.1 shows, based on the preceding chapters, potentially relevant goals. Figure 9.1 can be thought of as a "menu", the number of goals and KPIs being too large to include all. Figure 9.1 includes frequently mentioned goals of PDCs in strategy documents and annual reports; case-by-case selection of the most relevant goals and KPIs is required.

DOI: 10.4324/9781003630784-9

A strategy map

A strategy map is a tool to show the interrelations of the goals and performance indicators in a balanced scorecard. Such a strategy map can help to move strategy away from a small group in the boardroom to the whole organization. A strategy map helps in clearly defining measurable goals. Strategy maps are used by a huge number of public and private organizations. In the ports industry, the PMBs of Valencia and Rotterdam have used this framework. In Africa, Abidjan works with a balanced scorecard.

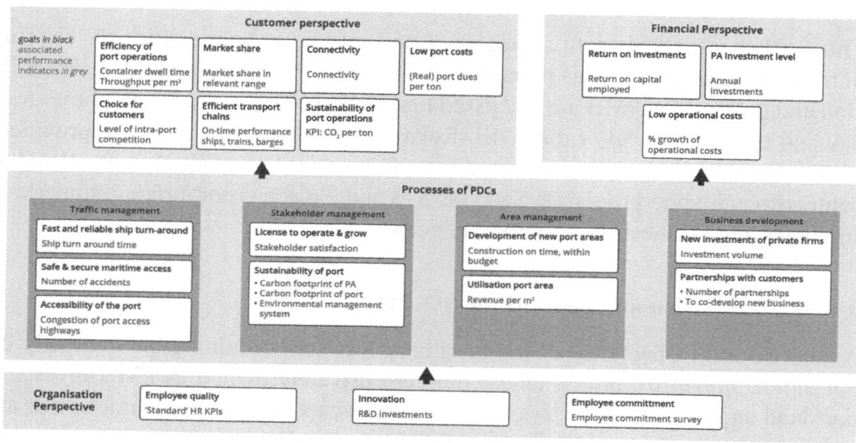

Figure 9.1 A strategy map for a PMB

The relevance of third-party investments

In line with the focus on the role of the PMB as developer of the business ecosystem, I advocate *focusing on attracting third-party investments*. In many ports in advanced economies, the *challenge of upgrading*, i.e., attracting investments to upgrade existing facilities, is at least equally important as attracting investments to new sites. As many existing assets are mature, the tenants and the PMB are faced with the choice between upgrading and closing down. The PMB thus has a risk of ending up with *stranded assets* in their PBE. As a general indication, for a PMB with a landlord business model, investments of third parties in the port are three to six times higher than the investments of the PMB. For instance, container terminal operators invest heavily in equipment, tank terminals heavily in tanks and industrial companies heavily in plants (either new plants or upgrading/modernization of existing plants). In a port like Huelva, with a large petrochemical complex, the required annual investments by third parties to ensure the long-term vitality of the port complex are around €300 to €400 million per year; in Europe's largest port, Rotterdam, the average level of third-party investments is around €2 billion per year.

9.2 Strategies of the PMB

Based on the work of scholars on the strategy of the "developer", "orchestrator" or "focal firm" of a business ecosystem, and especially Iansiti and Levien (2004) and Visnjic et al. (2016), the two core strategy choices relate to the business model (landlord vs a more integrated service bundle) and the efforts of the business ecosystem developer to enhance the productivity of the third parties active in the business ecosystem. Based on these two dimensions, the minimalist, integrator, platform provider, and ambidextrous strategy of and integrator and platform provider can be distinguished.

The minimalist strategy entails simply providing a service or asset required for an ecosystem to emerge. In the *integrator* strategy, the ecosystem developer controls the commercial interaction with buyers of the products and services provided by the ecosystem and integrates different activities in the value chain to secure its position as a central player in the ecosystem.

The *platform provider* strategy focuses on "providing an advanced platform in which other companies can thrive" (in the words of Iansiti & Levien, 2007, p. 7) without aiming for control over the commercial interaction with end users, but with a focus on developing services that allow third parties in the ecosystem to thrive by creating or enabling synergies and complementarities.

Fourth, ecosystem developers may both integrate upstream and downstream *and* develop additional services for firms in the business ecosystem. I use the term "ambidextrous" strategy for an integrator strategy combined with the development of services for third parties in the ecosystem.

These strategies for PMBs can be mapped by identifying "*minimalist*" *services* that are provided by all PMBs, because without these services, the "basic offering" (the provision of port infrastructure) is incomplete, "*integrator services*" and "*ecosystem services*" (see de Langen, 2023a for more details).

In the "integrator" strategy, the ecosystem developer has a central role in contact with customers. In this strategy, the PMB may outsource operational activities to third parties, but aims for direct commercial contractual relations with port users. As a consequence, in this strategy the PMB does not aim to attract third parties, like terminal operating companies, that serve port users independently. Six "integrator services" are part of a door-to-door logistics offering; by providing these services, the PMB moves toward a more "integrated" offering for port users.

The PMB may invest in services that enable third parties in the PBE to operate more efficiently. The core difference between the "integrator services" and the

Table 9.1 Minimalist, integrator and platform provider services of the PDC

Minimalist services	*Integrator services*	*Platform provider services*
Nautical port infrastructure	Inland ports	Intra-ecosystem infrastructure for exchange of flows between firms in the port area
Landside port infrastructure (road and rail connections in the port area)	Terminal operations	Intra-ecosystem transport services
Port land (lease/sale/ concession)	Hinterland transport	Intra-ecosystem energy infrastructure and services
Traffic management services[1]	Logistics and commercial real estate	Data exchange services
Stakeholder support[2]	Warehousing services	Interorganizational transport planning services
Port marketing	Nautical services (e.g., towage, pilotage and mooring)	Services to accelerate innovation (adoption)

"ecosystem services" is that the ecosystem services aim to increase the efficiency and productivity of the operations of the third parties active in the ecosystem. Thus, these services make the PBE more attractive for third parties. In contrast, the "integrator services" expand the bundle of services the PMB offers to port users (not third parties operating in the PBE).

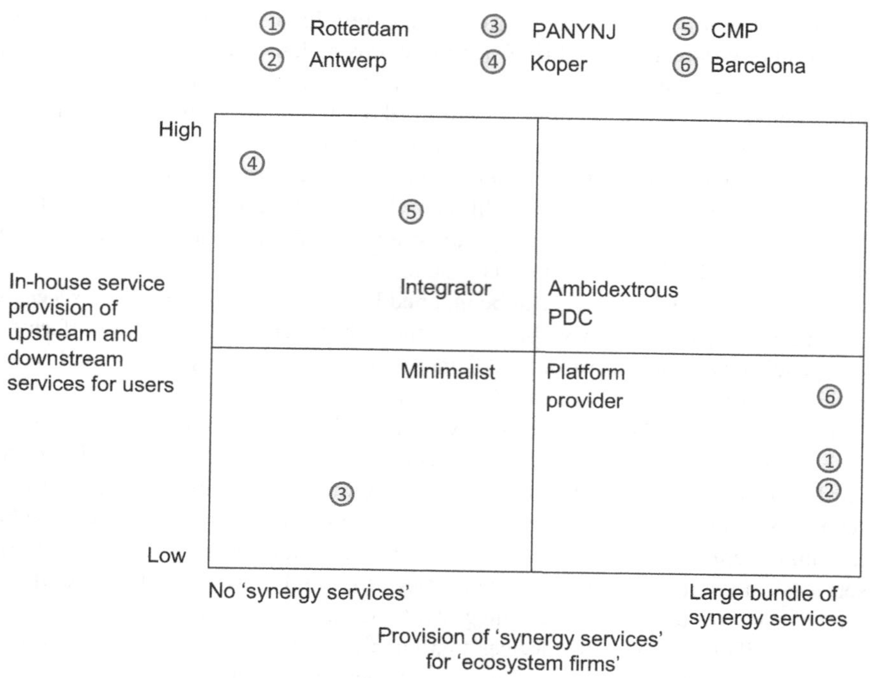

Figure 9.2 The stylized distinction between PMB strategies and positions of some PMBs

Based on the services as identified above, PMBs can be positioned in the framework presented in Figure 9.2. Figure 9.2 shows how some SO-PDCs are classified, based on an analysis of their annual reports.

PMBs increasingly position themselves as developers of the PBE. Many PMBs define their strategy in terms similar to the platform provider strategy. For instance, PMBs increasingly stress the importance of innovation for the port complex, suggesting that they regard the "port innovation system" as a part of the platform they offer. One of the challenges of the PMB is that it seeks to develop a world-class port business ecosystem, while most of the firms in this ecosystem are multinational corporations that are active in various port business ecosystems. Thus, the scope of the PMB to set standards and impose rules is rather limited.

Comparison with airports

In the context of the "platform provider strategy", the comparison with airport (development) companies is relevant. In various aspects, airports have a more active and assertive role in developing the airport ecosystem. More specifically, they often focus on ensuring that the interests of all third parties in the ecosystem are aligned with their interests. Some examples:

- Concessions of airport shops: Concessionaires generally pay a very significant share of their revenue (often as much as 30 to 40%), and revenue metrics are used to manage the relations with the concessionaires (i.e., contracts with those that perform under par are not prolonged).
- Taxis and buses: The airport company often shapes the structure of "inland transportation" through licenses or concessions to specific service providers.
- Value capture: Airport companies generally co-develop services such as hotels and commercial real estate in partnership with third parties, instead of "just" leasing land to such third parties.

9.3 The business model of the PMB

This section addresses the choice between the landlord business model and the integrator (service port) business model discussed above. As argued previously, the PMB should, in principle, be free to choose the business model; this is a strategic choice (see Figure 9.3).

At the "pure landlord" side of the spectrum, the PMB develops port land and infrastructure and leases out the land to terminal operating companies and other companies with logistics and/or manufacturing operations. Likewise, nautical services are also provided by separate companies. At the "full-service PMB" side of the spectrum, the PMB provides all operations (terminals as well as nautical services) in-house.

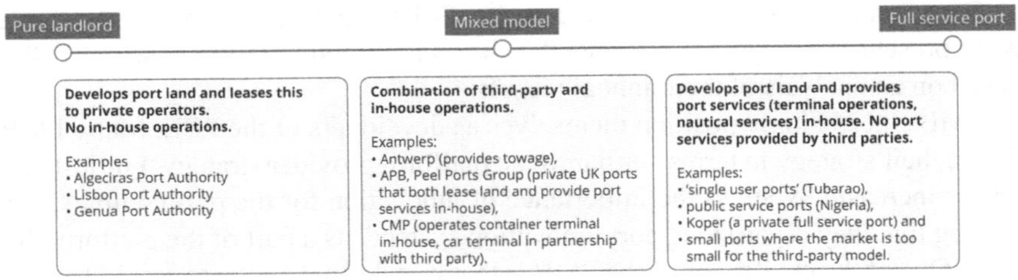

Figure 9.3 The business model choice: landlord, service port and mixed model

These "extremes" may not be the most attractive; here, there may be valid arguments to move toward a *mixed model*. A landlord PMB may consider engaging in operations (such as towage) for which there are synergies with the traffic management activities. In addition, in-house service provision of activities with sufficiently low levels of complexity may be more attractive than working with third parties. An example could be a terminal for roll-on–roll-off (RoRo) traffic.

At the other extreme, the full-service port model requires a vast range of capabilities. It would generally be beneficial to "outsource" service provision of some activities to third parties in the ecosystem. This may apply to container terminal handling, a segment in which increasingly advanced capabilities are required. In line with these arguments, most PMBs, state-owned and privately owned, operate mixed models, in which some services are provided in-house and others with third parties. Examples include:

- Antwerp Port Authority has a landlord model but an in-house provision of towage services.
- Rotterdam Port Authority has a landlord that offers (in partnership) industrial pipeline services.
- ABP is an integrator port that leases land to industrial companies and offshore wind companies.
- Peel Ports operates terminals (the integrator model) but acts as a landlord for industrial users.
- Tubarao (Brazil) is an integrator port owned by Vale, where nautical services are provided by third-party service providers.

In a substantial port business ecosystem, the developer will generally not operate all activities in the ecosystem itself. Therefore, at least for some activities, a PMB will act as a landlord. The experience with the fully private PDCs in the UK shows that these companies lease part of their land to third parties, as this strengthens the ecosystem. The most relevant considerations in the choice between in-house and third-party are provided in Figure 9.4.

The first two considerations, on synergy and capabilities, apply across the board for companies considering broadening the scope of the services they provide.[3] On top of these, four considerations emerge from the "business ecosystem perspective"

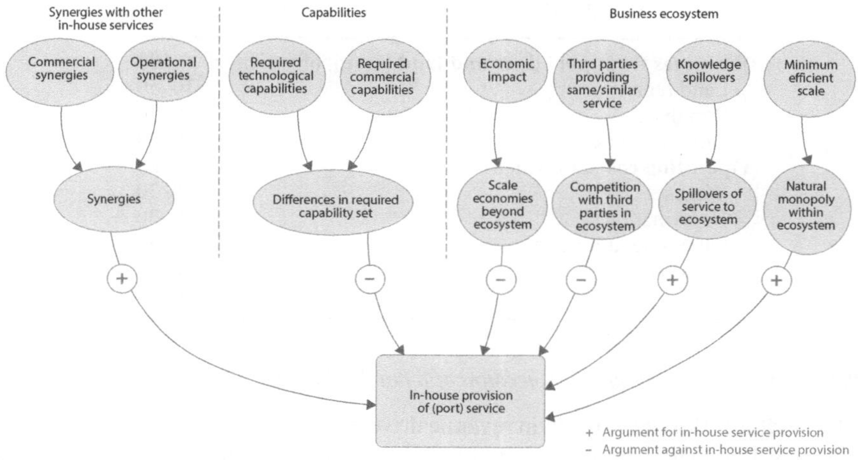

Figure 9.4 Relevant considerations for in-house vs third-party service provision

and thus are specifically relevant for the PMB. First, as most PMBs focus on developing *one* port ecosystem, they need to consider the relevance of scale economies from operations in various port business ecosystems. For instance, there are obvious scale economies from operating numerous container terminals (purchasing of equipment, terminal operating systems, commercial capabilities) as compared to operating just one terminal. This is an argument against the PMB aiming to provide container handling services in-house in one specific port, as is, for instance, done by the PMB in Koper and Copenhagen/Malmö.

Second, the PMB would need to consider the effect of competing with its own customers, i.e., other companies operating in the ecosystem. If various companies lease warehousing space, that would be an argument against the PMB starting to offer warehousing space in-house.

Third, the PMB needs to consider positive spill-overs to other firms in the ecosystem. For instance, providing incubation services may lead to such spill-overs, which would be an argument in favor of providing these in-house. Note that there is a specific type of "synergy services" (discussed in paragraph 9.5) which are treated separately, as these synergy services generally cannot be effectively provided in a "for-profit model".

Finally, a relevant consideration is whether a specific service is a natural monopoly. A third party that provides a natural monopoly service in the ecosystem is unattractive for the PMB, as this third party will extract "economic rents" from the users of the ecosystem. For instance, in small to medium-sized ports, towage may be a natural monopoly. Regulation or a tendering mechanism to create competition *for* the market in the absence of competition *in* the market are imperfect mechanisms to prevent rent extraction, so in case of natural monopolies, the PMB has an argument for providing such services in-house.

Table 9.2 An indicative profit and loss account of a landlord PMB

Revenues from port dues and land leases, of which	**100**
Land rents	30–50
Port dues	50–70
Other revenues	0–20
Operating costs, of which	**60–80**
Wages	20–30
Depreciation	20–30
Other operating costs	20–30
Capital costs	**10–20**
Profit	**0–20**

9.3.1 A stylized profit and loss account of a landlord PMB

The landlord PMB has two main revenue drivers: the *land value* and the *throughput volumes*. Land value translates into higher land lease fees, while a higher throughput leads to higher revenues through port dues. Table 9.2 shows the relevant components of a profit and loss account of a landlord PDC and rough estimates of the weights of the different items.

The operating costs generally consist of personnel costs (mainly wages), other operating costs (e.g., vessels operated by the port development company, annual dredging costs, marketing costs and so on) and depreciation. Since a landlord owns valuable assets such as port sites, infrastructure and quay walls, depreciations are generally substantial. Like all companies, the PMB has capital costs for their loans.

As PMBs generally have large volumes of invested capital (they develop and own port assets), profit as a percentage of *turnover* generally is high, even when the WACC is low.[4] These profits are often to a large extent re-invested to keep the port business ecosystem vital. Figure 9.5 shows the ratio of investments as a share of turnover for some large PMBs.

The weighted average cost of capital (WACC) of the PMB

The PMB needs to make a profit to be able to invest in port development. For understanding the required profit level, *the weighted average cost of capital* (WACC) is relevant. In general, the return of invested capital should be at least equal to the WACC. The WACC indicates the costs of the PMB for attracting capital, through loans, equity from shareholders or bonds. Most privately owned companies have a WACC somewhere between 7 and 20%. Given the relatively high stability of revenues (especially those from long-term land lease agreements), the WACC of a PMB is substantially lower (between 7 and 10%). The WACC can be considerably lower than that range, as PMBs frequently receive loans from governments or non-commercial development banks (such as the World Bank or the Asian Development Bank). In the case of government-owned PMBs, the dividend expectations or agreements of the shareholders influence the WACC.

If shareholders do not require dividends, this is an implicit "subsidy"; the same applies for guarantees for loans. For instance, if the Spanish state, the owner of Valencia Port Authority (APV), guarantees the loans of APV, the interest rates for these loans will be relatively low. This is implicit public funding, which may well be justified based on the "value for society" of port development.

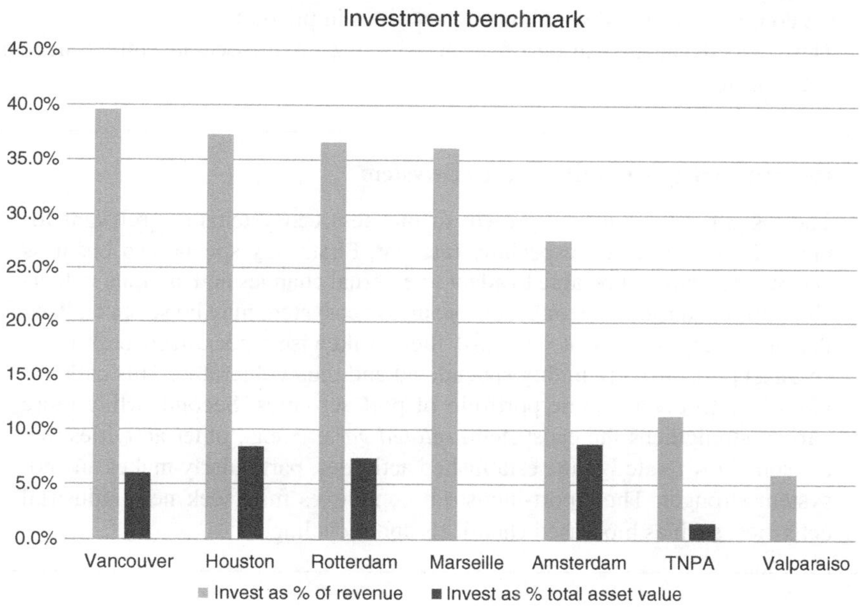

Figure 9.5 Ratios of investments as a share of turnover for some large PMBs

Source: own analysis based on data provided in the Annual Report.

A part of the profit of a PMB may be paid as a dividend to shareholders, the remaining part being available to be re-invested in the port. A port development company focused on the vitality of the port complex may annually invest 20–40% of its revenues in the port complex.[5] Smaller investment volumes of a state-owned PMB may suggest that *it has not succeeded* in developing sufficient investment projects; this has a negative impact on the long-term development of the port.

9.3.2 The port business ecosystem as a portfolio of activities

The PMB, as the developer of the port business ecosystem, needs to make choices about the "portfolio" of activities in the business ecosystem. For instance, the PMB may aim to develop a certain part of the port into a tank terminal, a site for bio-based chemicals or a site for warehousing. Given the long-term impact of such choices, it makes sense to not follow a "first come first serve" approach. In an alternative approach, the "strategic value" of potential new activities for the ecosystem is taken into account; in addition to financial considerations, the PMB prioritizes activities with a high strategic value. The following factors determine the strategic value:

- The life-cycle phase and competitive position of an activity: "waste to chemicals" has a higher strategic value than "oil to chemicals". This is also due to the potential to develop "first mover" advantages in new industries.
- The effects of specific activities on other activities in this ecosystem. A biorefinery may attract downstream chemicals; a container terminal may improve the competitiveness of warehousing activities in the port.
- The societal value creation of an activity, e.g., expressed in employment or externalities.

Related variety strengthens the ecosystem

The insights regarding the growth of business ecosystems are relevant for ports. Two insights are especially relevant. First, very specialized business ecosystems may not be able to adapt to external changes and are thus vulnerable. For instance, Houston's port business ecosystem may be so specialized that it is very dependent on fossil fuels. Likewise, specialized bulk (processing) ports also are highly specialized and thus vulnerable. This calls for initiatives to diversify the portfolio of port activities. Second, while more variety strengthens the ecosystem, *related variety*, e.g., other activities that are somehow related to the established activities, particularly makes an ecosystem stronger. Thus, port-industrial complexes may seek new industrial activities, such as bio-based chemicals and recycling.

9.3.3 Portfolio analysis

With regard to the life cycle and competitive position, portfolio analysis is a useful instrument. In the most widely used model for portfolio analysis (see Figure 9.6), segments are classified along two dimensions: the growth prospects and the market shares.

The framework above is best applied to all (potential) activities to be included in the port business ecosystem. Thus, in addition to activities like "container terminals" and "tank storage", it is relevant to include activities such as "warehousing", "recycling" and perhaps even "data centers" or "sustainable energy production". As argued in Chapter 4, in many PBEs the growth prospects of these activities are higher than for most terminal handling activities.

9.4 Relations with third-party service providers

For landlord PMBs, selecting third parties for land lease agreements and concessions are core strategic decisions. There are two methods to select third parties: *competitive bidding* and *direct negotiations*. As argued in Chapter 6, regulation should establish open and transparent procedures as the rule, with scope for the

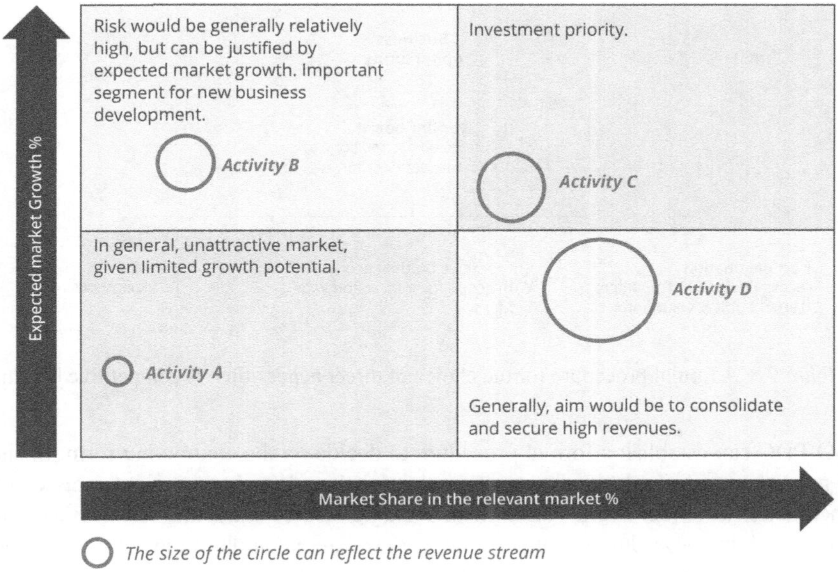

Figure 9.6 Portfolio analysis for the PBE

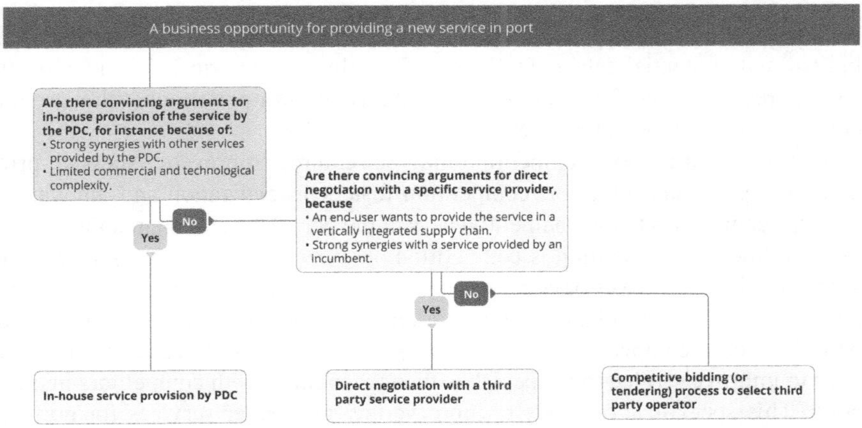

Figure 9.7 SO-PDC choices for new activities in the port business ecosystem

PMB to deviate from this rule. In such regulation, parties can appeal against contracts signed through direct negotiations. Such an approach gives PMBs scope for developing strategic deals with customers but places the burden of justifying this approach on the PMB.

9.4.1 A tender board to limit risks of unjustified direct contracts

The risk that a SO-PDC signs agreements with politically connected third parties is relevant, in addition to the risk of outright corruption. To develop safeguards for that, the

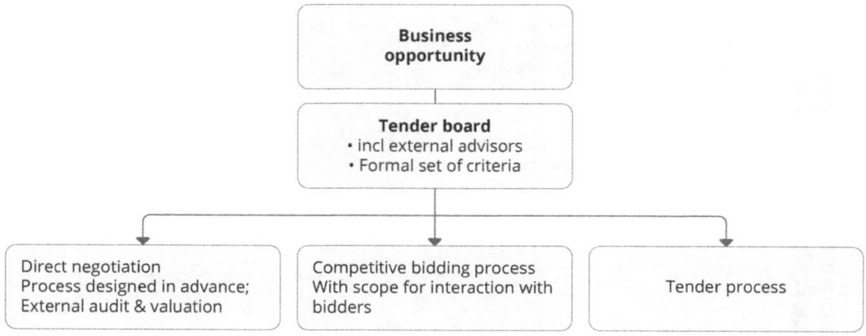

Figure 9.8 A formal procedure for the choice of direct negotiation vs competitive bidding

SO-PDC can establish a formal procedure to decide on the contracting form. In such a procedure, a formal set of criteria can be developed, and external advisors can be included in a "tender board" tasked with deciding on the contracting form. As a second safeguard, the procedure can include an *ex post* external audit of the contracting form in case a non-competitive process has been chosen. Figure 9.8 shows such a procedure.

9.4.2 Relations with third parties and intra-port competition

As discussed in Chapter 5, competition between service providers in ports is often limited, with potential detrimental effects for volumes and prices. For a PMB, the choices regarding the feasibility and desirability of intra-port competition are important port development choices.

Introducing intra-port competition may be required to prevent excessive pricing. On top of that, intra-port competition fosters specialization and innovation, and thus contributes to the competitiveness of the port. This argument applies in all cases. Intra-port competition is competition on a *perfect level playing field* in the sense that the cost curves of competitors are very similar. Competitors in the same port face the same regulation, labor market conditions, trade costs, and supplier base. In such a competitive environment, service providers have stronger incentives to improve services and specialize than when faced with competitors in other ports. This specialization leads to more variety and better services for port users. Intra-port competition thus fosters innovation and presses competing firms to constantly improve services to their customers. This dynamic process keeps ports competitive, as the benefits of innovation and specialization are passed on to port users. This argument for promoting intra-port competition is relevant *even when inter-port competition is fierce*. Thus, *whenever possible, introducing intra-port competition is beneficial for port competitiveness*. Introducing intra-port competition is also the commercially most attractive strategy for a PMB, under the assumption that a regulator disciplines service providers in the port as well as the PMB.

An important condition for the viability of intra-port competition is that *the market should be at least twice as large as the minimum efficient scale* (MES)

for providing a port service. A small market size relative to the MES prevents intra-port competition as the market in the port is a "natural monopoly". In such a market, scale economies are only fully realized with *one* supplier of port services. As an example, in a port that handles on average one seagoing vessel per day, the market is too small to accommodate two separate towage companies.

The MES of port services depends on cost curves: the MES is reached when marginal and average costs no longer decrease when capacity is expanded. For port services such as a container terminal or an iron ore terminal, this MES is clearly quite large, and intra-port competition may be feasible in large ports but unfeasible in small ports. Given the relatively large MES, intra-port competition generally will involve two or three competing service providers, often with a somewhat distinctive specialization.

A PMB may be able to *reduce* the MES by investing in assets and leasing those assets to competing private firms. In such an arrangement, scale economies are ensured, while relatively small firms can provide port services. Such an arrangement may, for instance, be viable in pilotage, where groups of pilots can use "public" assets for providing pilotage services. Figure 9.9 shows the available policy options and shows which policies are required in different circumstances.

Figure 9.9 suggests that concessions for providing port services may incur *competition for the market*. The bidding process can be developed in different ways. From a port competitiveness perspective, a process where interested parties have to bid for the lowest price for the port services is the most attractive. However, a PMB may be tempted to invite bids for the highest price. In case of limited inter-port competition, this approach is a form of "economic rent extraction" by the PMB, which is not in the interests of port users – nor in the public interest.

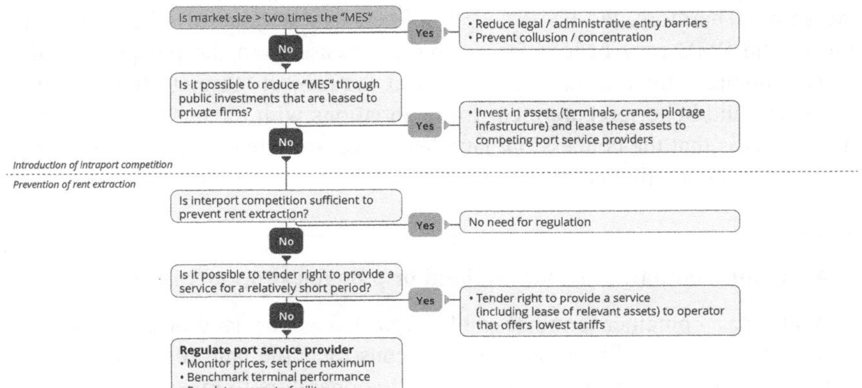

Figure 9.9 Strategies to introduce intra-port competition and prevent rent extraction

Source: Adapted from de Langen and Pallis (2006).

9.4.3 Competitive bidding to grant concessions/land lease agreements to third parties

A typical competitive bidding procedure consists of three phases (see Theys et al., 2010):

- *Pre-bidding phase*: The PMB needs to develop a business opportunity for a third party and needs to create interest in this business opportunity. In this phase, the rules of the bidding process are established.
- *Awarding phase*: This phase entails the qualification and selection of the winning bid.
- *Post-bidding phase*: The phase where, based on a contractual agreement, the third party is providing the port service. Disputes frequently emerge in this phase.

Developing the business opportunity for third parties

The value of a business opportunity that is offered to a third party (as an example, a container terminal) depends on many factors; some of the most important ones are:

1. Market and growth potential
2. Competitive position *vis-à-vis* competing terminals
3. Operational efficiency

The PMB deeply influences these factors. The growth potential often heavily depends on such items as customs performance, information availability in ports, quality of hinterland connections and so on. The competitive position depends on the price and quality of other port service providers (bunkering, towage, pilotage, hinterland transport), and operational efficiency depends on the terminal dimensions, the quality of VTS systems, coordination among all port service providers and so on. Therefore, the PMB deeply influences the value of a business opportunity. The PMB may benefit from a business case from the perspective of the concessionaire. This allows them to look at the project "through the eyes of the customer" and better prepare them for negotiations with the customer. An important insight is that the concession/ land lease fees are often a relatively minor part of the overall operating costs.

A site for a container terminal: land or a business opportunity

A site for a container terminal can be regarded as port land or as a business opportunity. In the first case, the PMB constructs the land for leasing to an interested operator and expects prospective operators to make sure the permits are obtained, design the terminal, attract cargo and develop a hinterland network.

When the PMB develops the container terminal as a business opportunity, it will develop forecasts, make sure (through lobbying) that the transport infrastructure can accommodate the expected traffic growth, ensure that environmental licenses will be granted, co-develop intermodal access to the port, invest in a port community system and so on.

In the first case, a prospective operator will see a piece of land that may be developed into a terminal, with considerable risks for the operator. In the second case, a prospective operator sees a business opportunity with limited risks.

This difference is reflected in the willingness to pay of an operator, which in general will be much higher for a business opportunity than for port land. An open assessment process, where bids are invited from competing potential operators, is potentially attractive, as in such a process, bids will reflect the value of the business opportunity, not "just" be compensation for the port land.

Loss-making business opportunities

SO-PDCs and PAs will also consider commercializing business opportunities with a *negative* business case if this creates sufficient value for firms in the port complex. Collective transport services serve as an example. SO-PDCs or PAs – like municipalities or regions – can invite bids for collective transport services, even when they are loss-making. In such a case, the SO-PDC would then have to pay a fee to an operator for providing collective transport services. This may be justified by reduced congestion on the highway and better access of firms in the port to labor markets. Note that in this approach the SO-PDC is still focused on creating value for firms in the PBE.

Bidding procedures

The aim of awarding processes is to maximize a set of specified objectives. A PMB generally would aim for a high concession fee (e.g., a fee per TEU handled or the percentage of revenue).[6] In preparing the bidding process, it is sensible to include a reserve price that allows the PMB to suspend the awarding procedure if no satisfying bid has been offered.

In most concessions (especially the lease contract and BOT type contract), the PMB will have to make decisions on the duration, fees and fee structure. In general, the duration of the concession will vary with the amount of the initial investment required. The duration of the agreement is of crucial importance to both terminal operators and the PMB.

Service level clauses and minimum throughput guarantees

Concession agreements can include performance levels, such as terminal productivity (e.g., total moves per ship per hour). The PMB may be tempted to develop very specific performance even though this may limit an operator's flexibility and may be costly to monitor. Therefore, more general indicators are best. As one example, moves per crane may be too detailed, in which case moves per ship may be better.

Likewise, the PMB may want to ask for minimum throughput guarantees, both to reduce its risks (as a minimum revenue stream from port dues is guaranteed) and to incentivize the operator to optimize the use of the terminal. Not meeting the minimum guarantees implies a financial penalty and may be sufficient basis to terminate the contract.

Renegotiations

Renegotiation can seriously undermine the efforts made in aiming to design a competitive awarding procedure. The OECD (2007) mentions in this respect:

> Renegotiation, whether due to contract incompleteness or opportunism, can eliminate the benefits of a competitive allocation mechanism; essentially, the winner of an auction will be the best negotiator, not necessarily the best infrastructure operator … Strenuous efforts should be made to restrict renegotiation to situations where renegotiation is not opportunistic, that is, to situations where unexpected events, outside the control of the parties, have occurred.

A renegotiation is considered to have occurred if a concession contract underwent a significant change. The World Bank analyses the occurrence of renegotiations and concludes (based on a sample >100 concessions) that the average number of renegotiations is 3.22 over the lifetime of the concession. Renegotiations generally are beneficial for the concessionaire. PMBs should be aware of the frequent occurrence of renegotiations. It is essential to acknowledge that the "regulatory regime" is both the factual concession contract and the commitment of the concession-granting agency to that contract. An important signal that the concession-granting agency is committed to the contract is a stipulation in the contract that a significant fee will need to be paid for a renegotiation request.

High leverage and the risks of renegotiation

Concession is done mostly with a "special purpose company/project company". This implies financing is required for the project, not for the company that operates the project (non-recourse financing). Two sources can be used to finance a project: equity and debt. Investors prefer as much debt as possible but an upper limit is imposed by the increasing threat of bankruptcy – as banks are not willing to provide loans. Projects have a leverage ratio (the ratio of liabilities over assets, high leverage thus indicating a high level of debt). The leverage is amongst others related to the commercial risk. When commercial risks are high, a project may not be bankable. Concession-granting entities can develop mechanisms to improve the bankability of a project, such as revenue guarantees. Alternatively, bidders may be asked to submit bids for the minimum net present value of revenues (PVR). The concession contract then ends not after a fixed number of years but when a fixed amount of revenues is reached.

If the entity granting the concession is averse to bankruptcy and/or fears service disruption, it may be willing to renegotiate to allow more profit (higher prices by the concessionaire) when leverage is high. Knowing this, firms will have an incentive to increase leverage. If firms know that they can renegotiate whenever they are in financial difficulty, they will have incentives to increase leverage, as the bankruptcy risk is held not by the concessionaire but by the concession-granting organization willing to renegotiate. Thus, port authorities may either design bidding processes where this effect does not occur or demand/incentivize bids with less leverage.

9.4.4 *A competitive bidding best case: Rotterdam's Rotterdam World Gateway (RWG) terminal*

In view of past and projected growth in the container market, Port of Rotterdam (PoR) started the port expansion project Maasvlakte II (MVII), aiming to enable Rotterdam to expand the port and attract cargo flows and investments. PoR decided to use competitive bidding for one of the newly developed terminal sites; for the other site, direct negotiation was used, with APMT, an operator already active in the port. The purpose of the second terminal (now the RWG terminal) was to attract a consortium of leading players in the container industry, capable of attracting new cargo volumes to Rotterdam. The scope was a container terminal of around 200 hectares and a capacity of 5 to 6 million TEU, to be developed in two phases. Port of Rotterdam provides the port infrastructure and the terminal site; the private partner is responsible for investments in superstructure.

Given the huge financial risks associated with starting this project without customers, prior to starting construction works, a competitive bidding process was launched in 2005 to attract a "*launching customer*" for MVII.[7] The interest in the right to operate the terminal was huge; after a process of about two years, a lease agreement was signed in the summer of 2007, with an international consortium consisting of DP World and the shipping lines APL, MOL, HMM and CMA CGM. Even though the 2008–2009 global financial and economic crisis dramatically changed the outlook for global trade, shipping and ports, the contract was honored; after a construction and testing period from 2012 to 2014, the consortium opened RWG in 2015, and the terminal handled almost 3 million TEU in 2018.

The process to select a container terminal operator was termed "open assessment" by the Port of Rotterdam. The three main characteristics of this process are:

- The process is transparent, non-discriminatory and open for all qualified candidates.
- *Initial proposals* were solicited from pre-qualified parties. Based on discussions between PoR and interested parties, these were re-submitted as *modified proposals*.
- The two best modified proposals were further developed into *best and final proposals*, based on negotiations. The most attractive best and final proposal was granted the concession.

Figure 9.10 summarizes the competitive bidding process. An important novel feature of this process is the dialogue between interested parties and PoR, with the aim of improving the proposals.[8] This is the key difference between the competitive bidding process and a tender procedure.

The terminal opened in line with the planning in 2015. RWG operated at 90% of capacity in 2017, implying an annual throughput of over 2 million TEU. Figure 9.11 shows the evolution of the market share of Rotterdam in the HLH range before and after the opening.

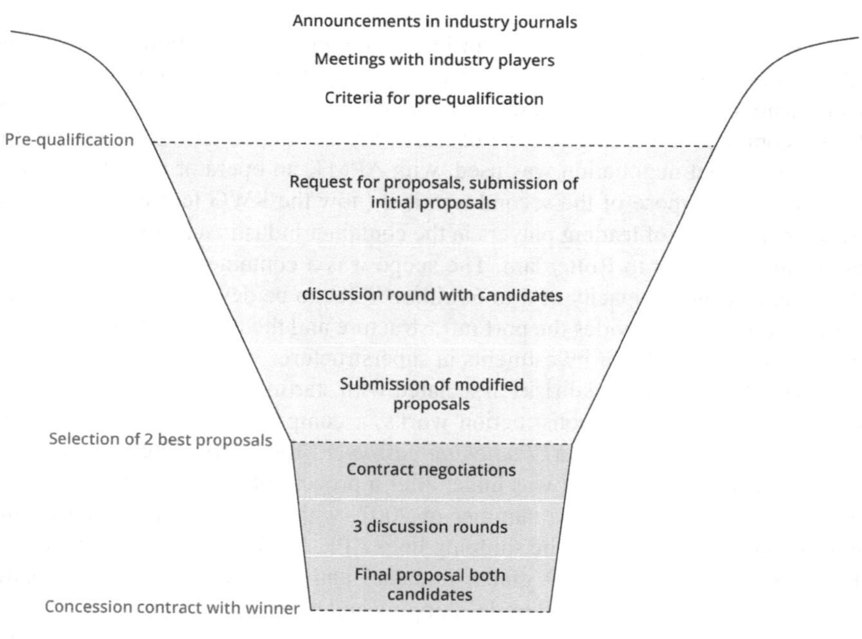

Figure 9.10 The competitive bidding process

Source: Figure adapted from de Langen et al. (2012).

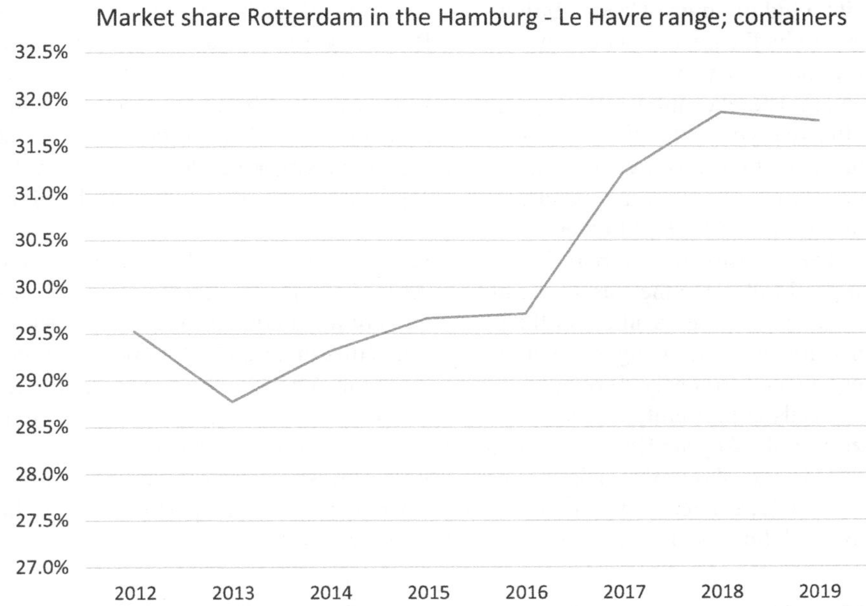

Figure 9.11 The market share of Rotterdam in the HLH range and the opening of RWG

Source: own analysis based on container volume statistics published by the PMBs.

Even though RWG accounts for less than 20% of Rotterdam's throughput, these data suggest that RWG's rapid success has contributed to a strong development of Rotterdam's market share. Less than five years after its opening, the terminal operated at around 90% capacity. In 2023, the expansion with phase 2 was agreed, and in 2025 a part of the additional capacity became available.

9.4.5 A failure case in competitive bidding: the port of Izmir (Turkey)

In Turkey, the transfer of port operations to the private sector in a PPP model was decided in 1994. The Turkish State Railways (TCDD) was the state-owned enterprise operating the major ports, because of the importance of railway connections. However, it was clear that this set-up was hampering the quality of service provision in the ports, while Turkey increasingly aimed to improve the export performance of the country. The reform in the ports sector was a part of a wider shift toward a smaller role for government-owned entities. The port reform initiative started in 1994 and worked well in virtually all ports except Izmir. The most widely followed approach, also followed in Izmir, was to select one private operator for the whole port infrastructure in one specific port.

TCDD invited bids for a concession to operate the ports in 2007. This process was applied to all six TCDD ports, including Izmir. In Izmir an international consortium including Hutchison as the main partner won the tender process in 2007, with a bid of almost US$1.3 billion.[9] The outcome of the bidding process was approved by the government. However, the Port Worker Union and the Development of Public Management Foundation (KIGEM) went to court to litigate to cancel the tender. The execution of the agreement was suspended by the Council of State. After two years, the lawsuit was settled in favor of the Turkish government, and the consortium was invited to sign the agreement in November 2009, yet due to the global financial crisis and other port developments in the region, they declined, as did the second-highest bidder.

The investments in port infrastructure, superstructure and equipment were stopped following the start of the bidding procedure. This situation continued during the legal process and after the cancellation of the bidding process. This lack of investment caused congestion at the port and shifts of cargo both to ports in other regions and to newly developed ports near Izmir. After 2009 two new container terminals in proximity to Izmir started operations. As a result, the market share of Izmir in the Aegean Region decreased from 24% in 2005 to 15% in 2015.

This case shows that delays in competitive processes to select a private partner increase legal uncertainty and have a detrimental effect on the performance of the port and thus also the value that the port assets represent.

9.5 The importance of "ecosystem services"

A part of the investments of a PMB (roughly between 25 and 50% of total investments) are aimed at improving the vitality of the port for all port users. Often, these investments are done without a *direct* mechanism to (fully) recover them.[10] Examples include investments in access roads in the port, a port community system and a port innovation network, "open access pipelines" between different companies in the ecosystem for the exchange of liquid bulk flows, and infrastructure to share and exchange energy, heat and CO_2. Some of these investments can be considered

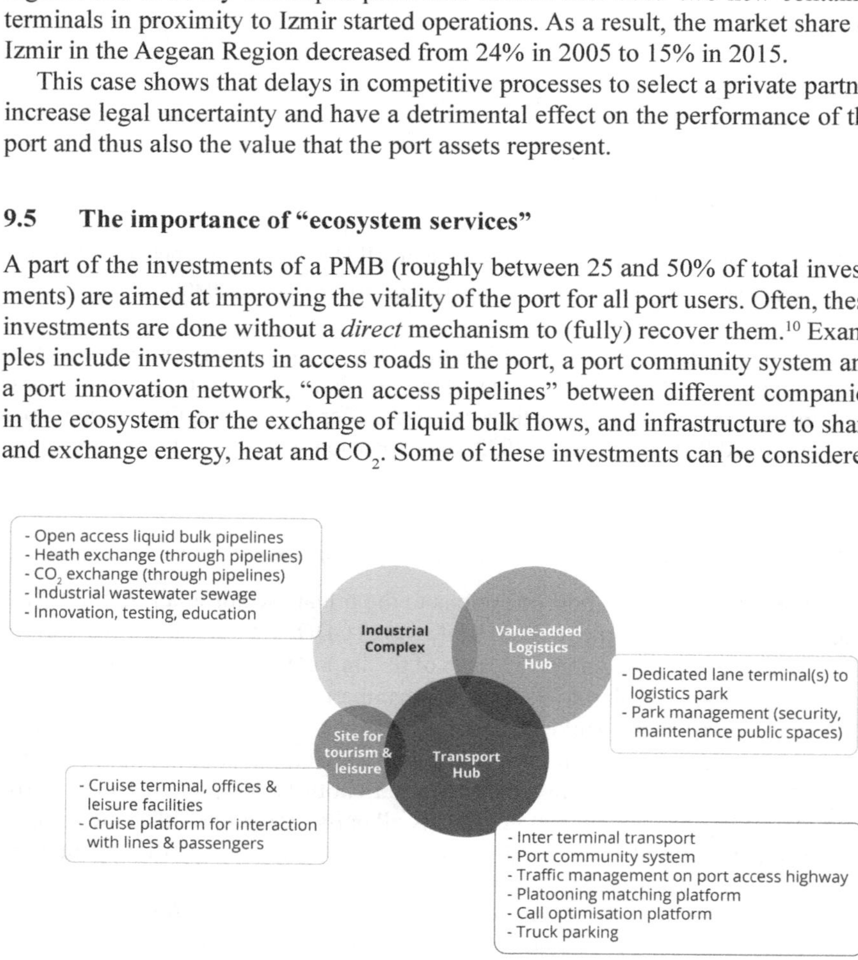

Figure 9.12 Examples of synergy services for the port business ecosystem

as services that the PMB provides to the firms in the port business ecosystem, i.e., "*ecosystem services*".[11] Synergy services can be defined as services provided to a group of companies in the PBE that allow these companies to create synergies. Figure 9.12 shows examples of such synergy services for each of the four components of the port business ecosystem.

Energy management as a "business ecosystem service"

Around 30% of the more than 60 European ports that provided data for a study on the investment pipeline and investment challenges of European ports intend to invest in developing energy management services.

Energy management services can for instance allow the optimization of the use of available electricity grid capacity for various companies, or even the whole "port business ecosystem" together. Such services can also enable companies to exchange any surplus of self-generated electricity or create value for port companies by joint facilities to store electricity when prices are low and use these when prices are higher.

The logic for the PMB as provider of such services is compelling: these services help improve the collective efficiency of all the companies that operate in the port. At the same time, commercial companies may not be too eager to develop these services (with the associated investments) because of an unattractive risk/return profile and because such energy services can only be developed in an often costly and lengthy process to secure buy-in of the companies in the port that stand to benefit from these services. These characteristics make energy management a "port business ecosystem service" in the same way a port community system is a port business ecosystem service. The PMB in my view should be eager to develop these "ecosystem services", primarily because they create value for the companies in the port and this help to attract new investments, which in turn generate financial return for the PMB. The road to successful introduction of such services requires "intrapreneurship", experiments and commitment. But value for port users and society at large awaits at the end of the road.

9.5.1 Creating and capturing the value of "synergy services"

The core challenge of developing synergy services is creating value for users, and, more complicated, capturing (a part of) the created value through charges. As the value of the synergy services often increases with the number of users, capturing value directly through pricing may not be attractive, as it reduces the number of users. In addition, users may be deterred by the risk of becoming dependent on the synergy services. Finally, synergy services generally create "value for society" (e.g., reduction of emissions, truck movements, congestion and the like). This justifies partial public funding for such services. For these reasons, a "for-profit approach" for synergy services is often problematic and a "not-for-profit approach"

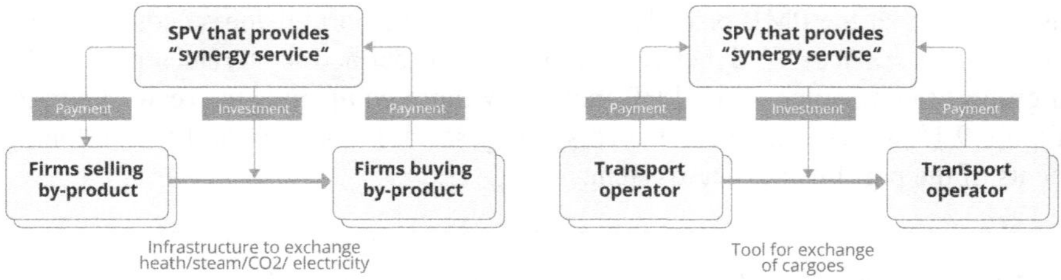

Figure 9.13 Synergy services provided by a special-purpose vehicle

may be more effective. In such an approach, the PMB may seek to recover part of the investments directly, and another part indirectly, as part of a broader "service bundle" or through attracting public funding. In addition, a "not-for-profit approach" may lead to service provision through a "special-purpose vehicle" (SPV) (see Figure 9.13).

In each of the models depicted above, a special-purpose vehicle invests in an asset (which may be an IT tool) that enables users to create synergies. The core challenge is that the more users, the higher the benefits, but users may be deterred by the risk of becoming dependent on the synergy services. For this reason, and because of the "value for society" that synergy services create (e.g., reduction of emissions, truck movements, congestion and the like), often a not-for-profit approach is most effective.

Bundling or unbundling: a port as a hotel

The choices about pricing for specific services are not unique to ports. For instance, a hotel may include breakfast in one all-inclusive price, or charge for it specifically. Attraction parks have similar pricing choices. Is parking free with the entry ticket? And toilets? And the attractions themselves: are all of them for free, or are there additional fees for the most popular ones?

The parallel for ports is straightforward: is pilotage included in the bundle of port services, for which the port dues are charged? And waste disposal? Is road infrastructure provided for free, or do users have to pay charges? How about charges for a port community system?

These questions show that the services of the PDC can be considered as a bundle, and the choice of what to include in the bundle is highly relevant. There are no "applies to all ports" answers to the above questions, but three general principles are relevant:

- In principle, prices send the right signals. So specific pricing for specific services is in general advisable.
- However, pricing may lead to free riding, e.g., firms may opt out of collective initiatives when asked to commit in advance (for instance the use

of a port community system may be low when directly priced, which reduces the value of such a system).

- Furthermore, costs for collecting fees may prevent direct pricing. While charging road users for specific port roads may send the right signals, costs of collecting such charges may outweigh the benefits.

For "synergy services" that are truly collective, including these services in the "service bundle", without (or with low) direct charges to users, is often sensible. In cases where a specific group of firms will benefit most, arrangements to (partly) recover investments through direct fees are more sensible. For instance, new infrastructure can be (partially) recovered with tolls or other direct charges, a port community system can be (partially) recovered through a fee for transactions, and shore power facilities can be (partially) recovered through user charges. Whether or not to recover investment costs directly is an important choice for a PDC. Figure 9.14 shows the four different ways to make and recover investments in synergy services, each with examples.

In some cases, partnerships for the provision of synergy services are best signed with public authorities (for instance, for transport infrastructure). In other cases, partnerships with private companies are sensible (for instance, for *port marketing*). The PMB needs to make decisions on whether and, if so, how to develop partnerships. Regardless of the partnership structure, the synergy services can only be successful if they are widely used by the firms in the port business ecosystem.

While many of those firms have ideas about services they would like to receive, not all of those ideas have a positive "value case". For instance, port users may express a desire for port marketing, but the value created by port marketing may not be significant. Thus, an important challenge is to select the most promising ideas

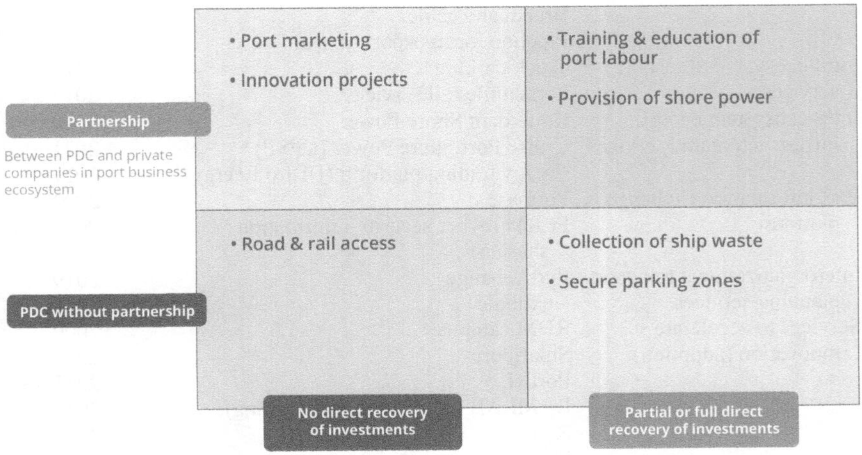

Figure 9.14 Four different ways to make investments in synergy services

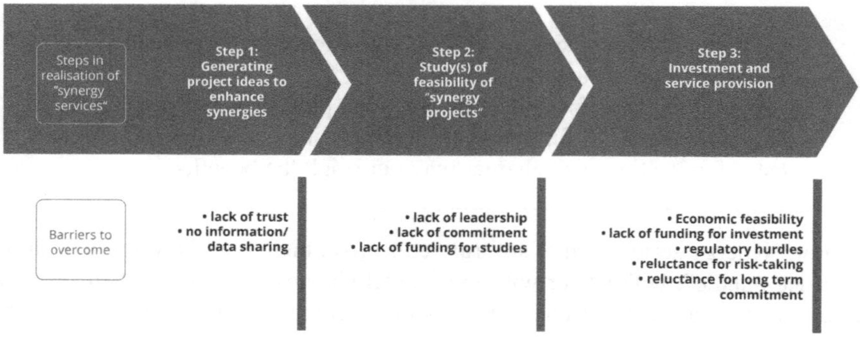

Figure 9.15 Synergy services: three steps and associated barriers

Source: Adapted from Siskos and Van Wassenhove, 2017.

and turn these into projects. However, various hurdles have to be overcome along the way. Figure 9.15 shows a distinction of three steps with specific barriers for each of those hurdles (Siskos & Van Wassenhove, 2017).

As discussed previously in this chapter, the SO-PDC tasked with developing Rotterdam's PBE (named Port of Rotterdam NV, or PoR for short) follows a "platform provider" strategy and has developed various synergy services. Table 9.3 shows these services and the year in which PoR introduced them.

Table 9.3 Timeline of introduction of ecosystem services by PoR

Service type	*Services provided by PoR*	*Year established*
Intra-ecosystem infrastructure	Multicore pipelines for fuels and chemicals	2003
	Broadband cable	2007
	Pipeline for transport of heat	2018
Intra-ecosystem transport services	Truck parking	2012
	Portshuttle rail services	2015
Intra-ecosystem energy infrastructure and services	Rotterdam Shore Power	2019
	Cruise Port Shore Power (CPSP)	2021
	Energy trading platform (Distro Energy)	2021
Port information exchange platform	Portbase	2003
	FERM (cyber security information sharing)	2016
Interorganizational transport planning services	PortXchange	2019
	Nextlogic	2011
Services to accelerate innovation (adoption)	RDM campus	2009
	Smartport	2015
	PortXL	2015
	RAMLAB (additive manufacturing)	2016
	Rotterdam Port Fund	2016
	Blocklab (blockchain)	2017

Source: Own elaboration, based on Port of Rotterdam (2025).

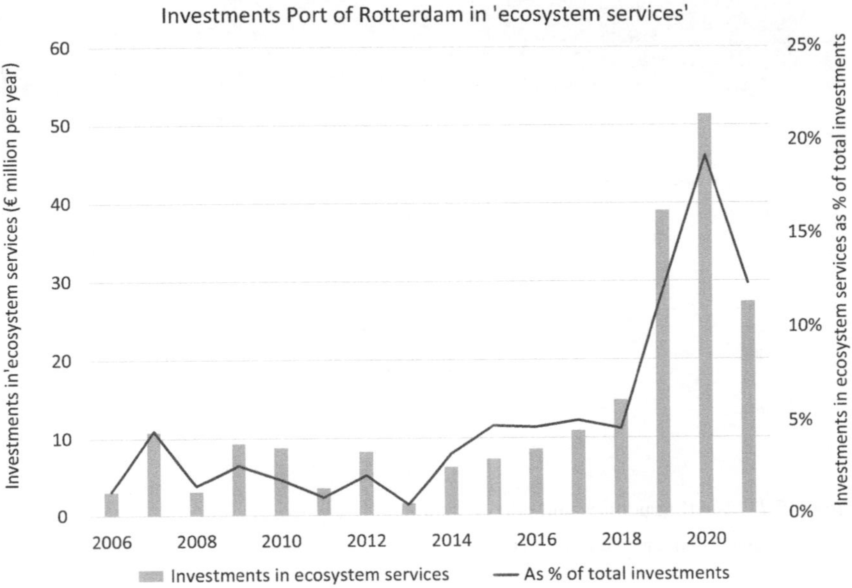

Figure 9.16 The total yearly investments of PoR in "ecosystem services"

Source: de Langen (2023a).

Table 9.3 shows PoRs efforts to develop additional "ecosystem services" that strengthen Rotterdam's PBE have grown over time. The expanding number of synergy services went hand-in-hand with larger investments in these services (see Figure 9.16).

For the years 2019, 2020 and 2021 (the latest years included in the analysis), the investments in "ecosystem services" accounted for more than 10% of PoR's total investments. This is a substantial increase compared to the share of below 5% in the period 2006–2016. This shows that PoR increasingly follows a "platform provider" strategy. It provides an increasing number of "ecosystem services" aimed at improving the productivity and efficiency of the port business ecosystem. PoR is not focused on capturing the value from the ecosystem services it provides directly, but rather regards the port dues and land rents as the "price carrier" for a broader service bundle.

9.6 Port pricing

While there is a lot of attention for the question of *how much* PMBs (should) charge, to recover costs and generate return, there is less attention for *what pricing structures* PMBs (should) use to charge their users. However, pricing structures are a key strategic decision of a PMB.

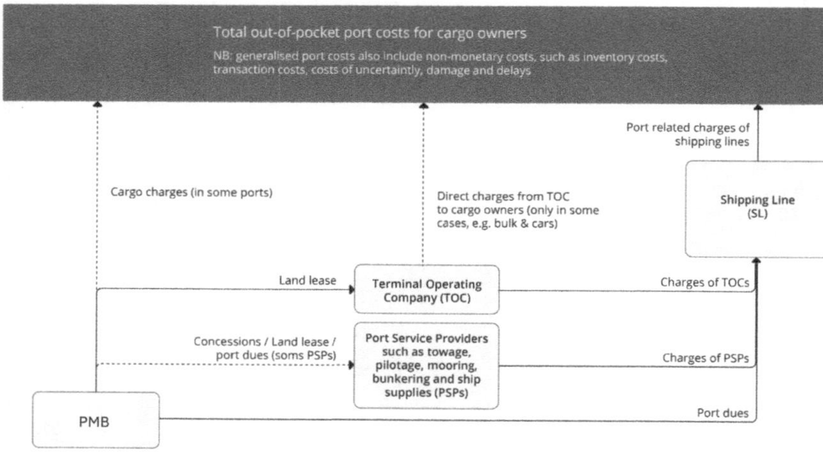

Figure 9.17 Tariff structures and port costs for cargo owners

Source: adapted from Van den Berg et al. (2017).

Regardless of contractual arrangements, importers and exporters are the final users of the port. Generally speaking, they pass on their *generalized port costs* to their customers (often consumers). Various potential structures of charges from the landlord port developer to port users are shown in Figure 9.17.

Importers and exporters receive a charge from shipping lines that generally includes (part of the) port costs. Furthermore, port users may directly pay handling fees to terminal operating companies. This is generally the case in bulk transport and in the transport of cars, but not in the container industry, where the shipping line pays the terminal operator and charges so-called "terminal handling charges" to port users. Finally, port users may be directly charged by PMBs. Such direct charges are often termed "cargo wharfage". In a large number of ports, such cargo wharfage charges do not exist. In these cases, shipping lines and port service providers charge importers and exporters, and exporters do not pay directly to PMBs.

For most PMBs, the port dues are the principal revenue stream. Table 9.4 shows some indicative figures on the average port dues per ton.[12]

Table 9.4 Port dues per ton for selected European ports

Port	*Port dues per ton (2023, in €)*
Barcelona	1.41
Riga	1.33
Amsterdam	0.86
Rotterdam	0.74
North Sea Port	0.68
Hamburg	0.56

Source: Own analysis based on annual reports published by the PMBs

Table 9.5 Rough estimates of port costs per ton for different commodities

	Liquid bulk	*Dry bulk*	*Containers*
Terminal costs	€8–12 (including storage)	€4–6 per ton	€8–12 per ton
Pilotage and towage costs	€0.5–1.5	€0.5–1.5	€0.5–1.5
Hinterland transport	Roughly 0,01-0,02 per ton/km (€12 per ton for 100 km)	Roughly 0.02–0.04 per ton/km (€2–4 per ton for 100 km)	Roughly 0.5–1.5 per ton/km (€50–150 to bring a container 100 km away from the port)

To put the port dues per ton in perspective, the port dues per ton can be compared to the total port costs per ton. This varies widely per commodity. The following figures are indicative (for a port in an advanced economy[13]).

These numbers show that the port dues per ton are relatively small compared to total cargo costs in a port, generally <10% and in many cases as small as 1–2%. This does *not* imply that port volumes are not sensitive to port dues. But it does suggest that investments of the port development company to make the area more attractive can be recovered through the port dues – as long as investments create value for port users. In principle, a PMB should invest in all projects that create more value for port users than the investment costs and recover costs with increased port dues and/or land rents.

9.6.1 Land rents

As a second revenue stream, landlord PMBs receive land rents (or concession fees) from companies that lease port land. Table 9.6 shows some indicative figures on the average land rents per m^2 of leased land in some ports.[14]

To put the land rents per m^2 in perspective, Table 9.7 shows some indicative figures on the turnover per m^2 of companies that lease port land.

These numbers show that the land rents per m^2 are also relatively small (in general <5%, often around 0.5–2%) compared to the revenue per m^2 generated by the private tenants. This is because the tenants generally invest substantially more than the PMB per m^2 (in terminal equipment, storage facilities or energy plants). This comparison does *not* imply that port dues or land leases can be raised without impact on port users. But it does suggest that investments of the PMB that lower

Table 9.6 Estimates of annual land rents per m^2 in some ports

Port	*Land rents per m^2 of leased land*
Rotterdam	Around €4.5
Antwerp	Around €2.5
Hamburg	Around €3.5
Barcelona	Around €5.5
Melbourne	Around €6

Table 9.7 Estimates of annual turnover per m² of activities in the PBE

Activity	*Turnover per m² per year*
Container terminal	€250–500
Dry bulk terminal	€150–300
Liquid bulk terminal	€200–400
Energy plant	>€1000
Warehousing company[15]	€100–300

operational costs (e.g., through pipelines, re-use of heat, reliable and cheap provision of energy) or increase revenues of the tenants (e.g., better hinterland connections) may create sufficient value to allow PMBs to charge higher land prices and/or port dues.

The diversity of port pricing mechanisms is huge. In most industries, pricing *structures* are fairly uniform in the sense that prices may differ, but all industry

Cargo dues?

Most port authorities have port dues and land rents as principal revenue streams. In some cases, in addition to port dues (charged to shipowners) *cargo dues* are charged to shippers. Such cargo dues are often related to the value of goods. This is for instance the case in South Africa, Australia, Spain and Brazil. In such a charging system the relation between the tariff and the provided service (efficient and safe access for ships and inland transport modes) is unclear.

Through port dues, ships pay for the use of a port. Large ships pay more than small ships, which is sensible given dredging costs. Land rents are also sensible to compensate for investments in the development of these sites.

However, with cargo dues based on the value of goods, port users pay a fee that has no relation to the port service: a container of paper pulp and a container are handled in the same way. As a consequence, cargo dues lead to a high burden for the import and export of expensive goods, and cross subsidies to imports and exports of low-value commodities. This pricing structure does not send the right signals: it penalizes moving to higher-value export products and subsidizes low-value exports. Finally, such pricing structures reinforce the perception of port dues as a tax, instead of a price for a service.

players have similar pricing structures, including the types of customers that are charged. In contrast, in ports, various users are charged, in varying proportions. Shipping lines and tenants are charged in all cases, but their relative contributions differ significantly. For example, in Singapore shipping lines generate more than 98% of the total revenue, compared to 18% in Vancouver. The contributions of tenants in the total port revenue also strongly differ per port. In Vancouver this group of port users accounts for 66% of the total revenue generated. Moreover, in some ports, shippers are charged and generate a rather large share of total revenues. Finally, the Dutch ports generate revenue from charges to inland transport operators.[16]

9.6.2 *Eight pricing principles*

The above-mentioned diversity suggests that analysis of pricing is highly relevant in the ports industry. We present nine pricing principles for PMBs. For each of the pricing principles, we provide examples of PMBs that apply them. Each specific port has its own unique characteristics. Therefore, these broad guidelines do not suggest that pricing structures of PMBs should or will converge to one standard. Instead, given the differences between ports, diversity of pricing structures is the expected outcome of the application of these principles.

1 Include part of the costs of "ecosystem services" in a bundle for shipping lines and tenants

Port users too often consider port dues as a kind of tax, not as a price for a service. That ignores the important positioning choice of the PMB. Figure 9.18 shows in stylized form the spectrum of price/quality ratio positions. On the one extreme is a port where only nautical access and land are provided. On the other extreme is a port where a broad range of services are provided, including collective transport for port workers and secure parking facilities for truckers.

The services listed in Figure 9.18 are examples and may not be relevant in all cases. The important insight is that port dues can be considered as a *price* for a *bundle of services*, and ports can aim for low prices and a limited bundle of services, or a higher price and a larger bundle of services. In general, it makes sense to include some synergy services in their bundle, with no or only partial recovery of investments/expenditures through direct fees.

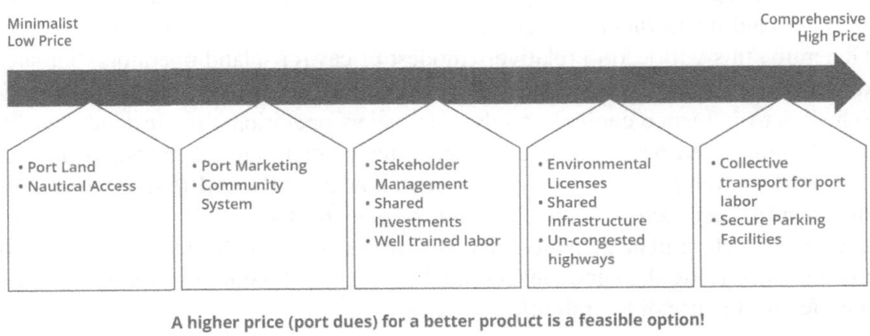

Figure 9.18 The price/quality positioning choice of the PMB

I previously argued that a "platform provider" is often the most attractive strategy for a PMB. However, for the "platform provider" strategy to work, its revenues need to be related to the productivity of the PBE. For instance, if the PMB owns only a part of the land in the PBE, as is for instance the case in Suape (Brazil) and Antwerp (Belgium, where various chemical and logistics companies do not lease land but have the full ownership), the ecosystem developer cannot capture the value it creates, but instead third-party landowners benefit from the investments in ecosystem services. In addition, the long contract duration, with fixed prices for tenants, reduces the link between the quality of the business ecosystem and the revenues of the PMB. In this respect, revenue-sharing mechanisms, as are used in airports (Gillen, 2011), may be an alternative value capture mechanism or could be used in addition to land rent contracts.

2 Broadly follow a direct "user pays" approach

This pricing principle implies that charges to direct users, such as the terminals and shipping lines, are generally more effective than charges to shippers-indirect users. This is for two reasons. First, PMBs do not really provide a direct service for shippers, whereas they do provide such a service for shipping lines (maritime access and vessel traffic management), terminal operators (port land) and inland transport operators (transport infrastructure). Thus, it is hard to find a legitimate commercial reason for charging shippers. Indeed, in countries where cargo wharfage is charged, it is regarded (and in some cases, like Italy, also legally arranged) as a tax charged by a public agency, rather than as a price for a service. In most countries with cargo wharfage charges to shippers, pricing reform has reduced the level and share of such charges. Relevant cases include Melbourne and South Africa. Second, charges to shippers have as a disadvantage that shippers are not involved in transport operations. Therefore, incentive schemes to improve port operations are unlikely to be successful. In contrast, as will be discussed later, incentive-based pricing schemes for shipping lines and terminal operators may be effective in improving port operations.

This pricing principle also suggests that in cases where PMBs make investments in hinterland infrastructure, inland transport operators are to be charged directly. Generally, this will lead to relatively modest prices for inland operators, but such direct charges offer the advantage of providing PMBs with the ability to use price schemes to influence choices of inland transport operations, for instance by differentiating based on environmental performance or through congestion pricing. The Port of Rotterdam Authority was shareholder in Keyrail (the infrastructure manager that between 2007 and 2015 was responsible for rail the rail infrastructure and infrastructure management of the Betuweroute, the dedicated freight railway line between Rotterdam and the German border), but did not push for a differentiated fee for the use of the rail infrastructure.

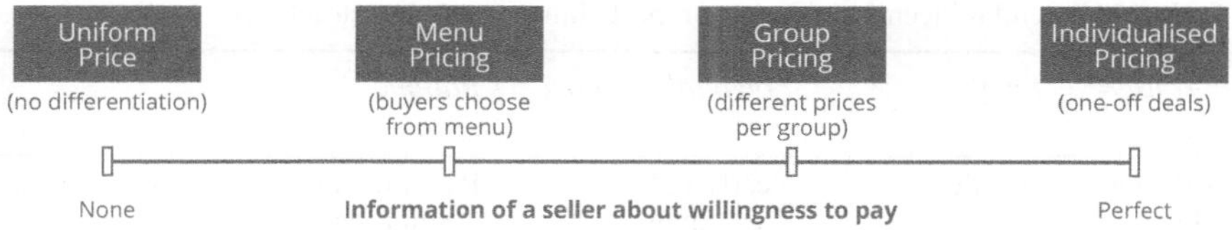

Figure 9.19 Types of price differentiation

3 Where feasible: differentiate based on price elasticity

An assessment of the price elasticity of the port services can be used for price differentiation. Price elasticity indicates the sensitivity of customers to changes in pricing, which in turn affects quantities, revenues and profits. Optimal pricing policies *charge what the market can bear* through price differentiation, charging the lowest prices in the most price-sensitive segments and higher prices in less price-sensitive segments. Figure 9.19 below shows types of price differentiation.

Most PMBs charge uniform prices for ships with the same ship characteristics. However, it may be an option to introduce differentiation through menu pricing, for instance, based on the day of the week (especially relevant for containers) or the month of the year (especially relevant for cruise).

4 Capture value from "non-core" tenants

The PMB can be considered to be a "multiproduct company", a company that offers different products. Theories of multiproduct firms have led to three main insights. First, differentiated pricing is unlikely to be effective if a single customer buys different products. Second, differentiated pricing is only beneficial for products or services that are non-perfect complements. In other words, it is only beneficial for a PMB to use different price allocations when its products or services are considered to be non-perfect complements. The "core users" – terminal operators and shipping lines – are perfect complements: both are required for freight transport. Potential imperfect complements include warehousing, port-related industries and other port-related service providers (such as maintenance, ship repair and office buildings in the port).

Thus, it makes sense to charge relatively high prices to non-core tenants, as these do not create externalities but do benefit from externalities created by others (shipping lines that create maritime connectivity and hinterland operators that create hinterland connectivity). This differentiation is, to a limited extent, applied in the port of Barcelona. Concessionaires need to pay a so-called tax based on the land usage. Companies which provide port activities (e.g., terminals) or port-related activities (e.g., nautical activities) pay lower rates than companies that provide complementary activities like logistic activities and warehousing. Third, differentiated

Table 9.8 Potential incentive schemes in port authority pricing structures

Port user	*Tariff*	*Potential incentive schemes*	*Rationale*
Shipping lines	Port dues	Yearly volume discount[17]	Rewards for large and performing shipping lines
		Large call size	Contributes to efficient utilization of port assets
		Call frequency	Rewards high connectivity
		On-time performance	Reward reliability of service and contributes to efficient utilization of the terminal
Terminal operating company	Land rents/ concession fee	Fast turnaround time	Contributes to efficient utilization of port assets

Source: Adapted from Van den Berg et al. (2017).

pricing may be relevant if the competitive forces in specific product markets differ. In this respect, it is relevant to note that shipping lines generally operate in very competitive markets, whereas the competition between terminal operators is imperfect – unless there is intra-port competition. Thus, in cases where intra-port competition is lacking, PMBs may benefit from charging higher prices to terminal operators and lower prices to shipping lines.

5 Use incentives to create alignment in the overall transport chain

PMBs may develop incentives in pricing. The use of incentives to align the interests of contracting parties is widespread in many industries. Options to realize ship efficiency through port pricing are priority pricing and slot actions. Table 9.8 presents some potential incentive schemes in PMBs pricing structures for shipping lines and terminal operators.

6 Differentiate pricing to promote maritime and intermodal connectivity

The sixth principle is to promote maritime and intermodal connectivity through differentiated pricing. This argument is based on the vertical externalities created by more connectivity. For maritime connectivity, one option is to reduce port dues for feeder vessels or for mother vessels with a relatively high transhipment share. The logic of such a pricing policy is that transhipment volumes are the most volatile freight volumes and – as volumes translate into connectivity – attracting such volumes will improve maritime connectivity. Likewise, for small and medium-sized ports, differentiated tariffs for deep-sea services (cheaper than short sea services, or discounts for services with new destinations) may be an option.

Various PMBs have taken different measures to stimulate maritime connectivity. The port authority of Rotterdam gives a discount for every transhipment container. The port authorities of Antwerp, Bremerhaven and Gdansk stimulate maritime connectivity by giving discounts on port dues for new deep-sea services, additional volumes and/or more frequent port calls. More specifically, the Port of Antwerp gives a discount of maximum 20% on tonnage dues for new container trade with a minimum of 100,000 TEU per year and a frequency reduction up to 30% reduction per call on tonnage dues for deep-sea lines (>200 calls), up to 40% for feeder line (>104 calls) and up to 50% for short sea lines (>52 calls). Bremerports give discounts up to 50% on tonnage charge for additional traffic through the deployment of larger vessels, the introduction of new services or an increase in the number of port calls.

With regard to intermodal connectivity, pricing to promote intermodal connectivity as opposed to road transport options may be appropriate. Possible pricing schemes include a specific charge for truckers that enter the port, without a similar charge for rail and barge operators, or (temporary) incentives for shipping lines that develop new intermodal services. In 2009, the port authority of Los Angeles introduced a discount program of US$20 per TEU to reward shipping lines for additional intermodal containers transported by rail compared to the previous year.

7 Maximize revenue from long-term lease agreements, price port dues competitively

There is an important difference between land lease agreements that are fixed for a long period, and port dues that are revised annually. Given the fact that land lease agreements are fixed in the long term, tenants regard these costs as *sunk costs*, i.e., costs that have already been incurred. In making investments and pricing decisions, companies do not (or not fully) take these sunk costs into account.[18] Thus, a lease agreement does not affect the pricing decisions of the terminal operator. Consequently, a price below the market value for a lease agreement will not lead to more competitive pricing by the terminal, but it does affect the financial results of the PMB – and thus the investment resources of the PMB. Therefore, maximizing revenues, next to securing environmental performance and potentially other criteria, is a valid goal when granting a concession or signing a lease agreement. An approach aimed at promoting a competitive port through land lease prices below market value is not effective.

On the contrary, port dues are revised yearly, thus allowing for adapting these to market conditions and the competitive position of the port. PMBs may have valid

Table 9.9 Average port dues per ton and land rents per hectare, PoR 2003–2023

Year	*Revenue per hectare*	*Port dues per ton*
2003	€30,000	€0.61
2007	€38,000	€0.65
2010	€47,000	€0.64
2012	€49,000	€0.67
2017	€73,000	€0.62
2020	€77,000	€0.65
2023	€81,000	€0.69

Source: Updated from Van den Berg et al. (2017).

reasons to set port dues below profit-maximizing values, as lower port dues are passed on to port users and thus create real economic benefits. Table 9.9 provides, as an illustration, an overview of the development of the average income on port dues and land rents for the Port of Rotterdam, which clearly shows a tendency toward maximizing revenues from concession contracts and setting port dues competitively.

8 Consider differentiation of charges based on environmental performance

PMBs may consider differentiation of charges based on environmental performance. Such price differentiation is feasible for port dues but may be more complicated for lease contracts. With respect to port dues, various PMBs give discounts based on the Environmental Ship Index program as part of the Worlds Port Climate Initiative. Empirical examples of incentives for greening inland transport exist in Rotterdam and Los Angeles. The port authority of Rotterdam introduced in 2012 a discount on inland port dues to vessels with environmentally friendly engines. The port authority of Los Angeles introduced a so-called Clean Truck Fee. Shippers need to pay a fee when they transport a container by truck in or out of the port of Los Angeles, only when the truck does not meet the demanded specifications in relation to the environmental impact.

9 Price aggressively for activities with a high strategic value

The last pricing principle is to price aggressively for activities with a high strategic value. This requires an understanding of the strategic value of different activities in the port business ecosystem, as was discussed in section 9.3. Figure 9.20 provides an overview of the main considerations that are relevant in the pricing of the port land.

Three pricing considerations included in Figure 9.20 merit elaboration. First, the PMB increasingly needs to consider the opportunity costs of the emissions (noise, particles, CO_2 and potentially others), so that uses of port land with high emissions are priced higher than those with low emissions. Second, as most PMBs generate revenue from cargo volumes, a cargo-generating effect (for instance, a new steel plant) should lead to a lower land price, as it generates additional revenues for the PMB. Third, for the state-owned PMBs (so the SO-PDC and the PA), the "value for society" is relevant.

9.7 Hinterland strategies

The quality of hinterland services is a core element in the competitiveness of the port as a transport node. Thus, strategies for improving hinterland access are relevant. Shipping lines, terminal operators and PMBs develop such strategies. Many ports aim to expand their hinterland reach; however, this is generally an "uphill battle".

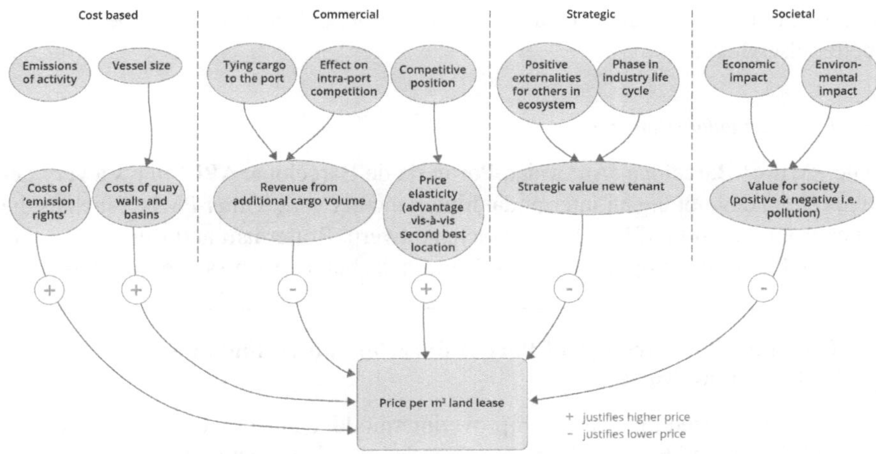

Figure 9.20 Considerations for the pricing of the port land

The port of Algeciras aims to serve the Madrid metro area (where Valencia is currently dominant), Rotterdam and Antwerp aim to improve competitiveness in Bavaria (where the German ports, especially Hamburg, are dominant), and various US east coast ports aim to expand their hinterland to destinations such as Chicago and Indianapolis, especially for trans-Pacific cargo, where currently the west-coast ports are dominant, but US east coast ports may benefit from the expanded Panama Canal locks. However, such ambitions often are not achieved. Cases where the ambitions were achieved generally succeed because of two factors.

First, a widely recognized development that favors a shift of cargo. For instance, the Panama Canal may be such a disruptive development. Likewise, the development that North Adriatic ports started to attract deep-sea calls was disruptive, and it enabled them to slowly gain market share in middle European countries such as Austria. But while the potential was already widely acknowledged in the 1990s, the shift has taken a long time and gained momentum in the last ten years: the port of Koper (Slovenia) surpassed Rotterdam as Austria's most important import port in 2009, and Hamburg as Austria's most important export port in 2011.

Second, a significant shift often requires involvement of some major shippers or hinterland operators. Mercedes made the choice to shift substantial volumes of car exports to Koper, while CN Rail enables the northern West Coast port of Prince Rupert (Canada) to reach the US Midwest market.

While these examples have succeeded, many other ambitions to expand market share have failed. If both factors mentioned above are not in place, the ambition to expand the hinterland is easy to formulate but very hard to achieve. Perhaps that should not stop port development companies from trying, but quite often port development companies turn to governments to support investments aimed at expanding the hinterland. In such cases, as a rule, public money can be deployed better elsewhere.

9.7.1 Intermodal strategies

The PMB of Barcelona (Autoridad Portuaria de Barcelona, APB) plays a very active role in developing an intermodal hinterland network. Other PMBs (such as the ones from the ports of LA, Long Beach, Antwerp, Rotterdam and Reijka) are also involved in the development of inland terminals, but not to the same extent as APB.

The hinterland strategy of Port of Barcelona: investing in a hinterland network

APB recognized the need to improve intermodal connectivity, for extending their hinterland beyond their home market, Cataluña, where truck transport has always been the dominant hinterland transport mode and rail traditionally had a very low market share.

APB developed its hinterland network with terminals and is also active in developing rail shuttles to increase connectivity with the port of Barcelona. Rail services are necessary to be able to compete with other ports that are closer to a specific hinterland region. Therefore, in 2009 APB decided to invest in a rail shuttle to Lyon, outside the traditional hinterland of Barcelona, together with Renfe (Spanish rail operator) and Naviland (French rail operator). Lyon was mainly served by Marseille, Antwerp and Le Havre. Although compared to Marseille, Barcelona is located 300 kilometres further away from Lyon, APB believes that cargo can be attracted. APB decided to invest in this shuttle as the companies operating in the port were not willing to take the risk. The hinterland activities have resulted in a modal shift from road to rail (Table 9.10). Despite the decrease of container volumes, rail transport increased between 2007 and 2009.

These data suggest that the active strategy of APB has had a significant impact. Market share has been gained in new hinterland markets through promotion and investments in terminals and rail services. APB understood

Table 9.10 Container traffic Barcelona

	2007	*2010*	*2011*	*2017*	*2023*
Total container volume (*1000 TEU)	2,610	1,946	2,034	2,969	3,280
Transhipment volume (*1000 TEU)	989	634	667	1,068	1,407
Volume, excl. transhipment (*1000 TEU)	1,621	1,313	1,367	1,901	1,873
Total rail transport (*1000 TEU)	42	104	147	244	217
% rail transport of total hinterland volume	2.6%	7.9%	10.7%	12.8%	11.6%

Source: Port of Barcelona (2024).

that it had to play a leading role, to reduce uncertainty and develop opportunities for private companies. With the possibility of working with lower return on investments and longer pay-back periods in comparison with private companies, APB has been able to make the described investments. These investments also show that the port authority has a long-term interest which reduces uncertainty for other firms in the chain.

9.8 Business development in ports

This section deals with business development in ports. Co-developing business opportunities is a central challenge for PMBs. The PMB is well-positioned to take the initiative to co-develop business opportunities, often in partnerships with other firms. This requires deep insights into trends and developments in the industry and a long-term vision for port development.

The value proposition of a PMB: land or a business opportunity?

PMBs traditionally think of port land as their value proposition. In such an approach, PMBs focus on developing port areas, and wait for private companies to approach them to lease the port land. This approach is essentially reactive: when potential customers see a business opportunity, they approach the port authority. The PMB starts negotiations with such parties to see if they can provide port land to them. PMBs can also co-develop business opportunities. In this approach, PMBs co-develop concepts and translate these into business opportunities for companies. In this approach, PMBs take the initiative in developing business opportunities, and market those to private companies.

The key differences between the value propositions land and business opportunities are that business opportunities need to be actively co-developed, often in partnership with others. While port land is a general asset that can be used for different purposes, a business opportunity is clearly defined.

9.8.1 Preconditions for successful business development

Five general requirements for the success of a PMB in business development can be distinguished:

1. "Leadership status" in the port community, which allows it to take initiatives and risks. Such leadership status is not a given, but needs to be developed carefully. One challenge, similar for every company that develops an "economic ecosystem", is to prevent a "dominator" attitude. Dominators are focused on capturing value instead of creating value. Therefore, dominators do not have

a sharing value with others in their "organizational DNA". This goes at the expense of a leadership status as a central organization in developing an economic ecosystem (in this case, a port complex). Another challenge, specifically for SO-PDCs, is not to confuse leadership with authority. Leadership is earned; authority derives from power. No SO-PDC can be successful in business development based on power alone.

A port vision as part of the process of developing business opportunities

A port vision that is widely accepted by relevant stakeholders is an important instrument for developing business opportunities. *A shared vision reduces the risks of business opportunities that are in line with this vision.* For example, to develop a business opportunity in "energy production" it helps when governments agree with the vision of the port as an important site for energy production – and back up this vision with investments in the electricity grid. Furthermore, it helps when clear sustainability targets are agreed with (public) stakeholders, so that firms have a societal license to operate and can count on public investments to enable a transition to more sustainable operations.

This argument is especially for firms that customarily operate in or are from countries with a strong government involvement in economic development, such as the BRIC countries. Such companies (one can think of the national oil companies as well as large mining companies) are used to public sector led visions – and actions to back them up.

2. Deep insights into relevant industries. Business development requires a deep understanding of the supply chains that ports accommodate and create value for. Such deep understanding goes beyond recognizing "increasing ship sizes" as a trend in port development and calls for strategic interaction with major players in relevant supply chains.
3. An organizational structure and culture in which committed teams can thrive, and risk-taking is accepted. Business development is a team effort, and inevitably requires risk-taking. Especially, government-owned organizations traditionally stay away from risk-taking. That implies business development is unlikely to be successful.
4. Ability to hold on to a long-term view. This is especially relevant when business opportunities are not viable in the short run, face delays and so on. Port development in ports generally involves substantial capital investments that cannot be retrieved. And it involves the development of scarce port land. That means decisions will have an impact for a long period of time; an overall port development vision is required to create a well-functioning port complex.
5. The ability to get stakeholder support for port development initiatives. Stakeholders, not least regional and national governments, are often deeply involved

in ports given their economic importance and external effects. Thus, government support, in some cases backed up with subsidies/funding, is needed.

Government support for new business development in ports

Port development companies frequently seek and get government support for developing business opportunities. PMBs receive EU, national and local grants for port expansion programs. Furthermore, specific projects are also often partially funded by governments, as with these few examples:

- The grant of roughly €50 million from the local government to Peel Ports, for the development of the container terminal Liverpool 2.
- The grant of roughly €2,5 million for the further development of the Dutch port community system.
- The substantial EU funding for port expansion projects in such ports as Riga, Piraeus, Gijon and Livorno.
- The significant funding for private initiatives to re-use heat and CO2 produced in ports.
- The EU funding for the development of a shuttle Barcelona – Lyon.

These examples clearly show the importance of government support for business development in ports.

9.8.2 Business development of the PMB: what scope?

In general, PMBs are most active in the developing sites for terminals in the port. However, they increasingly also co-develop business opportunities in the other domains to strengthen their port complex. Figure 9.21 shows a distinction in four

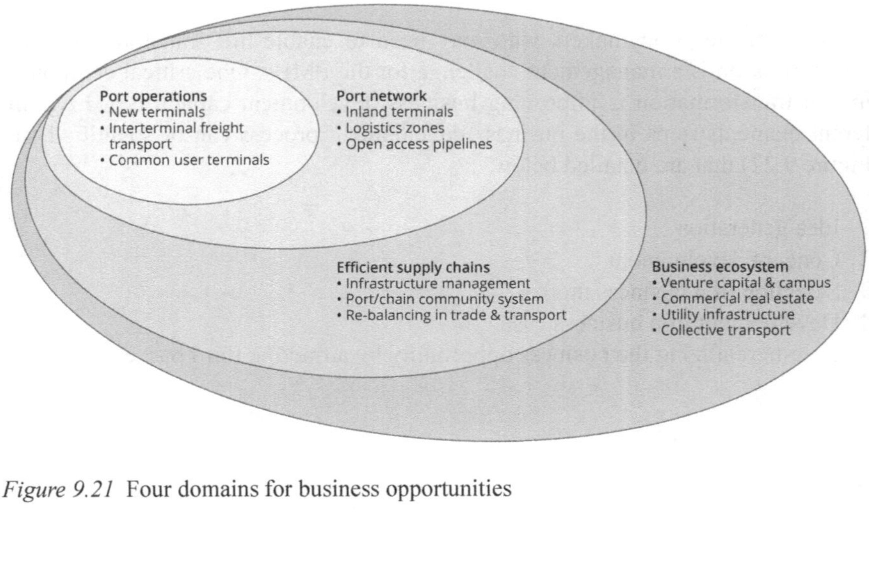

Figure 9.21 Four domains for business opportunities

different layers that represent increasingly broad scopes of potential value-creating activities. In the first layer, the focus is on port operations; the second layer extends this to the efficiency of the (inland) port network. In the third layer, the scope includes the whole supply chain, and the fourth domain includes the complete port-related *business ecosystem*.[19]

Business opportunities in *port operations* often remain at the core of port development, and include new terminals, systems for transport of goods between different terminals or sites and maritime/nautical services, such as towage, pilotage, mooring and information services in ports. Business opportunities that strengthen the port network may include inland terminals, logistics zones, feeder/rail/barge connections and pipelines to the hinterland. Business opportunities that add to the efficiency of supply chains include a port community system and empty repositioning systems. These business opportunities are aimed at creating value for the end users, shippers and forwarders.

Finally, the fourth domain consists of all kinds of business opportunities that make the *port business ecosystem* stronger. Examples include wind energy, smart grids, commercial real estate and collective passenger transport services.

9.8.3 Business development: five stylized steps

Many government-owned PMBs have historically not developed business development capabilities, but are transforming in this respect. As stated by an ESPO manifesto (2012):

> The traditional role of port authorities needs to be fundamentally revised. Port authorities that confine their role to conserving port land and regulating nautical safety will be unable to make a difference … Port authorities essentially have to become dynamic port developers and policy-makers need to give them the necessary means and tools to perform this role.

Apart from the policymakers who may need to enable this transformation, the transformation is a management challenge for the PMBs. One critical component in that transformation is improving business development capabilities. Five different elements/steps in the business development process can be identified (see Figure 9.22) that are detailed below.

1 Idea generation.
2 Concept development.
3 Selection of a business model.
4 Development of a business case.
5 Commercializing the business opportunity by attracting third parties.

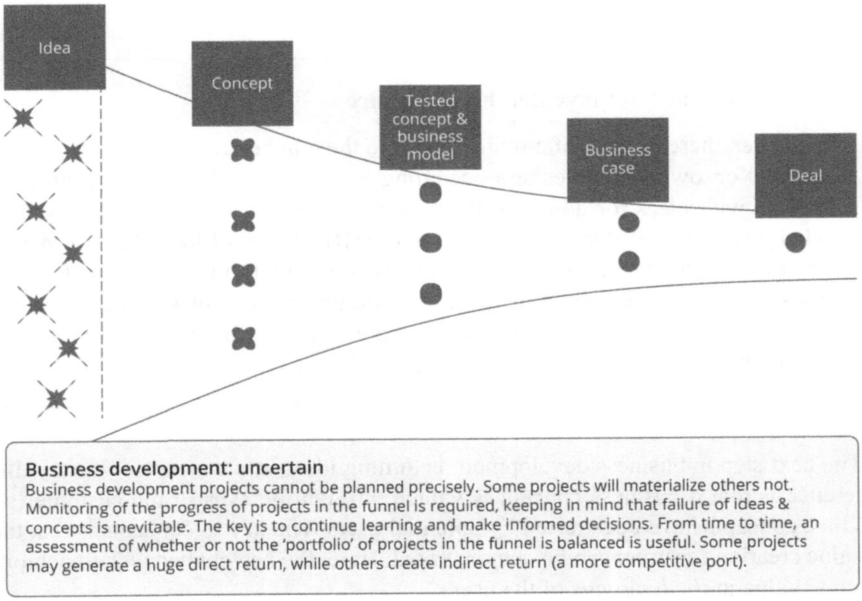

Figure 9.22 Five different steps in the business development

Idea generation

The first step in business development is idea generation: developing new ideas for potential business opportunities. In this phase, the key challenge is to get a rich portfolio of project ideas. Generating ideas requires deep insights into the *drivers of change* in the ports industry. Furthermore, and potentially more complicated, idea generation requires recognizing the pre-fixed mental maps of both individuals and organizations. These fixed mental maps prevent the identification of disruptive new ideas.

Various examples show how organizations tend to ignore signals that disruptions may impact the industry. For instance, various studies in the late 1960s dismissed the value of containers in maritime transport. Likewise, various fruit terminal operators stuck to classical reefer port facilities even though containerization increased rapidly in this segment. The energy companies invested in LNG facilities in the US, even though shale gas later destroyed the value of such facilities.

Thus, in the idea generation phase, the challenge is *to organize for* challenges to mental maps and to embrace uncertainty, rather than predicting 20 years ahead. Idea generation is best organized as a purposeful process, instead of assuming the organization will generate ideas for business opportunities "spontaneously".

Concept development

Preventing the "not invented here" culture

However, there is a risk of moving too far to the other extreme and becoming focused on own initiatives and becoming *unresponsive*. Firms that contact a PMB with ideas for doing business need to be taken very seriously, even when their ideas differ from those of the PMB. When all too often a PMB responds with something like "we have thought about that before, but the market is not big enough", it has fallen victim to the "not invented here" culture, which goes at the expense of responsiveness. The key challenge is combining initiative and responsiveness.

The next step in business development is turning ideas into concepts. The key difference is that a business concept is valued through the eyes of the customer(s). Thus, concepts have been tested by potential users. The key to concepts is that the value creation for users can be demonstrated. Here, the key challenge is to demonstrate value in *the language* of the users.

As an example from the Port Authority of New York and New Jersey (PANYNJ), warehousing next to the terminal increases drayage moves from about 2.5 to about six a day. This equals a cost reduction of roughly US$200 per box. Such value creation justifies significantly higher prices for warehousing next to the container terminals.

An important issue in the concept development phase is the distinction between different market segments and the assessment of potential value creation in these segments. A sound market segmentation leads to a detailed understanding of the service preferences in specific segments. As one example, in the cruise market there may be an important difference between turnaround cruise calls (which require huge parking facilities) and cruise ports of call (which require centrality to the main attraction or attractions). Table 9.11 gives some widely used market segmentations in port markets.

Concept development requires open interaction with industry players, especially end users, since they drive changes in supply chains. As an example, developing LNG as bunker fuel requires close interaction with shipping lines, as they are the end users of LNG as bunker fuel.

Tight relations with end users

PMBs often have strong relations with terminal operators and shipping lines. However, they are often rather loosely connected to end users. Such end users drive commodity flows and are therefore important end users. Thus, their current and future supply chains need to be understood to be able to analyze the potential for new terminals.

Table 9.11 Examples of market segmentations

Market	*Segment 1*	*Segment 2*
Container throughput	Transhipment cargo (easy switching between ports)	Gateway cargo (often more captive to specific ports)
Tank storage	Industrial storage (limited volatility)	Trading storage (highly volatile)
Freight ferry cargoes	Accompanied trailers (drivers influence route choice)	Unaccompanied trailers (transport planners make route choice)
Terminal operators	Dedicated terminals (volume commitment, specific customers)	Common-user terminals (neutral option for all users)
Container cargoes	Time-sensitive cargoes (willingness to pay for reliability and speed)	Not time-sensitive cargoes (cost-sensitive)
Rail services	Hub and spoke operators (place network central)	Direct shuttle operators (business case per shuttle)
Warehousing investors	Real estate investors (no risk-taking)	Logistics service providers (may build ahead of customers)

Table 9.12 Examples of end users

Commodity	*Important importers and exporters*
Containers	Large retail firms (e.g., Walmart, which is estimated to account for around 3% of all volume from/to the US) as well as large manufacturing firms (Heineken is estimated to account for roughly 3 to 4% of the total volume between northern Europe and the US). In smaller ports, the top five importers and exporters may account for 15–25% of all container volumes.
Iron ore and steel	Mining companies, such as Vale, Rio Tinto and BHP (together more than 35% of the total global mining volume, whereas in one instance, Brazil, the Vale share is >90%) and steel manufacturers such as Tata Steel and ArcelorMittal.
Coal and dry biomass	Energy producers (such as Eon in Europe with a market share of close to 10%).
Crude oil	Oil companies (for instance, Shell, Exxon and the large national oil companies).
Mineral oil products and chemical products	Chemical companies (BASF, for instance, accounts for >60% of the throughput of chemical products in Antwerp).
LNG	Energy companies.

Deciding on the business model

In every business development process, a decision on the business model[20] is required. For the PMB, the most relevant choice is the choice of in-house service provision vs third-party service provision.

In the business model phase, a deep understanding of the (changing) value network is also relevant. Business development by PMBs often involves cooperation with customers and/or service providers. Firms may expand into new activities, and new entrants may start providing services in the value chain. This may have important consequences for attitudes toward initiatives to enhance cooperation and coordination. Such developments are relevant for the PMB and especially for the viability of "ecosystem services". As an example, collaborative planning systems in which empties are not returned to the seaport can reduce empty container flows. Such a system becomes more viable if liner shipping companies shift away from individual container fleet management and toward cross-carrier container fleet management.

As a second example, a collaborative network design of barge services to and from the hinterland may have substantial benefits. For instance, part of the containers could be handled at an intermediate hub. Such an initiative is very hard to realize if barge companies focus on achieving a competitive advantage *vis-à-vis* distinctive barge service networks. Such initiatives may become more feasible if barge companies turn into intermodal logistics providers. In such a case, collectively improving utilization of assets (inland terminals as well as barges) may be perceived as a competitive strength compared to logistics service providers without such assets.

The need for alignment

In the understanding of the value network, *alignment at interfaces* is a relevant concept. Alignment of the business models of various players in the value chain is relevant, as more alignment leads to more efficient overall value chains. Such alignment does not emerge spontaneously; there is a risk of friction in supply chains due to misalignment between business models. Such friction becomes visible at the *interfaces*, places with transactions between different companies that are part of the value chain. As an example, there is friction at the interface between a terminal operator that earns money from storage (for instance, a car terminal) and a PMB that earns money from land leases and port dues. Their business models are not aligned as the PMB aims for throughput maximization, while the operator receives revenues from storage, not from "flows". In this case, a minimum throughput agreement can be used as a mechanism to create more alignment. Other frequently relevant bottlenecks at interfaces in the port are given in Table 9.13.

Developing the business case

A business case is a core element of business development. Such a business case shows whether or not the revenues are sufficient to recover costs and earn a profit. It is relevant to develop rough "back of an envelope" calculations from the start of the business development project. Such calculations need to be scrutinized and detailed, but a rough financial indication at the start is crucial in the business development process. For instance, detailed conversations with (potential) clients are often needed to identify the value from the customer's perspective and to assess whether or not the value creation is sufficient to capture value and recover the required investments.

Table 9.13 Examples of bottlenecks at interfaces in the port business ecosystem

Interface	*Issue*
Terminal – inland transport companies	Congestion at the inland gate. No contractual relations, so no straightforward way to ensure service levels.
Terminal – shipping line	Unreliable and unpredictable arrival patterns of ships at the terminal, which complicate terminal planning.
Forwarder – shipping line	Insufficient information to ensure efficient planning of empty containers.
Transport company – warehousing company	Limited opening hours of the warehousing company, which prevents efficient transport operations.

Business cases for investments of PMBs

The key challenge for the landlord port development company is to have an investment portfolio that is balanced, including customer-specific investments with business cases, and investments with collective but often (partially) indirect benefits and consequently negative business cases. Too many of the latter put the profit at risk, while too many of the former may put the long-term vitality of the port at risk, *and thus the capacity to continue to generate attractive customer-specific business cases*. Ensuring a continuous and high-quality stream of both types of investment projects is a key challenge for a PMB. The majority of investments of the port development company lead to direct increases in revenue streams. For these investments, the PMB makes *business cases* to calculate the return on investment based on the required investment and the revenues from these investments.

The basic structure of a business case is for an additional investment for one specific customer (for instance, an additional jetty or a quay wall), as given in Table 9.14.

The net present value (NPV) is the sum of the NPV of all expenses and revenue streams. The NPV is calculated with a given discount rate, which expresses the cost of capital. The internal rate of return (IRR) is the return on investment, expressed as the annual return on the invested capital. In case the NPV is 0, the IRR is equal to the discount rate.

The assumptions about the annual increase of land rents (often equal to inflation) and port dues (a commercial decision of the port development company) have a huge effect on the NPV.

Key success factors of business opportunities: some examples

Similar terminals often have similar critical success factors. We do not provide a comprehensive overview, but provide two examples of success factors for a specific type of terminal.

For container transhipment terminals, a central location in maritime networks is an important success factor. Second, fast and reliable turnaround time of deep-sea (and feeder) vessels is a key success factor. This has implications for the lay-out and scale of a terminal. Finally, given the fact that labour costs are close to 50% of the operating costs of a container terminal, and given the fierce cost-competition for transhipment, low labour cost is a key success factor.

As another example, for a multi-user LNG terminal, connection to the landside gas grid is an obvious success factor. Next to that, opportunities to re-use the cold required for keeping the gas liquid may be an important success factor, as this can help reduce the energy costs – which are >60% of the operational costs of an LNG terminal.

Table 9.14 The structure of a business case of a customer-specific project

Item	*NVP (*1 million)*
Investments	
Quay	–50
Terminal site	–50
Maintenance costs	
Port basin	–10
Quay wall	–10
Site	–10
Revenues	
Additional land lease	70
Additional port dues	100
Total NPV	**40**
IRR	**12%**
Parameters of the business case	
Discount rate	8%
Project period	25 years
Annual inflation (land lease income grows with inflation)	2%
Annual increase in port dues	2%

Drivers of return

A good business case also leads to an understanding of the drivers of return. This is important as in most cases the business case needs to be modified and adapted various times, and these insights are critical in developing a positive business case. Some important drivers of return in a business case are:

- The provided "service bundle" and the related investment level. For instance, a PMB may fully develop a port site, but may also invest in a quay wall and sufficient draft, while leaving the surface works to the customer.
- The timing of investments, as postponing investments reduces costs. That may, for instance, be relevant for dredging.

- The mix of revenue streams. For a landlord PMB, the mix between port dues and land leases influences the revenues in the business case.
- The projected throughput volumes.

In the course of a business development project, as well as in the execution phase, a project can be managed as a business case, with updated versions of the business case to test whether the financial return is still sufficient and an analysis of potential actions to improve the business case.

Spill-overs: the need for an "ecosystem business case" or even a "societal value case"

One issue that is often relevant in ports is the fact that investments may "spill-over" to other companies in the port. In other words, an investment may create value that cannot be captured in the business case. This requires a "business ecosystem" business case that includes the value creation that cannot be captured. For instance, developing pipeline infrastructure between tank terminals, refineries and chemical plants may allow tank terminals to reduce investments in handling facilities for trucks, trains and barges. In addition, shifting the transport of oil, oil products, and chemicals to pipeline may free up capacity at rail terminals. This may result in savings if such rail terminals are congested. The above examples are cost savings that would be included in an "ecosystem business case".

As argued previously in Chapter 2, investments in ports often create societal value. This may provide a basis for attracting public funding. For instance, a secure truck parking facility may in itself be loss-making, but reduce congestion in areas where trucks are parked, nuisance from truck parking in residential areas near the port, as well as thefts from trucks – with a value through reduced deployment of police resources. Some other examples of societal value creation are given in Table 9.15.

Commercializing the business opportunity: attracting third parties

The commercialization of new concepts is the final phase of business development (even though these phases are iterative, i.e., the business development process is not linear, and commercialization already starts in the concept development phase).

In the commercialization of new business opportunities, a focus on *change* is often sensible. Specific projects benefit from placing them in a larger *story*. This is

Table 9.15 Examples of societal value creation of investments

Investment	*Societal/ecosystem value creation*
Rail terminal	Reduced congestion levels on roads around the port, reduced CO_2 emissions and reduced costs of road incidents.
Cruise terminal	Increased tourism expenditure in the port city.
Dry port	Increased land value around the dry port.

especially relevant given the complex stakeholder environment for port projects. Such a story highlights how change affects the industry and how a specific business development initiative creates value in the new market environment. A story also benefits from placing initiatives in a shared long-term vision.

9.8.4 Strengthening business development capabilities of PMBs

Many PMBs shift from PAs to commercially operating SO-PDCs. In many cases, this transition involves strengthening business development capabilities. For instance, many SO-PDCs have only recently established a commercial department or a team focused on business development. Figure 9.23 shows the business development capabilities most relevant for PMBs.[21]

PMBs aiming at improving business development capabilities can use this framework for an assessment of the gaps between the aspired-to level of capabilities (what is needed to be successful) and the current level of capabilities. For instance, with the use of this framework, the Panama Canal Authority (ACP) made the assessment that the most relevant gaps at the time (2016) were in the speed of decision-making (i.e., it took too long for decisions to be made) and the capabilities

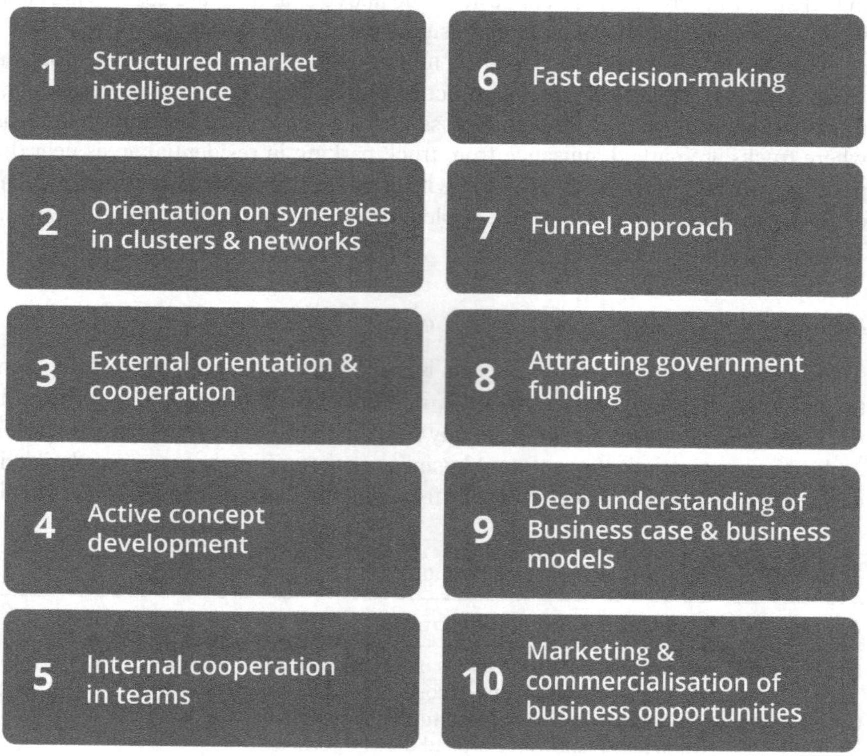

Figure 9.23 Ten business development capabilities for PMBs

for marketing and commercialization. This is partly due to the fact that ACP is used to working – and obliged to work – with tenders and concessions, and traditionally did not involve potential customers sufficiently in business development initiatives.

Insights regarding business development success

For the PMBs engaged in a transformation towards a more commercial approach, the following insights regarding business development success are relevant:

1. Business development involves risk. A SO-PDC needs to be comfortable with taking risks and thus also with some failed business development projects, in the sense that ideas are explored and turned into concepts but ultimately do not lead to a deal and investments. This does not mean that resources have been wasted or that in hindsight the idea was wrong in the first place – failure means learning.
2. The business development process benefits from a structured funnel approach, whereby it is acknowledged that for every ten ideas, only a few are turned into successful projects. That is acceptable. In such an approach, it is important to "fail fast"; instead of keeping ideas in the funnel for long periods, work with teams to test and dismiss/select ideas rapidly.
3. Top management support can contribute substantially to the success of new business development. Frequent and informal interaction with a business development team is more helpful than time-consuming formal management reporting.
4. Business development requires teams with different capabilities: creative and analytical capabilities in the early stages, externally oriented staff for the interaction with customers and other stakeholders and result-oriented managers in the implementation stages. Given the required team effort, one employee cannot successfully develop new business alone.
5. Successful business development requires an organization structure in which teams are central. "Silo" organizations in which "departments" are central and cooperation between departments is not fluid are unlikely to be successful in business development.

9.9 Common business development projects in ports

In this final section, I provide examples of business development initiatives that are pursued in a substantial number of ports, in each of the four domains (port operations, port network, supply chain and the port-related business ecosystem). Terminal operations and nautical services are well-established industries, with specialized companies, and a well-functioning market where companies compete (often through bids) for business opportunities. For the two relatively new business opportunities discussed below, port call planning and interterminal transport, ports are still in the process of finding out whether and how to develop such services.

9.9.1 Port call planning

Well-coordinated port call planning creates value for shipping lines. It enables fast and reliable turnarounds. Well-coordinated port call planning requires coordination between the shipping line, terminal operating company, towage company, mooring company, pilotage company, bunkering company and PMB/harbor master. Such coordination, for instance, would enable a better response to contingencies that often characterize a port call (e.g., vessel arrives too late, terminal handling takes longer than expected, the ship cannot be moored as the quay is still occupied by another ship, bunkering takes longer than expected and so on). Thus, a well-coordinated port call creates value.

Different companies contribute to such a seamless port call. The shipping line (in some cases represented by a ship's agent) has the highest stake in a seamless port call and thus places efforts in removing bottlenecks or inefficiencies. However, shipping lines have a rather lean global organization and are often not equipped to develop port-specific tools and routines to ensure a seamless port call.

Consequently, there may be a business opportunity for services to ensure a seamless port call. For PMBs, even if this business opportunity in itself is not profitable or even generating revenue, indirectly it adds to the competitiveness of the port. Various companies provide solutions for seamless port calls.

9.9.2 Interterminal transport

A second emerging business opportunity in port operations is interterminal container transport. This involves the transport of containers between different terminals: in some cases between maritime terminals, in other cases between maritime terminals and nearby rail terminals. Given the increasing volumes and the emergence of more dedicated terminals, traffic flows between terminals are growing.

Moving containers between terminals may be more cost-effective than calls at various terminals of trains, feeders or inland shipping barges. For instance, if a small feeder vessel needs to collect a small number of containers at one terminal and the majority at another terminal, interterminal transport of the small number of containers so that the feeder vessel only needs one call may be more cost-efficient than calls at both terminals. Similar issues are also relevant for trains and barges. Thus, in ports with multiple container terminals, *interterminal transport services* may be a business opportunity. Rotterdam and Singapore are two examples of large ports that have established interterminal transport services. Figure 9.24 shows an example with just two terminals; the need for interterminal transport becomes higher with additional facilities, such as empty depots or rail terminals where trains/feeder vessels/barges can make stops.

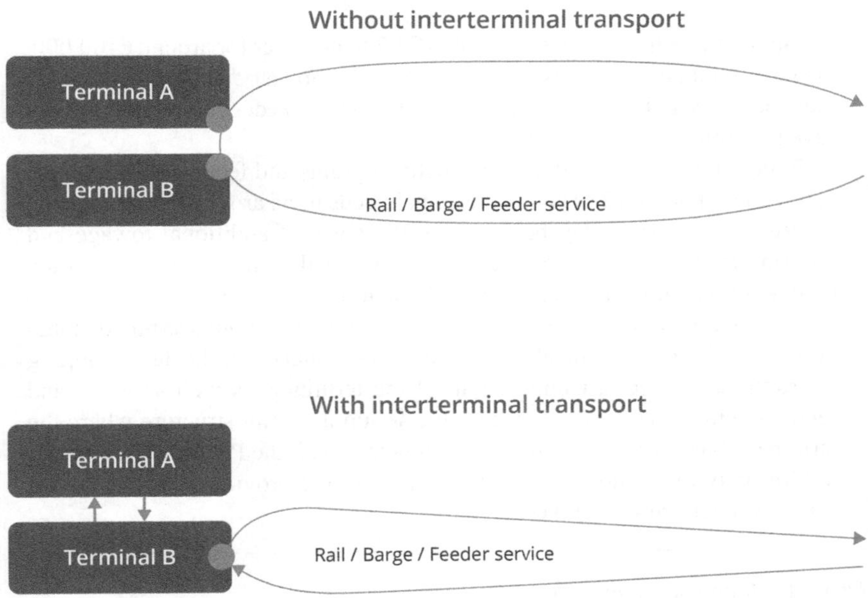

Figure 9.24 The value of interterminal transport

Interterminal transport between container terminals – a tentative calculation

As illustration, a tentative calculation for interterminal transport between container terminals is provided. Assume a port with 1.5 million TEU and two terminals of equal size. Next to the deep-sea calls, both are called at by feeder vessels and by trains. Either these call at both terminals, or the terminals exchange containers to enable a feeder vessel or train to (un)load at just one terminal. This option may be attractive when the volumes per train or feeder vessel at one terminal are lower than a certain minimum. The trade-off is whether the costs of additional port time for the feeder/train and the handling cost reduction as only one crew is required offset the costs for interterminal transport. Especially when the terminals are of a similar size, a rule "the feeder/train is handled by the terminal where most containers need to go" is likely to lead to roughly equal flows in both directions (terminal A to B and terminal B to A).

As a further assumption, take 10% of the annual volume as potential for interterminal exchange. This amounts to 150,000 TEU, or roughly 400 TEU per day. This enables investments in trucks and an interterminal planning system. With adequate planning, one roundtrip of a 4 TEU truck per hour may be feasible. With these assumptions, around five trucks would be required.

Assuming these trucks can be operated 24/7 in one year for around €100,000, the costs could be as low as €5 to €10 per TEU. So an operator that provides these services and charges such a fee (to the barge/feeder companies, as they save port time) may create value.

Following this calculation, the benefit for trains and feeders of skipping a call with around 100 TEU at one terminal needs to be around €1000 to make a case for ITT. This may be the case: the costs of additional towage and mooring for a call at a second terminal, combined with additional port time (and additional uncertainty), may easily be more than that.

This overview means to illustrate the potential for interterminal transport. Many issues (organizational, legal, operational) complicate developing interterminal services. Commitment of the terminals as well as barge and feeder operators is required. A possible set-up is a joint structure where the terminals, barge and feeder operators, together with the PMB, invite bids for a third party to provide this service and select the provider with the lowest prices of interterminal moves.

9.9.3 Business opportunities in port networks

Business opportunities in *port networks* may include inland terminals, logistics zones, and feeder/rail/barge connections to the hinterland. It is increasingly well understood that, on top of the attractiveness of the port itself, the attractiveness of the port network is central to port competitiveness. The port is "just" one transfer point in a whole network. Port development companies as well as terminal operators, shipping lines and forwarders increasingly invest in an attractive port network. In this section, we discuss business opportunities in port networks that have been developed, with cases from Barcelona (an inland terminal and a rail shuttle), Shanghai (an inland network) and Rotterdam (a "transferium"), as well as a potential new business opportunity in feedering.

9.9.4 Inland terminals

In some markets (north-west Europe and the US), intermodal transport is a mature industry. However, in many emerging economies (Brazil, Nigeria, Kenya, …) and in ports traditionally served by road (Santos, Lagos), there is a huge potential for inland terminals (served by inland waterways or rail). The rise of oil prices, road congestion and road pricing, more attention for sustainability and investments in rail infrastructure, create huge business opportunities for developing inland terminals. The inland terminal market potential critically depends on the presence of potential volumes in a – tentative – 50-km radius around the inland terminal. The development of an intermodal terminal attracts investments in warehousing facilities. So if a potential inland hub is well located to serve large consumer/manufacturing markets, it will attract logistics companies to the vicinity of the terminal. As an example, the municipality of Tilburg (the Netherlands, more or less between the ports of Rotterdam and Antwerp) invested in an intermodal terminal and an adjacent logistics zone. In 12 years, the warehousing capacity in the municipality doubled from around 800,000 square meters of warehousing space to over 1.6 million m^2 of warehousing space. This huge increase has led to a similar huge increase in volume handled by the intermodal terminal to well over 120,000 TEU per year.

Various firms may develop inland terminals. These include (road) transport companies, as they can shift cargo from truck to intermodal; large shippers, as they can guarantee stable volumes for such a terminal; regional governments, as they may want to invest in reducing truck traffic in the region; deep-sea terminal operators, to provide more attractive services to shipping lines; and port development companies, to strengthen their port network.

9.9.5 New intermodal connections

Especially in the container industry, companies compete for the development of new intermodal services. However, for intermodal services, *new service development* involves substantial risks. For a container shuttle service by train, just running *one* train incurs a cost of >€20,000. However, an attractive product for shippers would be at least a weekly train, guaranteed for at least one year. Therefore, the costs involved in developing new services are huge, and returns are uncertain, as potential customers will generally take a "wait-and-see" approach and be reluctant to contractually commit volumes in advance. The Barcelona case shows that, given the uncertainties and required operational losses in the first year(s) of operation, private initiatives for new service development may be limited. Contrary to other industries, where it is widely understood that a substantial part of all new services will fail, rail operators seem risk-averse in their approach to the development of new rail services. This suggests that a PMB may need to step in to co-develop new rail services. The PMB generally does not aim for a permanent involvement but may provide support in the start-up phase.

For instance, the port of Zeebrugge has developed and financially supported a barge service to Antwerp, while Barcelona co-developed a rail service to Lyon, and Koper invests in train services to Austria and the south of Germany. Port of Rotterdam had a "rail incubator" program for the support of new services.[22] Examples abound outside Europe as well: the port authority of New York and New Jersey co-developed and financed barge services, and the port of Melbourne co-developed rail services. Often, new services are developed in partnerships between rail operators, terminal operating companies, shipping lines, forwarders, shippers and port development companies.

9.9.6 Logistics zones

Logistics zones have emerged rapidly in the past decade. In mature economies, such as the US and the UK, logistics is one of the fastest-growing industries. Whereas the *manufacturing floorspace* (the number of m^2 of plants) has declined, *logistics floorspace* has grown substantially and is expected to continue to grow.

The recognition that co-location of logistics activities has economic *and* societal benefits is growing. Developing logistics zones requires a partnership with local public agencies to secure planning permits and public infrastructure investments.

The benefits of co-location in logistics

The benefits of co-location in logistics increasingly receive attention amongst others due to the work of MIT professor Yossi Sheffi on logistics clusters. Research shows that being located in a general logistics cluster provides benefits over being located outside a cluster, while being located in a specialized cluster provides additional advantages compared to a location in a diverse logistics cluster (Van den Heuvel et al., 2015).

Co-located companies more often share transport and storage than other than co-located companies. Companies co-located in specialized logistics clusters (e.g., fresh produce logistics clusters or medical product logistics clusters) do so more often than companies in diverse clusters. Next, such companies also exchange knowledge and trade more often within the cluster.

These findings are relevant for port development in at least two ways. First, logistics clusters do not emerge spontaneously, but often require combined public and private investments, for instance in intermodal terminals. Second, evidence shows that firms tend to re-locate to logistics clusters. This drives up the land value in such clusters. For the development of such clusters this means that an intermodal terminal may create land value around the terminal. Thus, firms that develop such terminals (PMBs, terminal operators and others) may be able to capture that value through also aiming for a stake in the logistics land surrounding the terminal.

9.9.7 Logistics zones in the port – transloading

For the PMB, it is especially relevant to understand the potential of attracting investments in logistics to the port business ecosystem. For specific segments in logistics, ports are attractive investment locations. Logistics chains in which ports are used for value-adding activities are sometimes termed "*port-centric logistics*" chains. For example, ports may attract value-added logistics services in supply chains in which containers are *transloaded*, i.e., shifted from maritime containers to "normal" trucks (or continental wagon cars). Facilities where these activities take place are sometimes referred to as "Container Freight Stations". Transloading is often used due to the larger capacity of trucks compared to container trailers. For instance, in the US, the cargoes of three standard 40-foot ocean containers fit in two 53-foot domestic trailers. Transloading also often takes place in countries where shipping lines charge high fees for inland container moves. As an example, containers that go to Central Asia (e.g., Kazakhstan) generally are loaded from containers into trucks, for instance, in the ports in Georgia.

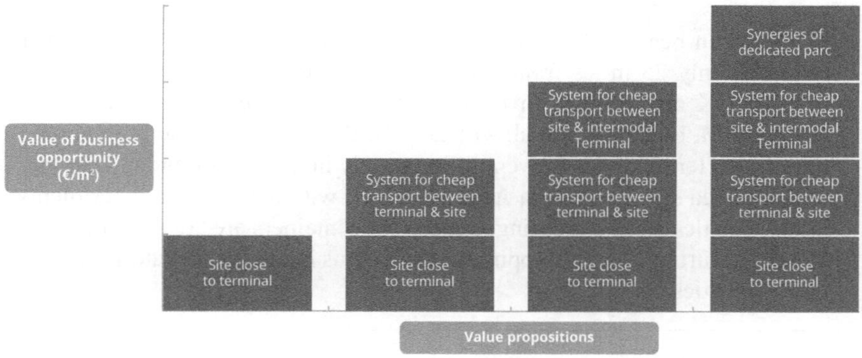

Figure 9.25 The value creation for transload facilities

Transloading is often combined with cross-docking and deconsolidation. Instead of transferring all goods from one ocean container into one domestic trailer destined for one location, cargoes are deconsolidated and reconsolidated into separate trailers for several destinations. A transload facility in a port can be used to bypass an inland distribution center and to ship cargoes directly to end users. Ports can develop attractive sites for transload facilities: close to the deep-sea terminal, connected with intermodal terminals and accessible by road. A transload facility with secure and cheap transport to/from the seaport is a potentially valuable business opportunity for logistics service providers. Figure 9.25 shows four very stylized propositions and their respective values.

A site that is "just" close to a terminal has limited value as it is not fundamentally different from a site, say 20 km away from the terminal. Value increases when a system is in place for smooth and cheap transport of containers between the terminal and the warehousing facility (e.g., through a secure lane). Additional value is created if a similar connectivity with an intermodal facility is created. Finally, such a facility embedded in a logistics zone with similar activities creates additional synergies and thus increases value.

The increasing recognition of the benefits of concentrating logistics zones in proximity to intermodal terminals has led to the emergence of various private developers of logistics zones.

Logistics zones in ports – the case of London Gateway

The benefits of an integrated development of a container terminal and a logistics zone are clearly illustrated with the case of London Gateway. This port development by DP World began in 2010; the first stage was opened in 2013, consisting of a terminal of three berths and the logistics park of around 230 hectares.

The main benefit of this logistics park is that it is next to the container terminal, only 25 miles from central London, and with intermodal access to other UK destinations. Investors in the logistics zone include Prologis, CMA-CGM, Lidl and UPS, all with large-scale facilities. Attracting shipping lines to the terminal has proven difficult; only in 2017 did London Gateway add deep-sea service to/from Asia. However, with the ongoing investments in the logistics park, increasing volumes of containers are "tied" to the port, thereby securing calls of shipping lines and thus increasing the attractiveness of the logistics park.

9.9.8 Business opportunities in supply chains

The third domain for business opportunities is in supply chains.[23] There is clearly potential to further improve the efficiency and sustainability of supply chains. Waiting times at terminals, congestion on port infrastructure, unreliability of scheduled services, high transaction costs associated with information exchange and limited utilization of transport equipment are commonplace. Various business opportunities can help increase efficiency and sustainability. Central to many of these is that they aim to improve coordination and alignment of transport operations. As discussed in Chapter 7, such coordination does not emerge spontaneously (due to unequal distribution of costs and benefits, limited willingness to invest, strategic considerations and risk-averse behavior). Two business opportunities are discussed below.

9.9.9 A chain community system as a business opportunity

A chain (port) community system aims to streamline information flows in the port and broader supply chain. In various ports, such a community system (PCS) has been developed. A PCS can be defined as a digital platform that connects the information systems of companies and institutions in the port (or supply chain) community.

A PCS facilitates the sharing of information between the actors involved in a port supply chain in an efficient and safe way. A PCS contributes to port efficiency by increasing the use of data standards in terminal operations. A PCS can provide at least five kinds of services (from simple to advanced):

1. Notification of ship arrival. This service allows shipping lines and ship agents to electronically notify the PMB (e.g., for the payment of port dues), harbormaster and customs organization of the arrival of a ship.
2. Other ship arrival notifications. These services allow shipping lines and ship agents to electronically notify of their waste and hazardous materials aboard the ship.
3. Customs-related information flows for import and export cargo. These services allow forwarding companies and importers/exporters to meet the data

requirements of the export control system (ECS) as well as the import control system of the EU electronically through one platform. Various firms (shipping line, terminal operator and forwarder) provide relevant data for customs.

4. Data exchange for efficient cargo handling. These services streamline information exchange between shipping lines/ship agents and terminal operators. Services include sending a list of cargo to be (un)loaded through the PCS. Generally, these services re-use some of the information provided to customs.
5. Data exchange hinterland modes. These services allow data exchange between truck, barge and rail operators (for instance, order of train wagons, pre-arrival notification of trucks) and terminal operators (e.g., customs status of cargo).

Many ports have developed port community systems. Most of these are organized as separate judicial and organizational entities. Most of these are not-for-profit but do aim to recover costs. However, some others do operate based on a for-profit model, such as MCP in the UK and Dakosy in Hamburg.[24] 36 PCS operators worldwide (including Portnet in Singapore, Dakosy from Hamburg, 1 Stop from Australia and Dubai Trade from West Asia) have founded or joined the International Port Community Systems Association (IPCSA).

PORTIC, the PCS active in Barcelona, is owned by all relevant stakeholders. PortBase is the port community system in the Port of Rotterdam and the Port of Amsterdam. PortBase is jointly owned by the SO-PDCs of Rotterdam and Amsterdam and offers services for efficient and simple information exchange between companies (B to B) and between companies and the government (B to G). About 2.5 million messages per month are exchanged through PortBase.

9.9.10 Managing infrastructure access

Congestion is a key impediment to efficient transport chains. Highways and rail tracks are often congested. Such congestion incurs costs to cargo owners, reduces reliability, increases the turnaround time of trucks and trains in the port and creates pollution. For this reason, many port development companies are concerned about congestion. One of the central strategies to combat congestion is to *actively manage infrastructure access*. Congestion is the result of peak arrival patterns. Active management of infrastructure access can influence these patterns, for instance, through road pricing, with differentiated tariffs (high in rush hours, lower outside these hours). There are many other initiatives to influence travel patterns, including a ban on empty trucks in rush hours, a ban (or additional charge) on polluting trucks, a ban on trucks without a handling slot at the terminal (through a truck appointment system), a bonus for commuters who change their travel behavior and so on. All these initiatives can only be taken by an organization that has the authority to manage access to the infrastructure. In most countries, (road) infrastructure is owned by governments and not actively managed. Allowing a partnership of organizations with an incentive to reduce congestion to do so can be beneficial for a port.

Such a partnership can be thought of as a *business opportunity*. It may be able to invest in alleviating congestion and collect revenues from infrastructure users – provided that travel time targets are met. Some ports have considered introducing charges for trucks to enter the port area, as in Melbourne; the Ports of LA and Long Beach introduced such a charge. In both cases, the idea is that the charge is used to alleviate congestion and mitigate environmental impact. In Valparaiso, the movement between a logistics zone outside the urban area and the port, which is located in the center of the urban area, is managed by the Valparaiso SO-PDC to secure efficiency and minimize environmental impacts.

The case of LA/LB – the development of Pierpass

PierPass is a not-for-profit company created by the container terminal operators at the Port of Los Angeles and Port of Long Beach to address multi-terminal issues such as congestion, air quality and security. Drayage trucks caused severe congestion on the roads and highways around the ports, with detrimental effects for air pollution.

PierPass launched regular night and Saturday work shifts to handle trucks delivering and picking up containers at the 12 container terminals. These additional opening hours are financed with a Traffic Mitigation Fee (TMF) levied on cargo movement during peak hours. This initiative has substantially increased the capacity of the gate handling and alleviated congestion. The program also includes incentives for clean trucks.

9.9.11 Business opportunities in the port business ecosystem

In addition to the previously mentioned new developments, PMBs increasingly aim to strengthen the port business ecosystem. Various ports take initiatives to strengthen the ecosystem. Four important business opportunities are discussed below.

Campus/innovation district

Attracting start-ups and new entrants, especially those with strong innovative capabilities, can contribute significantly to the ecosystem. Ports may co-develop a kind of campus for firms in the ports industry, like Dubai's maritime city campus, or Shanghai's maritime campus. Both cases may be larger than viable in other ports, but the general concept can also be applied at a smaller scale.

Utility infrastructure

The port complex needs an increasingly advanced utility infrastructure (electricity, water, broadband, industrial gases, and others). New technologies may give rise to new business opportunities, such as smart grids for electricity, CO_2 pipelines, LNG bunkering stations, shore power for ships and steam pipelines to re-use the heat produced at one facility in another facility. As with the other examples of business opportunities that we discussed, developing these business opportunities requires building partnerships that involve the users of utility infrastructure, prospective operators of utility infrastructure, regional governments and the PMB.

The value of utility infrastructure

The following utility infrastructure cases show the potential for business development.

- The multicore project in Port of Rotterdam, to develop "open access pipeline infrastructure" (as opposed to the pipeline infrastructure dedicated for one specific company), has created value for its users and financial return for the asset owners and managers.
- The "heat network" that connects various chemical companies in the port of Antwerp. The network consists of a pipeline for steam (400°C and 40 bar) and a regular pipeline for water. This infrastructure increases the energy efficiency substantially. For this reason, regional governments have subsidized the investments in this utility infrastructure.
- A planned aviation fuel pipeline between Dublin port and Dublin airport. The project, proposed by a company called Independent Pipeline Company, is backed by various stakeholders and potential users.

Commercial real estate

Ports often are attractive sites for real estate developments. In many ports, waterfronts have transformed from "working waterfronts" to "living waterfronts". Such transformations are attractive for port cities. However, housing does not strengthen the port ecosystem, so it is not further discussed. We do argue that well-developed *office space* for port-related activities can strengthen the port ecosystem, for the following reasons:

- Developing attractive office space for port-related businesses may lead to synergies between different companies. This strengthens the port community.
- As many port activities are located outside urban centers, they may not be attractive for "white-collar" workers (e.g., due to limited facilities, long travel distances). Shared office spaces may make working in the port complex more attractive.
- Next to the competition between ports for cargo flows and investments, port cities compete for port/maritime services. These services strengthen the port ecosystem.

Thus, there may be a case for co-developing waterfront office locations for port-related firms. This business opportunity requires partnerships between private developers, regional governments (permits, public transport infrastructure) and the PMB (as a substantial user of office space as well as developer of the waterfront). Examples of ports where office space has been developed specifically for port and maritime companies include Amsterdam, Barcelona, Marseille and Dubai.

Collective transport

A final potential business opportunity that can be developed is collective transport. Especially medium-sized and large ports often consist of port areas with substantial numbers of employees. Many of these employees commute to work by car during rush hour. That increases congestion and decreases the attractiveness of working in the port. Thus, establishing a form of collective transport can potentially create value.

To provide some very rough figures: in advanced economies, the "mobility costs" borne by the employer often are roughly 5–7% of annual I costs, for employees without a company car[25] (and much higher for employees with a company car). Additional mobility costs for employees are substantial and include commuting time. Thus, in a hypothetical case of a port area in Europe with say 15 companies and a total of 2500 jobs, the mobility costs of the port area are about €7.5 million (excluding the societal costs of the contribution of these commuting flows to congestion). These costs are borne by the individual companies and employees. All initiatives that can reduce these mobility costs create value and may be a business opportunity. Such initiatives can range from collective bus transfer for all firms in the port area to a park-and-ride facility or transport by boat. As previously discussed, some business opportunities may even be viable when the business case is negative, because governments may be willing to subsidize such efforts as part of an overall approach to alleviate congestion.

9.10 Good practices in crafting port strategies

In summary, various good practices can be distilled from this chapter on strategies for PMBs.

Strategy and business model

1. Develop a strategy map to visualize key goals and performance indicators.
2. Take the landlord model not as a given, but as a *business model choice*; consider in-house activities based on strategic considerations.
3. Benchmark the investment level of the PMB (investments as a percentage of total revenues) with peers.
4. Analyze the PBE as a portfolio of activities and develop an active approach to transitioning "decline activities". Invest in innovation capabilities to attract start-ups and scale-ups to the PBE and to be better positioned to address transition challenges.
5. Install a "tender board" to assess when competitive bidding is used and when direct negotiations are used to select and develop a partnership with third parties.

Investment projects

1. Invest substantially in new business development by taking the *initiative and risks*.
2. Develop a structured "funnel approach" for business development, so that progress is traced and the PMB can assess whether the pipeline is "healthy".
3. Secure user commitment prior to final investment decisions.

New services

4. Develop a structured approach to developing new "ecosystem services" and secure a healthy set of service development projects.
5. Invest in common infrastructures that lead to/increase synergies between companies in the port business ecosystem.
6. Invest in digital services that lead to/increase synergies between companies in the port business ecosystem.
7. Include part of the costs of "ecosystem services" in a "service bundle" for shipping lines and tenants.
8. Provide "synergy services" in an explicitly not-for-profit model.

Notes

1 While in most ports the harbor master is a part of the PDC and operates a vessel traffic management system, in some ports, a specific public agency is responsible for vessel traffic management. This service is included in the "minimalist" set of services as the PDC does not have a choice with regard to providing the service, whether or not this service is provided depends on the relevant national regulations.

2 Port marketing and developing stakeholder relations with the aim to secure stakeholder support for the port activities are included in the "minimalist" set of services, as both are provided by all PDCs and can be considered basic activities for developing an ecosystem; a port developer needs to make users aware of the value that the port business ecosystem can provide (i.e., port marketing) and needs to secure the port activities are acceptable for stakeholders (Dooms, 2010). Conceptually, both services can be considered as "ecosystem services" in the sense that the PDC engages in these activities in the shared interest of third parties in the PBE.

3 These two factors are loosely related to theories on boundaries of the firm as developed by Coase (1937), Williamson (1981) and other scholars in (New) Institutional Economics. The widely used factors to assess whether to use a market to purchase services or to provide them in house in a corporate hierarchy, frequency, uncertainty, asset specificity, can be considered to be encompassed with the items "synergy" and "capabilities".

4 As a numerical example: a landlord port with 1 billion of assets, a turnover of 250 million and a WACC of 10% needs to make an annual profit of 100 million (40% of turnover!) to be sustainable in the long run.

5 Generally, the free cash flow is larger than the profit, for instance, because port authorities depreciate their assets. In principle these depreciation costs are free cash flows, which can be re-invested in the port.

6 The OECD (2011) argues that bidding procedures for the highest fee are generally preferred, based on the argument that market environments are uncertain, so that fixing tariffs for long periods of time is complicated and more likely to result in renegotiation.

However, in the Chilean ports of Valparaíso and San Antonio, concessions were granted based on the bids for the lowest tariffs, and the process has worked well.

7 MVII consists of roughly 1000 acres of port; total construction costs were around €2.7 billion. The Port of Rotterdam (PoR) bears the costs and risks of building Maasvlakte II and receives the revenues from concession contracts and port dues. The project was developed with a business case approach: the revenues (port dues, land rents) are sufficient to cover investment and operational costs and generate sufficient returns. This port development approach prevents the publicly funded development of port sites that later prove of limited value. The project is financed entirely by PoR, partly with equity and partly with loans from banks (in total around €2 billion) and the Dutch state (around €700 million). The loan from the state is specifically to fund investments in public infrastructure and will be paid back –with interest – from the revenues (port dues and land rents) of MVII. Part of the equity (around €500 million) became available through a deal in which the state purchased roughly one third of the shares of PoR.

8 See Siemonsma et al. (2012) for more details.

9 This bid can be regarded as the land lease fee the private partner is willing to pay upfront for the entire period.

10 Note that some initiatives with collective benefits, such as marketing, training and maintenance dredging, are not treated as investments but as operational costs. Such activities are not discussed here.

11 See Siskos and Van Wassenhove (2017).

12 These figures are indicative only. Three "disclaimers" are relevant: first, differences in pricing structures blur this comparison. For instance, in some ports the costs of nautical access (e.g., entrance channel) are included in the port dues, while other ports charge separate *channel fees*. Likewise, some ports provide mooring services and include these in the port dues, while others do not. Next, port dues are divided by the total tonnage of a port. Thus, differences in commodities are ignored. Third, these data are from publicly available reports (mostly annual reports), which may report on gross (without discounts) or net port dues.

13 Labor costs are an important component of total costs and may be significantly lower in emerging economies.

14 Again, disclaimers apply: these data are publicly available and may not treat discounts equally and the quality of port land may differ (e.g., is the land paved or not).

15 Land surface, not m^2 warehouse space.

16 In the most similar industry, the airports industry, airport managing bodies have a much more uniform pricing structure with a distinction between aeronautical and non-aeronautical revenues. The shares of revenue types differ between airports, for instance in relation to the size of the airport (in larger airports the share of non-aeronautical revenues is higher), but there are widely applied principles regarding who is charged for what.

17 To be more precise, we argue for absolute and "dynamic" volume discounts. The absolute discounts reward huge-volume customers, while the "dynamic" discounts reward above-market growth. Such an incentive scheme can be transparent.

18 Experiments show that in some cases investors do take sunk costs into account, but we assume rational decision making applies to the decisions of terminal operators that influence the competitiveness of a port. For instance, if a terminal operator decides on investing in new terminal equipment, it would not make sense to include the level of land rents in the decision-making.

19 Of course, as with most conceptual distinctions, precise borders between these areas are hard to draw.

20 The choice of a business model is not the same as the choice of a strategy. For instance, a company can make the strategic choice to change a business model, to achieve its mission. For instance, companies can decide either to outsource activities that they currently do in-house (a shipper that sells a dedicated terminal) or to enter new markets

(an inland terminal that starts offering transport to/from a seaport). As another example, firms with the same or similar business models compete and can have different strategies. Shipping companies with the same business model can have different strategies, such as focusing on scale economies vs focusing on niche markets.

21 This framework is built on insights from studies on success in new product development and new service development (see, for instance, Thomke & Fujimoto, 2000; Jong, de & Vermeulen, 2003; Henard & Szymanski, 2001; de Brentani, 1995).

22 See www.portofrotterdam.com/en/doing-business/logistics/connections/intermodal-transportation/rail-transport/rail-incubator

23 The distinction between port network and transport chain is blurred; we limit the port network to three components (inland terminals, connections and logistics zones) and include all activities to develop efficient and sustainable services on this network as part of the next domain: supply chains.

24 It is worth noting that the origins of MCP can be traced back to when ABP was still a government owned entity, so while it was transformed into a for profit entity one could argue it grew out of a public sector initiative. Dakosy is owned by firms in the Hamburg ports industry. This is relevant as I argued previously that a PCS is unlikely to emerge as a private for-profit initiative.

25 Source: Data from www.mobiliteit.nu (in Dutch).

Appendix 1

Two best cases and two worst cases in port governance

Below, the most relevant findings of four cases in port governance, three of which are based on in-depth studies published previously (see de Langen & Visser, 2005; de Langen & Nijdam, 2009; de Langen & Heij, 2014), are discussed.

Best case: the cross-border merger of Copenhagen Malmö Ports

On 1 January 2001, the ports of Copenhagen and Malmö merged to become Copenhagen Malmö Port (CMP). Copenhagen and Malmö are separated by the Öresund, the strait between Sweden and Denmark. Because of the historically intensive interaction between the two sides, it was decided to build a bridge across the Öresund in the early 1990s. This Öresund Bridge opened in 2000.

The development of the Öresund Bridge would lead to the loss of virtually all ferry traffic between Copenhagen and Malmö. This threat was one of the drivers of the merger process. Ferry traffic accounted for roughly 20% of the turnover and 50% of the profits of both organizations. A merger was identified as an option, with important advantages summarized in Table A1.1.

The throughput figures of both ports declined after the opening of the Öresund Bridge, due to the loss of ferry traffic (and some container traffic). Since the merger in 2001, throughput has grown consistently. Key figures of CMP show that the turnover, productivity, profits and solvency all have increased following the merger, as did the CMP market share. Figure A1.1 indicates how the market share of CPM, relative to all Danish and Swedish ports, has steadily grown since the port merger in 2001.

The data clearly show that the post-merger performance of CMP was very good. Turnover per employee, profitability, throughput and market share all increased. Thus, it comes as no surprise that this merger is widely regarded as the best case in the industry.

Worst case: fragmented port governance in the lower Mississippi

The Mississippi River is a major transport corridor in the United States. The river is accessible by relatively large seagoing vessels (up to 40,000 "deadweight" tons) up to 233.5 nautical miles inland. This whole stretch of the river is one integrated port

Table A1.1 Identified important advantages of the CMP merger

Advantage	*Relevance for CMP*
Better utilization of resources	CMP can use resources (labor, land, capital) more effectively, especially since it has its own terminal operations. These benefits could be quantified in advance relatively accurately; in the first three years, a cost reduction of around 10–12% was achieved. The CMP labor force works on both sides of the Öresund.
Port infrastructure	CMP can provide facilities "on the other side" when capacity on one side is fully used. This is especially relevant in the cruise market, where ships that cannot be accommodated in Copenhagen are handled in Malmö. Consequently, Malmö handled the first cruise vessel ever in 2005. For containers and finished vehicles, the same mechanism applies.
Scale economies in management and administration	Cost savings have been achieved, but are less relevant than savings on operational costs.
Specialization, no double investments	Facilities on both sides of the Öresund can specialize in specific commodities. This leads to scale economies, while all major commodities can still be accommodated.
A new selling point	CMP can claim to serve the whole Öresund region, roughly 3,8 million consumers, effectively.
Professionalization of port management	CMP is a stronger player, with more financial resources. This is relevant in an industry with large and international customers. Due to the scale increase, especially the quality of the middle management has improved, according to respondents from the industry.

Source: De Langen and Nijdam (2009).

complex.[1] In throughput volume, the LMPC is one of the largest port complexes in the world and the largest in the US, with a total throughput in 2024 of covering 500 million tons, representing nearly 20% of all US cargo volumes. Even though the lower Mississippi functionally is one port cluster, it is administered by five independent port authorities, which are each responsible for part of the riverbanks.

All five port authorities are governed by politically appointed commissioners from their own jurisdiction. The five deep-sea ports in the LMPC compete in three ways. First, they compete for investments from private operators in their jurisdictions. All have land available for either lease or sale. Second, the port authorities compete for cargo; they support firms to attract more cargo to the port, e.g., through marketing. Even though the five ports form one integrated complex, they market their ports individually. Third, port authorities compete for state investment funds. The lack of coordination between the port authorities and the resulting competition has the following disadvantages:

1. Underinvestment in activities with benefits that spill-over to other port jurisdictions. The Port of Plaquemines provides a good example: the port hardly invests because the advantages (in terms of competitiveness, added value and

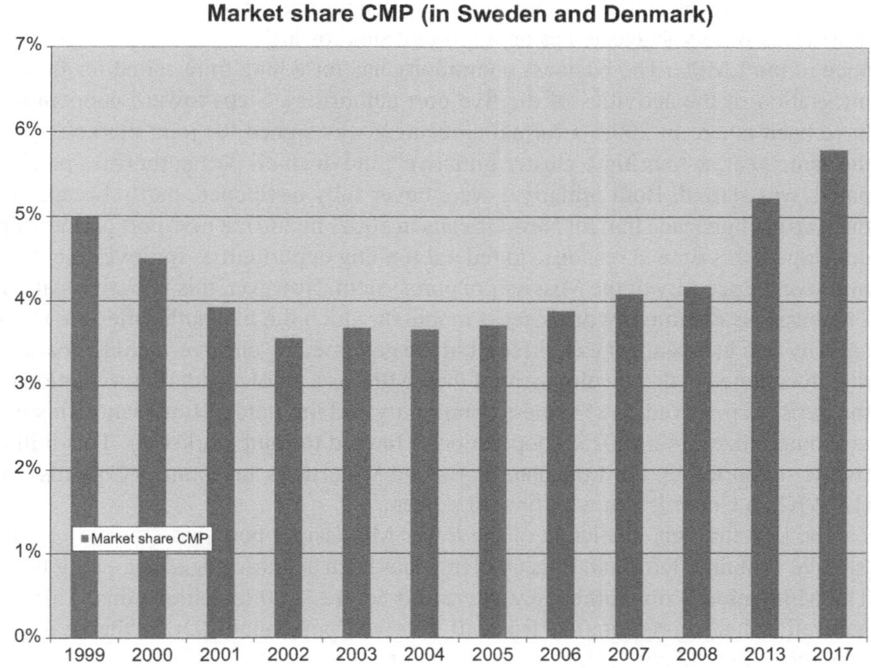

Figure A1.1 The evolution of CMP market share

employment) of such investments are to a large extent "external" to Plaquemines. Since the local community, consisting of nearly 25,000 inhabitants, indirectly governs the port authority, these external benefits have not been taken into account in investment decisions.

2. Spatial misallocation of investments. Since port authorities try to attract business, they invest in facilities in their jurisdiction, even when alternative locations make more sense from a business point of view. The investments of the Port of New Orleans in container facilities are an example. Two sites were developed, both at questionable locations, relatively far upstream and with moderate landside access. The locations were developed because the port owns only a limited amount of land and did not have better alternative locations *in its own jurisdiction*.
3. Overinvestment in similar port facilities. Competition between port authorities leads to a high willingness to invest in facilities within their jurisdiction, even if these investments duplicate existing facilities elsewhere in the LMPC.

The port governance in the lower Mississippi is not effective, with two major shortcomings. First, *different port authorities govern a part of one integrated port complex*. Second, and related, these port authorities have *limited autonomy and investment capabilities*.

Considering the above, it is not surprising that more cooperation between the authorities is widely suggested as an important step toward a more effective governance of the LMPC. The business community has for a long time called for further integration of the activities of the five port authorities. Steps toward cooperation have been taken. In 2002, a formal agreement was signed for joint marketing. In the same year, a "maritime cluster initiative", in which all port authorities participated, was started. Both initiatives were never fully developed, partly because of the Katrina hurricane that hit New Orleans in 2002. In 2007, a new port partnership developed, this time in response to federal funding opportunities for investments to improve the security of the Mississippi port system. However, this initiative stalled. The business community proposed a model in which the five authorities are managed by five independent executives, but are governed by one overarching board of directors aimed at the development of the LMPC as a whole, with representation of the parishes involved, the business community and the state of Louisiana. This did not materialize. As of 2025, cooperation is limited to joint marketing. This initiative is supported by the Louisiana Ports and Waterways Investment Commission (LPWIC), a Commission with limited powers.

The key strategic challenge of the lower Mississippi ports is to develop an attractive container terminal. This challenge has been acknowledged for a long time. The Millennium Port Authority was created before 2000 to achieve this. This organization had representation from all involved port authorities in the board of governors, but did not achieve its ambition of a new port facility and re-focused on improving (the security of) existing terminals. In 2012, the governor of Louisiana took the initiative to develop an attractive container facility and formed the Louisiana International Deep Water Gulf Transfer Terminal Authority. The fact that this was not a joint initiative of the port authorities is clearly a sign of the weak port governance in the lower Mississippi. The project has not advanced much; as of 2025, construction has not started, and no operator has committed to the project. Another initiative is under development: APMT signed an agreement in 2021 with the Port of Plaquemines to develop a terminal. This intention was renewed in 2024, but a final investment decision has not yet been taken.

The weak port governance has contributed to a weak port performance. Both the total volumes and the container volumes reveal a downward trend. The LMPC lost market share between 1990 and 2010, falling from 18% to 17.3% of total USA throughput. In the same period, Houston, the other important Gulf Coast port, managed to increase its market share from 5.8% to 9.2%. In container traffic, the decline was much stronger: New Orleans went down from a market share of 48% for the Gulf region in 1980 to a market share of well below 20% in 2017. Between 1980 and 2010, total container traffic through US ports almost quadrupled, and container flows through US Gulf ports nearly tripled, but the number of containers handled in the LMPC remained stable. This is a dramatic loss in market share, and very uncommon in the industry globally. Of course, this is not due solely to the ineffective port governance model, but this case does suggest that *port governance matters*. Ports where port governance structures are not effective face a serious risk of falling behind.

Best case: the corporatization of the Port of Rotterdam Authority

This case of the post-corporatization performance of the Port of Rotterdam Authority (PoR) is a case of a government-owned but corporatized port development company, which does not aim for maximum profits, but does operate commercially. In January 2004, the institutional position of PoR changed from a *municipal department* to a *public corporation*. All major stakeholders, such as the port business association, supported the corporatization. The municipality of Rotterdam is still the majority shareholder of PoR; the national government acquired a minority share of PoR. This transaction was agreed to in part to finance the €2 billion port expansion project, Maasvlakte II. The agreement involves a financial contribution of the state to the Port of Rotterdam Authority in return for a minority share. Thus, instead of providing a state subsidy to port development, the state has become a shareholder in making an investment in the equity of the company. Given the fact that PoR provides dividends, this investment is being recovered.

Since the corporatization, the management (executive board) of PoR is no longer controlled directly by the municipality, but by a supervisory board. The profile of the supervisory board members is such that the board "must be capable of working in the hybrid setting of a private company with public accountability". The shareholders have a formal influence at the annual shareholders' meeting and have periodic shareholder committee meetings. The shareholders appoint new members of the supervisory board. The supervisory board is the sole body involved in monitoring the executive board, including the appointment of new executive board members.

Prior to the corporatization, the management of PoR had successfully claimed more autonomy. In autumn 2004, just after the corporatization, it became apparent that the previous lack of monitoring had enabled the CEO to engage single-handedly in risky and questionable activities. The CEO had withheld important information on bank loans from the municipality and engaged in highly questionable transactions. These events demonstrate that the city council did not effectively monitor PoR.

Next to the organizational changes, the profile of senior managers changed. Prior to corporatization, new senior managers often came from the public sector. Many managers were internally promoted, within PoR or the municipal administration in a broader sense. This changed after corporatization. Table A1.2 shows the post-corporatization performance at PoR in two seven-year periods, 1997 to 2003 as well as 2005 to 2011.

In addition to the data above, the market share of Rotterdam declined substantially in the period 1997 to 2003.[2] After corporatization, the market share first stabilized and later started to increase. This growth was realized in the existing port area, not including Maasvlakte II, a major port expansion project, where the first terminals became operational in 2015. A related indicator of the commercial performance is customer satisfaction, which also has increased, from roughly 7.0 in 2004 to 7.3 in 2009.

EBITDA ("Earnings Before Interest, Taxes, Depreciation and Amortization", roughly equal to the free cash flow from operations) is an important financial

Table A1.2 Post-corporatization performance at the Port of Rotterdam

Variable	*1997*	*2003*	*2005*	*2011*
Total revenue (millions)	€453	€457	€486	€588
Port dues (millions)	€246	€228	€253	€291
Land rents (millions)	€153	€197	€203	€267
Employees	1,165	1,304	1,268	1,220
Turnover per employee (millions)	€389	€350	€383	€482
Operating costs (millions)	€210	€238	€245	€226
EBITDA (millions)	€242	€219	€241	€362
Net profit (millions)	€62	€64	€81	€195
Profit per employee (millions)	€53	€49	€64	€160
Investments (millions)	€167	€127	€149	€494

Source: De Langen and Heij (2014).

indicator. It has grown rapidly, in line with turnover growth. This is mainly driven by growing throughput volumes and operating costs reduction since corporatization, with 0.4% per year (correcting for inflation), compared to growing operating costs prior to 2004. These factors combined explain the substantial growth in EDITDA as well as net profit (>14% growth per year since corporatization!). The operating cost control was due partly to reduced employment after corporatization. Employment used to rise by close to 2% per year prior to corporatization. These figures suggest that PoR's financial strength and weak monitoring allowed for growth in employment size prior to corporatization, a typical result of an organization with a "soft budget constraint". Strongly put: PoR was "burning money" through employment growth. This trend has been reversed after corporatization. The following insights from the above case are relevant for PMBs in general:

1. Politicians (at the local level) have insufficient capabilities as well as incentives to tightly monitor PMBs. The operating environment of PMBs is so distinct from most public activities that PMBs that are monitored by politicians (or public sector professionals alone) run the risk of becoming self-governing organizations.
2. PMBs increasingly need commercial capabilities. A corporatized setting may lead to an inflow of senior managers with a commercial background, partly as a result of a supervisory board with commercial experience, partly because corporatized organizations are more attractive for private sector executives.
3. Corporatization of a PMB may enhance its performance, among others, through tighter operational cost control, more investments and better investment decisions.

Worst case: Chittagong's inability to take reform steps

There are various indications that port services in Chittagong are not in line with international standards. Container vessel service times in Chittagong are well above average (World Bank, 2025b). A World Bank study (Dappe & Suárez-Alemán, 2016) also shows Chittagong's poor operational performance and finds exports take twice as long to load as imports at the Chittagong Container Terminal, largely because of lack of enforcement of official cut-offs for exports and an inadequate tariff scheme on container stacking, leading to insufficient stacking capacity. In addition, dwell times for containers (the time spent in port) are exceptionally high: they averaged 17 days in 2012 compared to the 3–4 days typical at efficient ports. The World Bank study states that according to shipping lines and other port users, the main reasons for these patterns include complicated customs procedures, slow processing of documentation and payments by importers and poor connectivity with Dhaka.

Finally, the infrastructure characteristics also suggest Bangladesh's infrastructure is inadequate: Bangladesh has just two international ports, Chittagong and Mongla (with a limited role). Chittagong is the deepest port in Bangladesh, but the draft of under 10 meters is much less than Colombo (18), Karachi (>15 at its newest terminal) and JNPT (after dredging is completed, 16). In addition, substantial container volumes are handled at general cargo berths without specialized containerized handling equipment. These berths mostly handle geared vessels.

The root cause of the inefficiencies is the dominant position of the Chittagong Port Authority (CPA). CPA is a state-owned entity with weak corporate governance (Dappe & Suárez-Alemán, 2016) and operates a "mixed model" in which it retains control over terminal tariffs and has not introduced competition between service providers. CPA has over 6000 employees,[3] well over what seems reasonable based on international comparisons.

CPA outsources terminal operations to private stevedores, who operate under relatively short-term (typically three- to five-year) contracts with CPA. The main private operator is SAIF Powertec;[4] it operates the Chittagong Container Terminal and the New Moorings Container Terminal. SAIF Powertec is a Bangladeshi conglomerate.

The business community has repeatedly expressed the desire for support for more private sector involvement. Initiatives to enlarge the private sector role have been a constant in the last 30 years, but progress has been limited. Consequently, Bangladesh is the only country on the Indian subcontinent in which specialized internationally operating terminal operators are not active.

SAIF Powertec was given an increasingly large role as container terminal operator, even though allegations were made of irregularities in the selection process, as the bidding process stifled the interest of international players, while SAIF Powertec was the only qualified party, with operating experience in Bangladesh. In 2024, a new government started an effort to bring in international operators, more specifically DP World.[5] That process has not concluded as of the end of 2025. In the meantime, SAIF Powertec has signed an agreement with AD Ports, the relatively new state-owned port company from Abu Dhabi. This case shows the need for effective corporatization and a competition regulator that promotes competition.

Notes

1 A detailed description of this complex is given in de Langen (2004).

2 However, one has to keep in mind the impact of the *commodity effect* on the market share. Rotterdam has a large share of crude oil and dry bulk throughput, in 1996 more than 60% of total throughput. Both market segments are mature, with low growth rates. And Rotterdam has a very high market share in these markets. Competing ports, especially Hamburg and Antwerp, are more specialized in container trade, the fastest growing market segment. *Thus, even if Rotterdam maintains its market share in all segments, overall market share decreases*.

3 Including an in-house training center as well as a training center specifically for women. This is a characteristic of a state-owned entity with a soft budget constraint.

4 Other private operators provide container-handling services at the general cargo berths.

5 One interesting issue regarding the selection of DP World as preferred candidates was stated by an advisor of the Ministry of Shipping and Ministry (M. Sakhawat Hossain) as follows: "DP World is owned by the UAE government, where more than 1.9 million Bangladeshi expatriates are employed. Turning down their proposal outright would have been risky. If even half of our expatriates were sent back in protest, it would severely impact our economy". This demonstrates the relevance of the leverage of SOEs discussed in Chapter 6.

Appendix 2

Analyzing throughput drivers: crude oil, coal and steel

Throughput drivers of commodities

The changing landscape discussed in Chapter 4 has important implications for future maritime transport volumes. Below, I discuss the *throughput drivers* for three important commodities (crude oil, iron ore and coal) and relate these to the changing landscape discussed in Chapter 4.

Crude oil

Crude oil is the largest single commodity handled in ports. The throughput drivers of crude oil are straightforward. Crude oil is refined in oil refineries. Figure A2.1 provides details of the different uses of refinery products and the relative share of these types of use. For oil, the key throughput driver is the *refining capacity*. For import ports, the import volumes are directly determined by the oil demand of refineries. Refining capacity also determines exports worldwide.

Transport fuels are clearly the dominant type of use of refinery products. Given the fast rise of car ownership and mobility demands, major companies, such as ExxonMobil, with their well-known *Energy Outlook*, foresee a rise in demand for refinery products until 2050, mainly driven by a growing demand in developing economies, and consequently a rise in refinery capacity.

A second throughput driver, especially relevant for ports, is the share of oil trade by pipeline. Even though in most cases, pipeline infrastructure is complementary to

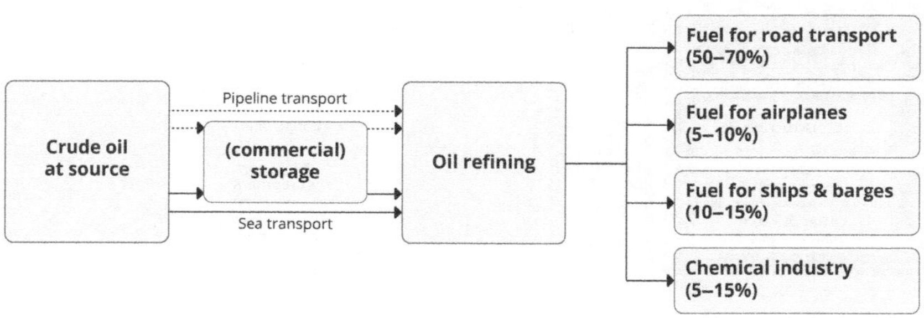

Figure A2.1 Throughput drivers of crude oil

maritime transport, in some cases additional pipeline infrastructure can change the volume as well as the routing of oil flows. For instance, the development of new pipelines led to a substantial reduction in the oil volumes of the ports of Georgia, which used to handle substantial oil volumes for Central Asia.

The third driver of oil volume is commercial storage volume. In volatile markets, oil traders as well as others invest in oil stocks. These volumes are stored temporarily, in the expectation of higher future prices. This leads to a demand for temporary storage of oil, often in ports. This third effect is quite relevant: in the economic crisis of 2009, profits of virtually all large companies in Europe declined, in many cases dramatically. Vopak, the world's largest independent tank storage provider, was one of the rare exceptions, mainly because of the huge demand for temporary storage of oil and oil products that resulted from the economic crisis.

Iron ore

The second largest commodity flow worldwide is iron ore. Figure A2.2 shows the main throughput drivers of iron ore. Iron ore is used in steel plants. The output of steel plants is used predominantly in three industries: the automotive industry, including parts producers, the construction industry and manufacturing of other durable consumer goods (e.g., kitchen equipment, audio equipment, etc.). The key throughput driver is the *industrial production* in these three industries. As these are all durable consumer goods (houses, cars, kitchen equipment), their sales are closely related to *consumer confidence*. Consequently, these products are sensitive to economic recessions, making iron ore throughput also sensitive to recessions. Indeed, the throughput of iron ore and steel fell rapidly in most countries in 2008–2009.

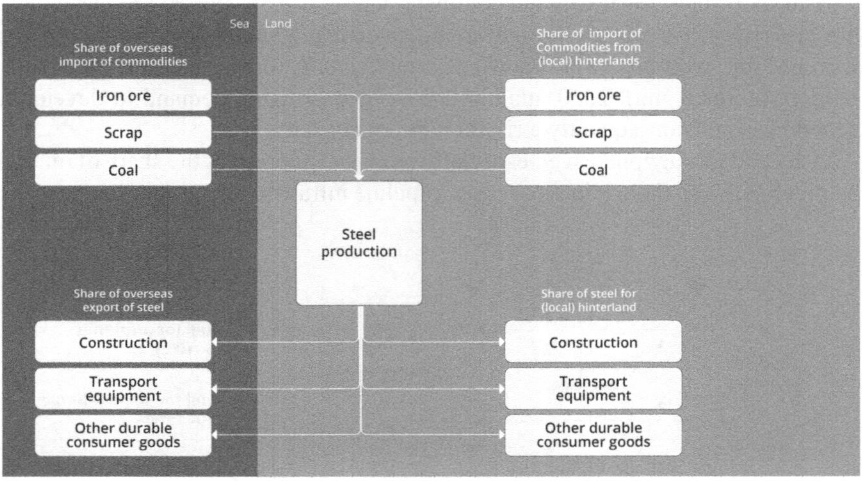

Figure A2.2 Throughput drivers of iron ore

The second throughput driver for iron ore relates to the mix between iron ore and scrap as sources for steel production. As most (>85%) steel is recycled, but with a substantial time lag, the share of scrap as a source for new steel has gradually increased *vis-à-vis* iron ore and has reached around 35%. This reduces imports of iron ore. In some advanced economies, the share of scrap is higher than 35% and expected to increase further, putting downward pressure on iron ore volumes. For instance, in Türkiye, around 90% of all steel is produced from scrap (World Steel Association, 2025).

The annual global production of crude steel was about 1.8 billion tons in 2024.[1] In the past decade, production of crude steel grew by around 5% per year. This growth was driven mainly by strong demand in emerging economies. The demand for steel in developed economies (Europe, North America and Japan) is stable. The main raw materials required for producing steel are *iron ore* and *coal*.

Steel production in the developed countries (Europe, North America and Japan) has been roughly stable in the last 15 years, while production has exploded in China, so that China now produces over 50% of the global output. Production in Brazil and India has also increased, but at a much lower pace. A very substantial increase in both countries is widely expected.

Currently, more than 80% of all steel is recycled. This percentage is expected to rise further. This may lead to a volume of recycled steel of over 1 billion tons in the next decade, from currently about 400 million tons. This will profoundly change steel supply chains; in advanced economies, steel mills based on iron ore and coal have closed down, and further closures are widely expected.

For ports, steel and related products are important commodities. Iron ore is the second largest commodity shipped worldwide, while intermediate and finished steel products are also traded in huge quantities (see Table A2.1).

The demand for and trade of iron ore has increased substantially, in line with the demand for steel. The most significant demand for iron ore has been from China, which imported over 600 million tons of iron ore in 2008, more than 1 billion in 2018, and more than 1.2 billion in 2024, accounting for more than 60% of global iron ore imports.

Two different production methods are used to produce steel: blast furnace steelmaking (roughly 70% of total production), which uses iron ore, coal and in some cases recycled steel, and electric arc steelmaking, which uses recycled steel only and electricity. Iron arc production accounts for a little under 30% of total steel

Table A2.1 Trade of steel commodities

Commodity	*Global trade 2008*	*Global trade 2024*
Iron ore	About 930 million tons	About 1730 million tons
Finished and semi-finished steel products	About 420 million tons	About 450 million tons
Scrap[2]	About 100 million tons	About 100 million tons

Source: World Steel Association (2010, 2025).

production. In the European Union, almost 60% of Steel is produced with recycled steel; in the US, this figure is almost 70%.

The difference between current steel production volumes and recycling volumes is caused mainly by a *time lag*, as steel products generally have a long life-cycle. In the long run, a steel industry based *fully* on recycled material is feasible. For this reason, steel is environmentally friendly compared to alternatives such as concrete. Over time, the importance of scrap as a resource will increase, at the expense of iron ore. Regional imbalances lead to intercontinental scrap flows. In 2018, around 60% of scrap trade (around 60 million tons) was extra-regional trade. As the majority of export flows are containerized, scrap exports benefit from container imbalances. Given the "empty leg" between the US and China, scrap freight flows from the US to Asia increased rapidly. However, scrap exports are likely to have peaked at around 18 million tons in 2021. The addition of significant "electric arc capacity" has increased the potential for domestic consumption, and additional increases of clean steel production are expected, the majority of these relying on scrap as its primary input. The US trade policies also discourage scrap exports. The transition of the steel industry implies volumes of iron ore, slabs, scrap and finished steel are likely to change substantially in the coming decades.

Coal

The third largest commodity shipped worldwide is coal. The main drivers of coal throughput are given in Figure A2.3. A part of the coal imports, roughly 30% worldwide, is so-called "coke coal", which is used in steel production. The majority of

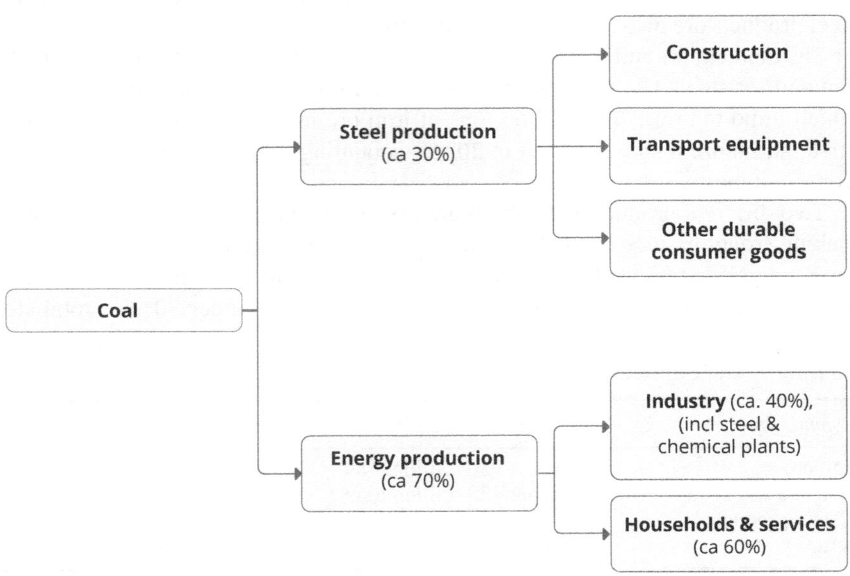

Figure A2.3 Throughput drivers for coal

coal is used in coal-powered electricity plants. Electricity is consumed by households (roughly 60%) as well as industries. The steel and chemical industries are heavy users. This explains the significant drop in electricity demand during the economic crisis – heavy electricity users stopped producing. A continued increase in electricity demand is widely expected. The share of coal-fired energy plants is uncertain, heavily influenced by political decisions, but widely expected to decline (see, for instance, ExxonMobil, 2025).

Notes

1 See www.worldsteel.org
2 Some additional figures on scrap: the external trade of scrap of the European Union grew from €800 million in 2000 to €3 billion in 2009 (over 20% per year)! For the EU, scrap, with an estimated volume of around 400,000 TEU, is one of the largest single commodities in containers.

Appendix 3

Details of relevant port performance indicators

Number of ship calls

The number of ship calls is a basic indicator of the utilization of the maritime infrastructure. These data is available in all ports as vessel arrivals are logged. Numbers of ships are often collected for different ship types; this makes the data more useful for market analysis.

Total volume of goods handled in the port

The most widely used indicator is available in virtually all ports. Relevant as the main revenue driver for terminals and the PMB. Often available for specific commodities, such as containers, oil and coal.

Containers: share of transhipment and transit of total cargo

Container volumes are widely available. Precise transhipment shares (based on volume) are available in only a few ports. Data on transhipment are needed for an objective distinction between transhipment ports – where the majority of traffic is transhipment – and gateway ports – where the majority of traffic is to or from inland destinations.

Port or terminal productivity

In the container segment, the emerging global standard for port or terminal productivity is the annual World Bank report, produced with data from S&P Global Market Intelligence. The report can be found here: https://openknowledge.worldbank.org/.

Liner shipping connectivity

In maritime transport, the liner Shipping Connectivity Index (LSCI), developed by the United Nations Conference on Trade and Development in 2005 (Hoffmann, 2005), has measured the container connectivity of countries for almost a decade. LSCI has been published by UNCTAD each year since its starting year of 2004.

It is developed to measure countries' connectivity in terms of access to regular and frequent liner services. LSCI is constituted of five components:

1. The number of ships that national and international liner shipping companies deploy on the liner services from and to the country's ports.
2. Deployment of container carrying capacity (number of slots for 20-foot equivalent units (TEU) of the ships used in these services).
3. Maximum vessel size that calls at a country's port (TEU).
4. The number of different services provided by the shipping lines.
5. The number of liner companies providing services to the country's ports.

All of the components are calculated on a yearly basis, and each of the components is normalized by the value of the highest component in 2004. The obtained values are then averaged and once again normalized by the maximum average for 2004 and multiplied by 100. The data are available at https://unctadstat.unctad.org/datacentre/dataviewer/US.LSCI.

Roll-on–roll-off connectivity

In Europe, roll-on–roll-off (RoRo) trade is as important for short-sea shipping as container shipping. Roll-on, roll-off is not used for deep-sea shipping because roll-on, roll-off is not cost-competitive for this segment (since the key feature of roll-on, roll-off is that trucks or trailers, sometimes with drivers, are transported by ship, enabling fast and cheap loading and unloading). For short-sea trades, RoRo is often potentially competitive; the connectivity of a port through regular RoRo services can be assessed in a similar way to liner shipping connectivity.

Intermodal connectivity

Intermodal connectivity is an important indicator. Intermodal terminals allow for efficient transfer of cargo and containers from one high-volume mode of transportation, such as rail or river barges, to trucks that link to final destinations. The connectivity of intermodal transport thus refers to the number of rail or barge inland terminals that can be reached from a port. Intermodal connectivity can be calculated when container train and barge[1] schedules are publicly available, which is increasingly the case because publicly providing schedule information is part of the marketing efforts of train and barge service providers to attract individual shippers. This type of data is often available on platforms that have schedule information from multiple service providers. With such data, several methods can be used to express a port's intermodal connectivity. The simplest indicator is the sum of the unique directly served destinations from a port.[2]

Bulk cargo: tons per (working) hour

Like for containers, the most relevant PPI from a shipping line perspective is the turnaround time in a port; a substantial part of this time is the time of loading/unloading. Thus, a metric of the speed of (un)loading is relevant.

Tons per berth meter

For the terminal operator and PDC, utilization of the expensive assets involved (cranes, equipment, quays and basins) is critical. An indicator of utilization is the volume handled per year per berth meter.

Containers: modal split (shares of rail, road and inland waterways)

Modal split is an increasingly widely used indicator. While it is also used for all volumes passing through the port, it is most widely used and most valuable specifically for containers because the modal split figures at a port level are deeply influenced by fluctuations of volumes of specific volumes and because the "value for society" of a *modal shift* with a reduced share of road transport is clear for containers but less clear for an aggregated indicator, as many bulk cargoes are processed in the port itself.

The container modal split shows the share of total *hinterland* container volumes[3] to/from the port that is transported by rail and or barge[4]. In most countries, calculating this indicator requires data from the container terminal, as they measure the "hinterland volume" and data from the rail terminals in the port, as they measure the volume by train. In some countries, statistical agencies derive modal split statistics from transport manifests or customs declarations.

Containers: dwell time

As an additional indicator, the dwell time, i.e., the average length of the stay of containers in the terminal yard, is relevant. Such dwell times, especially for import cargo, suggest inefficiencies in the last leg, either administrative or operational. High average dwell times often imply crowded container yards, which reduces the operational efficiency of the terminal.

Containers: terminal CO_2 emissions per TEU

From a supply chain perspective, the emissions at the terminal are rather small compared to emissions in both the maritime and the hinterland leg. Nevertheless, in view of accurate CO_2 emission data, the emissions per TEU are also increasingly relevant.

Presence of third-party terminal operators

Even though port governance is not a port performance indicator in the strict sense – that is, it is not an outcome of port activities but a description of how the governance of a port is organized – it is relevant because various studies have shown its effect on outcome indicators such as productivity.[5] Reform of state entities that provide terminal services (public service ports) to landlords, with private specialized companies providing terminal services, has proven beneficial. Thus, the presence of third-party terminal operators is a performance indicator. In addition, the number of competing terminal operators is a relevant PPI.

Independent SO-PDC

As discussed in Chapter 5, the presence of a truly independent SO-PDC is beneficial for port performance, compared to an ineffectively corporatized PDC or a public sector embedded PA,[6] and is therefore a relevant indicator.

Corridor governance

Especially for ports that serve foreign hinterlands (such as the port of Maputo in Mozambique that serves South Africa and the ports in Georgia that serve Azerbaijan and Armenia), the presence of "corridor governance structures", i.e., structured and lasting cooperation between parties from various countries involved in developing the corridor, can be considered a port performance indicator as the absence of such structures negatively impacts the port's ability to serve transit destinations.

Average ship waiting time

Shipowners as well as shippers benefit from a fast turnaround time of ships. For shipowners, this means they can make more trips with their vessels; cargo owners have their cargo available earlier. Therefore ship turnaround time is an important performance metric in ports. It is important to understand that the ship TAT is influenced by all kinds of services to the ship, such as loading and unloading, pilotage, towage, competent master, bunkering and ship supplies. From the port perspective, the ship TAT should include as many relevant elements of a port call as possible. Ideally, the TAT should be calculated from the moment the ship arrives at the entrance point to a port until the ship leaves this entry point.

Average truck waiting time

Especially for container terminals, trucks are often confronted with waiting times. These waiting times both reduce supply chain efficiency and truck utilization and have negative environmental impacts. Thus, truck waiting times are a relevant PPI.

Burden of customs procedures

The Logistics Performance Index on the quality of customs analyses the efficiency of customs and border management clearance. As with all of the LPIs, it indicates the relative ease and efficiency with which products can be moved into and inside a country, and it is calculated (as the other five LPIs) on the basis of interviews with international, national or regional logistics and warehouse operators, or freight forwarding companies.

Notes

1 The remaining analysis focuses on trains because the number of ports with high inland barge traffic is very limited. Of the identified EU core ports, less than 5% have container barge services.

2 More complicated indicators would attribute a link quality to each link and then sum the link qualities of all unique destinations.

3 It is important to express this indicator in relation to hinterland traffic, since the hinterland mode is not relevant for transhipment cargo. Including transhipment volumes in the denominator would mean that the modal split indicator changes with shifts in transhipment volumes. For instance, if Barcelona loses transhipment volumes, its modal split indicator would go up.

4 The calculation method is: (Rail + barge container volume) / (Total container volume – transhipment volume).

5 See, for instance, Cheon, Dowall, and Song (2010).

6 This is not a black or white distinction: port authorities can have some but not full autonomy. The analysis draws on the composition of the supervisory board (if any), hiring practices of the port authorities, and their commercial freedom to negotiate prices.

References and further reading

References

Acciaro, M., Ghiara, H., & Cusano, M. I. (2014). Energy management in seaports: A new role for port authorities. *Energy Policy*, 71, 4–12.

Aritua, B., Chiu, H., Cheng, L., Farrell, S., & de Langen, P. (2022). *Developing China's Ports: How the Gateways to Economic Prosperity Were Revived*. World Bank Publications.

Arvis, J.F., Vesin, V., Carruthers, R. C., Ducruet, C. and de Langen, P.W. (2018). *Maritime Networks, Port Efficiency, and Hinterland Connectivity in the Mediterranean*. World Bank Group. http://documents.worldbank.org/curated/en/508771540319329808

Ashford, N. A. (2002). Government and environmental innovation in Europe and North America. *American Behavioral Scientist*, 45(9), 1417–1434.

Asteris, M., & Collins, A. (2010). UK container port investment and competition: Impediments to the market. *Transport Reviews*, 30(2), 163–178.

Barros, C.P., Felício, J. A. & Fernandes, R.L. (2012). Productivity analysis of Brazilian seaports. *Maritime Policy & Management*, 39(5), 503–523.

Baier, S.L. & Bergstrand, J. H. (2007). Do free trade agreements actually increase members' international trade? *Journal of International Economics*, 71(1), 72–95.

Balsmeier, B., Buchwald, A. & Stiebale, J. (2014). Outside directors on the board and innovative firm performance. *Research Policy*, 43(10), 1800–1815.

Baumol, W. J. (1964). External economies and second-order optimality conditions. *Amer. Econ. Rev*. 54: 358–372.

van den Berg, R., de Langen, P.W. & Van Zuijlen, P.C. (2017). Revisiting port pricing: a proposal for seven port pricing principles. *WMU Journal of Maritime Affairs*, 16(3), 421–438.

Bichou, K. (2021). Development of a strategic plan for port performance improvement in South African container terminals, report for the SA-TIED program. https://sa-tied.wider.unu.edu/sites/default/files/SA-TIED-Bichou-Report_0.pdf

Blanchard, J.M.F. (2023). *Chinese Overseas Ports in Europe and the Americas: Understanding Smooth and Turbulent Waters*. Routledge.

Boardman, A.E., & Vining, A. R. (1989). Ownership and performance in competitive environments: A comparison of the performance of private, mixed, and state-owned enterprises. *The Journal of Law and Economics*, 32, 1–33.

Bolevics, V. (2017). The impact of governance on the efficiency of the Baltic states' major ports. *Journal of Business Management*, 14.

Bryan, J., Munday, M., Pickernell, D., & Roberts, A. (2006). Assessing the economic significance of port activity: Evidence from ABP operations in industrial South Wales. *Maritime Policy & Management*, 33(4), 371–386.

Brown, P.H. (2009). *America's Waterfront Revival: Port Authorities and Urban Redevelopment*. University of Pennsylvania Press.

de Brentani, U. (1995). New industrial service development: Scenarios for success and failure. *Journal of Business Research*, 32(2), 93.

Castro, J. V., & Millán, P. C. (1998). Port economic impact: methodologies and application to the port of Santander. *International Journal of Transport Economics/Rivista internazionale di economia dei trasporti*, 25(2), 159–179.

Chen, J. M., Petrick, J. F., Papathanassis, A., & Li, X. (2019). A meta-analysis of the direct economic impacts of cruise tourism on port communities. *Tourism Management Perspectives*, 31, 209–218.

Cheon, S., Dowall, D.E. & Song, D.W. (2010). Evaluating impacts of institutional reforms on port efficiency changes: Ownership, corporate structure, and total factor productivity changes of world container ports. *Transportation Research Part E: Logistics and Transportation Review*, 46(4), 546–561.

Christiansen, H. (2013). Balancing commercial and non-commercial priorities of state-owned enterprises. *OECD Discussion Paper*. www.scispace.com/pdf/balancing-commercial-and-non-commercial-priorities-of-state-1dvcsicubp.pdf

Clark, X., Dollar, D. & Micco, A. (2004). Port efficiency, maritime transport costs, and bilateral trade. *Journal of Development Economics*, 75(2), 417–450.

Coase, R.H. (1937). The nature of the firm. *Economica*, 4(16), 386–405.

Cohen, W. M., & Levinthal, D. A. (1990). Absorptive capacity: A new perspective on learning and innovation. *Administrative Science Quarterly*, 35, 128–152.

Cuadrado, M., Frasquet, M. & Cervera, A. (2004). Benchmarking the port services: A customer oriented proposal. *Benchmarking: An International Journal*, 11(3), 320–330.

Damman, S., & Steen, M. (2021). A socio-technical perspective on the scope for ports to enable energy transition. *Transportation Research Part D: Transport and Environment*, 91, 102691.

Dappe, M.H. & Suárez-Alemán, A. (2016). *Competitiveness of South Asia's Container Ports: A Comprehensive Assessment of Performance, Drivers, and Costs*. World Bank Publications.

Debrie, J., Lavaud-Letilleul, V., & Parola, F. (2013). Shaping port governance: the territorial trajectories of reform. *Journal of Transport Geography*, 27, 56–65.

Drewry Shipping Consultants (2025) Global container terminal operator annual review and forecast 2025/26. www.drewry.co.uk/maritime-research-products/global-container-terminal-operators-annual-review-and-forecast-202526

Ensley, M.D. & Hmieleski, K.M. (2005). A comparative study of new venture top management team composition, dynamics and performance between university-based and independent start-ups. *Research Policy*, 34(7), 1091–1105.

ESPO (2012). ESPO manifesto; Brussels, no longer available online

ESPO (2016). Trends in EU ports governance, Brussel. www.espo.be/publications/trends-in-eu-ports-governance-2016

ESPO (2018). The infrastructure investment needs and financing challenge of European ports, available at https://www.espo.be/media/Port%20Investment%20Study%202018_FINAL_1.pdf

ESPO (2022). Trends in EU Ports' Governance 2022, available at https://www.espo.be/media/ESPO%20Trends%20in%20EU%20ports%20governance%202022.pdf

ESPO (2024). Port Investments Study 2024: the investment pipeline and challenges of European ports.

European Commission (2006). Communication from the Commission on a European Programme for Critical Infrastructure Protection, available at http://eur-lex.europa.eu/legal-content/EN/TXT/PDF/?uri=CELEX:52006DC0786&from=EN.

European Court of Auditors (2016). Special report No 23/2016: Maritime transport in the EU: in troubled waters—much ineffective and unsustainable investment, Brussels.

Eurostat (2025a). Port statistics. https://ec.europa.eu/eurostat/statistics-explained/index.php?title=Maritime_transport_of_goods_-_annual_data

Eurostat (2025b). Maritime transport of goods – quarterly data. https://ec.europa.eu/eurostat/statistics-explained/index.php?title=Maritime_transport_of_goods_-_quarterly_data, last accessed 29 October 2025.

ExxonMobil (2025). 2025 global outlook. https://corporate.exxonmobil.com/sustainability-and-reports/global-outlook/introduction, last accessed 29 October 2025.

Flyvbjerg, B. (2007). Policy and planning for large-infrastructure projects: problems, causes, cures. *Environment and Planning B: Planning and Design*, 34(4), 578–597.

Fugazza, M. & Hoffmann, J. (2017). Liner shipping connectivity as determinant of trade. *Journal of Shipping and Trade*, 2(1). https://doi.org/10.1186/s41072-017-0019-5

Fujita, M., Krugman, P.R. & Venables, A.J. (2001). *The Spatial Economy: Cities, Regions, and International Trade*. MIT press.

Galal, Ahmed, Leroy Jones, Pankaj Tandon, Ingo Vogelsang (1994). *Welfare Consequences of Selling Public Enterprises*. Oxford University Press.

Gillen, D. (2011). The evolution of airport ownership and governance. *Journal of Air Transport Management*, 17(1), 3–13.

Goss, R.O. (1990). Economic policies and seaports: The diversity of port policies. *Maritime Policy & Management*, 17(3), 221–234.

Global Solar Atlas 2.0 (2025). A free, web-based application developed and operated by the company Solargis s.r.o. on behalf of the World Bank Group, utilizing Solargis data, with funding provided by the Energy Sector Management Assistance Program (ESMAP). https://globalsolaratlas.info.

Government of Germany (2025). National strategy for sea and inland ports. www.bmv.de/SharedDocs/EN/publications/national-strategy-for-sea-and-inland-ports.pdf?__blob=publicationFile

Haney, A. B., & Pollitt, M. G. (2013). New models of public ownership in energy. *International Review of Applied Economics*, 27(2), 174–192.

Henard, D., & Szymanski, D. (2001), Why some new products are more successful than others. *Journal of Marketing Research*, 38(3).

Herrera Dappe, M. & Suárez-Alemán, A. (2016). *Competitiveness of South Asia's Container Ports: A Comprehensive Assessment of Performance, Drivers, and Costs. Directions in Development*. World Bank. https://doi.org/10.1596 /978-1-4648–0892-0

Herrera Dappe, M., Lebrand, M. & Stokenberga, A. (2024). Shrinking economic distance: Understanding how markets and places can lower transport costs in developing countries. https://hdl.handle.net/10986/42061

van den Heuvel, F., van Donselaar, K., de Langen, P. & Fransoo, J. (2015). Co-location synergies: Specialised versus diverse logistics concentration areas. *Tijdschrift voor economische en sociale geografie*. https://doi.org/10.1111/tesg.12152

Hoffmann, J. (2005). Liner shipping connectivity. *UNCTAD Transport Newsletter*, 27(1), 4–12.

van Der Horst, M.R. & De Langen, P.W. (2008). Coordination in hinterland transport chains: a major challenge for the seaport community. *Maritime Economics & Logistics*, 10(1–2), 108–129.

Huat, C.B. (2016). State-owned enterprises, state capitalism and social distribution in Singapore. *The Pacific Review*, 29(4), 499–521.

Hummels, D. (2007). Transportation costs and international trade in the second era of globalisation. *The Journal of Economic Perspectives*, 21(3), 131–154.

Iansiti, M. & Levien, R. (2004). *The Keystone Advantage, What the New Dynamics of Business Ecosystems Mean for Strategy, Innovation and Sustainability*, Harvard Business School Press.

IEA (2025). World Energy Outlook 2025. hwww.iea.org/reports/world-energy-outlook-2025

IRENA (2025). Renewable power generation costs in 2024. www.irena.org/Publications/2025/Jun/Renewable-Power-Generation-Costs-in-2024, last accessed 29 October 2025.

Isenberg, D. (2014). What an Entrepreneurship Ecosystem actually is. *Harvard Business Review*, May 12, 2014. http://hbr.org/2014/05/what-an-entrepreneurialecosystem-actually-is/

Jacobides, M.G., Cennamo, C. & Gawer, A. (2018). Towards a theory of ecosystems. *Strategic Management Journal*, 39(8), 2255–2276.

Jones, C. I., & Williams, J. C. (2000). Too much of a good thing? The economics of investment in R&D. *Journal of Economic Growth*, 5, 65–85.

International Energy Agency (2018). World energy outlook. https://www.iea.org/weo/

International Federation of Robotics (2017). Executive summary world robotics 2017 industrial robots. https://ifr.org/free-downloads/

Jacobides, M.G., Cennamo, C., & Gawer, A. (2018). Towards a theory of ecosystems. *Strategic Management Journal*, 39 (8), 2255–2276.

Jia, N. (2017). Should directors have term limits? – Evidence from corporate innovation. *European Accounting Review*, 26(4), 755–785.

Jong, P.J. de & Vermeulen, P.A.M. (2003). Organizing successful new service development: A literature review. *Management Decision*, 41(9), 844–858

Juhel, M.H. (2017). *Container Terminal Concession Guidelines*. World Bank. https://documents1.worldbank.org/curated/en/108731501220267086/pdf/117776-WP-PUBLIC-Container-Terminal-Concession-Guidelines.pdf, last accessed 29 October 2025.

Kyllönen, M. (2017). Can the EU's circular economy apply to ports? *The Parliament Magazine*, 19 May. www.theparliamentmagazine.eu/articles/opinion/can-eus-circular-economy-apply-ports

de Langen, P.W. (2004). The performance of seaport clusters; A framework to analyze cluster performance and an application to the seaport clusters of Durban, Rotterdam and the Lower Mississippi (No. ERIM PhD Series; EPS-2004–034-LIS).

de Langen, P.W. (2008). Analysing training and education in ports. *WMU Journal of Maritime Affairs*, 7(1), 5–16.

de Langen, P.W. (2025). Investments and financing challenges of the EU's port managing bodies: Findings from a comprehensive survey. *European Transport Studies*, 2, 100019.

de Langen, P.W. (2023a). The strategy of the port development company; a framework based on the business ecosystems perspective and an application to the case of Port of Rotterdam. *Maritime Transport Research*, 4, 100089.

de Langen, P.W. (2023b). Advancing public interests through state ownership: the case of Port of Rotterdam. *GeoJournal*, 88(6), 6507–6521.

de Langen, P.W. & Heij, C. (2014). Corporatisation and performance: A literature review and an analysis of the performance effects of the corporatisation of port of Rotterdam authority. *Transport Reviews*, 34(3), 1–19.

de Langen, P.W. & Nijdam, M.H. (2009). A best practice in cross-border cooperation: Copenhagen Malmö Port. In *Ports in Proximity: Competition and Coordination among Adjacent Seaports*. Ed. Th. Notteboom, C. Ducruet, & P.W. de Langen, 163–174. Ashgate.

de Langen, P.W. & Pallis, A.A. (2006). Analysis of the benefits of intra-port competition. *International Journal of Transport Economics/Rivista internazionale di economia dei trasporti*, 33(1), 69–85.

de Langen, P. & Saragiotis, P. (2018). Getting port governance right. In *Handbook of International Trade and Transportation*, 500–517. Edward Elgar Publishing.

de Langen, P.W. & Sornn-Friese, H. (2019). Ports and the circular economy. In *Green Ports*, 85–108. Elsevier.

de Langen, P.W., Turró C. M., Fontanet, M. & Caballé, J. (2018). The infrastructure investment needs and financing challenge of European ports. ESPO report. www.espo.be/media/Port%20Investment%20Study%202018_FINAL_1.pdf

de Langen, P. W., Van Den Berg, R. & Willeumier, A. (2012). A new approach to granting terminal concessions: the case of the Rotterdam World Gateway terminal. *Maritime Policy & Management*, 39(1), 79–90.

de Langen, P.W. & van der Lugt, L.M. (2017). The role of public shareholders in government owned port development companies: Insights from the Dutch case. *International Journal of Transport Economics*, 44(4), 589–609.

de Langen, P.W. & E.J. Visser (2005), Collective action regimes in seaport clusters: The case of the Lower Mississippi Port Cluster. *Journal of Transport Geography*, 13, 173–186.

Levinson, M. (2016). *The Box: How the Shipping Container Made the World Smaller and the World Economy Bigger*. Princeton University Press.

Levitt, T. (2008). *Marketing Myopia*. Harvard Business Review Press.

van der Lugt, L., de Langen, P. & Hagdorn, L. (2015). Beyond the landlord: Worldwide empirical analysis of port authority strategies. *International Journal of Shipping and Transport Logistics*, 7(5), 570–596.

Marshall, A. (1890). *Principles of Economics*, 8th edn (1920). London, McMillan.

Maersk (2025). East West Network, Trans Suez, route network brochure. www.maersk.com/~/media_sc9/maersk/campaigns/east-west-network/files/maersk-trans-suez-ocean-services-overview_v7.pdf?h=64&w=64&hash=3C2EE14206C8252130800EFD982009A5, last accessed 29 October 2025.

McEvily, B. & Zaheer, A. (1999). Bridging ties: A source of firm heterogeneity in competitive capabilities. *Strategic Management Journal*, 20(12), 1133–1156.

Megginson, W.L. & Netter, J.M. (2001). From state to market: A survey of empirical studies on privatisation. *Journal of Economic Literature*, 39, 321–389.

Mendes Constante, J., de Langen, P.W. & Furió Pruñonosa, S. (2023). Innovation ecosystems in ports: A comparative analysis of Rotterdam and Valencia. *Journal of Shipping and Trade*, 8(1), 18.

Mintzberg, H., & Waters, J. A. (1985). Of strategies, deliberate and emergent. *Strategic Management Journal*, 6(3), 257–272.

Moore, J.F. (1993). Predators and prey: A new ecology of competition. *Harvard Business Review*, 71 (3), 75–86.

Morgan, W. (1951). Observations on the study of hinterlands in Europe. *Tijdschrift sociale en economische geografie*, 42, 366–371.

Munim, Z. H., & Schramm, H. J. (2018). The impacts of port infrastructure and logistics performance on economic growth: the mediating role of seaborne trade. *Journal of Shipping and Trade*, 3(1), 1–19.

Musacchio, A., Lazzarini, S. G., & Aguilera, R. V. (2015). New varieties of state capitalism: Strategic and governance implications. *Academy of Management Perspectives*, 29(1), 115–131.

Musso, E., Ferrari, C., & Benacchio, M. (2006). Port investment: Profitability, economic impact and financing. *Research in Transportation Economics*, 16, 171–218.

Normann, R. (2001). *Reframing business: When the Map Changes the Landscape*. John Wiley & Sons.

OECD (2011). Competition in ports and port services, DAF/COMP(2011)14. www.oecd.org/regreform/sectors/48837794.pdf

OECD (2015). The impact of mega-ships. www.itf-oecd.org/impact-mega-ships

OECD (2015). Guidelines on corporate governance of state-owned enterprises, 2015 edition. www.oecd.org/daf/ca/OECD-Guidelines-Corporate-Governance-SOEs-2015.pdf

OECD (2018). The impact of alliances in container shipping. www.itf-oecd.org/impact-alliances-container-shipping

Ollivier, P. Prasad Sahu, S. & Saragiotis, P. (2024). *Port Community Systems: Lessons from Global Experience*. World Bank Group. http://documents.worldbank.org/curated/en/099092624152038561

Pallis, A.A., Notteboom, T.E. & de Langen, P.W. (2008). Concession agreements and market entry in the container terminal industry. *Maritime Economics & Logistics*, 10(3), 209–228.

Peng, M.W., Bruton, G.D., Stan, C.V. & Huang, Y. (2016). Theories of the (state-owned) firm. *Asia Pacific Journal of Management*, 33(2), 293–317.

Pigou, A.C. (1920). *The Economics of Welfare*. Macmillan and Co.

Port of Barcelona (2024). Memoria Estadística 2024. www.puertos.es/sites/default/files/2025-09/Memoria%20Anual%202024%20AP%20Barcelona.pdf, last accessed 29 October 2025.

Port of Rotterdam (2019). Annual report 2018 (in Dutch). www.portofrotterdam.com/en/about-port-authority/finance/annual-reports

Portugal-Perez, A. & Wilson, J. S. (2012). Export performance and trade facilitation reform: Hard and soft infrastructure. *World Development*, 40(7), 1295–1307.

Rentsch, C. & Finger, M. (2015). Yes, no, maybe: The ambiguous relationships between state-owned enterprises and the state. *Annals of Public and Cooperative Economics*, 86(4), 617–640.

van Riessen, B., Negenborn, R.R. & Dekker, R. (2015). Synchromodal container transportation: An overview of current topics and research opportunities. In *International Conference on Computational Logistics*, 386–397. Springer.

Rietveld, P. & Bruinsma, F. (2012). *Is Transport Infrastructure Effective?: Transport Infrastructure and Accessibility: Impacts On The Space Economy*. Springer Science & Business Media.

Rothschild, M. (1990). *Bionomics: Economy as Ecosystem*. Fitzhenry & Whiteside Lts.

Rohrbeck, R., Hölzle, K. & Gemünden, H.G. (2009). Opening up for competitive advantage–How Deutsche Telekom creates an open innovation ecosystem. *R&D Management*, 39(4), 420–430.

Schoemaker, P.J. & Day, G.S. (2009). How to make sense of weak signals. *Leading Organisations: Perspectives for a New Era*, 37.

Schulz, V., Bell, M.G., Rose, J.M. & Geers, D.G. (2025). From fossil fuels to biofuels: Circular economy diversification for fossil fuel ports. *Transportation Research Part D: Transport and Environment*, 144, 104796.

van Son, L., Arkhipov-Goyal, A., Van den Berghe, K.B.J., den Ouden, B., van Vliet, R.-J. & Jacobs, W. (2023). *CommodipHy: The Commodification of Ammonia and the Role of Rotterdam as a Global Pricing Centre*. Delft University of Technology.

Suárez-Alemán, A., Sarriera, J.M., Serebrisky, T. & Trujillo, L. (2016). When it comes to container port efficiency, are all developing regions equal? *Transportation Research Part A: Policy and Practice*, 86, 56–77.

Suárez-Alemán, A., Serebrisky, T. & de León, O.P. (2017) Port reforms in Latin America and the Caribbean: where we stand, how we got here, and what is left. *Maritime Economics & Logistics*, 20, 1–19.

Shirley, M.M. & Walsh, P. (2001). Public vs. private ownership: the current state of the debate. *World Bank Policy Research Working Paper*, 2420.

Sappington, D.E. & Stiglitz, J.E. (1987). Privatisation, information and incentives. *Journal of Policy Analysis and Management*, 6(4), 567–585.

Sheffi, Y. (2012). *Logistics Clusters: Delivering Value and Driving Growth*. MIT Press.

Shleifer, A. (1998). State versus private ownership. *Journal of Economic Perspectives*, 12(4), 133–150.

Shafer, S.M., Smith, H.J. & Linder, J.C. (2005), The power of business models, *Business Horizons*, 48, 199–207.

Sheng, H., Hong, S., & Zhao, N. (2013). *China's state-owned enterprises: Nature, performance and reform. Series on Chinese Economics Research, Vol. 1*. World Scientific Publishers.

Siemonsma, H., Van Nus, W., & Uyttendaele, P. (2012). Awarding of Port PPP contracts: the added value of a competitive dialogue procedure. *Maritime Policy & Management*, 39(1), 63–78.

Siskos, I. & Van Wassenhove, L.N. (2017). Synergy management services companies: A new business model for industrial park operators. *Journal of Industrial Ecology*, 21(4), 802–814.

Taaffe, E.J., Morrill, R.L. & Gould, P.R. (1963). Transport expansion in underdeveloped countries: a comparative analysis. *Geographical Review*, 53(4), 503–529.

Talley, W.K. & Ng, M. (2022). Cargo port choice equilibrium: The case of shipping lines and cargo port service providers. *Transportation Research Part E: Logistics and Transportation Review*, 164, 102817.

Taneja, P., Walker, W.E., Ligteringen, H., van Schuylenburg, M. & Van Der Plas, R. (2010). Implications of an uncertain future for port planning. *Maritime Policy & Management*, 37(3), 221–245.

Theys, C., Notteboom, T.E., Pallis, A.A. & de Langen, P.W. (2010). The economics behind the awarding of terminals in seaports: Towards a research agenda. *Research in Transportation Economics*, 27(1), 37–50.

Thomke, S. & Fujimoto, T. (2000). The effect of "front-loading" problem-solving on product development performance. *The Journal of Product Innovation Management*, 17(2), 128–142.

Tongzon, J. & Heng, W. (2005). Port privatisation, efficiency and competitiveness: Some empirical evidence from container ports (terminals). *Transportation Research Part A: Policy and Practice*, 39(5), 405–424.

Tribunal de defensa de la libre competencia, Republica de Chile (2020). Informe n° 18/2020.

UNCTAD (2012). How to utilize FDI to improve transport infrastructure – ports: Lessons from Nigeria. http://archive.unctad.org/en/docs/diaepcb2011d8_en.pdf

UNCTAD (2025a.). Review of Maritime Transport. https://unctad.org/en/pages/publications/Review-of-Maritime-Transport-(Series).aspx

UNCTAD (2025b). Port call and performance statistics. https://unctadstat.unctad.org/datacentre/dataviewer/US.PortCalls, last accessed 29 October 2025.

Valls, J.C., de Langen, P.W., Alonso, L.G. & Pinto, J.Á.V. (2020). Understanding port choice determinants and port hinterlands: Findings from an empirical analysis of Spain. *Maritime Economics & Logistics*, 22(1), 53–67

Verkehr (2020). Seehafenbilanz. www.verkehr.co.at/category/epaper/seehafenbilanz/, last accessed 29 October 2025.

Verhoeven, P. (2010). A review of port authority functions: towards a renaissance? *Maritime Policy & Management*, 37(3), 247–270.

Vickers, J. & Yarrow, G. (1991). Economic perspectives on privatisation. *The Journal of Economic Perspectives*, 5(2): 111–132.

Visnjic, I., Neely, A., Cennamo, C. & Visnjic, N. (2016). Governing the city: Unleashing value from the business ecosystem. *California Management Review*, 59(1), 109–140.

Wang, Y. & Wang, N. (2019). The role of the port industry in China's national economy: An input–output analysis. *Transport Policy*, 78, 1–7.

Williamson, O.E. (1981). The economics of organisation: The transaction cost approach. *American Journal of Sociology*, 87(3), 548–577.

World Bank (2014). *Corporate Governance of State-Owned Enterprises: A Toolkit*. World Bank. License: Creative Commons Attribution CC BY 3.0 IGO. http://hdl.handle.net/10986/20390

World Bank (2025a). The logistics performance index. https://lpi.worldbank.org/, last accessed 29 October 2025.

World Bank (2025b). *The Container Port Performance Index 2020 to 2024: Trends and Lessons Learned*. World Bank. http://hdl.handle.net/10986/43744, last accessed 29 October 2025.

World Bank (2025c). World development indicators. https://databank.worldbank.org/databases, last accessed 29 October 2025.

World Bank (2025d). Port reform toolkit. www.worldbank.org/en/topic/transport/publication/port-reform-toolkit, last accessed 29 October 2025.

World Shipping Council (2025). Data online. www.worldshipping.org/top-50-container-ports, last accessed 29 October 2025.

World Steel Association (2010). World steel in figures 2010. www.worldsteel.org

World Steel Association (2025). World steel in figures 2025. www.worldsteel.org

Further reading on trends and developments

Digitalisation

- WEF (2016). World Economic Forum White Paper – Digital transformation of industries: Digital enterprise. http://reports.weforum.org/digital-transformation/wp-content/blogs.dir/94/mp/files/pages/files/digital-enterprise-narrative-final-january-2016.pdf
- ISLI – KEDGE Business School Whitepaper – digitalisation of maritime supply chains. www.porteconomics.eu
- Fruth, Markus, Teuteberg, Frank, & Liu, Shaofeng (2017). Digitisation in maritime logistics – What is there and what is missing? *Cogent Business & Management*, 4(1). www.tandfonline.com/doi/citedby/10.1080/23311975.2017.1411066?scroll=top&needAccess=true

Autonomous transport

- TNO (2018). TNO Whitepaper – truck platooning: Driving the future of transportation, www.tno.nl/en/about-tno/news/2015/3/truck-platooning-driving-the-future-of-transportation-tno-whitepaper/

- www.eutruckplatooning.com/
- Rolls Royce (2018). Remote and autonomous ships: The next steps. www.rolls-royce.com/~/media/Files/R/Rolls-Royce/documents/customers/marine/ship-intel/aawa-whitepaper-210616.pdf
- Tavasszy, L. & Janssen, R. (2016). On the value case for truck platooning in Europe. www.researchgate.net/publication/312116529_The_value_case_for_truck_platooning

Energy transition

- International Energy Agency (2018). World energy outlook. www.iea.org/weo/
- http://www.energy-transitions.org
- Oxford Institute for Energy Studies (2018). Power-to-gas: Linking electricity and gas in a decarbonising world? www.oxfordenergy.org/wpcms/wp-content/uploads/2018/10/Power-to-Gas-Linking-Electricity-and-Gas-in-a-Decarbonising-World-Insight-39.pdf

Additive manufacturing

- Wu, B., Myant, C. & Weider, S.Z. (2017). The value of additive manufacturing: Future opportunities. www.imperial.ac.uk/media/imperial-college/imse/IMSE-Briefing-paper-2-AM.pdf
- Johnston, Trevor, Smith Troy D. & Luke Irwin, J. (2018). *Additive Manufacturing in 2040: Powerful Enabler, Disruptive Threat*. RAND Corporation. www.rand.org/pubs/perspectives/PE283.html
- McKinsey (2018). Additive manufacturing: A long-term game changer for manufacturers. www.mckinsey.com/business-functions/operations/our-insights/additive-manufacturing-a-long-term-game-changer-for-manufacturers
- http://additivemanufacturing.com/

Robotization and Industry 4.0

- Scheer, A. W. (2015). Industry 4.0: from vision to implementation. www.researchgate.net/publication/281447305_Whitepaper_-_Industry_40_From_vision_to_implementation
- Rojko, A. (2017). Industry 4.0 concept: Background and overview. *International Journal of Interactive Mobile Technologies (iJIM)*, 11(5), 77–90.
- International Federation of Robotics. https://ifr.org/
- https://www.roboticstomorrow.com/whitepapers.php
- http://news.mit.edu/topic/robotics

Circular economy

- Geissdoerfer, M., Savaget, P., Bocken, N.M. & Hultink, E.J. (2017). The circular economy – A new sustainability paradigm? *Journal of Cleaner Production*, 143, 757–768.

- Kyllönen, M. (2017). Can the EU's circular economy apply to ports? *The Parliament Magazine*, 19 May. www.theparliamentmagazine.eu/articles/opinion/can-eus-circular-economy-apply-ports
- Preston, F. (2012). A global redesign? Shaping the circular economy. *Energy, Environment and Resource Governance*, 2, 1–20.
- United Nations (2011). Recycling rates of metals – A status report. www.wedocs.unep.org/handle/20.500.11822/8702
- https://circulatenews.org/
- https://circulareconomy.europa.eu/platform/
- State of Green (2017). Denmark as a circular economy solution hub. www.stateofgreen.com/publications

Geopolitics

- Hillman, J.E. (2018). China's Belt and Road Initiative: Five years later. Statement before the US–China Economic and Security Review Commission, January, 25. www.csis.org/analysis/chinas-belt-and-road-initiative-five-years-later

Societal and demographic developments

- United Nations (2018). World urbanisation prospects 2018. https://population.un.org/wup/

Natural resources and ecosystems

- FAO (2018). The future of food and agriculture: Trends and challenges. www.fao.org/3/a-i6583e.pdf
- McKinsey (2018). Mining & metals scenarios 2030, report for the World Economic Forum. www.mckinsey.com/~/media/mckinsey/dotcom/client_service/Metals%20and%20Mining/PDFs/mining_metals_scenarios.aspx
- WEF (2015). Mining & metals in a sustainable world 2050. www3.weforum.org/docs/WEF_MM_Sustainable_World_2050_report_2015.pdf

The international economy and trade flows

- NZIER (2017). Is peak globalisation upon us? Globalisation is much more than trade in goods. Working Paper 2017/1. https://nzier.org.nz/static/media/filer_public/6b/c8/6bc89ea8-996e-45df-9521-9aa183ae030b/2017-01_gobalisation.pdf
- https://www.wto.org/english/forums_e/public_forum18_e/public_forum18_e.htm

Supply and value chains

- APEC (2012). Concepts and trends in global supply, global value and global production chains, APEC#212-SE-01.4. www.apec.org/Publications/2012/05/Concepts-and-Trends-in-Global-Supply-Global-Value-and-Global-Production-Chains
- PwC (2018). Transportation & logistics 2030. www.pwc.com/gx/en/transportation-logistics/tl2030/assets/pwc-tl2030-pub.pdf

International freight transport

- UNCTAD (2018). Review of maritime transport. https://unctad.org/en/PublicationsLibrary/rmt2018_en.pdf
- Arvis, Jean-François, Vesin, Vincent, Carruthers, Robin, Ducruet, César, & de Langen, Peter. 2019. *Maritime Networks, Port Efficiency, and Hinterland Connectivity in the Mediterranean. International Development in Focus.* World Bank. https://openknowledge.worldbank.org/bitstream/handle/10986/30585/9781464812743.pdf
- OECD (2018). Information sharing for efficient maritime logistics. www.oecd-ilibrary.org/transport/international-transport-forum-policy-papers_24108871
- ITF (2018). Decarbonising maritime transport: Pathways to zero-carbon shipping by 2035. *International Transport Forum Policy Papers*, No. 47, OECD Publishing. https://doi.org/10.1787/b1a7632c-en
- ITF (2017). Local governments and ports. *International Transport Forum Policy Papers*, No. 31, OECD Publishing. https://doi.org/10.1787/820a7ecb-en

Index

Note: **Bold** page numbers refer to tables; *italic* page numbers refer to figures and page numbers followed by 'n' refer to notes.

For Product Safety Concerns and Information please contact our EU representative GPSR@taylorandfrancis.com Taylor & Francis Verlag GmbH, Kaufingerstraße 24, 80331 München, Germany